THE BIBLE OF:
WEALTH
SECRETS

THE BIBLE OF WEALTH SECRETS

BY: Louis Rubin, Author & Research Editor
Copyrighted 2017 by Wealth Achievers, Inc.

List of Revelations

	Page Number
Title Page	1
Table of Contents	2
Preface	3-6
1) You Can!	7-8
2) Motivation	9-20
3) Vision and Imagination	21-36
4) Brainpower	37-50
5) Opportunity	51-59
6) Chance	60-66
7) Goals	67-77
8) Keeping Informed	78-84
9) Human Relations	85-101
10) Personality	102-111
11) Observation	112-116
12) Listening	117-132
13) Negotiation	133-142
14) Persuasion	143-161
15) Leadership	162-168
16) Inflation	169-180
17) Challenge	181-192
18) Capital	193-212
19) Decisions	213-225
20) Health is Wealth	226-237
21) Organize	238-254
22) Entrepreneurship	255-269
23) Deception	270-274
24) Business Philosophy	275-282
25) Turn Ideas into Wealth	283-284
26) Go Forward	285-286
27) Risk and Chance	287-288
28) Business Capital	289-290
29) Control Personal Problems	291
30) Investing	292-293
31) Hypnotic Meditation	294-295
32) Investing Soundly	296-297
33) Know Yourself	298-327
34) Advertising Campaigns	328-329
35) Persistence and Perseverance	330-344
36) Wealth is Health	345-362

PREFACE

As a shortcut to wealth, the author, Louis Rubin, offers his life time of business experience as an investor, financier, and researcher. His keen observation and study of the successful moguls of yesteryear is the product of this bible.

It is the intent of the author, Mr. Rubin, to share some of his most valuable success secrets with seriously ambitious people. The content of which can be considered to be very valuable and helpful to people seeking wealth. Most people think of wealth as accumulating capital in some lucky way rather than the hard work and discipline a person is required.

The foregoing writings are referred to as a Bible. The title " " refers to money. In the modern day world, The Bible is associated with religion. It seems that money is more prevalent as a religion then we readily realize. Money is almost worshiped and justly so because we cannot survive without it and that is how this Bible of Wealth Secrets became a source of valuable information.

The task of obtaining wealth secrets went beyond Mr. Rubins' vast experience. He had researched how the original Bible which was written 200- 300 be. The leader at that time was Ptolemy Philadelphus as research reveals realizing that a guide for living was important. He commissioned those 70 scholars to write valuable information in the form of stories. The subject matter of each legend or happening is what comprises the Old Testament and as time changed different religions adopted their own version into a Bible.

Mr. Rubin in modern times has sought to take advantage of the knowledge and experience of the most outstanding business professionals of the last century. He has extensively researched many documents and public domain literature interjected with his own views to make these writings the most worthwhile for any aspiring business minded person. The result of this work will hopefully make a shortcut for ambitious people to achieve success.

These exclusive works outline the formula for creating and maintaining wealth. It is necessary for a person to govern themselves in a manner of learning more and having a better business philosophy than his peers. Hopefully, this work can help accomplish such goals set by the reader. Success in life starts with an attitude of determination and willingness to strive towards accomplishing the goals that you have determined. There is no easy way or magic wand that can accomplish success. The outcome and result of the work you put into establishing good plans is the only formula that will determine the outcome of your success.

Whatever you read and study here has to be thought of and practiced in your mind in order to establish your own guidelines for reaching your goals. Everybody has a different background and so one has to evaluate themselves as to how diligent they have to work to accomplish learning the information presented in these writings.

One important point that the individual has to remember is that everyone has the equal chance to become unequal. In a sense, that means that nobody is really ahead of you in striving for success.

The author wishes you the best in your life and with that sincere wish may you have God speed.

Introduction

What is Wealth?

The Webster dictionary defines wealth as "one's worldly possessions." The Webster dictionary defines abundance as "adequacy, enough, plenty, sufficient." Our Wealth Society defines wealth as making enough money to pay all of your living expenses including vacations and income for a bright future of retirement.

Wealth does not necessarily mean that you can have all the money that you can spend. It means that you can be considered wealthy if you do not have to worry about where your next meal or living expenses are coming from. It also means that your children will feel secure in knowing that their education or college is provided for without struggle. Wealth also means that you have the joy of life by virtue of knowing that you have the knowledge to preserve your estate for the rest of your life.

You do not need, as found by the author, to have a million dollars or multi millions to be considered wealthy. Our Wealth Society is called the "WEALTH SOCIETY" founded by and established by Mr. Karples. The only requirement is to take a pledge to oneself to study and learn the contents of this Bible plus any specialized knowledge for your pursuit.

THE BIBLE OF WEALTH SECRETS contains helpful guidance towards the goal of becoming wealthy or wealthier than you are at the present time. The Wealth Society now considers you a member. That is to say that it should be shared by your family and even limited to only your close friends. The purpose being that keeping the information exclusive and confidential as much as possible will give you the exclusive and confident edge of becoming unequal or have risen to a level financially above your peers. Status actually is when you are compared financially to others. If everyone had a million dollars, for example, theoretically everyone would be poor rather than rich. Think about what was just said to realize the significance of that statement. That is the reason that you would be unselfish to yourself and family keeping the information confidential and limited.

These works are on me with the United States Government Library of Congress in Washington, D.C. as copyrighted and exclusive material which protects the original writing and also protects your Wealth Society from unauthorized reproduction of these writings. The Wealth Society is dedicated to its members, being that you are a member.

Another significant philosophy that a wealth member should adhere to is the fact that he or she knows that any task is to be taken seriously. A person is well rewarded knowing that they have to put their best foot forward and have performed
With their best efforts. This does not mean that the outcome has to be perfect. When a person knows in his heart and gut that he performed with the most energy, care and diligence than his or her individual feelings should be satisfied without any regrets that he or she has performed their best.

People, who dedicate themselves to their commitment to the philosophy of doing their best, can expect to receive the best rewards of accomplishment. So from this time forward a Wealth Society member is expected to do his best and they can expect the best to come back to him.

A few surveys made during the last decade indicate that people that reach retirement age should be earning between $35.000 & $75,000 a year from their investments if they hope to retire in a "comfortable" manner.

It is expected that most people will be shocked to realize this fact. Many people retire having to be already dependent upon their children for their welfare. This shocking realization will hopefully reinforce your purpose of earning and saving adequate sums of money to be self-sufficient.

The author's credentials are to be noted as significant in the fields of business, investments and management. He had the spirit of becoming wealthy at an early age and has become involved with many businesses.

He was well known for his work and diligence and had accomplished in that field everything he wanted at the time. He knew then there were better ways to become wealthy. His family had an interest in real estate and that caught his fancy along with stock market investing, financing and as a building contractor. He studied at the University of Miami and various trade schools as well as working on the different projects. In his early 20's, he became State licensed as a general contractor and also a Real Estate Broker. This led him into becoming a developer and investor which gained him specific knowledge from working in these fields. Because of his knowledge, he published many books and articles as well as writing numerous reports that were published and sold worldwide. These writings are not a how-to-do book but rather how-I-did-it. The information is first hand from study, doing it and managing it. There are very few other writings that encompass all the necessary vital facts. Now that the author is retired, he reveals all of his insider's experiences and know-how. Even in my day, I would hear a lot of negativism for example; it cannot be done; you think the world is waiting for you; all of those things have tried and do not work, and it isn't possible to do this or that. There is no replacement for actual experience and actually taking somebody by the hand and teaching them better ways of learning than just reading.

In this world, you will find that the most important accomplishment is learning how to do many things that are not even written or talked about. The purpose of these writings is to make wealth objectives most tenable by disclosing in simple language how to handle difficult people and situations.

As you study the contents of this special Bible, you will find duplications of references to different subject matter. The author intends to show you by repetition the important different views that should be studied from many different angles. The additional viewpoints are more important than the mere mention of the idea.

In pointing out various viewpoints on the subject, you are actually studying in greater depth the meaning of the introductory idea. It should be considered as having additional and broader meaning which should be viewed in the broader sense.

REVELATION #1
YOU CAN!!

Your knowledge is your power. Your destiny depends upon your knowledge. This is a factor that only you control. Achievers realize that obtaining knowledge is a vital key to success and wealth. Knowledge is the power to put your plan into action. THE BIBLE OF WEALTH SECRETS is a compilation of many revelations that comprise the ingredients that create wealth. Success is not an accident. If you were to ask a successful man who was a self-made millionaire or multi-millionaire what he attributes his success to, he may tell you there was a lot of luck involved. But if he is honest and aware, he would think back and attribute his success to the fact that he recognized opportunity and took advantage of it. He would probably think back and add to his statement that he had the ability to recognize opportunity and prepare himself by observing, studying and applying good judgment to make many good small decisions. In his analysis, he would then begin to realize that luck belongs to the best players, meaning one that is prepared to recognize opportunity and knows how, when, where and why his gut feeling tells him to proceed to create wealth. In looking back, he will agree with the fact that luck belongs to the best players.

So, success to gain wealth is really an attitude that the person must have to do whatever is necessary to prepare himself for his goal. When one is prepared, opportunity will become their opportunity and their enthusiasm will almost automatically be increased invigorating their appetite to expand that success into greater success. So, the attitude of determination becomes almost automatic and raises one's sights to achieve higher levels of success. This self-propelling attitude is the basis for creating wealth and success. Success in itself creates the ambitions of a person to achieve higher and better things and thusly is the seeds for creating many successes. If one's mind has been cultivated early on with wealth secrets information, there is virtually no limit to the enthusiasm that is then almost automatically stirred.

This Bible of Wealth Secrets contains all the ingredients that an individual human being can use to achieve wealth. A serious and diligent effort must be made to mold one's conscious thoughts along the parameters. It is like baking a great cake; the good ingredients must be mixed together to create a prize winning recipe. The more you learn, the more you will earn. It is entirely up to the individual to study this business Bible with the proper attitude, diligence and consistency, and to practice the concepts learned in your mind in order for you to be ready, willing and able, to take on the challenge of an opportunity and turn your dreams into wealth. It can be said with great truth that your desire for wealth has to be so embedded in your mind that you eat, sleep and think opportunity and success. There is nothing casual that is going to happen if you just depend upon luck. Anything you do in life can only be measured by the work that is accomplished and it is what you put into your efforts that will determine what you can take out and establish what you and your family life would be like. As a human being, most people desire wealth but do not know how to achieve it or have any plan. This Bible of Wealth Secrets will help you make a plan and also work your plan and can accomplish more in life than possibly beyond your wildest dreams. If you think that just owning this Bible of Wealth Secrets will do the trick, you are well mistaken. It requires a sincere commitment to accomplish learning about business wisdom and have a yearning desire to study it continually, rather than just reading it.

By this time and point in time of reading this segment, you should be convinced that the greatest secret to cultivating and achieving wealth is all dependent upon you and your attitude. You are the main player in this objective. The best investments that an ambitious person can make are knowledge gained. A person can invest in all types of investments and risk losing it; but when you invest in acquiring knowledge, you cannot lose it, no one can take it from you, it is yours for the rest of your life so that you and your family can enjoy it.

One of the most important things you can do is learn the lingo of business. Learning the definitions of business terms will give you a firm basis in order to build your knowledge. Learning the vocabulary of words used in every phase of business will give you a comprehension of the subject matter. The definitions of business words will give you greater insight and stimulate your imagination in order to apply greater meaning and understanding of your ideas and planning business activities. It is suggested that you obtain the glossaries of terms used in conducting stock market trading, real estate operations, accounting procedures, and business law, etc. Finding a text book glossary on these subjects can be done from the computer and/or your library.

The time and effort expended in this pursuit of increasing your knowledge will pay off like no other investment could.

Good luck as this is the first Revelation in THE BIBLE OF WEALTH SECRETS

REVELATION #2
MOTIVATION

There has to be a purpose in accumulating wealth. The purpose, of course, is to add to you and your family's security. Wealth, itself, is having more money than you need to pay all your expenses. It is the excess money that you do not use that you can accumulate into investments or a more enjoyable retirement. Making money will increase your enthusiasm to invest to make more money. Therefore, the objective is to accumulate wealth. Working for a salary, wage, or commission, is rewarding for many but the greatest rewards can be achieved from running a business. Of course, running a business can be much more involved and a personal sacrifice is usually required because it is not simply a 9-5 job. The choice, of course, has to be your own. It is possible to manage your life having a job and having a business as an avocation. This, of course, requires a larger sacrifice.

Profit as an economic motive. Throughout history, the hope and expectation of making a profit has been the most powerful incentive to economic advancement. This motive does not appeal to all men since it carries with it the chance of failure. Profits are not fixed in advance, as are salaries and wages. They may be high, or low, or non-existent, depending upon whether the business is a success or a failure. If the business meets with some degree of success, profits are what is left over for the owners after all expenses have been paid. No one can say what this excess over cost will be in any given year.

Because working for profits entails taking a risk, the multitude of men prefer working for wages. They are able to do so, however, only because the profit motive has first created wage-paying jobs. To the adventurous few who are willing to take a business chance to assume the risk of success or failure--economists have applied the term entrepreneur, or enterpriser. These are the men who start new businesses, launch new products upon an uncertain market, and assume collectively the task of industrial expansion.

Some measure of adventurousness is required, also, in the management of an established enterprise. Being established does not free the enterprise from the factor of risk. Profits are the most variable item on a company's balance sheet. Sales may drop off, unexpectedly and even unaccountably, without a corresponding reduction in operating costs. Certain elements of expense either remain fixed or can be reduced only gradually. Under some circumstances, consequently, a drop of only 10 per cent in sales may produce a decrease in profits running as high as 50 per cent.

Nevertheless, despite their uncertainty, profits are earned frequently enough to appear a glittering reward of business enterprise. Impressive figures are collected by the statisticians showing the high rate of mortality in this or that industry or the percentage of businesses that will not survive past their first or second year, but these figures rarely deter a man from starting an enterprise upon which he has set his heart. The enterpriser who is convinced of the merit of his product or service is quite willing to gamble on his ability to succeed against all obstacles. Who is influenced by the profit motive? The lure of profit is evident enough in the case of the enterpriser launching a new business, or in the instance of the small business owned by a single individual or by a few partners. What is not so evident is the working of the profit motive in the case of the large corporation, whose owners are the thousands of stockholders scattered over half the globe, having little to do with the actual management of the company. The men responsible for the day-to- day operations are on a salary; perhaps own no shares in the company. Who, in the corporation, is being influenced by the profit motive in the way that it influences the enterpriser?

Strange as it may seem, it is probable that the managers of a corporation, even though they may not be numbered among its owners, are more profit-conscious than the individual who owns and operates his own business. Profits-and costs-are watched very closely in the corporation. An accounting department collects and analyzes the necessary sales and cost data, then presents the cumulative results weekly or even daily to the managing executives. The latter are practically compelled to follow the curve of rising or falling profits, cannot help becoming cost and profit-conscious. In contrast, the busy owner of a small business can scarcely find time to take his financial soundings-sometimes does not know where he stands, or how well he is doing, for weeks at a stretch.
It must be remembered, also, that while the managers of a corporation are working for salaries and may or may not own stock, they are keenly aware that their positions and salaries, present and future, depend upon the success of the company in making profits. So, too, the thousands of investors who put their money into the company's stocks and bonds are counting upon continued profits; otherwise, they would not invest.

Profits as a condition for growth. If a going concern is to thrive, its profits must be more than merely nominal. Breaking even is not enough, nor is low profits much better. Profits must be high enough to pay some return to the stock holding owners of the business, and also to add to the company's capital resources available for the purchase of new equipment, the modernization of old plants, or the building of additional facilities. New inventions and scientific discoveries may call for the scrapping of existing machinery and the installation of new units, for all of which money is required. But the company's savings, if any, come only from its profits-if there are profits. From its undivided profits-the profits not paid to stockholders in the form of dividends--the company takes the capital needed for its improvements and growth.

It is true that companies can and do borrow funds for needed improvements or expansions, either through loans from financial houses or through an approved issue of new bonds to the public. But these loans involve heavy obligations which in turn must be met from profits. Some companies make it a matter of policy to finance improvements from their own earnings. Thus, United States Steel, for a long time among the largest corporation in the world and the first billion-dollar company in existence, financed almost all of its huge expenditures for improvements and new construction from its own earnings up to World War II. The owners (the stockholders) had to be content with a market value of their stock scarcely higher than what it had been in 1902 when the corporation was organized. No company can afford to stand still unless indeed it has a monopoly, and even then, the consuming public, through its government, will find ways of enforcing progress. Growth is not only the normal desire of a business enterprise but it is the goal that must be realized if the enterprise is to survive. But growth depends upon new and more capital, which directly or indirectly must come from the company's earned income. Profits, therefore, are both a condition for survival and a test of business efficiency. It's like rowing a boat upstream against the current. If you stop rowing or slow up the rowing, the boat will go backward. That is the reason you have to keep the momentum going forward.

Profits are not easily come by. A fallacy held by too many people outside of business circles is that most enterprises make huge profits. Growth does not always mean that more profits are produced even though one would assume that more profit is produced. So, growth in itself has to be watched and guided with great concern and skill. Pleasant as it might be for business men if these imaginary profits were only real, the facts must be faced as they are, and they tell an altogether different story.

For example, during the ten years that preceded World War II, fewer than 50 per cent of all the business enterprises in the United States earned a profit. That particular decade included years of depression but it also included some years that were considered good, and the percentage of profit-making enterprises stayed under 50 in good years as well as bad.

The precarious status of a business enterprise is authoritatively shown by the data collected since 1900 by Dun & Bradstreet, widely known for their annual listing of credit ratings. Their reference books, covering all types of business concerns except the smaller service enterprises, furnish a reliable guide to what may be termed the "vital statistics" of American business. They list business births -new enterprises or new ownerships or new reorganizations. They also list business deaths, whether by simple withdrawal from business, changes in ownership, or outright commercial failures.

Reviewing all these changes back to 1900, Dun & Bradstreet found that one-fifth of the business population undergoes some change annually. Thousands of concerns go out of existence during their first, their second, or their third year, and the average life of a business enterprise is only about sixty-six months.
It is true, of course, that when dividends are passed up, as we learned from the depression years, wages and salaries are sometimes cut or men are let go. Jobs, after all, depend upon profits and are created by profits. The employee's stake in business profits is a very real one; moreover, it is all the larger from the fact that the employee is a consumer as well as a worker. Profits invested in newer machines and techniques cut the costs of production and reduce the price of consumers' goods.

These reductions directly benefit the employee-consumer. The history of almost any industry over the past few decades will furnish illustrations of how this process works.
The beneficiaries of profits are not individuals only; entire communities share in the rising standards made possible by the accumulation and use of capital to build up or expand business enterprises. Every such expansion means a larger payroll and more purchases of materials and supplies, many of them purchased from suppliers within the community. New employees added to company payrolls contribute their payments for housing, clothing, food and other personal supplies to the total working capital of the community.

The attack on profits. Despite the need of profits for industrial growth, despite their beneficial effects upon individuals and communities and the difficulty with which they are acquired in actual practice, profits have been eyed with suspicion by many persons outside the world of business.
"Service" as a substitute for the profit motive. The activities of business result in services rendered, and the business man gets a keen satisfaction from the

contemplation of the good he is accomplishing. As we have seen, he is not the sole beneficiary. A going enterprise, under normal conditions, benefits employees, consumers, other business men, the community and the nation. Consequently, the idea of service is never absent from normal business enterprise, but is, in fact, a genuinely compelling motive.

There is no reason for critics of business to try to separate the motives of profit and service, or, worse still, to contrast them as if they were deadly opponents. The two motives can be held by the same man, and actually are. It is the profit motive that leads the business man to plan and launch his commercial enterprise, but it is the service motive that broadens the original motive of profit-seeking to make it fruitful of economic and social good. Business men should understand this relationship very well and by and large have lived up to their understanding of it. To brand the profit motive as selfish and immoral. and to ask that production and distribution be conducted solely from the motive of service is to ask for what is neither necessary nor possible. The one exception to this statement is a time of war or some other calamity endangering the existence of community or nation. In such a time, the service motive is transformed into the patriotic motive, and miracles of production are performed without regard to costs, whether of material or of labor. When peace returns and national danger is less obvious, appeals to patriotism notoriously meet with less success. The service motive by itself is too vague for the ordinary man to visualize. Just whom is he supposed to be serving, he asks, and why should he toil for them? There may be good answers to these questions, but it is doubtful whether they would have much motivating force.

The Ethics of Competition. Underlying much of the critical attitude toward the profit motive held by people who are neither Communists nor Socialists, is the assumption that there is something wrong about competition-something smacking of the jungle wherein animals prowl about seeking other animals that they may devour. So much is heard about "unfair competition" that many people, outside the business world, tend to think of all competition as unfair.
Without competition, the world would take on a monotonous sameness, such as may actually be observed on the streets of Moscow, according to American visitors. No signs, no window displays, and no newspaper advertising call attention to the merits of competing products. Blasé consumers who think themselves allergic to advertising, U.S.A. style, would probably soon lose their allergies if they could not get improved products, but had to stand in line for the few models authorized by an all-powerful government.

There is nothing like having an alert, progressive competitor in the same line of business to keep a man on his toes. Your competitor adds an improvement to the product, or works out a more attractive design, or installs new machinery enabling him to cut costs and reduce prices a little. Or perhaps he launches a sparkling advertising campaign or offers dealers better display material. Whatever he does, you must evaluate its effect on your own dealers and customers.

If you judge that the effect is likely to be permanent and serious, you take steps either to emulate him or, if possible, to surpass him. In the end, you find yourself doing what you had supposed to be impossible, with results beneficial to everybody. This is the way in which fair, healthy competition operates; obviously, it is not only ethical but highly desirable.

Doing Without Competition-and Liberty. In their efforts to blueprint a new kind of economic order in which the disadvantages of the present order would be overcome, socialists of every hue have made much of the slogan, "Production for use." Their idea is that the state should own the machines and operate them for the benefit of everyone. Are hats needed? Very well, count the heads, and make as many hats as there are heads. Then distribute them.

Improvement of the profit system. If some people are enthusiastic about the benefits of dictatorship, it is because they were neglected or oppressed under previous authoritarian governments, or was the butt of racial or religious hatred. Soviet Russia, for example, appears to have greatly improved the living standards of certain Asiatic nomads and the long-persecuted peoples of the Caucasus, such as the Armenians. Millions of simple people in the Old World, for centuries the victims of tyranny and exploitation, do not understand the privileges of democracy or the operation of a free economy but do understand the contrast between the life of the toiling masses and that of the privileged few. They understand, also, the tenacity of the few in hanging on to their privileges, and are easily convinced that force alone (the so-called "class struggle") will secure them a share in the good life. The dictator, or the dictatorial party, who promises to use force for the benefit of the many, appears as a benefactor from heaven. Relying on his promises, the peoples, like the Faust of legend, sign away their liberties.

There is a lesson in this for all who believe in the superiority of democracy and free enterprise. That lesson is, of course, that business men must never lose sight of the social effects of their plans and activities-the service motive must reinforce and guide the profit motive. The human consequences need always to be visualized, and to do this, business men must cultivate and strengthen their powers of the sympathetic imagination-a form of the imagination of importance. The economies of all nations depend greater upon the policies and practices of the government. People living in the United States of America have proved that opportunity is boundlessly rewarding to those people that have the courage and convictions of their ideas.

It must be granted, nevertheless, that the effort to extend a higher standard of living is incomplete, that not all people have been reached. There are still economic frontiers to be pushed back.

There are also obstacles to competitive enterprise arising from the sad fact that some men will not play the game fairly, but will try to circumvent the law and flout the entire code of business ethics. To control these business mavericks, it is necessary that there be policing by government and by business itself-by government, through such agencies as the Federal Trade Commission, the SEC (Securities & Exchange Commission) and the Interstate Commerce Commission, by business, through trade associations and bureaus to detect fraud or unfair competition.

It should not be thought that the individual business man has no part to play in securing economic stability. On the contrary, he has a very important part to play, well expressed by a contemporary business leader in the statement, "The greatest contribution any business man can make toward stability is to operate his business profitably." Recall what profits mean, and who benefits from them, and the truth of this quotation will become apparent at once.

Why do some business owner/managers hit the profit target more often than others? They do it because they keep their operation pointed in that direction. They never lose sight of the goal to finish the year with a profit. This revelation gives suggestions that should help an owner/manager to zero in on profit as needed.

It points out that you must keep informed, make timely decisions, and take effective action. In effect, you must control the activities of your company rather than being controlled by them.

A beginner rarely shoots a hole in one, hits a bulls-eye, or hooks a prize-winning trout. Topnotch performance in golf, shooting, and fishing requires knowledge, practice, and perseverance.

Similarly, in small businesses, year-end profit comes to the owner/manager who strives for top-notch performance. You achieve it by knowing your operation, by practicing the art of making timely, balanced judgments and by controlling the company's activities.

Know Your Business. The time-honored truth "Knowledge is power" is especially pertinent to the owner/manager of a small business. To keep your company pointed toward profit you must keep yourself well informed about it. You must know how the company is doing, make the use of surveys among your employees and professional team of lawyers and accountants before you can improve its operation. You must know its weak points before you can correct them. Some of the knowledge you need you pick up from day-to-day personal observation, but records should be your principal source of information about profits, costs, and sales.

Competition is a fact and justly so that has to be contended with. The benefits are many. Being competitive is to produce a better value to the public. It also improves products. We have all heard that if you can build a better mouse trap then more sales can be realized than your competitors. So, the goal for every business or service is to perform better than the now existing system. So, the secret is to do a lot or a litter better than your competitors.

Know Your Profit. The profit and loss statement (or income statement) prepared regularly each month or each quarter by your accountant is one of the most vital indicators of your businesses worth and health. You should make sure that this statement contains all the facts you need for evaluating your profit. This statement must pinpoint each revenue and cost area. For example, it should show the profit and loss for each of your product lines as well as the profit and loss for your entire operation.

It is a good idea to have your profit and loss statement prepared so that it shows each item for the current period, for the same period last year, and for the current year-to-date.

Know Your Costs. An owner/manager should know costs in detail. Then you can compare your cost figures as a percentage of sales (operating ratio). Be certain that your costs are itemized so that you can put your fingers on those that seem to be rising or falling according to your experience and the cost figures of your industry.

When costs are itemized, you can spot the culprit when the overall figure is higher than what you had budgeted. Take advertising costs for example. You can catch the offender if you break out your advertising expenditures by product lines and by media. In addition, a thorough check of inquiry returns from advertising will help to avoid unproductive publications. In knowing your costs, keep in mind that the formula for profit is: Profit equals Sales minus Costs.

Know Your Product Markup. Be certain that the pricing of your products provides a markup adequate for the kind of profit you expect to achieve. You must keep constantly informed on pricing because you have to adjust for rising costs and at the same time keep prices competitive. There are two ways to go out of business. One way is having your goods priced too low and the other way is pricing your goods too high. So, it becomes necessary to stay informed about competition. Knowledge about your markup also helps you to run close outs with your eyes open. Continuing to make a product that only a few customers want is an effective merchandising tool only when you use it on purpose-for example, to hold or attract buyers for other high markup products. Don't hesitate to drop a loser from your line.

Predict Your Future. Don't use a crystal ball to make forecasts of your business. By carefully analyzing the historic trends of your business, as shown in your records for the past five years, you can forecast for the year ahead. Your record of sales, your experience with the markets in which you sell, and your general knowledge of the economy should enable you to forecast a sales figure for the next year. When you have a sales forecast figure, make up a budget showing your costs as a percentage of that figure. In the next year, you can compare actual P & L figures to your budgeted figures. Thus, your budget is an important tool for determining the health of your business.

Effective decision making in the small business requires several things. The owner/manager must have as much accurate information as possible. With these facts, you should determine the consequences of all feasible courses of action and the time requirements. When you have made the judgment, you have set up your business so that the decisions you make can be transmitted into action.

Control Your Business. To be effective, the owner/manager must be able to motivate key people to get the results planned for within the cost and time limits allowed. In working to achieve results, the small business owner/manager has an advantage over big business. You can be fast and flexible while many large firms must await committee action before a decision is made. You do not have to get permission to act. And equally important, bottlenecks to implementing new practices can receive your personal attention.

One of the secrets is in deciding what items to control. Even in a small company, the owner/manager should not try to be all things to everyone. You should keep close control on people, products, money, and any other resources that you consider significant to keeping your operation pointed toward profit.

Manage Your People. Most businesses find that their largest expense is labor. Yet because of the close contact with employees, some owner/manager of small businesses do not pay enough attention to direct and indirect labor costs. They tend to think of these costs in terms of individuals rather than relate them to profit in terms of dollars and cents. Here are a few suggestions concerning personnel management:

Periodically review each position in your company. Take a quarterly look at the job. Is work being duplicated? Is it structured so that it encourages the employee to become involved? Can the tasks be given to another employee or employees and a position eliminated? Can a part-time person fill the job? Beware of theft and mishandling of merchandise and/or any employee consciously or unconsciously revealing company trade secrets.

Play a little private mental game. Imagine that you must get rid of one employee. If you had to let one person go, who would it be? How would you realign the jobs to make out? You may find a real solution to the imaginary problem is possible to your financial benefit.

Use compensation as a tool rather than viewing it as a necessary evil. Reward quality work. Investigate the possibility of using raises and bonuses as incentives for higher productivity. For example, can you schedule bonuses as morale boosters during seasonal slacks or other dull periods?

Control Your Inventory. Don't tie up all your money in inventory. Use a perpetual inventory system as a cost control rather than a system just for tax purposes. Establish use patterns or purchase patterns on the materials or items you must stock to keep the minimum number required to supply your customers or to maintain production. Excessive inventory, whether it is finished product or raw materials, ties up funds that could be used to better advantage, for example, to open up a new sales territory or to buy new machinery.

Control Your Products. From control of inventory to control of products is but a step. Make sure that your sales people recognize the importance of selling the products that are the most profitable. Align your service policies with your markup in mind. Arrange your goods so that low markup items require the least handling.

Control Your Money. It is a good policy to handle cash and checks as though they were perishable commodities. They are. Money in your safe earns no return, and it can be stolen. Bank promptly. Use credit wisely and take advantage of discounts. One of the hallmarks of a successful business owner/manager knows how much credit you can afford to extend over any period and how much you have already extended. Grant credit willingly, but keep it on a systematic basis. Insist on a written credit application and see that the credit application contains a promise to pay according to the credit practices in your industry.

Get Help When You Need It. It is good practice to use your outside advisors as you go along rather than calling on them only in emergencies. For example, your accountant can help you analyze the financial position of your business to help you avoid problems rather than to get you out of them.

Sometimes an owner/manager needs to call in a management consultant. For example, help may be needed in isolating and solving a problem that the owner/manager senses but can't quite put a finger on. In other instances, the consultant's professional background may be needed to supply skills that do not exist in the company-for example the capability for doing market research or for setting up an inventory control system. In many cases, the management consultant can provide the time that the owner/manager lacks to implement a solution.

"WHAT IS IT? WHO HAS IT? WHERE DID THEY GET IT? HOW CAN WE GET SOME?"

It's magical for those who have it-various ingredients bring about business success: operating capital, experienced management, being in the right type of business at the right time, having a business plan-these are among the most important. But all other ingredients can be right and the business will fail unless the one in charge possess the determination to succeed. Eighty-five percent of all new enterprises will fail. Is there a way for the entrepreneur to judge whether he or she has what it takes the determination to forge a successful business? There just might be a way.

Diverse qualities and assets make for business success-but the magical factor is determination. No business succeeds without it and any successful business that loses it withers away.

So, what is this thing called determination? Who has it? Where did they get it? Why didn't they teach Determination 101 in college? How much is needed to launch a successful business?

Does determination, in fact, have markers that will let us say, "Yes? We have it!" Or no "We don't"?

Starting a business-becoming an entrepreneur-is certainly for the tough minded. Most people lack the kind of determination it takes to launch and carry an enterprise to success. For them, happily, there are limitless wonderful, rewarding occupations that do not involve entrepreneurship. But those who do possess strong determination and have a bent to own their own business rarely will be denied their shot at the golden ring.

"I am determined to make it work" is the credo of the entrepreneur and the tap root of most entrepreneurial success. Wishing hard for something is not the same as having the determination to get it. Wishing rarely works; determination almost always works. It is, therefore, good effort to figure out just how very determined people use routinely to get things done and succeed.

The passion in our core beliefs makes us determined; goals are the natural and only tool of determination. Thus, a goal- oriented person is a determined person and a determined person is goal-oriented. The goal-oriented management technique is at the heart of every ambitious person and successful executive.

It is this degree of specificity in our goals which define the extent of our commitment and gives us verification into our core values.

Saying "I am determined to make it work," can be ruinous overconfidence for those short on determination, having confused it with a wish. With strong determination, there is a serious chance for the successful enterprise because the effort will be goal- oriented - the orientation vital to business success and unfortunately all too often missing in start-ups.

It is expected that you will be successful at your goals for accumulating wealth. The more important part of life is enjoying the fruits of your labor which encompasses having a life's style of quality. The accomplishment of your pursuits will give you more gratification and joy with more incentive.

We all are aware that every animal including human being has a limited life span on our planet. We all will realize, if not already, that it is not the quantity of life but the quality of life that is our greatest achievement. The best formula for living happily and productively is to enjoy each day with the things that offer you the most pleasure.

The best physiological attitude to have is to count your blessings and function by enjoying all the faculties that you have.

REVELATION #3
VISION AND IMAGINATION

Vision to a business man is really the foresight of a new idea or undertaking. It is a challenge to develop a plan of a business entity using all of his business acumens to develop a profitable business.

Visions come into focus when a man's knowledge and sub consciousness experiences are attracted to a single thought of making money. This encompasses all the experiences and knowledge that he has stored up in his mind and combines with the consciousness of desiring to turn a profit or lucrative enterprise into reality. Everybody has the latent power as well as the ready to use instincts to visualize an opportunity, especially when their thinking is always searching for profitable opportunities. If you study and emulate successful businessmen and women, you will quickly realize the uplifting experience of enthusiasm and drive when you have a vision of making a lucrative business. To give you some actual examples of men and women who have channeled their thinking of exercising their vision to promote extraordinary business successes, we are going to review a few of the most widely known enterprises that have been born by creative people with simply a thought and a vision.

It has been said that imagination is an underrated power. Business men, as a rule, do not realize their indebtedness to the imagination. That power is commonly thought of, not as a workhorse, but as a thoroughbred to be driven only by the poet, the artist, the story-writer. The imaginative man is thought of as a dreamer. He may entertain us with the beautiful pictures his mind creates, but we do not expect him to be alert in practical affairs. Few parents would think their son fitted for a business career because his teachers had discovered that he possessed a vivid and active imagination.

This popular view of imagination is erroneous because it rests upon an inadequate conception of the nature of this mental ability and upon a superficial idea of business. No person of feeble imagination ever achieved a lasting success in business.

By imagination is meant the mind's ability to recall past experiences -sensations, emotions, feelings, perceptions-and to cause these to reappear in the consciousness of infinite variety of newly learned principles and concepts. All people possess the power of imagination, and in most people, it is a very active power, yet much of its activity is purposeless and useless.

The imaginations of many people reproduce most easily sight images, things that have been seen with the eye. This power is the basis of what is commonly called "visual" memory. Some people quickly forget words that are spoken to them but will easily commit to memory a poem or an oration from a printed page. It is not unusual for a man or woman to recall something that he read as a young person in his geography or history, and to remember exactly whether the fact was stated on the left-hand or right-hand page, or at the top or the bottom of the page.

For example: Two men of equal ages open a clothing store in the same business district. Both men, full of enthusiasm, are compared in progress years later. One is still struggling at the same location; the other is successful with a chain of stores. The main difference can be wholly attributable to creative imagination. It is often said that "imagination" is the only capital that every person starts with and that every person possesses. Imagination results in progress it transforms; as an example, a row boat into a sailboat. A stuffy of progress itself makes imagination the key. It takes imagination to perceive imagination.

We all can relate the person who was not a very good singer although he was good in a church choir. Even if the singer did not sing for 20 years, the person could recall the key of tune. The imagination reproduces before them the page and musical notation of the hymn book. If the music were not actually before them, they could not sing a tune unless their imagination reproduced the notes as they appeared on the page. They had visual memory or imagination.

A person differs greatly in their power to visualize. It is a source of pleasure to the possessor and, as we shall see, can be made to do useful work in business. Without its aid, an inventory would be as helpless as the builder who has no tools, or bricks, or lumber.

Sound and other Sense Images: The ability to recall sounds-impressions on the consciousness produced through the ear-is believed to be rarer than the visual memory or imagination. It is highly developed in the blind, for their visual imagination receives no stimulus. It must be especially strong in the musician. The aural imagination of the deaf Beethoven was able to recombine sounds in his consciousness and produce marvelous harmonies. We say of such a person that the music is in his soul. People with an "ear for music" are often able to reproduce a melody after hearing it only once. Similarly, we are able to reproduce more or less vividly the sensations of touch, taste and smell, and various painful and pleasant emotions that we have experienced in the past.

Memory Supplies the Materials: The imagination in its constructive efforts is limited to the materials which memory can furnish. It creates no totally new images of any kind, no new states of consciousness. Imagination is a marvelous builder, but it can accomplish nothing without its faithful hood-carrier. the memory. It is clear, therefore, that the imagination of a person who has had little or no experience in business can build for them no new plans or visions that will be of much value. When such a person, not knowing the limitations under which their imagination must work, plans great ventures in business, they fail time and again and are called a visionary. Colonel Sellers, Mark Twain's immortal visionary, had a scheme every few days and there were always "millions in it." He knew nothing about the details of the business, yet he had superb confidence in his ability as a fortune builder. Colonel Sellers is still alive; you can find him in almost every town. We may think of imagination as a Pegasus in harness, but the driver must be a person who knows every twist and turn of the road.

Imagination in Science: The aim of science is knowledge or understanding. Some of the readers may say: "Of what possible use can imagination, the builder of air castles, be to the scientist? He is seeking for truth and of course, can get some aid from his memory. But imagination does not think or reason and therefore can be of no help to him."

As a matter of fact, the scientist who is exploring new realms of knowledge employs his imagination as much as he does his reason or judgment. When a person is seeking to explain a phenomenon, it is the imagination that constructs the necessary hypothesis. It was Newton's imagination that discovered the law of gravitation; it was his reason that verified it and finally accepted the law as the truth.

The theory of evolution had been in existence for many years as a product of the imagination before the patient studies of Darwin and Wallace brought forth data which satisfied the reason. Copernicus, who is credited with the discovery of our planetary or solar system, undoubtedly in his imagination pictured the planets moving around the central sun, and the moon about the earth, before his reason and judgment had weighed and sifted all the phenomena and accepted as true the hypothesis which his imagination had created.

Imagination and memory have played their important parts in the demonstration of all mathematical truths. A person of weak imagination is never a really great mathematician. The arithmetical processes, multiplication and division, which are short processes of addition and subtraction, were suggested by the imagination of man thousands of years ago. Both algebra and geometry, when properly taught owe their charm almost entirely to the play they give to the student's imagination. If imagination, an ability apparently so irrational, can be made of so much use to the scientist, it would be strange, indeed, if it could not be drafted into the service of the business man.

The Building of Ideas: Imagination constructs for men more or less definite ideas or pictures of the things which will give them greatest satisfaction for a person whose chief joy is eating, his imagination plans a dinner which no cook ever sets before him. It is his ideal dinner, and he hopes to eat it when he gets to heaven.

The great artists are never quite satisfied with their creations. Their imagination has built for them an idea which they cannot quite convert into reality. The ideal is the highest product of the imagination. Using those past experiences which have given us the most pleasurable emotions, or have proved themselves of golden worth to our reason, the imagination, spurred sometimes by our pleasure-loving senses, sometimes by our conscience, sometimes by our desire for success and happiness, pictures those experiences to us in a combination which seems absolutely perfect. Thusly, it is that we get the idea. It is a human product and may be far from perfect, yet to every person, their idea has all the qualities of perfection. Unconsciously, the imagination of every person is forever at work building ideas that charm his soul and stir him to activity. The ideas of one person may seem base, vulgar and commonplace to a man of a higher type, whereas the ideals of the latter may seem foolish, impracticable, and worthless to the man of cheaper tastes.

No man can subdue his imagination and keep it from building ideas. A person's imagination keeps forever at its work and constructs for him those imaginings in accordance with which he must live. In the firmament of every man's soul, there is a polar star-it is the idea that dominates his life.

Such being the case, it is important that each of us give some thought to the character of the ideas which our imagination is building. If we examine them critically with our judgment, we may discover that their perfection is only apparent. While we cannot chain our imagination, or hitch it to a post, yet we can, if we will, supervise its marvelous work and make it build for us ideas toward which we may struggle without disloyalty to our reason or to our conscience.

If a business man's idea is no more than the accumulation of a great fortune, is he not merely chasing the pot of gold at the end of the rainbow? Should he not envision the idea of service and its rewards, rather than material gains without thought of social duty or public service? It is the consciousness of duty well performed that will give the most enduring satisfactions.

Vision and Judgment: The reader will have already discovered that imagination is an activity that serves no useful purpose unless bridled and guided by judgment and common sense. To get an idea of what imagination can do by it, a person has only to recall one of their dreams. During our sleep, the will and reason are at rest, but imagination, particularly if we have overeaten before going to bed, often amuses itself by galloping around the universe. In our dreams, imagination shows us nothing new, but it often creates most startling combinations out of the materials consciously and sub-consciously stored in our memories.

The subconscious mind is always working even when we sleep. Therefore, some of your best ideas are cultivated in a dream when sleeping. For this reason, you will often hear upon awakening in the morning, "I had the answer."

The subconscious mind is always working even when we sleep. Therefore, some of your best ideas are cultivated in a dream while sleeping. For this reason, you will often hear upon awakening in the morning, "I had the answer."

Let us recall here that the mind is a unit, a single entity, and that what we call imagination is a name we give to one of its powers or activities. Reason is another activity, memory another. Just as with our bodies, we can crawl, walk, run, climb or lift, so with our minds, we can reason, feel, suffer, enjoy, remember, imagine. The whole mind is occupied in each one of these forms of its activity.

Sometimes, being weary, the mind may lazily indulge in the pleasures of imagination and not seek to make the pictures presented conform to the rules of reason or to the facts of memory. When the imagination is permitted to work in this haphazard, uncontrolled fashion, we call it phantasm. Aladdin's lamp, the Lilliputians in "Gulliver's Travels," the yesterdays and tomorrows of Alice in Wonderland," are all delightful creations of the phantasm, that is, of an imagination over which reason has deliberately held a very loose rein.

We cannot measure or estimate the importance of imagination. We know how much our physical comfort and well-being depend upon our eyesight, and what fearful calamity blindness is, but the loss of our inner vision-our imagination-would be a greater calamity than the loss of physical eyesight.

Vision and Ambition: Many people seem quite satisfied with life if only they have a job which yields them what they consider a decent livelihood. After school days are over, they strive for no further mental development but are content to devote what leisure they have to social pleasures, sports and amusements of various kinds. They like to feel certain that their job is secure. They may grumble now and then because their salary is not raised, for their family expenses increase as time goes on, but they give no thought to self-improvement or to plans for bettering their lot. Such people lack ambition. They bear a very close resemblance to animals of the field; they have a definite number of wants and are fairly content when those wants are satisfied.

Being content with an ordinary job is a wonderful state of mind. However, very few blue collar workers are really content. Many are in denial and really wish for a better life style. The world is full of mediocrity simply because they have fears of taking on other challenges. Being a business man is not for everyone but for those who crave to have more wealth challenge is irresistible.

Ambition is a purely human quality, not possible to the slightest degree in a beast. It makes a man dissatisfied with the present status and eager to climb to a higher level. It is the child of vision and desire. The imagination, aided by judgment and memory, creates for us a more attractive, an ideal environment, and pictures in it a stronger, wiser and happier self. It contains for us all the promise of Canaan to the Israelites and beckons to us with such compelling charm that we struggle toward it with all our energy and will. Sacrifices, fatigue, hunger, misfortune, criticism by our friends, the cajolery of temptation-all these things mean nothing to us and fail to stop us. Then we are people of purpose, of ambition. An idea has taken possession of us.

A person who lacks vision will never feel the desire for great ambition. He may greatly desire riches and honor, but they cannot earn them, although by miserly methods they may accumulate a small fortune. It is quite possible for a person to possess vision and yet not be ambitious. He perceives the idea, but does not feel irresistibly drawn toward it. They are content to admire it or to talk about it to others. A person of this type usually lacks energy and will; he may get his greatest pleasures out of reveries and reflection and care little about achievement. These people sometimes become poets and philosophers and write books which stimulate the imagination of thousands of other men, thus bringing to others the beauty of the idea and the energy and push of ambition.

Ideas and Enthusiasm: The person of real enthusiasm puts their heart and soul into their work. They do so, not because they love their work per se, but because the idea back of the work has made them captive. A so-called matter-of-fact man, a man who prides himself on taking things as they are, who has no use for theories, dreams or speculations of any kind is never an enthusiast; in fact, he may scorn enthusiasm as a stigma of an ill-balanced mind. He is sure that an ounce of common sense is worth a ton of enthusiasm. No great idea ever tempts him from his moorings. He may be a faithful, industrious, intelligent worker all his days, but his career in business or in a profession will be mediocre, commonplace, uninteresting. Enthusiasm is the most dynamic of all human qualities. In a sense, it is the ideal descended on earth to battle with realities. People instinctively recognize its influence. That is why we say that enthusiasm is contagious. A salesman not charged with enthusiasm could not sell a cake of ice in the tropics. A business organization lacking enthusiasm does not get out of its men fifty per cent of their potential efficiency. The enthusiasm of a manufacturer of funeral caskets, or a mortician, may appear a bit gruesome, but it is a necessary part of his equipment if he is to succeed.

Vision and Will: The will is a complex mental power, and weakness of will often has its origin in indecision, in the reluctance of the judgment to make choice between two alternatives. A person who thinks clearly and feels strongly should have a strong will. A person of high purpose, born of clear vision, will have an aggressive will. The person of muddled vision, on the contrary, works without a clear-cut purpose in view, and this confusion of purpose is likely to bring about a weakening of will.

If therefore, we would strengthen our willpower, we must cultivate our imagination and encourage it to build for us an idea that will bring our whole being into action. The person, who wants something with their whole soul, wills irresistibly. He whose desire or purpose is drab, lackadaisical, sentimental, has the will of a jelly fish.

The Fixed Idea: A strong mental power perverted or wrongly used is necessarily harmful. Hence a person of vigorous imagination, if his judgment happens to be biased by prejudice, religion or convention, and especially if he is conceited or obstinate, sometimes clings to an idea with the devotion of a fanatic long after he should have learned from experience that it is inadequate and imperfect. He is a victim of what the French call the Idee fixe-"the fixed idea.''

If a person gazes blankly for a certain length of time at any object, seeking to think of nothing at all, he may pass into a hypnotic state and temporarily lose control of his mental faculties, accepting as true and pleasant whatever may be suggested by prolonged contemplation of an idea in which they believe. It may be a curious religious faith, or an idea that death awaits them at a certain age, or the idea that some specific peril threatens society.

The idee fixe is a symptom of mental disorder. If you feel that one of your friends is becoming a victim to it, do not argue with him-that will make him worse. Keep him from solitude. Give him plenty of company and plenty of other things to talk and think about, so that his mind may recover its poise.

Vision At Work: The reader's own imagination or memory has doubtless already supplied him with illustrations of the way in which vision helps a person in business, and perhaps of instances in which failure has come because imagination had not done its part. Yet a few illustrations here may help to clear the reader's thought.

In the 1870's when the telephone was invented, most people could see in it only an interesting plaything. Capitalists saw little chance for profit in its exploitation, but the imagination of Alexander Graham Bell pictured it in every business house and residence. He could hear the voices of people talking with their friends far away, or concluding a business negotiation in a few minutes, with miles of travel and personal interviews no longer necessary. He preserved and lived to see his vision become reality.

In its earlier years, the automobile was a luxury enjoyed only by the rich. Henry Ford's imagination pictured to him what the automobile could do for people of ordinary means. Spurred on by his vision, Mr. Ford at once began to plan an automobile selling at a price within the reach of the average man. For several years, his cars had no competitors in their field.

But further illustrations are not necessary. The reader will find himself surrounded by examples of vision at work, ideas that have become realities-the alarm clock that wakes him in the morning, his electric razor or his shaving cream, the rubber heels of his shoes, his fountain pen, his computer, the streamlined train which takes him to work, the airplane which carries him to a distant business engagement in a couple of hours, and soon.

While he will recognize the importance of vision in the creation of such products, the reader may object that these are all in the nature of inventions and that they mean nothing to him because he is not an inventor. But every new idea is an invention. Frederick Winslow Taylor, introducing new methods of efficiency into the industry, was an inventor. Pierpont Morgan, creating great financial combinations, was an inventor. The department store is an invention. The supermarket is an invention.

In brief, all business progress is the result of invention, the working out of ideas; imagination is the product. If the person in business wishes to be successful, they should hold before themselves a vision of accomplishment in business and prepare themselves to convert their vision into reality.

Mary Kay Products was started by a dynamic lady who envisioned the importance of a woman looking her best in society and to satisfy her own mind and body. Starting from mediocrity, she developed a multi-million-dollar industry simply employing her vision, imagination, courage of her convictions and a plan to proceed. Mary Kay has left her legacy which comprised of all the things she accomplished into a book written by her entitled The Mary Kay Way. She left her mark in the industry and more importantly, has shown the world that a woman had the vision, foresight and business acumen to accomplish one of the greatest business enterprises catering to women and helping women look their best.

Another impressive business mogul was Sam Walton. Sam Walton was an American businessman. In his early twenties, he began his training with J. C. Penney in Des Moines, Iowa. In 1962, he opened his first retail store, Wal-Mart, in Rogers, Arkansas. By 1992, he had more than 1,700. Unlike other discount retailers, he opened stores in small towns where there was little competition. At the time of his death, he was the wealthiest man in the United States.

A pioneering businessman who broke convention and showed that large discount stores could thrive in small, rural areas, Samuel Moore Walton was born March 29, 1918, in Kingfisher, Oklahoma. He was the first son of Thomas Walton, a banker, and his wife, Nancy Lee. Early in his life, Walton and his family moved to Missouri, where he was raised. An able student and a good athlete, Walton quarterbacked his high school football team and was an Eagle Scout. Upon his graduation from Hickman High School in Columbia, Missouri, in 1936, his classmates named him "most versatile boy." Following college, Walton got his first real taste of the retail world when he took a job in Des Moines with the J. C. Penney Company, which was still a relatively small retailer.

After serving as an Army captain in an intelligence unit during World War II, Walton returned to private life in 1945 and used a $25,000 loan from his father-in law to acquire his first store, a Ben Franklin franchise in Newport, Arkansas. In 1962, Walton opened his first Wal-Mart store in Rogers, Arkansas. Success was swift. By 1976 Wal-Mart was a publicly traded company with share value north of $176 million. By the early 1990s, Wal-Mart's stock worth had jumped to $45 billion. Wal-Mart surpassed Sears, Roebuck & Company to become the country's largest retailer.

Another notable person is Ray Kroc and his story. He exclaims a very notable statement, "If I had a brick for every time I've repeated the phrase Quality, Service, Cleanliness and Value, I think I'd probably be able to bridge the Atlantic Ocean with them."

In 1917, 15-year old Ray Kroc lied about his age to join the Red Cross as an ambulance driver, but the war ended before his training finished. He then worked as a piano player, a paper cup salesman and a multi-mixer salesman. In 1954, he was surprised by a huge order for 8 multi-mixers from a restaurant in San Bernardino, California. There he found a small but successful restaurant run by brothers Dick and Mack McDonald and was stunned by the effectiveness of their operation. They produced a limited menu, concentrating on just a few items- burgers, fries and beverages-which allowed them to focus on quality at every step.

Kroc pitched his vision of creating McDonald's restaurants all over the U.S. to the brothers. In 1955, he founded the McDonald's Corporation, and 5 years later bought the exclusive rights to the McDonald's name. By 1958, McDonald's had sold its 100 millionth hamburger.

Ray Kroc believed in the entrepreneurial spirit and rewarded his franchises for individual creativity. Many of McDonald's most famous menu items-like the Big Mac, Filet-O-Fish and the Egg McMuffin-were created by franchises. At the same time, the McDonald's operating system insisted franchises follow the core McDonald's principles of quality, service, cleanliness, and value. Because of Ray Kroc's imagination the fast food industry and franchise system was emulated by dozens of other companies. Seemingly, there was a big impetuous to the fast food restaurant business as is apparent nationally and continuing to grow larger encompassing world markets.

From his passion for innovation and efficiency to his relentless pursuit of quality, and his many charitable contributions, Ray Kroc's legacy continues to be an inspirational integral part of McDonald's today.

Another famous establishment was Nathan's Famous Frankfurters. Nathan's Famous was founded by a Polish immigrant, Nathan Handwerker and his is truly an authentic "only in America story." He started his business in 1916 with a small hot dog stand in Coney Island, New York. He sold hot dogs that were manufactured based on a recipe developed by his wife, Ida.

In the over 95 years that have passed since opening day, Nathan's has gained worldwide recognition for the unequaled quality and taste of its product. Today,

Nathan's has gained reputation for being among the highest quality hot dogs in the world.

Nathan's popularity was almost instantaneous and in its earliest days had legendary characters such as Al Capone, Eddie Cantor, Jimmy Durante, and Cary Grant as regular customers. It gained its first international exposure when President Franklin Delano Roosevelt served Nathan's Famous hot dogs to the King and Queen of England in 1939. Later, Roosevelt had Nathan's hot dogs sent to Yalta when he met with Winston Churchill and Joseph Stalin. Years later, Nelson Rockefeller, Governor of New York, stated that, "No man can hope to be elected in his state without being photographed eating a hot dog at Nathan's Famous.

Politicians, show-business personalities, and sports celebrities are often seen and photographed munching Nathan's dogs, and heard dinging its praises. Barbara Streisand, actually had Nathan's hot dogs delivered to London, England for a private party.

A trip to Nathan's was the focus of a Seinfeld episode created by comedian Jerry Seinfeld. More recently, the ex-mayor of New York City, Rudy Giuliani declared Nathan's the "World's best hot dog."

Shortly after that, Nathan Handwerker was named to the city's top 100-joining the ranks of Joe Namath, Irving Berlin, Andrew Carnegie, Joe DiMaggio and others. Even Jacqueline Kennedy loved Nathan's dogs and served them at the White house. In his final last will and testament, actor Walter Mathau requested Nathan's hot dogs to be served at his funeral - and they were! The point is Nathan's is not just a hot dog, it has history and it is American!

"Where there is an open mind there will always be a frontier," says Charles F. Kettering. You face your competitors, your fellow workers and your community on a threshold of your own making--the frontier of imagination. How freely and how wisely you use your imagination may be the difference between success and failure. A psychologist once said that even our most renowned thinkers seldom call into play more than a fraction of their true capacity for thought. Millions of people travel from the cradle to the grave without thinking at all.

Every individual with a normal "head on his shoulders" and possessing normal energy, normal ambition, and normal curiosity, is potentially a thinker. The overwhelming tragedy is that so few people ever realize their potential-which so many, in fact, never come even close to it. They simply do not have the habit of thinking.

We believe that the thinking habit can be cultivated. We are concerned primarily with creative imagination; that, too, can be cultivated. For more than 30 years we worked in one of the toughest "idea processions" in the world-selling, being highly disciplined in the use of imagination. This experience convinces us that imagination is not a gift; it is a habitual way of using one's mind.

Many times, people have said, "I can't think up ideas. I guess I was born without imagination." With this kind of thinking, you will never perform effectively. But don't be too grim about it. Don't tighten up, too much heavy concentration will stifle your imagination and give you a headache. New ideas will come from your ability to turn your mind loose, give it plenty of rope, and let it play with fugitive thoughts even if apparently, they have no immediate relation to your problem. It is a mistake, in your eagerness, to focus on your original notion, to place aside what may seem at first to be irrelevant or even silly ideas. Did not Charles Darwin often play with what is called ''Fool's Experiment?''

Don't lose sight of your objective, of course, but, concentrate only to the extent of keeping your thoughts moving toward your desired end. "Nearly all creative men, "Woodrow Wilson once said, "are dreamers."

Grim bulldog concentration isn't meditating but quite the reverse. So close your eyes and dream, explore the back rooms of your mind for memories-for it is memories of what you knew yesterday compounded with what you know today that produce fresh ideas. Recollection of a long succession of small experiences, old and new, is the stuff imagination is made of. Such recollection is throttled when your mind, "grooved" by movement and spontaneity. A literature professor once remarked that a friend of his, when in pursuit of a desired idea, was always helped by letting his mind, "wander in random directions."

Free and fertile play of the imagination - not the kinked and furrowed brows, not the taut pose of Rodin's "Thinker" is the outstanding characteristic of the truly creative brain. Relax. Keep your mind open. Edison, when asked if he sat down and thought things out, replied: "No, not always. Often they just happen. I start here with the intention of reaching here (Edison was tracing with his finger) in an experiment, say to increase the speed of the Atlantic Cable; but when I arrive part way in my straight line, I meet with a phenomenon and it leads me off in another direction and develops into a phonograph."

Often you will find it helps to pick up a pencil and play with words. Thought engenders thought. Place one idea on paper, another will follow it, and still another, until you have written a page. There is a well of thoughts which has no bottom; the more you draw from it, the clearer and more fruitful it will be. This is not a new technique. George Augustus Sala, a great English war correspondent, wrote that over 100 years ago. There is this plus -advantage to the pencil-and-paper method. If you catch yourself writing down the same word or thought over and over again, you'll see that your mind has a fixation and is whirling around hopelessly in a tight little circle. This is the time to loosen up and start writing down anything that comes into your head.

Perhaps you may have the idea by now that using imagination is enough to assure your success in any venture you undertake. And it is - provided you link up imagination with information to make the unbeatable team.

Unfortunately, there have been many men and women who have used the most brilliant imagination possible, but have failed because they have not added information to their formula. It takes both. It takes imagination to give life, and force to a project. It takes information to make sure that this life and force will be directed where it will do the most good.

You see, imagination is like any powerful force in that it can be used improperly so that its vast powers do harm. Dynamite is a useful explosive which, when properly directed, works miracles of force; ignorantly, improperly used, it has blown many of its users into dust. Electric energy is undeniably a powerful factor in serving man, yet thousands of persons have been electrocuted because they used it improperly. It is the same with imagination.

One brilliant user of imagination was forever conceiving ideas which anyone could see were miracles of imagination. He was an inventor. He died in poverty. The reason for that was his unwillingness to link facts with his ideas, to mix information with his imagination and stir well before using.

To illustrate: he at one time spent several years perfecting an invention he was sure would serve mankind. Reading of a disastrous flood which had washed away a railroad bridge and caused a long train to plunge into a river, drowning over 50 persons, this kind-hearted inventor decided he would put a stop to such violent deaths. He invented life rafts to be carried on every train. Whenever a car went into a river all the passengers had to do to save them was to board the rafts. It took imagination to conceive such an idea. But there was no information involved. The inventor disregarded the fact that so few railroad passengers are drowned that it is a negligible factor. He could have saved himself hours and hours of work and scores of heart breaks if he had inquired before he acted.

The archives of the United States Patent Office are idled with equally grotesque ideas, and the life stories of millions of men and women contain tragedies of persons who put their money, their time, and their energy upon projects that were doomed to failure because they lacked the backing of information.

All such catastrophes could be avoided by making information a partner in any undertaking and seeking a background of facts.

If you were marketing a toothbrush and wanted increased demand for it, what would you do? Assuming that your brush was as good as it could be made, by what act of imagination could you cause it to stand out competitively? That was the problem that faced John T. Woodside, president of the Waco Company. Most toothbrushes were then anything but clean; they were displayed "nude" in open baskets, and customers would sell them by thumbing the bristles. Woodside decided to sterilize his brushes and package them clean in sealed glass containers believe it or not, a brand- new notion. He now had an inviting, fresh-looking product, one that the public took to so readily that sales have quadrupled since the revolutionary introduction of the sparkling glass bottle. Many things have contributed to its success, of course, but none so much as this single act of one man's imagination. Such is the stuff that all merchandising ideas are made of; little plus-values that often mean the difference between mediocrity and brilliance. How simple they seem -after the event!

Another single act of imagination - a very simple idea - turned a small Detroit jewelry firm into a company of national repute. It was again a clear case of relating one thing to another. For a long time, Ernest E. and Carl O. Bross, the company's president and vice-president, respectively, had felt that there might be a countrywide market for a decorated wedding ring to take the place of the customary gold and unadorned band. But the Bross Brothers have only half an idea; the other half was how to decorate this new ring? When the other half of the idea, and once thought of, it was astonishingly simple. Was not the orange blossom the traditional wedding flower? "Why," asked Ernest of Carl, "didn't we think of it years ago?" Many designs were made. The problem of putting a suitable design on a narrow band was not easy and almost everybody insisted the old plain band was best. Finally, even the prejudice of the cler.gy was overcome by a beautiful design of orange blossoms chased on a band of gold or platinum.

Through the years since then there have been changing styles; diamonds have become more generally used for decorative purposes. Today there are a variety of designs numbering in the hundreds but it was the orange blossom flower which changed it all - an idea so obvious nobody thought of it before. Today leading jewelers everywhere sell "Orange Blossom Wedding Rings by Traub."

Perhaps there is no greater challenge in business than the selection of a trade name. Often the appeal of the name is a primary force in attracting customers. The quality of imagination in the naming of a great many products and services is appalling second-rate. Nobody has ever made a count, but there must be thousands of public eating houses know by such names as Brown's Restaurant, Rochester Restaurant, Main Street Cafe, Harry's Cafe, Joe's Place, and - worse of all - just plain Eats.

Let us now take a business, a spectacularly successful one, and observe in considerable detail the reason for its amazing growth. Conrad N. Hilton was unquestionably the most successful hotel man in America. Let us take a look at the workings of his mind - at the reach and depth of an imagination that has spread a string of Hilton Hotel across America from coast to coast which are host to more people than any other group of hostelries on earth.

The amazing thing is that it has all been done in 26 years. Conrad N. Hilton, the man who did it, had his first "hotel" experience as a boy of 16 in little San Antonio, New Mexico, when he fixed up five rooms over his father's general store, took in guests, earned and saved enough profits to put himself through college. Then, enlisting, he fought in World War I, came back a lieutenant, got in the hotel business in earnest by buying his first hotel in oil-boomed Cisco, Texas. That was in 1919. At that time, a seventy-million-dollar property, of which Conrad Hilton was head man and principal owner, ranks him unquestionably the number one man in the United States hotel business.

How did he do it, this boy from a backyard New Mexican village? What quality of mind and character does he have that has made him so successful? What, in short, makes him "tick"?
Countless people have asked that question - just as they have always asked it about every man or woman of outstanding achievement.
The answer can be summed up in one word - imagination. Conrad Hilton had a powerful lot of it, and from it came his idea, which you shall hear about presently; his vision of how far this idea would take him; and the courage he displayed in seeing it through.

At the very outset of his hotel career, Hilton sensed that the age of leisure, of hotel management by the "servant- proprietor," was over. America was speeding up and he saw long before most hotel men that techniques in hotel keeping were not keeping pace. Few hotels were making money, and about 85 percent of them went to the wall during the hard years following World War 1.
Conrad Hilton - and here you see imagination at work - was always able to see things with the other fellow's eyes. He was unfailingly objective in his viewpoint. Thinking of himself as a hotel guest - not as a hotel owner - he studied his patrons with vast curiosity, saw them as fast - stepping, go-getting impatient Americans with no time for the leisurely inefficiency of the old time innkeeper. What sort of hotel service does modern America want, he asked himself day in and day out, and what will it want in the future?

What they want above all else, he was convinced is efficiency - modern, streamlined efficiency on just four counts: comfort, speed, courtesy and cleanliness. Out of this conviction comes Hilton's philosophy of hotel-keeping. Here it is, the big idea that was building his empire: The only hotel that can be really a good hotel - good in the quality of those four things guests want - is the hotel that operates at a profit.

Conrad Hilton has been referred to as a "balance sheet operator," and he truly is that. He determinedly ran his hotels to make money, not only because he likes to make money for himself and his shareholders and his employees, but also because he knew there is no other way to give his guests fine hotel service.

Hence, it is that Hilton's first consideration was the caliber of business management when he added another hotel to his string. The man he installed to run it did not have to be a connoisseur of rare wines, but he had to be a connoisseur of business statistics. Hilton is said to be the first hotel man anywhere to introduce a daily profit-and loss statement, a detailed report ranging from such vital matters as every single penny spent for food to the prevailing state of the weather.

Hilton waged continuous war on waste. He contended that one reason so many hotels lose money is that their eyes are shut to many golden opportunities to turn waste into money. He says they can't "visualize." Particularly keen on making profitable use of "dead" space, his lively imagination served him well.

The Plaza Hotel in New York is a striking example of the Hilton brand of imagination. It was on the rocks when Hilton took it over. The old owners declared it couldn't make money, but Hilton felt that it could, and the deal was closed. The Plaza Hotel in New York is a striking example of the Hilton brand of imagination. "Visualization" was a sort of a hobby with Hilton. Gazing at a dreary stretch of ocean sand, he sees big umbrellas in gay colors and lovely maidens plunging into the water. He seems to do it instinctively, almost without thinking.

In his earlier days, Hilton survived many heartbreaking crises. On one occasion, he hurried at night to the home of a postmaster, begged him for the return of a check that had accidentally been mailed too soon. Hilton's bank account was down to zero and he knew the check would bounce back. The postmaster, affected by Hilton's earnestness and enthusiasm about his future, not only returned the letter but loaned him enough money to starve off the sheriff.

This enthusiasm of Hilton's is extremely contagious. It is busily planning better ways to be a better host. He is unhappiest when Hilton service falls short of what he feels his guests expect. No form letters are used to answer complaints. Hilton personally wrote a sincere and friendly note to every complaining guest; and he lost no time in correcting the cause of the problem.

There have always been restless, curious, meditative men forever looking for better ways of doing things, and their businesses have prospered because their ideas have been of genuine service to mankind. Opportunity awaits the creative service to mankind. Opportunity awaits the creative thinker in every field of human activity. "There is no limit," said Henry Ward Beecher, "to the sphere of ideas."

The point of these success stories is mainly to demonstrate that average people can become very successful. One does not have to be a millionaire, multimillionaire or billionaire to be successful. There are hundreds of thousands of successful business people who have been innovated and creative to make more money than the average. Obviously, one does not have to be a super millionaire to be successful. The fact of the matter is that if you earn more than you can use, you are considered wealthy.

Good luck in your endeavors and enjoy living the good life.

REVELATION # 4
BRAINPOWER

Controlling situations especially in business is certainly an element for success. It is therefore vital that the businessman have a good understanding along the principals that add efficiency to the efforts exerted. Once the know-how is acquired - then self-discipline can be implemented. The power of concentration can be increased by anyone willing to put forth effort and discipline them. Concentration is like mustering up all of your accumulated conscious and subconscious knowledge that becomes a powerful force producing answers to solve problems and make good decisions.

EFFICIENCY COMMANDS ADMIRATION:
Observing an efficient mind at work is as fascinating as watching a smooth-running piece of machinery. One must admire the man who dispatches his day's work precisely on schedule, turning promptly from one problem to the next, concentrating completely on each. The process of analyzing data should proceed more rapidly and the decisions should proceed more expeditiously.
Everything is handled with a minimum of wasted motion. If a conference must be held, or someone called in to answer a question, the efficient executive displays a fund of clear, accurate information, with the ability to get at the heart of the problem. This is the analogy with an efficiently working machine. Every successful person wants for themselves to become this kind of human being, possessing mental mastery. Once realized, it becomes very powerful.
TAKE CHARGE OF YOUR MIND:
Developing an efficient mind is neither easy nor simple. It is not easy, because it demands much self-analysis and no end of patient, persevering practice. It is not simple, because mental efficiency involves a considerable number of individual abilities, each requiring development and strengthening. The first step is clear enough, however, and that is to take charge of one's mind, to stop drifting with the current.
It was a proud boast that the poet made who wrote, "I am the captain of my soul." It is not too proud a boast, however, if we interpret it to mean that he has become conscious of his abilities and disabilities, and has plotted a course for himself on the chart of self-knowledge. It is the attitude of awareness that is important and that will lead to progress.

A PROGRAM OF MENTAL DISCIPLINE

Assuming that the businessman is imbued with a strong, intelligently conceived purpose, we have to consider what he can do to develop his intellectual abilities to their maximum efficiency.

To simplify the problem, and to set up a truly workable program, we shall attempt to list the abilities that experience has shown to be important for most men. We shall call these abilities by their popular names, but it should be remembered that these so-called mental abilities are really groups or complexes of abilities, which the psychologist would analyze into more specific behavior patterns. The popular concepts will do very well for our purpose, however.

There is first the group of abilities going under the general name of concentration, which we may think of as the ability to give sustained attention, promptly and fully, to the tasks of the business day.

A second group centers around the abilities to get clear meanings, which we call learning, and to analyze ideas and problems so that we may prompt and correct decisions. The latter is the ability which we dignify as thinking.

A third group is included under the popular names of memory and habit, involving the development of the abilities to fix information for ready and accurate recall, and to repeat automatically useful actions that conserve what we have learned.

Any comprehensive program of mental discipline will include goals from these three groups. The emphasis will shift from one group to another, depending upon the individual man's knowledge of where he is weak or less efficient than he would like to be.

IMPROVING THE ABILITY TO CONCENTRATE

Long periods of intensive concentration, such as are required by the inventor or the mathematician, are not the usual requirement in business. What the business man needs is the ability to concentrate intensively for short periods, giving his attention to a succession of problems, often quite unrelated. Flexibility is the characteristic note of an executive's concentration.

The central ability involved in concentration is that of resisting the competition offered by distracting stimuli. These are internal as well as external ideas and thoughts as well as objects and persons. The factor of competition is present as long as a person is conscious, and even during intense concentration, as psychologists have discovered, distracting stimuli are not completely shut off from the mind.

Men do not possess the ability to resist distractions to the same degree or in the same way. A scientist may be unusually proficient in sustaining attention to a single problem over a long period of time. But he may not be able; on the other hand, to shift his attention quickly if he is given an administrative position wherein he is confronted with a daily barrage of problems requiring what the psychologist calls "impulsive" or flexible concentration. This is the type in which the businessman usually excels.

The encouraging aspect of this matter is that most men can cultivate either type of concentration, even though they may naturally excel in one type or the other. By a little daily practice, it is possible either to lengthen gradually one's span of attention, or to acquire a greater facility in dropping one problem completely and turning promptly and energetically to the next. For either type of concentration, knowing what we want to do is half the battle.

CUTTING DOWN ON DISTRACTIONS

The working environment helps or hinders according to the number and intensity of the distracting stimuli it may contain. The aim should be to create a setting as favorable as possible for concentration. Industrial psychologists have found the efficiency of workers to increase as much as thirty-five per cent when they were moved from a noisy to a quiet place. With the advancements made in building construction to deaden noise, and the availability of noiseless office appliances and restful, attractive office furniture, there is no reason for tolerating office conditions that multiply disturbing stimuli, reduce efficiency, and add to fatigue. Much has been done, also, to make the modern factory a more satisfactory working environment.

Some men hold the theory that a noisy, exciting environment acts as a challenge to a person's mental powers and calls forth his best efforts. There is an element of truth in this theory, but it can easily be carried too far. Production records show that work done in a noisy environment for long hours at a time will result in diminished efficiency toward the end of the business day. Such an environment should not be fostered needlessly.

ORGANIZATION TO REDUCE DISTRACTIONS

The working arrangements in the modern office illustrate how organization can be utilized to curtail unnecessary demands upon the businessman's attention. The executive has a desk to himself or a private office. A secretary guards his seclusion by handling personal telephone calls, ascertaining who is calling and the nature of his business. Many calls are taken care of without interrupting the executive at all. Department heads dispose of routine matters not requiring the executive's personal supervision. In large companies, besides the secretaries and department heads, there are assistants to the higher executives who further reduce the demands upon their chiefs. The arrangement of the executive's desk drawers, files, and the articles of convenience on the desk top is a further illustration of organization to reduce distractions and facilitate concentration.

The image and view of the executive by employees is amazingly different. The employees realize that the executive is an important figure yet is under the illusion that all he does is relaxed in a chair behind the desk all day. This is far from the truth. Actually, the executive is working mentally which is actually harder than performing something routine without problems.

Viewing the office as a whole, it is plain that from the opening of the morning's mail to the flow of work from desk to desk, the office is planned very definitely to secure the maximum of concentration for each worker. The executive who feels that too many petty demands are robbing him of time for more vital questions of policy- making may well pause to examine his office organization. If it is not serving him well, the chances are that it is not serving his subordinates any better. One part of the executive's job is to guard his fellow workers against the same distractions that hamper him in his work.

PLANNING AS AN AID TO CONCENTRATION

One successful businessman, the head of a nationally known company, is a strong believer in planning and scheduling devices as means for ensuring that his environment shall promote good concentration. Taking as his slogan, "One thing at time-the big thing-at the right time," he has trained his executive staff to submit, at definitely scheduled periods, the significant problems that should be referred to him and that cannot be handled within their various departments.

Planning one's work makes concentration easier, just because it is planned. A great mass of work tempts many men to procrastinate from its sheer burdensomeness, but if, through planning, the accumulation of problems has been divided into small, accessible units, the task of overcoming inertia becomes a great deal easier.

The man who does not plan or schedule carefully is likely to diffuse his efforts and even impair his ability to concentrate. The French educator, Payot, relates how, at the assumption of administrative duties, he was overwhelmed by the mass of communications crossing his desk. "I would cast a glance over the whole lot," he writes, "then look at one and another without making a decision on any." He soon saw that he was losing a great deal of time, and the discovery began to prey on his nerves. Then he took hold of himself, resolved to dispose of one communication before opening a second. The result was magical. He accomplished his work in much less time; his former poise returned, his nerves recovered their serenity.

Early in his career, the average businessman learns the lesson that Payot learned late, but perhaps not as perfectly as he imagines he has. Even when working by a schedule, there is a temptation to spread one's attention over too wide an area, perhaps with the excuse that one must obtain a "broad" view of a problem. Getting a broad view has its uses, but it should not be allowed to dissipate concentration. Once the problem is seen broadly, it should be broken down into its various sub-problems and each attacked separately.

Some men find that certain hours of the working day are more favorable than others for maintaining a high degree of concentration. It is often possible to arrange a schedule so that those duties requiring longer periods of concentration may come at the more favorable hours, with less danger of fatigue.

DEVELOPING INTERESTS TO AID CONCENTRATION

Procrastination usually implies that the task to be done is distasteful or difficult. We put off such tasks or attend to them poorly. Here we may draw upon the psychology of interest-formation-what is interesting secures attention easily and painlessly. Our problem, therefore, is to find some way of converting the distasteful task into an activity commanding spontaneous attention.

Work can be made interesting by making it seem more worthwhile. It may be related to the progress of the company, to one's personal advancement, to the expectations of associates and higher officers, or even to the discomfiture of competitors. Once we see that the accomplishment of an unpleasant task means a definite production or sales gain for the business, or that it will service notice to one and all that we "can take it, "or that this task, competently performed, will lessen outside competition, we shall have built up an interest in the distasteful job, enabling us to tackle it with a sort of grim pleasure.

Another method of making work interesting is to treat it as a contest. The executive may set quotas for himself - so many letters to be dictated within a given time, a desk to be cleared by a definite hour in the day, a schedule to be followed according to the dictates of a calendar or a tickler file.

These are non- essential interests, added to the work. In any event it establishes a short goal that the worker can strive for to achieve. To develop an interest growing out of the work itself, and hence essential to it, will usually involve getting to know more about it than we do - exploring its importance to other departments of the business, how it is being handled by other companies, the past and probable future of the activity, the possibilities of doing it better. Attending the meetings of trade or professional clubs and associations where the experience of other companies may be shared, or reading the weekly and monthly issues of trade and business journals in which other executives describe how they handle the same operations, will help materially in developing an intrinsic interest. The more we know about any job, the more interesting it is bound to become.

WILLPOWER AS A LAST RESORT

If information is not readily available, or if some other factor prevents the development of an interest in a distasteful task, recourse must be had to the old-fashioned quality of ''willpower'' -and staying power to accomplish the task. Perhaps our work seems difficult because we have built up habits of luxurious, enjoyable dawdling. In that case, stern measures are required, and at once. The fact must be faced that some pleasures are not to be indulged in business, and dawdling is one of them. To take ourselves in hand, to see whether we can take a reasonable amount of punishment, could become an interest in itself.

Will power is particularly needed to overcome the temptation to postpone action on the ground that we are not "in the right mood" and that later we can do better. Will power can be encouraged, for such emergencies, by recalling our boyhood reluctance to take the first plunge into cold water. The thing to do then was to brush aside every excuse and make the plunge.

It is the thing to do now. Once in, whether it is the old swimming hole or our present work, we become warm and exhilarated, and everything functions as it should.

It is possible to form a habit of "sticking," or refusing to quit. If a schedule is worth setting, it is worth following through with. Unless a company policy is shown to be wrong, it should be carried out to the letter. Dogged repetition of such acts as getting at work promptly, doing the unpleasant task first, and refusing to quit until it is finished, will form habits equivalent to will power.

THE OVERWORK DELUSION

The belief that we are overworked is more frequently a delusion than most men are aware. The testimony of those who have looked into the matter is a little surprising. It was observed that businessmen of several nations, declared that "the majority of decent, average, conscientious men of business (men with aspirations and ideals) do not, as a rule, go home of a night genuinely tired.

It is said that most people who are overworked are, more properly speaking, simply the victims of bad air, bad diet, poisons and worry. They believe that, because they are tired, it must be work which is hurting them. They are undoubtedly working beyond their working capacity; but their working capacity is only a fraction of what it would be if they took exercise, were not constipated, did not eat too much, abjured alcohol, or ceased to worry continually. Some men suffer from a constant sensation of fatigue, the remedy for which is personal hygiene, with special care to secure sufficient sleep."

This would seem to be very good advice for those who need it, but there are some businessmen who must be cautioned that the delusion of overwork is, for them, no delusion. They usually know it, having been warned by a physician to slow down.

IMPROVING THEIR ABILITIES TO GET AND ANALYZE IDEAS

Getting clear, precise meanings or ideas is basic to all thinking that leads to correct decisions, and the absence of clear concepts is responsible for hazy thinking in every walk of life. Many an argument is ended when the participants finally get around defining their terms, because it is then seen that they were not talking about the same things.

How does this familiar situation arise? In the first place, words have often acquired a rather long list of meanings and undefined connotations during their progress through the decades or centuries. One man emphasizes one meaning, another a different meaning and each too often assumes that everyone else has adopted the particular meaning that he cherishes.

In the second place, people are often hazy about the precise meaning of a word because it is one that has never been transferred from their reading to their speaking and writing vocabularies. The average person's reading vocabulary is much more extensive than either his speaking or writing vocabulary. He guesses at the meanings of many words that he reads, and because they occur in a printed context, associated with other words familiar to him, their general drift can be made out, with the result that he does not come to know the word in any real sense, or to make use of it in his speaking or writing.

One cure for a hazy vocabulary is to have a dictionary, a glossary of synonyms, or a book on English usage conveniently at hand, and to form a habit of browsing in it whenever time permits. Noting new words, or words that need clearing up, or good words known but neglected, will do much for a vocabulary, particularly if we take pains to give ourselves practices in using the new or recovered words.

GUARDING AGAINST STEREOTYPES

Even more dangerous than hazy words, and certainly harder to detect and eliminate, are the ready-made evaluations and judgments which have been well named "stereotypes." Such prefabricated judgments are commonly expressed in slogans, catch-phrases and word formulas, and are to be met with in every walk of life. The business world is perhaps less beset by them than some other departments of human activity, notably politics, where a great deal of alleged thinking is merely the repetition or juggling of time-worn platitudes.

However, business has its share of stereotypes, some of them true, some true only at times or with large exceptions. "The customer is always right" is one example of a stereotype which has an honorable origin and history, possesses considerable merit still, and yet has led to some outstanding abuses, as, for example, capricious returns of merchandise. Nearly every change or reform of business procedure has been opposed in the name of some stereotype -often only a prejudice or a set conviction that business must always be done in a traditional way, or that the proposed change will lead straight to bankruptcy.

To be forewarned is to be forearmed. Forming a habit of looking critically at our own conceptions as well as at those of others will put us on guard against the deluding effects of stereotyped thinking. "Is that true?" "What are the facts?" "Have you checked that, or are you merely assuming?" Questions like these will start us on the way to genuine thinking.

QUESTIONING ASSUMPTIONS

A manufacturer of a home appliance noted that orders were dropping off, particularly from the large department stores. The sales department had an explanation, but it was merely the old stereotype that competition was bound to cut down orders as the industry grew out of its infancy. The manufacturer decided to investigate.

Devoting six weeks to his study, he traveled from Chicago to Los Angeles and interviewed several dozen buyers and department store managers. What he found was startling - department stores were pooling their buying to an extent unsuspected by his salesmen, and the real buying was being done by apparently unrelated concerns in New York. The local buyers didn't want to lose face with the visiting salesmen by admitting the curtailment of their authority. It was not so much increased competition, as a shift in the market that had kept the manufacturer's salesmen from taking orders. As a result, the sales department overhauled its assumptions as to where to put its sales effort.

TESTING IDEAS UNDER BUSINESS CONDITIONS

The businessman is in charge of an organization that is not static but constantly moving; his decisions on the many questions laid before him each day must be made promptly. This means that he cannot analyze problems in the leisurely manner of a judge on the bench or of a scientist in a laboratory. On the other hand, since his decisions result in actions, he cannot afford to make mistakes. He must think accurately, as well as quickly. What tests can he apply?

First, he can see what the proposal, problem or idea means. This is the first step. To jump at the meaning of a proposal, as the busy executive is inclined to do, is to run the risk of error, waste, and expense. Ten minutes spent in examining the full meaning of an idea, in forecasting its effects on the various departments of his business, will save time and effort later. His decision may well be neither to accept nor reject, but to investigate further.

Secondly, a new idea should be tested with respect to the worth of its source. Who suggested it? What are his general intelligence and understanding, his knowledge of the matter, his sincerity and honesty? Is the proposal free of undue self-interest? If the idea has come from printed material, what is the author's reliability? Is he a competent witness?

SEEKING THE OVERLOOKED FACTOR

An idea may pass successfully these first two tests but fail to meet the third, namely, whether any factor has been overlooked either in the assumptions or in the line of reasoning leading to the conclusion that such and such an action should be taken. The careful executive will examine both assumptions and reasoning.

As for the assumptions or premises of a proposal, he will ask whether they are correct and whether they are complete. Perhaps the assumptions are not evident at first glance, in which case it is likely that they were not evident to the man offering the idea, or that he mistook assumptions for facts. To assume too much or to assume too readily are common errors; assumptions will nearly always stand investigation. An advertising campaign or a sales policy based on market research in which assumptions have played the main part, almost inevitably leads to grief, as any good advertising man will tell you. The same is true for finance or production or for any other department of business.

Once the basis assumptions of a proposal have been uncovered and checked, there remains the task of checking the line of reasoning leading to the conclusions or recommendations. The critical executive will ask: Has the point been proved? Do the premises really lead to the recommendations as set forth. Is this one more instance of arguing by analogy, of assuming that because A 1s similar to B, A will have the same growth as B, or meet with a like success? Reasoning by analogy is congenial because it is easy to see similarities and to connect them by a cause-and-effect relationship. Too often, the similarities are only superficial.

MEMORY AND ITS IMPROVEMENT

A retentive, reliable memory is a great asset to any executive, saying the time necessary to recover data once known but subsequently forgotten, and enablingthe executive to examine a proposal more quickly in search of overlooked factors. On the other hand, the businessman with a lazy, untrained memory labors under a serious handicap. Written reports, letter files, price lists and other memoranda relive memory of a part of its burden, but there are many important data that must be held in mind without the aid of records.

Strictly speaking, we have memories rather than a memory. Certain sets of experiences are more easily recalled than others; we become proficient in their recall, or develop "a good memory" for them, while failing to become proficient in the recall of other types of experience.

The essential factor in any memory seems to be the association of experiences in some kind of order - time, or space, or an order of cause and effect - or a tie-up with some strong emotion. How strong the association will be depends upon which of several factors is the prevailing one. Frequency is a factor; so, too, are the intensity of impression and its regency. Usually, the more recent the experience, the better it is remembered, but the aged tend to recall events of their youth more vividly than events of middle age. For them, it is primacy of experience that matters.

These factors, being external, are largely beyond our control, although we can juggle experience to some extent to secure conditions favorable for strong associations. By reading trade and business journals consistently, we are brought to think about certain important ideas or methods repeatedly. Using a new acquaintance's name frequently in a conversation helps to strengthen the original impression.

As a matter of fact, any improvement in memory is almost exclusively the product of improved learning. The more thorough the original impression of the data to be remembered, the greater will be its retention. We can repeat some experiences, as a further aid, but we cannot do much to change the native retentiveness of our brain tissues. That depends upon the health of our nervous system. Of course, anything we do to foster our general health is contributing to the better functioning of that system. For immediate results, however, we must improve our learning procedures.

AIDS TO BETTER MEMORIZING

Many men who were born with a relatively poor retentively of nervous structure. have overcome this handicap by concentrating on the improvement of their learning processes. They have developed these processes to a point where they often surpass men born with a greater native retentiveness. It is memorizing, rather than memory that is the point of attack in so-called memory training.

What can be done to improve one's learning procedures? The following suggestions will indicate the general line of attack:

Resolve to remember. The intention of learning a fact for later really is important for actual retention. Say to yourself, "I must remember this. A simple expedient, but experiments show that it increases the efficiency of memory from 20 to 60 per cent.

Give alert attention to new facts and ideas. Repel distractions, attend to one thing at a time, and get clear ideas.

Multiply the original impression where you can. Use as many senses as you can while you are getting the impression; speak a new work as you read it, for example.

Create occasions for repeating new ideas or facts as soon and as often as convenient.

Seek associated meanings. Tie up new ideas with older ones; classify your knowledge. Most adult memorizing is of the logical rather than of the rote type. Mechanical repetition is necessary for the latter, as in learning telephone numbers, but logical memorizing demands meaningful associations.

WHAT ABOUT MEMORY SYSTEMS?

So-called memory systems devises as a commercial product probably have been more profitable to their vendors than to those who bought and tried to use them. The main value of commercial systems lays in their teaching habits of useful learning and concentration, perhaps more or less incidental to the "system" proper. For the most part, memory systems expect the student to commit to memory (by rote methods) an artificial framework consisting of fifty or more unrelated words. These words are then made the basis for other associations, often quite fanciful, and into this framework the student fits any data that he wishes to remember. Most people find that the "system" demands an exorbitant amount of time for memorizing the necessary keys, and still more for finding applications of the keys to the material to be learned.

Homemade systems for memorizing telephone numbers or other rote material are as useful as the commercial systems to the average person, and the man who invents one is making no specious claim to be "training" his memory as a whole.

HABITS AS CONSERVERS OF EFFICIENCY

Throughout our discussions to this point we have referred to the importance of forming useful habits and habitual attitudes. Habits are in reality the end results of all our efforts to achieve mental efficiency. They conserve the gains we have made, guarantee that our efficiency will maintain at least its present level. Habits will not guarantee efficiency, however, unless they are the selected and controlled products of intelligent training. The man who is just beginning to investigate his mental status will find that his accumulated habits have "just been enhanced. Many have come into existence without his being aware of them, formed unconsciously, through imitation. Some are good, others are not. Some make for efficient work, others hinder it.

It is necessary, therefore, to take control of one's habits. The easiest way to begin is to study one's habitual methods of work, to make a rough survey of which procedures should be strengthened, which broken and replaced by better ones. Unless we get control of our habits, we shall not consolidate the gains from our attempts to improve any phase of mental efficiency.

FORMING AND BREAKING HABITS

The principles of habit formation are much the same as those for learning or for memorizing. We must first get clearly in mind the precise action or attitude that is to be made habitual, and begin the series of repetitions of the new habit with a strong resolution to succeed. Practice periods should be divided, if possible, letting several hours intervene between periods. The new habit should be used in as many associations as possible. No exception should be permitted until the habit is formed.

Breaking an entrenched habit is a difficult but not an impossible task. As a rule, it cannot be done directly, for if a direct attempt is made, the habit is often driven deeper into the nervous system. The direct attack, moreover, is more painful and takes more energy. The indirect attack of substitution is the better approach. New and more desirable habits should be substituted for the old.

To take an example from the realm of personal habits, suppose a man wants to break off smoking. Let us assume that he is a mild smoker, confining himself to a cigar after meals. Merely to refuse a cigar and sit grimly wondering how long he can stand the misery, is not likely to meet with any great success. He must 1md something positive to take the place of smoking - entering more actively into conversation, leaving the table and taking a walk, strumming a musical instrument, or some other activity. One psychologist reports knowing a man who broke off smoking after dinner by cleansing his teeth. The substitute habit does not matter, provided it is more desirable than the one to be broken.

In short, to break a habit, form a counter habit.

HABITS OF THOUGHT

Our accumulation of habits does not consist only of physical habits; we also have habits of thought. Certain thoughts about a large number of subjects have passed and reposed through our minds with increasing ease until at last, we accept them as obvious and self-evident. Emotional reactions are often tied up with these thoughts or judgments, and tend to repeat themselves when the thought is repeated. That circumstance makes it very difficult to question a habit of thought without arousing resentment - a difficulty often slowing down or preventing the introduction of some long overdue change of program or policy. The difficulty can be overcome only by patient publicity and re-education.

Ideally, of course, there should be no question which a reasonable man cannot permit himself to be asked, and no long-standing assumption that he is unwilling to have both questioned and investigated.

Mastery of mind, to a large degree, depends upon the physical condition. Few people except physicians realize that a good physical condition adds to the mental performance, and the contrary is also true, that a poor aching, out of condition body diminishes mental ability to concentrate. Physical unfitness should be guarded against. A good physical fitness program is called for in every case where top mental efficiency is demanded. Physical unfitness should be guarded against. A good physical fitness program is called for in every case where top mental efficiency is demanded. Proper exercise routinely, along with adequate sleep and rest is essential. A proper diet should be adhered to daily. Any overweight or underweight condition should be attended to with utmost diligence.

A good physical condition adds to the feeling of strength, confidence, and well-being which directly and indirectly affects the mental faculties. We hope that this report has highlighted some areas of benefit to you personally.
The foregoing information on Brain Power should be studied intensely for it is the habits we have formed that will make or break us in the pursuits of our goal.

Have the brains to employ the brains to solve problems and go forward. That is progress.

From the beginning of time problems have existed that demanded solutions.   The problems were in the path of progress and needed answers. It is inevitable as problems have always existed. Mathematics is the foundation of all knowledge.

The uneducated, as well as the brilliant encounter problems. Mathematicians always have a problem to solve. Finding the solution to the problem unveils another problem. It is an endless chain of progress to be made.

The problems of mathematicians are endless. Most mathematical problems will never be solved within our lifetime or even future generations. The smartest people in the world encounter the most complex problems which they may diligently work on most of their lives. Often times, solutions are not achieved and the problem perpetuates only to be challenged by future generations.

The quest to solve problems goes on indefinitely. As a matter of course, many experts are brought together to consult with each other trying to arrive at a solution.

Many meetings are arranged and years can go by before a solution or half of solution is discovered. All the efforts and time and expense are the price of progress. Answers are not cheap.

Because we know that problem result in pursuit to find a solution, we invite the challenge of having problems, simply because this leads to progress.

Donald Trump is a brilliant man when confronted with a problem. He uses his brain to hire brains to solve whatever problems he encounters. He does not take the position to depend solely on his judgement.

Every Government in the world is always seeking brain power talent to solve problems and make progress. The old saying "that two heads are better than one" is brilliant.

Revelation # 5
OPPORTUNITY

Significance of opportunity. The intensity of our nature, the quality of our character, and the tenacity of our purpose are all revealed by the vigor or sloth with which we pursue opportunity. It is one of the important words in the language. It means much more than chance. Chance comes to us unasked, unexpected, and often undesired, but opportunity comes only as the result of our desiring, willing and acting. It is a precious, golden thing and must be worked for.

Men who succeed in business somehow seem never to lack opportunity, while those who fail often complain that opportunity has been denied them. On account of its importance in business, it seems necessary to devote a chapter to a consideration of the various conditions that develop or create opportunity. Men who are trying to get ahead in business should have a clear idea of what the term means. They are too prone to think that their chances depend more upon "pull" or luck than upon preparedness.

Today's business opportunities. We often hear people remark dejectedly that business opportunities have almost disappeared, that the small man has little chance, that large corporations have absorbed all the opportunities for making money, and that most men cannot hope to be more than minor employees. That kind of talk is radically erroneous. It is true that a great part of today's business is conducted by corporations, but there is no ground for the statement that corporations kill opportunity. On the contrary, they create opportunities.

Some of the most successful business men of today, who have great executive ability and have accumulated comfortable fortunes, rose from obscurity from creating management of corporations where they were able fully to demonstrate their talents. Many of our successful business men began life as poor boys and worked up to the top, not in spite of corporations, but because of the opportunities opened up to their abilities by the corporate form of business operation. Of those who have built up businesses of their own, not a few previously acquired in large corporations the valuable training that was the groundwork of their success.

A hopeful outlook. In growing countries like the Americas, where conditions are constantly changing, where inventions are forever improving processes, and where markets are widening, business opportunities in normal times are plentiful. While geographical frontiers have largely yielded to civilization through the advent of railroads, highways and airlines, there are business, economic and social frontiers

many of which still have not even been explored. The bare needs of a large part of the human race remain yet to be reasonably satisfied.

Beyond the demand for these meager necessities there lie uncounted wants and desires for the supplying of which no means has yet been provided. Even though the rate of population growth slows down, this "backlog of unfilled orders" will require the united efforts of several generations to come before it can be filled to satisfaction.

The past growth of countries in the Western Hemisphere into business and industrial nations is due largely to the fact that in no other lands on earth is there such a genius for making use, to the full, of opportunities as they develop. Even in the "times that try men's souls" men and women of the Americas refuse to be daunted-they go on capitalizing on existing opportunities and creating new ones.

Is there a law of opportunity? Broadly speaking, a business opportunity is a combination of circumstances that creates a profitable market for something which we have to sell or may be able to produce. The business man himself, however, must perceive the conditions which make the opportunity, and then promptly take possession. If a man perceives an opportunity to increase his business or to start a new one, and does not act promptly, the opportunity is lost to him. Somebody else seizes it.

If our law of opportunity is correct, no man has any right to complain about his lack of opportunity, or to set up in defense of his failure the claim that he never really had a chance. Opportunity is clearly a relative term. On the one side are the business conditions pregnant with profit; on the other side is the fit man able to call the profit into existence. When these two meet, we have opportunity. For the untrained man of little will power and no worth-while experience and education there can be no opportunity. Nobody seeks his services, however cheaply he offers them. In the current of affairs, he is merely driftwood.

Rising to one's opportunities. It is important that a man in business-whether running his own enterprise or working for somebody else-should have correct idea of his mental power. He should not underestimate his ability, for then he will never do himself justice, being fearful lest he tackle a job too difficult for him. On the other hand, he must not overestimate his ability or depend upon a degree of luck for then he may undertake tasks for which he is not really fitted.

As a rule, however, it is wise to err, if at all, in the direction of self-confidence. A man who is working in company with men abler than himself, or who does not hesitate to attack a problem which seems a little beyond his powers, often will make mistakes, but in the long run, he will be more successful than if he practices excessive caution, for all the time he will be growing wiser and abler. Moreover, many tasks are less difficult on close inspection than they first appear.

No man, however, likes to admit that his mental powers are limited or below the average. As an English philosopher once remarked, "We are all willing to admit that our memories are defective, but no man will admit that his judgment is not sound." So, doubtless, many men who have not been promoted to positions of responsibility feel that they have not been appreciated. The companies, for which they work, of course, may have no better jobs which are unfilled and therefore cannot promote anyone at the time. But sometimes the executives for whom such men work have different options of these employees than the employees have of themselves.

A man who is anxious for advancement should first examine himself from the viewpoint of his immediate superior and that of his company. Perhaps he is not prepared to go higher without some further development. He may need to correct certain of his characteristics, and to stimulate and cultivate certain other qualities, before he will fit into a more responsible position. Often he needs additional training to broaden his knowledge of business and to widen his acquaintanceship with principles and practices in fields with which previously he has had little contact. The company can hardly be expected to take the risk of promoting him until he has begun to correct his deficiencies.

In no case, however, should he be discouraged. Ambition coupled with intelligent action is meritorious. He should continue his efforts to climb to attainable heights. Not all men are so eminently qualified that they can reach the very top. But all can rise to better jobs and/or create their own enterprise which they will be making the most of their talents in useful and remunerative service, and they will find happiness and satisfaction in these higher, constructive spheres of business. Seizing the opportunity at hand. It is a familiar human weakness to think of ourselves as not being in just the right place. Many a country boy feels certain that he could do great things if he could only get into a city. Doubtless many bank employees in small towns feel that they have never had a chance for development because of the limited local field in which they operate. The man in the East hopes to get into some marketing or industrial center in the West, or on the far coast. We are prone to think that opportunity, like happiness, lies in some distant place and that if we only could get there, we should be successful and content.

As a matter of fact, the secret of opportunity, like that of happiness, lies in us. No man who wishes to become a business man needs to travel far to make a start. For him the very best opportunities often are at his elbow. Many of our biggest business men got their first training in their home towns or villages-by clerking in a small store, by selling newspapers, by taking subscriptions to magazines, by acting as agents for manufacturers of farm implements, and in other simple pursuits. The needs of home folks are usually the needs of people elsewhere.

After a man has discovered opportunity near at home and has profited by it, then he will be fit for larger opportunities in other places, but often. even then, his next opportunity lies not far from him. This is naturally and logically the case for we are familiar with near-at-hand conditions and knows their possibilities. The glittering opportunities beckoning to us in the distance may be unreal. They may be like the sirens who sought to charm Ulysses from his true course. As Thomas Carlyle has said, "Our grand business is not to see what lies dimly at a distance, but to do what lies clearly at hand."

The fact that opportunity always lies near at hand does not mean that a man should not change from place to place, or from business to business. A change of location is often exceedingly desirable and advisable, but a man should not make a change because he is looking for opportunity, but because opportunity has made the change practicable and profitable.

Paying the price of progress. The proverb, "Where there's a will there's a way," receives abundant verification in the business world. The man who gets what he really wants in business, whether riches, position or honor, is the man who does more than wish hard for such things. Far more men could get what they want if they were willing to pay the price.

This statement doubtless looks extravagant to many readers. It may be read by a man of fifty who has been in business for over thirty years, and is even now barely able to do much more than support him and family. "Surely," he may say, "I wanted a fortune and I set out to make it. I have worked hard for more than thirty years, but here I am just able to hold down an ordinary position. In what way did I fail?"

Let such a man question himself along these lines: "In the thirty years of my business life have I ever voluntarily gone without food or sleep in order to further the interests of my employer or of myself? Have I turned my back on all pleasure which killed time that might have been profitably devoted to the study of my business, or to the seeking of opportunities to increase my business, or to developing of my own usefulness in business? Have I spent my money foolishly, or have I saved every penny possible in order that I might increase my capital, being content with the simplest and plainest manner of living? Have I deliberately sought the friendship of men who could be helpful to me in my business? In short, have I given my whole energy, physical and mental, to business with just enough time out to keep fit?"

To many men, large fortunes are not worth the price, for sometimes many fine things have to be sacrificed in merely getting rich. If a man has not the ability to make a great success in business unless he neglects his duties as a husband, father, and citizen and neighbor-foregoing what President Eliot of Harvard called "the enduring satisfactions of life"- he will be happier and more "successful" if he is content with moderate success in business.

But a man must not expect to find opportunity of any kind if he has not the will for doing and for sacrifice. Back of his will must be an intense desire, not just a milk-and-water wish or longing. The desire must be so consuming that it impels him to

act and to do anything and everything honorable that can possibly help him to conquer. Men cannot expect to fill positions for which they have not proved their fitness.

Opportunity accompanies age. It is event that the opportunities for which a man of forty or over is, or should be, fitted is entirely different from those open to the young man. But has the man of middle age already exhausted opportunity? Must he be content with his present rank in business? If he has been in business for himself, has he a right to hope that he can accomplish more during the next ten or fifteen years than he has accomplished in the past? Should a man of forty or fifty years of age enter a new business? Questions like these have come home personally to many men and have proceeded very difficult to answer.

Everything depends upon the man. Some men are old at forty-five; they have ceased to learn or to take an interest in new things, and are ambitious merely to maintain their present status, or to retain a position or a business which gives them a comfortable living. Such men should beware of severing old connections or of undertaking new enterprises.

Other men are still young at forty-five or fifty; their minds are on the future, not the past; they take no exaggerated pride in what they have accomplished, but are impatient for more work and bigger tasks; they still have vision and ambition. To men of this sort, if they have guarded their health, opportunity offers its biggest prizes.

A man of sixty-five-active, mentally alert and progressive-who had begun life as a farmer's boy and had built up a business of international scope, once said: "I wish I were twenty again. I see many opportunities in business of which I cannot take advantage, things that ought to be done, that would make the nation richer. It is not the money I think of-I already have more of that than I need-but I do not like to see opportunities for good business going to waste. Now, what I cannot understand is why I cannot make my two sons see these opportunities. I have given them both a good education, but they simply do not understand me when I try to show them how they can do as much as I have done, over and over again."

The man of fifty who has lost his job and does not know how to do anything particularly well, or who has failed in business, may not seem to have a particularly favorable outlook. But if he can only be made to seek opportunity with courage and ardor, the chances are that he will still succeed, despite the prejudice against his age. As a rule, men who are stranded at fifty have not mastered the art of rendering really valuable service and are suffering the hard, but inevitable, penalty of ineptitude and lack of training in business. Needless to say, the young man cannot protect himself against any such fate.

Learning by experience. Valuable as are the lessons learned from books and schools, and from those with whom a man comes in contact, it must never be forgotten that there are certain most important lessons which he can learn only by doing. A lawyer can learn how he can best influence a jury only by experience with a jury. He may have been taught the methods of appeal generally held to be the best, but which ones are best fitted to his own powers he must discover for himself through practice. So, a man preparing for business can learn much from books about the laws governing business phenomena, and about the methods and policies which have proved most successful, but he cannot be a master in any field until he has had actual experience in solving its problems.

The more a man has learned about business through experience, as well as through study, the keener his insight is into opportunity, and the more likely he is to avail himself successfully of an opportunity.

Earning the right to be "lucky." Opportunity and luck are not relatives or even good friends. The popular gospel which converts luck into the Goddess of Fortune has no basis in fact. There is a vast amount of loose talk about the part that luck plays in business success.

The essential element of luck is chance, and it is a mathematical certainty that chance is no respecter of persons. Chance is absolutely impartial. To say that a man has succeeded in business because of his luck, or because he was born under a lucky star, is as absurd as to say that some right angles are bigger than others. Chance helps the wicked and the good, the efficient and the inefficient, the lazy and the energetic, and it distributes its favors with the coldest kind of impartiality. Chance might be called a mathematical goddess who smiles and frowns alternately. If you catch her smile you are lucky, but if you incur her frown you are unlucky.

Undoubtedly men often make money in business as a result of luck. The outbreak of war may be lucky for some of the makers of ammunition and other war supplies, but unlucky for those in other industries which are cut off from materials by priority regulations. A failure of the wheat crop is "lucky" for the miller who happens to have a large stock on hand. A rise in the price of copper is "lucky" for the owners of copper mines. A man who seeks to make money in business must battle with the elements of chance, with the uncertainties of the seasons, with the changes of fads and fashions, and with the unaccountable and unforeseeable shifting of demand. but in the long run chance helps one business man quite as much as it does another.

When you carefully analyze the career of a man who seems to have been born lucky, you will find that he earned his "luck," that in all his undertakings he took every precaution to guard against evil chances. On the other hand, the man of notoriously bad luck will be found to have been lacking in some of the most important qualities essential to success. In baseball, the most "breaks" usually fall into the lap of the team that is most fit.

Be prepared. In conclusion, let us sum up the things essential to opportunity, and decide how a man may best fit himself for it. Externally, as we have seen, an opportunity in business consists of certain conditions which, if handled by the right man, may be made to yield a profit. But those conditions constitute an opportunity only to the right man. Large opportunity exists only for those who have the mental qualities, the will, and the knowledge necessary for its perception and utilization. For men of small powers, only small opportunities exist.
Can a man prepare himself for opportunity? Can a man of average intellectual ability hope ever to fit himself for large opportunities? Both these questions can be answered positively in the affirmative. There is practically no limit to what a man can accomplish in business, if he only will.
Here are the things he must do: work, study, read, think, observe-and then do more work.

So much stress has been laid on the importance of mental power or ability that some more diffident readers may have become a little discouraged. But no man, young or old, who can read business texts understandingly, need worry about his mental quality. He has brain power enough, and can accomplish anything he wishes in business, if he will work and equip himself to meet opportunity.
For such a man, study itself is an opportunity. Every man who will just believe so has an abundance of opportunity to develop and strengthens his mental power, store his memory with information about business, and train his judgment to an understanding of business opportunities. Any man who sets himself at the performance of these tasks diligently, faithfully and perseveringly, will rid himself courageously facing larger and larger opportunities as the years add to his experience in business.

Brain power is tremendously important in business. But a man gifted with only the normal amount of this valuable asset, if dominated by the higher type of character-the essential principle of which is a will resolute to know the truth, to do the right thing, and to work with all one's might for a worthy purpose- may rise to the top in business. First, however the brain must be properly trained, and the character must be such as inspires complete and absolute confidence among men. Therefore, let the man who wishes to prepare for opportunity put his brains into harness and, if necessary, rebuild his character. This any man can do. Hence, opportunity is potentially within the reach of all.

The world is full of needs and the needs are continually changing. The best formula for opportunity is to find the "need and fill it." Every problem has a solution. Make your work using the best answer to solve the problem. In so doing, you will be filling a valuable need and a creative mind can turn that into a fortune.

The trick is to fine tune your imagination and observation to recognize needs as opportunities that can be turned into a business opportunity. Scholars like Thomas

Edison knew there was a need for better lighting and therefore worked on developing what is now known as the "electric bulb." He tried over 1000 filaments that would not burn up and would last for many months and years. It is obvious that the effort paid off. Thomas Edison was a self-educated scholar with determination. He was discouraged by many who questioned him saying "when are you going to give up on this impossible idea?" He believed that it was going to work and increased his efforts and said he now knows over 1000 filaments that cannot work so he is making a lot of progress. Finally, he discovered Tungsten and lit up the world. He proved to everyone that genius is 99% perspiration and 1% inspiration.

J.P. Morgan, the greatest financier of his time, had a need for a revolutionary client to finance. His need was to find a brilliant scientist. He did by finding Thomas Edison.

Many stories of success can be told of opportunity from people finding a need and filling it. You can readily see by observation everyday needs that have to be filled to solve or improve problematic conditions, these are all opportunities. Train your mind to tune in your observation skills combined with your imagination and business acumen and opportunities will appear plentiful.

If you find the opportunity that you are enthused about and it gets you excited, the best action to take is starting and doing provided you have all of the main objectives worked out in your mind. Just thinking about it and keeping it on the shelf so to speak, will never accomplish the results you want. It is necessary to start implementing a plan to move forward and accomplishing your objective. One of two things will happen. Firstly, and most importantly, you will be moving forward and encounter the challenges that will have to be overcome and secondly, you may reach the point that you determine that your plan or idea is not as feasible and will not work at all. It is better to have gotten this far to determine some other direction or drop the whole idea in its entirety. It is better to drop the whole idea if that should be the case or rather just keeps it as an idea to be explored in the future. By simply harboring an idea, you now are in a position to work on other ideas that are more promising. The importance of starting is to determine whether the idea is workable or not rather than harboring an unworkable idea. This is what is meant

by "failing forward." You get rid of unworkable ideas and leave your energies ready for better and more promising pursuits.

REVELATION #6
CHANCE

Achievement is not a matter of pure luck. Undoubtedly, you have heard it said that "his" success was due to luck. In the real world, such a statement is more myth than truth. The fact of the matter is that luck for the most part is created. That is to say that one who succeeds has prepared oneself for success. It has accurately been said, "Luck belongs to the Better Players!" When one prepares themselves for opportunity, to recognize opportunity and act upon opportunity, then opportunity becomes their opportunity. Thusly creating the luck. Think about this concept for a few minutes, and re-read the foregoing again!

Earning the Right to Become "Lucky": Opportunity and luck are not really relatives. The popular notion which converts luck into the Goddess of Fortune has no basis in fact. There is a vast amount of suggested loose talk about the part that luck plays in business success.

When you carefully analyze the career of a man who seems to have been born lucky, you will find that he has earned his "luck," that in all his undertakings he took every possible precaution he could think of to guard against evil chances. On the other hand, the man of notoriously bad luck will be found to have been lacking in some of the most important qualities essential to success. In baseball, the most "breaks" usually fall into the lap of the team that is most fit. This is an example of creating luck.

Be Prepared: So much stress has been laid on the importance of mental power or ability that some more different readers may have become a little discouraged. But, no man, young or old, who can read business texts understandingly need worry about his mental quality. This brain power is enough to pursue accomplishing almost anything he wishes in business if he will work and prepare himself to meet the challenge of opportunity.

For such a man, study itself is creating the opportunity to recognize opportunity. Every man who will just believe so is lucky to see the abundance of opportunities to further develop and strengthen his mental power, and store his memory with information about business, and train his judgment to an understanding of business opportunities. Any man who dedicates himself to the task of these in a diligent manner, faithfully and perseveringly, will find himself courageously facing larger and better opportunities as the effort adds to his experiences in business and life. Brain power is tremendously important in business. Any man can further develop this valuable asset - the essential factor is a will resolute to know the truth, to do the right thing, and to work with all one's faculties towards a worthy goal. The attitude of determination can lift a person to the top in business. First, however,

the brain must be properly trained, and the character must be such as inspires complete and absolute confidence among other men.

Therefore, the man who wishes to prepare for opportunity put his brains into harness and, if necessary, rebuilds his character. This power exists within any man to do. Hence opportunity and luck is potentially within the reach of all to create.

Today's Business Opportunities: We often hear people remark dejectedly that business opportunities have almost disappeared, that the small man has little chance, that large corporations have absorbed all the opportunities for making money, and that most men cannot hope to be more than minor employees. That kind of talk is radically erroneous. It is true that a great part of today's business is conducted by corporations, but there is no ground for the statement that corporations kill opportunity. On the contrary, they actually create more opportunities and have more need for the smaller innovated man.

Some of the most successful businessmen of today, who have great executive ability and have accumulated comfortable fortunes, rose from obscurity into the management of corporations where they were able fully to demonstrate their talents. Many of our successful businessmen began life as poor boys and worked up to the top, not in spite of corporations, but because of the opportunities opened up to their abilities by the corporate form of business operation. Of those who have built up businesses of their own, not a few previously acquired in large corporations the valuable training that was the groundwork of their success. Successful people didn't fall into place by luck; they strived to reach that position. Clearly it is up to you to do the same thing, if that be your goal - create your own luck.

Many ambitious people have started their own business simply because they were not recognized with their talents thusly outperforming the company that they had worked for.

In enterprising countries like the United States, where conditions are constantly changing, where inventions are forever improving processes, and where markets are widening, business opportunities in normal times are plentiful. Abnormal times usually produce even more opportunities for the imaginative. While geographical frontiers have largely yielded to civilization through the advent of railroads, highways, airlines, and communications, there are businesses, economic and social frontiers, many of which still have not even been explored. The bare needs of a large part of the human race always remain yet to be reasonably satisfied.

Beyond the demand for these meager necessities there lie uncounted wants and desires for the supplying of which no means has yet been provided. Even if the rate of population growth slows down, this "backlog of unfilled orders" will require the perusal of great efforts for several generations to come before it can be partially filled to satisfaction.

The past growth of countries in the Western Hemisphere into business and industrial nations is due largely to the fact that in no other lands on earth is there such industrious genius for making use, to the full, of opportunities as they develop. Even in the "times that try men's souls" men and women of the free world refuse to be daunted - they go on capitalizing on existing opportunities and creating new ones. The more you know, the more opportunities will be recognized. Thusly, the more you learn, the more you will earn.

We may formulate a law of creating luck through opportunity in the following terms:

Opportunity offers itself to men in proportion to their ability, their will for action, their power of vision, their experience, and their knowledge of business. Inversely, opportunity is concealed from men in proportion to their slothfulness, their reliance upon others, their passion for imitation, and their ignorance of business. Evidently, opportunity in business is not merely a chance to make money which any man may act upon if he is worthy enough to discover it. An excellent opportunity may exist in the presence of hundreds of men, and yet not be seen by any one of them, or they may all lack the necessary ability or experience and therefore be unable to take advantage of it. To such men, owning to their unfitness, it is not opportunity which exists, but merely a set of business conditions awaiting the eye of another man, ready, willing and able to create his own luck.

If this law of opportunity is correct, no man has any right to complain about his lack of luck, or to set up in defense of his failure the claim that he never really had a chance. Opportunity is clearly a relative term.

On the one side are the business conditions pregnant with profit; on the other side is the fit man able to call the profit into existence. When these two meet, we have an opportunity recognized and ready to take advantage of, resulting in creating luck.

For the untrained man of little will power and no worthwhile experience, there can be no opportunity or appreciative luck. Nobody seeks his services, however cheaply he offers them. In the current of affairs, he is merely driftwood worthy only of his complaint of being without luck. Most failures in business blame lack of luck as the cause of their failure. The fact is that studying and learning eliminates all excuses. As a rule, however, it is wise to err, if at all, in the direction of self-confidence. A man who is working in company with men abler than himself, or who does not hesitate to attack a problem which seems a little beyond his powers, often will make mistakes, but in the long run he will be more successful than if he practices excessive caution, for all the time he will be growing wiser and abler. Moreover, many tasks are less difficult on close inspection than they first appear. Any action is better than no action, and in the words of the scholar Bernard

Baruch, "If you fail, then you fail forward," meaning the experience of learning the reasons for failure will carry you to future successes.

No man, however, likes to admit that his mental powers are limited or below the average. As an English philosopher once remarked, "We are all willing to admit that our memories are defective, but no man will admit that his judgment is not sound." So, doubtless, many men who have not been promoted to positions of responsibility feel that they have not been appreciated. The companies, for which they work, of course, may have no better jobs which are unfilled and therefore cannot promote anyone at the time. But sometimes the executives for whom such men work have different opinions of these employees than the employees have of themselves.

A man who is anxious for advancement should first examine himself from the viewpoint of his immediate superior and that of his company. Perhaps he is not prepared to go higher without some further development. He may need to correct certain of his characteristics, and to stimulate and cultivate certain other qualities, before he will fit into a more responsible position. Often, he needs additional training to broaden his knowledge of business and to widen his acquaintanceship with principles and practices in fields with which previously he has had little contact. The company can hardly be expected to take the risk of promoting him until he has begun to correct his deficiencies.

In no case, however, should he be discouraged. Ambition coupled with intelligent action is meritorious. He should continue his efforts to climb to attainable heights. Not all men are so eminently qualified that they can reach the very top. But all can rise to better positions in life which they will be making the most of their talents in useful and remunerative service, and they will find happiness and satisfaction in these higher, constructive spheres of business.

Seizing the Opportunity At Hand. It is a familiar human weakness to think of ourselves as not being in just the right place. Many a country boy feels certain that he could do great things if he could only get into a city. Doubtless many bank employees in small towns feel that they have never had a chance for development because of the limited local field in which they operate. The man in the East hopes to get into some marketing or industrial center in the West, or on the far coast. We

are prone to think that opportunity, like happiness, lies in some distant place and that if we only could get there, we should be successful and content.

The secret of opportunity, like that of happiness, lies in us. No man who wishes to become a business man needs to travel far to make a start. For him the very best opportunities often are in his own backyard. Many of our biggest businessmen got their first training in their home towns or villages - by taking subscriptions to magazines, by acting as agents for manufacturers of farm implements, and in other simple pursuits. The needs of simple folks are usually the needs of people elsewhere.

After a man has discovered opportunity near at home and has profited by it, then he will be readied for larger opportunities in other places, but often, even then, his next opportunity lies not far from him. This is naturally and logically the cases for we are familiar with near-at-hand conditions and know their possibilities. The glittering opportunities beckoning to us in the distance may be unreal. They may be like the sirens who sought to charm Ulysses from his true course. As Thomas Carlyle has said, "Our grand business is not to see what lies dimly at a distance, but to do what lies clearly at hand."

The fact that opportunity always lies near at hand does not mean that a man should not change from place to place, or from business to business. A change of location is often exceedingly desirable and advisable, but a man should not make a change because he is looking for opportunity, but because opportunity has made the change practicable and profitable.

Paying the Price of Progress. The proverb, "Where there's a will there's a way," receives abundant verification in the business world. The man who gets what he really wants in business, whether riches, position or honor, is the man who does more than wish hard for such things. Far more men could do what they want, if they were willing to pay the price.

This statement doubtless looks extravagant to many readers. It may be read by a man of fifty who has been in business for over thirty years, and is even now barely able to do much more than support him and family. "Surely," he may say, "I wanted a fortune and I set out to make it. I have worked hard for more than thirty years, but here I am just able to hold down an ordinary position. In what way did I fail?"

The man may think he really wanted a fortune, but if he did not do all these things, and many more, he is mistaken. Like many thousands of other people, he merely wanted to be rich. Desire alone without full-fledged pursuit is not usually adequate to expect achievement.

To many men, large fortunes are not worth the price, for sometimes many fine things have to be sacrificed in merely getting rich. If a man has not the ability to make a great success in business unless he neglects his duties as a husband, father, citizen and neighbor - foregoing what a University President called "the enduring satisfactions of life" - he will be happier and more "successful" if he is content with moderate success in business.

But a man must not expect to find opportunity of any kind if he has not the will for doing and for sacrifice. Back of his will must be an intense burning desire, not just a thought or wish or longing. The desire must be so consuming that it impels him to act and to do anything and everything honorable that can possibly help him to accomplish a goal. Men cannot expect to fill positions for which they have not proved their fitness.

Objectives Accompany Age: It is evident that the objectives for which a man of forty or over is, or should be, fitted are entirely different from those open to the young man. But has the man of middle age already exhausted opportunity? Must he be content with his present rank in business? If he has been in business for himself, has he a right to hope that he can accomplish more during the next ten or fifteen years than he has accomplished in the past? Should a man of forty or fifty years of age enter a new business?

Questions like these have come home personally to many men, and have proved very difficult to answer. Everything depends upon the man. Some men are old at forty. five; they have ceased to learn or to take an interest in new things, and are ambitious merely to maintain their present status, or to retain a position or a business which gives them a comfortable living. Such men should beware of severing old connections or of undertaking new enterprises.

Other men are still young at forty-five or fifty; their minds are on the future, not the past; they take no exaggerated pride in what they have accomplished, but are impatient for more work and bigger tasks; they still may have great vision and ambition. To men of this sort, if they have guarded their health, opportunity offers its biggest prizes. And so, it should be recognized that age can produce greater luck and opportunity due to the vast accumulation of knowledge and experiences.

Learning by Experience: Valuable as are the lessons learned from books and schools, and from those with whom a man comes into contact, it must never be forgotten that there are certain most important lessons which he can learn only by doing. A lawyer can learn how he can best influence a jury only by the experience of confronting a jury. He may have been taught the methods of appeal generally held to be the best, but which ones are best fitted to his own powers he must discover for himself through practice. So, a man preparing for business can learn much from books about the laws governing business phenomena, and about the methods and policies which have proved most successful, but he cannot be a master in any field until he has had actual experience in solving its problems.

The more a man has learned about business through experience, as well as through study, the keener his insight is into opportunity, and the more likely he is to avail himself successfully of an opportunity to create "luck."

We hope that you have had impact from this report that will give you the insight of creating your own luck.

Ambitious people sometimes are an obstacle in their own path. They adopt a phrase called "If I only had?" They don't realize they have just analyzed what the problem really is.

Whenever they would say to themselves "If I only had" they are using that as an excuse, as an obstacle. The point here is that once you realize what is missing that becomes the exact reason for overcoming and rising above what they now know what is missing to make a successful formula. In so doing, they are really eliminating their self-imposed obstacle.

REVELATION #7
GOALS

Self-Image: A good self-image acts to charge your mind and body positively. When you perceive yourself as confident, capable and diligent about your goals, have the proudest of a winner, you'll know you can win. You act like the person you want to be like. You can enjoy fantasizing about what you want to achieve as though you were watching a show with yourself as the main player. You enjoy emulating people you admire, pretending you are them.

Goal seeking (goal oriented) Achievers have a game plan for every objective which they may target. Both short-term and long-term goals are planned meticulously and thought about constantly. They not only plan for business but for their personal life as well.

Self-determination is a quality that is the backbone of accomplishment. One uses this attitude to overcome seemingly impossible obstacles. It is almost a fanatical commitment made to oneself to accomplish a given objective. These people feel confident of reaching any tenable goal.

Self-Discipline. The art of making your own body and mind a robot-like servant to your desires. Self-sacrifice is easy when your objective is paramount. Knowing that this quality of self-discipline is mastered gives the person a confident feeling beyond the norm. Self-discipline can affect a permanent change in you. One can override emotions and even current information in the subconscious. Self-discipline alone can make or break any habit.

Self Esteem. This is synonymous with self-confidence. People that possess this quality have an ever-present, deep-down feeling of being proud of their own worth. They recognize their own uniqueness, and have their own high principles and standards. Truly successful people believe in their own worth. The self-esteem quality is the pathway to happiness and achievement. They keep a continual self-improvement plan in action at all times. High self-esteem becomes part of your personality, and therefore increases the charisma which makes you shine like a diamond apart from the average person.

Courage, Integrity and Commitment. These qualities must be the basic foundation. All other qualities can be learned.

Perspective Vision. The person can view themselves within the entire "big picture" of things happening around them. They have learned to see themselves through their own eyes as others see them. They are great observers, being totally aware of time and their surroundings. They have a great awareness of time-past, present and future. With this understanding, they strive to live as fully as possible in the present while making calculated decisions. The spiritual power is woven into the very fabric of their mind, body and soul with a keen understanding

67

of the delicate balance of life around them. They understand the mortality of themselves with a sensible attitude of aging gracefully without fear or remorse. They are for the most part genuine humanitarians.

Positive Self-Awareness. People with this quality already know exactly who they are, where they stand at present and where their future is headed. They have learned and are continually adding more to their arsenal of knowledge. These people play the game of life from a position of strength and they avoid errors and seek to correct their own mistakes. They accept and recognize what cannot be changed but are eager and quick to change whatever can improve their life.

Self-Projection. You can improve the quality of communication. You will have the power to appraise and determine the qualities of other people along with noticing that they look you right in the eye when speaking and listen with the utmost interest showing a warm and close concern.

Leadership: Leadership most simply defined as taking individuals and groups from where they are to where you want them to be. Leadership is one trait that cannot be conferred. Let's face it, only titles can be conferred. One basic thing must happen before a person is truly a leader-he or she must be accepted as a leader. You can go around and give an individual a high-sounding title and call that person a leader if you wish-but if others aren't following, that person is clearly not a leader. A person may be "in control" because he or she has been appointed to a position. That position may have authority. But real leadership is more than having authority-it is more than having the technical training and following the proper procedures. It is being the person others will gladly and confidently follow.

Leadership is getting a job done-through other people. All of us have seen people appointed to a "control" position. But the true leader-an individual who climbs to a position of leadership on his or own without being appointed-has certain qualities. Here are the qualities or the "profile" of that kind of person.

A Leader Is Courageous. He is not afraid to risk. Nothing great has ever been built without risk-incredible risk at times. A leader is not rash, reckless, or impetuous. He puts as many facts together as he can; he builds a strong, carefully studied case. But eventually he must take the leap into the unknown, willing to risk everything to make his dream come true, AND HE MUST BE ABLE TO GET OTHERS TO TAKE THAT LEAP WITH HIM. This is why there are really so few leaders.

There are thousands of people with unusual talent who must forever remain in secondary positions because they are afraid to risk. Fearful of the consequences if they go sour, they must forever stay in the shadows. A leader is courageous-not foolhardy-but courageous. He makes a decision and calls the play, accepting all consequences. A leader is strong and willing to say (to borrow Harry Truman's phrase), "The buck stops here!"

All leaders are going to make one mistake-perhaps some real big ones! But a leader doesn't make the biggest one of all-a mistake of doing nothing because of indecisiveness. It was once said, man cannot discover new oceans unless he has courage to lose sight of the shore." To making no decision is in fact making a decision.

Walt Disney was a real leader. He was decisive and courageous. Is there anyone who hasn't heard of Disneyland, Walt's Magic Kingdom?" In the early days of Walt Disney's life, he envisioned a plan then made a plan and then proceeded to execute his plan and he was so dynamic that he promoted investors to invest in a mouse called Mickey. Now, you have to ask yourself would you invest in a mouse that did not exist. This gives you an example of salesmanship as well as convincing people of his ideas. Their objections seemed sensible: Costs too much time not right-location wrong. But Walt wasn't listening. The mere fact of his heightened enthusiasm as influenced all of those people on his team. In other words, he was a great salesman for getting everybody to work with him rather than for him. His enthusiasm was bubbling; his courage unflinching. The "Magic Kingdom" was born-after two decades continues to grow. Accidental? Not on your life. Success is never accidental-not in business, not in personal life. The steps are almost always the same.

Think, dream;
Work, work hard, and keep on working:
Don't give up!
Do a lot of thinking; Make your plan and set your goals and then WORK YOUR PLAN. Samuel Johnson who wrote the dictionary brilliantly made the point "that if all obstacles must be overcome before anything is ever attempted then nothing will be accomplished." Therefore, starting is the most important time of executing any plan.

"Optimism is a normal duty," said inventor/industrialist Edwin H. Land. It certainly is for a leader. The real leader must be a morale builder. When a person's morale is high, he or she will accomplish things they wouldn't even attempt otherwise.
A Leader Is Persistent. Nearly every great accomplishment was begun against a background of jeers with people saying it couldn't be done. I'm sure you know many like this. Such as, "it can be done in your territory, but not in mine." You have to be stubbornly persistent to win. Not only must you have an idea-you must have supreme faith in that idea and in your ability to bring it to life. Your faith must be strong enough to stand up against pessimistic head shaking. Attaining more

education is as important as being persistent in your pursuits. There is more to success than the one important ingredient of education.

Hundreds of file cabinets are bulging with super plans. These plans could increase the efficiency and upgrade the products of every company in the country. But getting the plan off of paper and into action is another thing. The action step is where persistence comes in. The best books haven't been written. The best products haven't been produced. The best companies haven't been built. The best presentations haven't been written yet. The best hiring talks haven't been completed yet. Why? Because they are stuffed back in the mind of some individual who doesn't yet have the persistence to write them, produce them and build them. There was a time in history when the government spoke about closing the patent office because they had misjudged the opportunities. We have in recent decades invented television, computers and the entire various computers driven machinery creating a new industrial revolution. Today there are more opportunities than ever before simply because each new innovation brings about new ways to fill needs particularly in medicine, electronics and communications. A secret to success is for an individual to find a need and a way to fill that need.

When former heavyweight champion James J. Corbett was asked what it takes to be a heavyweight champion, he answered, "Fight one more round." Then he added, "When your feet are so tired that you have to shuffle back to the center of the ring, fight one more round. When your arms are so tired that you can hardly lift your hands to come on guard, fight one more round. When your nose is bleeding and your eyes are black and you're so tired that you wish your opponent would crack you one on the jaw and put you to sleep, fight one more round - remembering that the "man who always fights one more round is never whipped." All of us have heard the old expression that when we're completely done with the day's activity, when we're bone tired and sick of making presentations, when we don't think that there's another order left in this town - pick up the phone or knock on that door and make one more call. Why? Do we have to tell you after the above? E.

Persistence:
Successful people have the philosophy that it is not how many times you get knocked
down but how many times you get back up. It is engrained in their thinking that a winner never quits and a quitter never wins. Winston Churchill said it this way, "Never, never, never, never gives up!" Persistence. Be courageous! Be optimistic! Be persistent! That's what it takes to be a success. And isn't that what you want to be?? Shakespeare said, "such as a man thinks - so he is."
Attitude and Commitment. Why is it that many people who are unemployed never seem to get the right breaks that allow them to get an interview? They try hard. They are committed. They are organized. They have a resume and they seem to have tried everything. Something is missing. For most, the missing ingredient is a

lack of a winning attitude. Sounds too simple, doesn't it? Yet, time and time again, people are getting interviews and getting hired despite a recessive economy. A winning attitude is made up of 5 parts. The first part hinges on the energy you give off when you interact with people. People that have a winning attitude are enthusiastic, excited, positive, happy and confident. Despite their situation, they seem to always believe that they will succeed. They expect to win. The path to success has many obstacles. The attitude for achieving success is to do whatever it takes to bypass those obstacles. Put your mind and imagination to work in circumventing obstacles. You can go over, under, by or through obstacles by many means. Here is where your imagination and striving can pay off. In the sport of wrestling, there are many holds and a break for every hold and the same holds true in business.

A second characteristic relates to their perspective. They see themselves as an agent for change instead of a victim of the economy. They generate an aura of optimism that keeps them in control.

A third part, and probably the most important, is their willingness to pay the price to succeed. Many people almost do enough to be successful. Without the total commitment to do it and do it and do it until they get results, they often never see success.

A fourth component to have a winning attitude is to have a plan to win. Having specific goals and daily realistic objectives provides a focus that guides them in the right direction. No one plans to fail, they just fail to plan. People with a plan look like winners and act like winners.

The next time you turn on a bulb for light think of the scholar Thomas Edison. We call him a scholar because he did not have a degree from any university or trade school. His knowledge was gained by the persistence of trial and error until he was successful. He was asked how many different materials did he try and he said, "well over a thousand." He was questioned why doesn't he give up and he replied "that he is making progress because he now knows over a thousand manners that do not work. Of course, we now know that he discovered Tungsten which gave the world light in place of the candles. Edison had numerous inventions in addition to the light bulb which shows us that success usually leads to more success.

Many people have been so disappointed and disillusioned with hopes and opportunities that have failed, that it sometimes seems impossible for them to believe in anything, including themselves. Today more than ever, you probably won't win until you make a total commitment. People who are consistent in their focus and drive will achieve success. More often than not, most of us quit too soon, never realizing the return on our investment of time and effort. You don't get something for nothing. When they say, "Success is not an accident" you can be reminded of Alexander Graham Bell in their pursuit to develop the telephone acid was spilled accidentally on the equipment they were making and a voice was heard over a wire,

Watson come here, I need you. Of course, the accident happened in the process of trial and error and persistence to develop the telephone. Similarly, latex rubber was strictly a rubber that had little use by itself except when they were trying to make it into a hardened elastic product and accidentally knocked over sulfur and when it mixed with the latex liquid, it became hard rubber. So, it could be said that innovation and invention is one percent inspiration and 99% perspiration.

Commitment: Commitment is often confused with sacrifice but real commitment is when you are thinking and your body is so dedicated to your objective that you eat, sleep and dream your goals. In so doing, it becomes a priority over practically everything else in your life. Your mind stays focused to be creative to drive your body and mind towards the objective that you want to achieve. In other words, commitment monopolizes your thoughts and actions towards achievement. The only problem that can result is that you may unknowingly sacrifice and trade-off some health or other healthy family commitments which have to be as important as your commitment.

Assertiveness: You are waiting patiently in line at the supermarket to pay the cashier when someone barges in ahead of you. The shirt you bought recently has a faded spot you didn't notice at the time of purchase - you take it back to the store, but the clerk states that she-cannot refund your money. Or, maybe you find yourself sitting through a movie because you really didn't speak up when your friends were deciding which movie to see. You must assert boldness only when it is necessary to make your point.

If these or similar incidents happen to you more frequently than you would like, perhaps you need to become more assertive. In other words, you need to learn to stand up for yourself. No one admires a push-over. More importantly, the person who is pushed around doesn't admire himself.
Being assertive is not the same as being aggressive. There is a big difference between the two. By being assertive, you stand up for your legitimate rights, without violating the rights of others. Assertive behavior is a direct and honest expression of your feelings, beliefs, and opinions. Aggressive action is frequently used to "put down," humiliate, or dominate others. Niceness is often misinterpreted for weakness and you must stand up for your rights.

Salient Rules for a Leader: To lead effectively, you need to create an atmosphere of mutual admiration and respect between yourself and your associates. If you give them this environment, the associates will respond by working with loyalty and diligence. The bottom line is a more comfortable and productive relationship. Everybody wins.

Through my years of working with people in the real estate profession, I've found that by following my own list of guidelines for effective broker-agent interaction, I have been able to maintain a productive professional atmosphere. Here are my 10 rules of effective leadership, designed to help you develop better relationships with your subordinates.

Always Criticize in Private. Keeping silent can sometimes be extremely difficult, especially when you see someone fouling up when the company can't afford any foul-up. In the heat of such a moment, it's very tempting to chew out the person on the spot. However, regardless of the nature of the offense, people find it uncomfortable and embarrassing to watch a manager scold a subordinate. More importantly, it's demeaning. When criticism is necessary, it should be done in private. Constructive criticism can help resolve problems and can help the individual who is criticized grow as a person. But remember, when criticism is used to embarrass or demean someone, it becomes a destructive weapon that will ultimately cost its user.

Always Praise in Public: If you have praise or compliments for a person, go out of your way to tell as many people as possible. When your people know that you are proud enough of their accomplishments to advertise them, they will feel a stronger tie to their work, which leads to company loyalty and higher productivity. Additionally, they'll be far more eager to take up your cause when you need them to "go to war" than will people who are dressed down in public or ignored.

Let Your Associates Be Independent: If you help your associates become independent, they become better associates and better people. How do you make people independent rather than dependent? Simply give them the job, explain the rules, state the desired end result and then let them do it. That's it. If they make a mistake, help them get up and do it again until they can do it right. Don't be too quick to dive in and do it for them.

Be a Boss, Not a Buddy: Sometimes, it's possible for managers and employees to get "too close" or get on each other's nerves. Socializing with subordinates is fine, to a point, but it can be overdone. Going out too often, staying out too late or drinking too much with them can bring your weaknesses to the surface-weaknesses that people don't generally see in the business setting. Your employees will notice them and, as a result, will respect you less as a manager. In this broker-associate relationship, your job is you're first and foremost responsibility. So, remember, don't be a buddy; be a boss. Everyone will be much happier in the long run.

Encourage Participation: Another way to boost morale and earn respect is by allowing associates to express their opinions in matters that concern them. People always want to throw in their two cents' worth, and sometimes it can amount to big bucks for the company. So, permit your associates to participate by giving them a project and asking them to provide you with their solutions before you make a final decision. Allow everyone from the highest to the lowest position to have a voice.

This will build confidence and self-esteem in the ranks and will make everyone feel more a part of the operation.

Set a Good Example: I've learned this one, time and time again, through painful experience. Many times, when, as a sales manager, I noticed that my team's morale was particularly low, I'd spend weeks trying to find out why. Finally, it would dawn on me that I was at least part of the problem by setting a bad example. When my morale was low, my team seemed to follow suit. If you want your associates to be cheerful, it's got to start with yourself. If managers set good examples, their people react accordingly. Examples can include a nice appearance, a positive attitude, even temperament, hard work and increased productivity.

Be a Good Communicator: Several key categories of communication are essential. The first category is listening. Listen to your people and encourage them to speak their mind. Allow them the opportunity and the freedom to come into your office and complain about you, about a company procedure, policy or about any phase of the organization in general. Let them know that, at times, they can "dump on" you. Let your associates know that your door is always open to them. The second essential area of good communication in the workplace is effective explanation of your expectations very clear and ask others to do the same. The third area is keeping your people informed of new policies or procedures that might affect them. When you hear of a change that affects your associates, let your team know about it as soon as possible.

Trust Your Associates: Give your workers some up-front, blind faith, and trust them until they prove they can't be trusted rather than withholding trust until they prove trustworthy. Many times, if you trust someone, he or she will go out of the way to prove you're right. A little unconditional trust up front can go a long way toward building an effective team.

Show That You Care: Your associates are people, not machines. Allow them to be human. If you know one of them is experiencing trouble at home with a sick child, express your concern. Or, if one has reached a particularly difficult professional goal, give extra recognition. Use your own imagination with the various individuals on your team to come up with other ways of showing that you care. Your people will care more for you and will respect you more if you treat them as human beings. And, they'll work harder for you in the long run.

Work as a Team: Teamwork, the working together of various individuals toward a common cause, can be fostered by defining a common cause, encouraging communication among team members, setting minimum standards for the entire team and encouraging individual commitments to accomplish the team goal. Teamwork is the essence of maximum productivity and the quickest way to get where you're going.

I believe that if you follow these 10 Rules of Effective Leadership, you'll have little problem managing a strong team of capable, committed individuals who will be as loyal as they are effective. You'll find out (if you don't already know) what it's like to lead a team of individuals who like and respect you; who will stay with you longer than average, who are happy and productive while they're there, and who, will, should the time ever come, go to bat for you when you need them most. And, if that should happen, the odds are good that you'll be fighting a battle that you'll win.

You now have the knowledge of what is required as the initial steps to becoming wealthy. The content of the complete Revelations will give you the insider's view points and analysis for obtaining the vital information to gain the power with knowledge of the numerous subjects.

Learning the insider's secrets will prove to be of the greatest value in your pursuits to achieve the maximum of the goals you inspire. Listed below are the vital insider's secrets that you will learn which will become your tools to gain wealth.

CONTENTS OF REVELATIONS FROM

REVELATION 1: YOU CAN There are more millionaires than Heinz has pickles. You can be one.

REVELATION 2: MOTIVATION: The purpose of success is to achieve a better life for you.

REVELATION 3: VISION: Your own ideas and ambition turned into profit for your whole life.

REVELATION 4: BRAIN POWER: The brain is a powerful computer. Learn how to use it.

REVELATION 5: OPPORTUNITY: Everyday numerous opportunities arise; find a need and fill

REVELATION 6: CHANCE: Moving forward. Rewards only come from a chance! Worthy of risk.

REVELATION 7: GOALS: Know how t-0 devise a feasible road map. Start now with good planning.

REVELATION 8: KEEPING INFORMED: Learn current trends politically and economically.

REVELATION 9: HUMAN RELATIONS: How to develop people power.

REVELATION 10: PERSONALITY: Charm and charisma have been the secret to control people.

REVELATION 11: OBSERVATION: The biggest opportunities can be obvious. REVELATION 12: LISTENING: An insider knows the value of listening and analyzing.

REVELATION 13: NEGOTIATION: Become aware of the effective ways for control.

REVELATION 14: PERSUASION: Learn the importance of selling yourself.

REVELATION 15: LEADERSHIP: Winning with the help of others is admired.

REVELATION 16: INFLATION: Learn about precious metals and avoiding fiat.

REVELATION 17: CHALLENGE Knowledge gives you courage how, when and why to proceed.

REVELATION 18: CAPITAL: Money talks & BS walks Learn how& where to obtain it.

REVELATION 19: DECISIONS: Educated thinking makes the best decisions. Learn the facts.

REVELATION 20: HEALTH IS WEALTH: Wealth is more valuable with good health.

REVELATION 21: ORGANIZE: Being organized is more than half the accomplishment

REVELATION 22: ENTREPRENEURSHIP: More business knowledge ensures success.

REVELATION 23: DECEPTION: Know how to protect your estate against fraud. REVELATION 24: BUSINESS PHILOSOPHY: Adopt brilliant and profound statements.

REVELATION 25: TURN IDEAS INTO WEALTH: ideas made millionaires do not your idea die.

REVELATION 26: RISK AND CHANCE: risk is necessary to learn how to win

REVELATION 27: MENTAL MASTERY: develop a superior mind.

REVELATION 28: ADVERTISING: the heart and soul of every new and existing business.

REVELATION 29: CONTROL PERSONAL PROBLEMS: avoid complications learn how to solve problems.

REVELATION 30: INVESTING: protect your wealth and make more money with knowledge.

REVELATION 31: HYPNOTIC MEDITATION: powerful phenomenon solves many problems.

REVELATION 32: INVESTING SOUNDLY: enjoy knowing the tricks of financing and investing.

REVELATION 33: KNOW YOURSELF: use your talents and wisdom to undertake profitable entities.

REVELATION 34: USE YOUR SIXTH SENSE: Your intuition is a valuable tool all based on experience.

REVELATION 35: POSITIVE MENTAL ATTITUDE: Your attitude is the captain to accomplish goals.

REVELATION 36: PERSISTANCE AND PERSERVERANCE: persistence is omnipotent you cannot lose.

REVALATION #8

KEEPING
INFORMED

It is imperative that a person intending to find opportunities and to run a successful business keep aware of current local decisions by government, changes in the country, the economics locally, and county, state-wide, countries and global. The economic conditions will dictate and present new opportunities that have to be met as conditions continually change. New technologies are innovated almost daily, making old axioms of thinking obsolete. Staying abreast of all the changes that occur will give you insight as to new and better ways to solve problems and create new business opportunities.

In the fast-moving world, today one should be aware daily of the economic conditions that affect almost everybody on the planet. An ambitious person should keep abreast of the stock market in general of all countries and industries particularly, the industry that you may be engaged in already or wish to pursue. A person should be aggressive in getting the news and being informed about everything to determine what the effects are and will be so that you can predict outcomes and new needs that will be required to meet the present situation or new situations.

This, of course, requires a lot of time and study to be well informed. Nevertheless, a person or business must be knowledgeable as to what is happening in the world they live in.

It is almost imperative that one utilize the technologies of communication to give them quick access to events that effect to make new laws and changes in each industry within improved technologies. A person with commitments to himself and his goals has to pursue information wherever and whenever possible. Newspapers, of course is the most logical source including Trade Journals, Radio and Television. Educational seminars for particular industries are a very good source of information for learning up-to-the-minute new thinking and determining the mood of the different markets.

This country, United States of America, is a leader of the whole world yet, the rest of the world is very innovative and one must expand their thinking to include all the happenings world-wide. Become aware and informed about what is happening of significance that affects the USA economy and learns what is happening world- wide in every field of endeavor. We all know that knowledge is power and that is the reason that we want to be aware of everything happening everywhere.

The computer has changed how we do business on the entire planet. The world has actually become smaller in the sense that everybody's business is our business. There is a big advantage in knowing the living conditions and the thinking of what used to be recognized as foreigners because every human being has the same needs, problems, desires, and complexities of life. Therefore, as a business person looking to indulge in business today, has to consider the world market as one or becoming consolidated into one. Of course, this is going to be an evolution of changes over a long period of time.

The world should be viewed by the business minded as being part of that great change. There are tremendous avenues of opportunity that go along with these world changes. We have evolved already to the point that learning a new language is important around the world for example, the Chinese are anxiously learning English and the South Americans are in great need of learning several languages. The Wall Street Journal has been a spectacular source of information not only to keep appraised of the Stock Market but most important happenings worldwide. It is recommended that you add this to your daily routine and provide the time to read it. Your decisions for starting, expanding or just maintaining a business, would be enhanced by having the management run by an informed person or group. Where to Start: The best place to start facilitating access to information is with your hobby. Gather all the information you can about this hobby. Create records and files. Write things down or record data electronically so you can begin to see interrelationships among the ideas and data.
Next, build your own network. Establish a link with other knowledge workers. Send them fact sheets about your information specialty.
Once you start getting paid for your information, then approach business owners, managers, and CEOs. They hire entrepreneurs to facilitate access to information to help free them to more effectively decide, act, or communicate.
The following steps should help you prepare and plan to become an entrepreneur that facilitates access to information.
Make information management your top priority.
Understand the management issues which relate to information overload.

Monitor all advancements and breakthroughs in applications of technologies that facilitate access to information.

Review your client's current information management system by noting methods of accessing, filing, storing, sorting, retrieving, and distributing information. Audit the operational effectiveness of your customer's current information noting areas that may require upgrading, expansion, or enhancement of information resources.

Specifically identify the types of information your client desires. Be sure to understand why it is needed (competition analysis, new product introduction, etc.). Provide your client with information in a concise format so it is clear and easy to understand.

Outline the measures your client should take to protect this information from loss, tampering, or destruction.

Reinforce the value of your role in facilitating access to information by quantifying your efforts on behalf of your client. Try to establish a return on investment factor in time and resources saved, as well as opportunities seized.

Make recommendations which will introduce more efficient ways to access and manage information among upper and middle managers.

A Look Ahead: The Industrial Age was known for its goods production. The Information Age will be known for its ability to organize these goods and the ideas used to produce them. As information becomes a resource in itself, people will need to learn new ways to view the information resource. The computer and the telecommunication infrastructure represent one of the world's most effective productivity raisers. They will be the keys to the biggest industrial change of the next few decades:

Another example of facilitating access to information through the infrastructure is in the use of on-line data bases. Not only can they help access information, but they eliminate duplicate research; introduce the exchange of new ideas, services, and technologies; help support the development of long-range plans; simulate economic scenarios; close the gap between buyers and sellers; identify support for a broad range of problem-solving situations.

Consider for a moment that the amount of information available today will double within the coming decade. The need for disciplined information access will more than justify its role in the business marketplace. Practically every scientist has been reduced to the point of just trying to cope with the amount of information being generated, let alone comprehending it. One entrepreneur developed a series of techniques for these scientists whereby they can access information that is not only relevant but actually worth reading. He uses an editorial peer-review process that weeds out the less valuable articles before they are published. He then produces only the cream of the published information for his clients.

Another approach to the problem of the information over-load is offered by a "low- tech" entrepreneur whose Financial Information Center houses racks of brochures, prospectuses and applications from about 50 companies, including mutual funds, insurance companies, mortgage bankers, accounting firms, and banks. Shoppers can browse among the racks, watch the Financial News Network on a giant screen, or check on stock prices using a stock-quote machine. There is a company that also provides information as to telephone with toll free speed dial. You can easily see that information is widely offered. You only have to research where and how to obtain it.

Companies are also getting customers to talk back to them as a means to facilitate access to information. By offering toll -free phone numbers, consumers are encouraged to call at the slightest hint of dissatisfaction over a product or service, in a survey of 700 companies, nearly half had established toll-free numbers for complaint handling. Toll-free and local telephone numbers are commonly seen for anonymous tips to stop crime and catch spies. They all work under the same principle-facilitate access to information. The entrepreneurs that successfully facilitate access to information are recognized by the following characteristics:

They are skilled technicians with the ability to instantly access hundreds of data bases.

They consider information a corporate asset to be quantified and accounted for on the balance sheet.

They understand the synergistic impact of information and actually suggest to clients how to get the optimum impact from their accessed data.

They have on-call information resources which provide instant answers to 80 percent of their requests.

They are organized and constantly on guard against information overload. They continually search out fresh information to update aging data.

Information is constantly being updated and revised so periodically it must be screened as to the sources that the information is derived from. Conversations with people in the same field is important because you can determine what problems they have as well as new information that you can learn from, in fact, conversations with any other well-informed person are always valuable to get their opinions and you may find a good friend at the same time. Your own records are very important especially if you are running a business. The records we are talking about is keeping track by bookkeeping your income and expenses. Following the basic accounting practices is a sure-fire way to keep you apprised of how your business efforts are paying off.

The reason for keeping good records is to evaluate where your best business is coming from, keeping adequate inventories, and having good detailed records which will assist with the accounting process. It will provide information to make a monthly or yearly balance sheet for filing tax returns. It offers a guide to replenish inventories as needed, offers a direction of where expansion is warranted as well as items that should be discontinued. Many businesses that deal in credit would need to determine who is behind in their payments and who is worthy of the credit you give.

As an owner/manager, your primary objective is to make a profit. This section is designed to ensure you have a simple, timely system of recording and reporting data -so that you can effectively control what goes on in your company and know that you really are making a profit. With the personal time, effort and money you

have put into your company, you owe it yourself to know what is going on and soon enough to do something about it if things are not going the way you want them to. While Planning for Success is concerned with planning the overall direction of your company, this section deals with the day -to-day control of the company-less fun, more detail, but just as important. If you can't effectively handle the present, there won't be any future.

You may have a background in sales, marketing or some other non-financial activity, and the detail and tedium of bookkeeping and accounting may be something you want to avoid if at all possible.

Nonetheless, no owner/manager can afford to remain ignorant of such an essential function-to do so could have extremely serious consequences. If your accounting function is already well-established, understanding it better can help you use accounting and financial analysis techniques to improve your profits. Perhaps you are operating on a smaller scale. As your business grows large enough to justify a double entry system, you will be able to hire a bookkeeper and have your taxes and reports handled on a part-time basis by an accountant. And, as your business continues to grow, you can then employ a full-time accounting staff. This section won't train you to be an accountant or bookkeeper but it will give you enough knowledge so that you can recognize what information you need and how it should be developed. It will also give you enough information to know what your bookkeeper is doing and whether the job is being done well. Most business owner/managers just starting out can get by with bound or loose-leaf books for their journals and ledgers and then progress to a simple "one write" system. Several copyrighted bookkeeping systems can be purchased directly from the publisher or through your office-supply house or printer.

Many owners now have personal computers to help them run their business more effectively. But regardless of the systems you use and the accounting

staff you employ, you must know enough about the system to:
1. Evaluate and understand results.
2. Recognize when an employee has strayed, intentionally or unintentionally.
3. Appreciate the need for controls.
4. Understand the recommendations made by the bookkeeper or accountant.

This section is divided into the following major parts:
Bookkeeping, including a description of the books of account, how they are made up, an explanation of "double-entry" and "debit and credit," and the process of bookkeeping up to "trial balance." (Improving Your Financial Prime will describe the process of preparing basic financial statements.)

Three types of information-operating, management accounting and financial accounting-and the purposes for which each of these may be used.
Efficient filing systems.
Internal control, safekeeping and security, including the handling of cash.
Whether you use a manual or computerized system, the basic concepts are the same. We want you to know what to look for and how to talk to outsiders, about your business. Most important, we want to help you strengthen your internal-control procedures, enhance the quality of your information- gathering and help you develop a standardized information-gathering routine.
Bookkeeping: Bookkeeping is the process of recording and classifying every transaction that affects a business, expressed in terms of money in the books of account in an orderly way.
Journals-The books of original entry: The following five books, or journals, are called "books of original entry" since they are the books in which transactions are entered as soon as they occur. These usually are the basic journals for a small firm. Larger companies may use many more than these. The purpose and use of journals are the same in all record-keeping systems. The following information will help you gain a basic understanding of the concepts of record-keeping.
Purchase journal to record: Goods or service bought.
Sales journal to record: Goods or services sold.
Receipts journal to record: Cash or checks received.
Disbursements journal to record: Checks paid out.
Payroll journal to record: Wages, salaries and deductions.
The practical purpose of the general journal is to record three types of transactions:
Correcting or adjusting errors. Errors are likely to occur in any bookkeeping system-for example, an item posted in the wrong journal or account.
"Closing" entries at the end of each business year. Closing the books may involve transferring entries between accounts or the setting up of accrued (accumulated)

entries for expenses and revenues.

All entries incidental to the commencement of a new business. This involves "non-cash" entries, including patents and copyrights.

It is necessary to hire a qualified CPA to set up your books according to your type of business transactions. The Certified Public Accountant will instruct you how to use these ledgers in the correct manner and also instruct you on any other record ledgers that would be helpful to you and to him in making an analysis as needed.

REVELATION #9
HUMAN RELATIONS

Human Relations can be defined as the study and understanding of individual human characteristics and needs. The more skillful you become at recognizing an individual's needs, traits and motivations, the better you will be able to deal with that person in any kind of situation. Human Relations here will aspire to teach you to modify your behavior in order to become more effective in relating to other human beings, especially in the area of work.

You must understand yourself first before you can start understanding others. Once you understand yourself, you should develop a high degree of objectivity, facing problems of human relations as if they were outside of you. This way you will be able to identify the actual problem or situation, get the proper information, and make a sound judgment. To get the proper information, you must become sensitive to the feelings and attitudes of others. You must be able to recognize the various human characteristics and have the knowledge and skill to relate to these people in a diplomatic manner.

These are people who have an extraordinary ability to relate to others, who show sensitivity and who will modify their own behavior in order to help other solve their problems or fill their needs. These people are probably unaware of the reasons for their success in dealing with others. They often go about their business without giving any thought to this quality.

What is the reason for their success? How can they communicate to a wide variety of individuals? The simple answer is they recognize the people they deal with as individuals, often assuming different characteristics and react properly to them. Your learning of human relations here will focus on the different characteristics you find in individuals, how you can recognize them and relate more effectively to these people. This is not an attempt to stereotype people, but rather, an attempt to better understand the many different faces, moods and feelings we all display at different times.

The Timid Characteristic: Many people that you deal with are overly cautious, indecisive and unsure of themselves. In many cases they would prefer to have others make decisions for them. They are frequently listless, have a weak handshake and generally lack aggressiveness. These are the main indicators of the timid character. You can probably think of many more.
The key to handling this character is to gently lead the individual. Since he is not

aggressive, he must be encouraged to open up, to express his opinions.

The Procrastinator Characteristic: We meet procrastination each and every day. Most often it takes the form of simply putting things off for another day. We all procrastinate from time to time. If you don't believe this just think of all the little repairs around the house you've been "meaning to take care of' Or how about that savings account you were going to start "one of these days." We often become true masters at avoiding or delaying decisions especially when it requires effort on our part. This same characteristic exists daily in the business world as well. Decisions are often delayed again and again until hours and even days of hard work result in a tremendous amount of wasted time and effort. Why? Because it is easy to be deceived by an individual who has decided to procrastinate.

When you first meet this individual, you may think that he is going to be a delight to do business with. He may give his full attention to everything you say. He may even give you his approval by nodding at every suggestion, at the end, however, the procrastinator will often respond, "Let me think it over" or "I'll take care of that when I get a chance."

The responses and characteristics are obvious. Behind the procrastinator's indecisiveness is often a lack of confidence in his ability to make correct decisions. Many times, he is just too lazy or disorganized to accommodate a decision. Your efforts may appear to be wasted.

Handling Procrastination: The best way to deal with procrastination can be found if we first discover why it occurs in the first place, if you stop and think about it, you most often fail to do things because they don't seem important at the time. At least they don't seem to warrant your immediate attention. Sometimes, it's just "too much work to bother with now."

Herein lays the answer to handling procrastination. Show why it is important... now. If you can convince an individual that it is to his advantage to do something now rather than later, he is less likely to choose tomorrow over today. If you can show an individual how the additional time or effort he must expend will mean greater profit or advancement, he is less likely to hold off on a decision. If you can point out that an individual cannot benefit from indecision, he is less likely to choose the well - worth path of "maybe tomorrow." Procrastination can cause both frustration and misunderstanding. Eliminate it by convincing the individual that his decision is important now.

The Curiosity Characteristic: Curiosity can be either a virtue or a hazard depending upon the individual. In a business situation, the curious individual wants to know everything but his desire for knowledge does not necessarily stem from a desire for education. Rather, the curious individual often times uses his curiosity as an end in itself. Once his curiosity has been satisfied, he has no further need for you.

The curious individual has one point in his favor. It is easy to arouse his interest. It is almost as if we had been waiting all day for the opportunity to hear you tell your story. It is easy to be encouraged by this characteristic since the individual seems to want to hear you talk - and you do. You tell him everything. Occasionally, the curious individual interrupts with "How interesting" or "What do you know about that." Why then does the curious individual so often refuse to buy your ideas? The answer is simple. If you tell him everything, you sate his curiosity. This is the principle pitfall with a curious individual. "It was sure nice meeting you," he will say. "Drop by again sometime."

Satisfying the Curiosity: The pitfall to avoid in dealing with the curious individual is telling him too much. Do not let his curiosity entice you into saying everything you have to say on the subject. Instead you must learn to direct the individual toward specific ends. Do not tell everything. Hold back some information. As you move along, gain commitment from the individual. Transform his curiosity into a surge of genuine interest in your idea. This interest can easily be converted into a desire. Remember, do not let the curious individual lead you along merely for the satisfaction you get out of your own words. Dig in and take over the control.

The Skeptic Characteristic: One of the most unnerving and challenging characteristics you face in the world today is skepticism. The very nature of the skeptic individual places you in a defensive position for he straightforwardly demands, "show me," Here our phrase "knowledge is power" becomes very important. The skeptic individual challenges your ability to prove what you say, or else challenges your proof source. If this kind of challenge makes you feel frustrated and defeated, you are over-reacting to the situation. The answer to the skeptic is not as difficult as you imagine.

The Talkative Characteristic: Frequently, you find yourself confronted with the talkative characteristic. He may talk all of the time. In fact, he talks so much that often you cannot get a word in edgewise. This is an extremely trying situation for if nothing is done; he will keep on talking until the end of the conversation, dismissing you before you have a chance to say a word. When confronted with this kind of situation, you risk the chance of wasting valuable hours and never having an opportunity to be heard. No matter what the person's reasons may be for his continuous talking, you must always be aware of the fact that unrelated conversation can only lead you away from the business at hand.

Directing the Talkative: The most logical question you might ask yourself when confronted by the talkative individual is "How can I get a word in edgewise without offending him or sounding rude?" Obviously, you must take the ball away from him and carry it toward your goal, not his. But how?

To begin with, you must realize that you cannot out-talk or out -shout the talkative person. If you make a contest out of it, he is sure to win - if for no other reason than that he has a head start. You must use more subtle strategy. The best technique is to channel his talk. Turn his wealth of words to a profitable subject- your product or service, naturally. One way to do this is to make use of the compliment. Tell him,

for example, that you admire anyone who can be as interesting and well-informed as he. "It must be gratifying to have such a fund of knowledge, Mr. Smith." Then listen for a break in the conversation, a high point which you can use in controlling the interview. Another way to channel his talk is to use the device called "capping the conversation." When your talkative friend has reached the point at which he has to pause, break in with something like this:

"Mr. Smith, your opinions upon conditions behind the Iron Curtain are certainly interesting, and I agree with what you have to say. It's evident that you've given the matter a lot of thought. Too bad that we can't get our leaders in Washington to see things through the eyes of a practical businessman and scholar." Then change the subject and turn the conversation to your specific goal, you might even hand hint a sample or a letter regarding your service. You can do this without appearing rude if you sum up his remarks and then change the subject quickly. This is called "capping the conversation."

Still another way to direct the talkative prospect is by the magic phrase, "You said something just then." Think about this phrase for a moment. What does it do? It gets him to listen to himself-a fascinating adventure for any man. "You said something just then, Mr. Smith," you might say. "You said something that strikes me as a most powerful reason for this improvement I ever heard!" Then quote some remark he has just made. He will listen because even the talkative individual will listen when his own words are the topic of conversation.

You can certainly think of many additional ways to redirect a conversation that had drifted from the subject at hand. This is a frequent occurrence not only in a business situation, but also in many social and civic functions which you have experienced. By maintaining an alert and positive attitude and by exercising the proper strategy at the right moment, channeling a conversation is not difficult at all.

"The Braggart Characteristic: It is a fact that everyone needs to flatter his own ego and boast of his past accomplishments from time to time. When we are well-versed in a subject, we are often eager to offer both our knowledge and opinion on the topic being discussed. In many ways, this places us in a key position - we are the focus of the conversation. This human tendency to demonstrate our knowledge is a frequent occurrence in the world. When it is carried to extremes, it can be a detriment to the smooth transaction of business. Often it is reduced to simple conceit and bragging.

We have all met the individual who seems to "know-it- all." No matter what the subject, he makes it his specialty. He brings forth all the facts and is Johnny-on-the - spot with the inside dope on everything and everybody. If you do not believe it, ask him - he will tell you personally. Although there may be a number of reasons why this individual has a need to brag at any given time, the situation can be frustrating to the man who lets it affect him.

Listening to the Braggart: There will undoubtedly come a day (if it hasn't already) when you will be seated across the desk from this kind of individual whom for some reason or other, insists on telling you all he knows on a variety of subjects. No matter what you say, he attempts to top it. Perhaps he had a deflating experience the day before or perhaps he is merely trying to impress you with his accomplishments. Whatever the case, you must first hear him out - LISTEN! The more this individual talks, the greater your chances of understanding him as well as his deficiencies. You already know that his ego is a big soft spot! When you make a conscientious effort to hear him out an interesting thing generally happens. He begins to take an interest in you.

Here is a man who dotes on praise. If others do not praise him, he praises himself. You come along - and listen, you open up and laugh at his jokes and take an interest in what he says. You hear him out. If he is convinced of your appreciation for him, you should have little trouble redirecting the conversation. He will soon find you an interesting person. After he has warmed up to you, remember to redirect the conversation to your idea, plan or service.

Remember, however, that in order to radiate sincerity-you must be sincere. This does not mean that you have to find him as charming as he finds himself. But look for the good in him, knowing that there is good in each of us. And since you have no proof that what he says is untrue, what harm does it do to let him know that you are impressed with his accomplishments? There is always an outside chance that he is telling the truth. Give him the benefit of the doubt. It will prove a valuable lesson in human relations.

The Perfectionist Characteristic: From time to time, you are confronted with a characteristic significantly different than any other - the perfectionist. The term is somewhat deceiving in that the perfectionist does not always demand perfection in everything he does. If, however, perfection is one of his key requirements in buying your ideas or service, this characteristic places you in a very trying situation. By this we simply mean that both your ideas and services will be carefully scrutinized.

The perfectionist will weigh and consider everything you say and do. You should not be deceived by his often slow, plodding manner. Since he is a methodical individual, he considers everything that is being said because of a low tolerance for ambiguity. He demands a rigid caliber of precision and clarity. He needs to feel that he completely understands what is said and what is implied. For this reason, the perfectionist is likely to interrupt frequently for further elaboration and discussion. By watching for these characteristics of his attitude, you will be able to mentally outline the manner in which you will deal with this individual.

Handling the Perfectionist: The chances are you have not met many total perfectionists in your business affairs but many individuals demand a certain amount of perfection. Whenever this is the case, you may find yourself confronting one of the most difficult persons to sell. Since they will frequently interrupt you at

any turn in order to clear up technicalities, you must be prepared to handle their questions before they occur. This is the real key to the perfectionist attitude-answer the questions before they are asked. Anticipate his key questions and cover them before they occur to him.

Selling the Wise Guy: You probably have a good idea of what lies behind the facade of the "wise guy" characteristic. It is a very common malady known as an inferiority complex. His attitude becomes that of a wise guy in order to compensate for this complex. Often, he does not see himself acting in this obnoxious manner. Consequently, it is impossible to argue with him or criticize his attitude openly; it can only lead to hostility and a separation of personalities. Instead, use his personality to help direct your ideas or service. He drinks up compliments like a sponge absorbs water, so compliment him - but in such a way that he must prove his assumed superiority by answering your questions the way you want him to. Above all, guard against one thing. Do not "buy the idea" -at the beginning - that he knows all the answers.

Do not try to break through his self-erected wall of wisdom. Let him think that he has you convinced of his superiority. Do not contradict him when he is wrong. Do not argue. Compliment him on his good judgment and wisdom. Ask his advice in such a way that he must sell himself. In brief, while you cannot force the "wise guy" to do anything, you can compliment him into selling himself on your ideas or services.

The Push-Over Characteristic: You probably know several people who have a terrible time saying "no" to anyone. They are true "push-over" to the indiscriminate person. You can often recognize the "push-over" by what you see in his office or home. If you find an ample scattering of such articles as encyclopedias, business calendars, desk paraphernalia and charity plaques -items usually sold by sales groups only-you know him for a "push-over," someone who buys from one and all.

Restraining the Push-Over: A question of moral standards always arises when you find yourself face to face with such an "easy mark." You can let your conscience take over and tell yourself, "My sworn duty to myself is to not take advantage of those who have no need for me or my service." We have no way of knowing which "voice" will win you over. We can only tell you, in all sincerity, that you will never be a complete success if you follow the dictates of your subconscious without discrimination. Gain at the expense of others is, in many ways, more loss than profit.

The Argumentative Characteristic: Argument for the sake of argument can place you in a difficult position in trying to present your ideas or service. The argumentative character is easy to recognize - he loves to argue and is always on the lookout for something to argue about. Often, he'll take issue on a point just for the sake of arguing whether he believes his position or not. On a psychological level, his

behavior is frequently caused by feelings of inadequacy. He sees life as one continuous battle to prove his worth to others. Every discussion and conversation is seen as a test of his ability to better his opponent. To make matters worse, the arguer usually possesses a hostile, sarcastic and aggressive attitude. This individual argues about almost everything you propose. He knows a better way of getting the job done, a better company than yours to do business with and even a better service than the one you offer him - or so he tells you. That is just the point. He is not really sure about the things he says, but he is taking this form of attack in the hope that he might be right enough to discourage you from selling him something. If the argumentative person can succeed in "shooting your ideas or service full of holes," he will know that you know little about your competitor and hence must be green.

Countering the Arguer: In working with this kind of individual keep one thing in mind: the argumentative person really wants to be sold. If he did not, he would not be wasting his time arguing with you, He wants to be proved wrong -but this proving must, of course, be done with a delicacy that will not injure his ego. You should handle his argument like this:

"Mr. Jones, I can see that you've given this matter much thought. Your arguments are based on good sound judgment. However, I feel sure that if I give you a few facts with which you do not yet seem familiar, I will be able to show you why you should alter your opinions."

When he tells you that he thinks one of your competitors is offering a better deal, you should counter with something like this: "I also think very highly of the company you mention. It's a fine business firm. And I'm glad to hear you know the full story of what they can do, for it will give you a better chance to use your sense of values to weigh their product merits of the one I'm going to explain to you." Always remember that if the argumentative person did not argue with you, he would not be a prospect. By arguing, he is indicating that he is in the market for a product or service like yours. As soon as you have him sized up, you should try to answer most of his arguments before he presents them. If what you have in your opinion is the best product - you will be able to sell it to the argumentative prospect. Use tact to turn his arguments into sales points. When you prove him wrong, give him an out by showing him how he was right before he knew about your product or service.

Selling the Stubborn: The study of psychology tells us that often a dogmatically stubborn person is that way because of an inferiority complex, He is afraid that if he gives an inch, he will never gain it back. A more confident person is not, afraid to give ground because he relies on his intelligence to help him gain ground on another point. So now we know this person's weak point- and we also know that he will not

buy because of any good logic you may present. What is left? Of course, it's his emotions and they are the key to the sale. He is most often an emotional buyer. So, use your emotional appeals in presenting your points. If he sets his heels in the ground and pulls away, congratulate him on his steadfast character and resolute firmness. Then use all of the emotional tools at your command to guide him toward your way of thinking. Here is where showmanship pays off in big dividends for you. Use stories that stimulate emotional reactions. Whether those reactions take the form of tears, laughter or shame, makes no difference. Once you have stimulated him emotionally, you can use your logical arguments with effectiveness.

The Overcautious Characteristic: One characteristic that succeeds in causing discomfort and frustration is the overcautious individual. This individual is afraid to make even the smallest move. Even the strongest sales points and appeals do little to move this kind of individual. He sits in his chair as if he were nailed to it. He thinks he "won't buy now." He gives no reason. He just strongly asserts that he has decided not to buy. No matter what you say or how long you say it, no matter how fervently you plead your case-the answer is the same. "I'm going to wait and see what happens." The problem is not one of disinterest, however. Rather this individual prefers to take great pains in studying every point before making a decision. His only problem is that he has taken his cautiousness to the extreme.

This can be sheer frustration to anyone.

Turning Caution to Confidence: Within the overcautious person are streaks of timidity that run his length breadth. You cannot, in the short time you are with him, make a courageous battler out of a man who lives by fear. But you can continue in some way to allay some of his fear long enough to turn him into a customer. And here is how we suggest you go about doing so.

What the overcautious person lacks most is confidence -confidence in him, confidence in you, and confidence in the world or anything in it. He is timid. Maybe he has reason for his mistrust, or maybe he is by nature what is called "the timid soul." At any rate, this total lack of confidence is his dominant characteristic. Your direction of attack should be obvious. If he will not buy as long as he lacks confidence -it is up to you to instill enough confidence in him to elicit an order. This then is your approach. Do everything possible to win his confidence.

One way to win it is to show him that he will save money, or at least not lose money in his transactions with you. There is a peculiar and fascinating relationship between money and confidence. If you can paint the money -making picture in bold enough colors, this man will forget his timidity long enough to buy from you. So, talk about the savings he will make, the profits in store for him, the satisfaction he can earn in dealing with you. Be personal but be aware that he doubts you too as well as your firm and your goals. He doubts everything- that is his nature. Be personal with him and assure him of your interest. Talk slowly and conduct yourself in a way that gains confidence.

Act the gentleman, the solicitous professional man who is equally skilled in recognizing problems and in solving them. Use testimonials and stories both unexcelled winner of confidence. And by all means, once you win his confidence do nothing to lose it. Keep your word, no matter what the odds or costs. Once you lose the confidence he gives you, you lose him as a customer.

"Like attracts like." It is the oldest law in the world. It governs every move we make, every facet of our daily lives. We cannot escape it. It surrounds us and rules us. It is a basic Law of Nature, a Law of God, and a law -of anything you wish to call it. But it is a fundamental law from which there is no escape. The great minds of the ages have accepted it. You will accept it too, after due reflection.

Your acceptance is of primary importance because we are going to carry the law one step further. You'll notice that we do not change the law or its meaning; that cannot be done. But we do change the wording. Let's phrase it like this:

Good Efforts get Good Results

And

Poor Efforts get Poor Results

Did we lose our basic law in our change of wording? No. This is still essentially the same law. This statement has been proven in experiments conducted by some of our leading scientists. Accepting this idea and seeing it at work everywhere is essential to your own personal happiness and success.

We're now ready for the most important law-for the Golden Key to Success. Think Only Thoughts of Success: Simple? Yes! It is so simple that men have spent their lives looking for it and have overlooked it. The simplest things are often the most important and the easiest to overlook.

It has been said that most people work harder at being a failure than they do at being a success. The statement is accurate. Applying the basic law "Like attracts like" and using it as our measuring stick, we can see these truths:

It is in everyone's power to bring success by thinking thoughts of success.

It is in everyone's power to bring failure by thinking thoughts of failure.

Your acceptance of these principles or laws can cause a remarkable change in your life. Give further thought to the ideas here until you fully understand them. Begin to apply them immediately to your everyday activities. You will soon see the true power your thoughts can have on yourself and those around you.

When you first meet someone, they decide unconsciously in the first few minutes whether to like you, dislike you, accept you, or reject you. Therefore, you must make the first few minutes count by using the foregoing ideas. First remember (Like attracts like). Find something you genuinely like about the person- his handshake, his nose, mouth, eyes, build, etc. If you find something you like about him, then he will feel this and like you in return. If you have done your homework on this person and know his likes, dislikes, hobbies, etc., then you have a further advantage. Use this knowledge to establish a rapport with the person and he will soon open up to you and be ready to help you or buy your ideas or plans.

You must show confidence and enthusiasm. This will also communicate itself to the person. Have a firm handshake and a pleasant smile. Do all these things and I can assure you that in those first few minutes, the person will decide to like you and if he likes you, he will listen to you and then you can influence his thoughts in the area that you wish without him realizing it.

It is beyond argument that in order to achieve worthwhile things when dealing with people, one must know how to handle the many different types of personalities. Influencing and controlling others is a matter of knowledge and application. Every successful undertaking can directly or indirectly be attributed to the dynamic influence of a leader, whether we are speaking about general business or specifically sales. The magic principle of salesmanship is: "Handling people successfully!"

People Must Be Studied: Almost everyone agrees that in order to become a stenographer one has to study lessons and practice them. Everybody knows that in order to become an accountant, one has to study lessons and practice them. The same holds true for law, medicine, engineering, and so on but very few peopleunderstand that it also holds true for human relations. Few people are born with a complete knowledge of how to deal successfully with people.

It must be realized that knowledge of people is not confined to business establishments. It is also outside of working hours that you develop skill in handling the people around you. From the time, you get up in the morning until you go to bed at night, you are dealing with people. From the time, you are born until the time you die, you are dealing with people; parents, brothers and sisters, other relatives, employers, supervisors and associates. A successful salesman in business is usually a successful salesman in his home and among his friends: he knows how to handle people.

What you will get in this world as regards (1) friendships, (2) wealth, (3) social standing, will depend to a large extent on how capable you are of selling yourself to people. If you are a good salesman, as a result of your knowledge of people, you will have many friends, considerable of this world's goods and will be admired and looked up to. If you are a poor salesman because of your lack of knowledge of people, you will fall far short of the above universally desirable achievements. Friendliness Is The Key: Friends are your most valuable asset, and knowledge of people enables you to make and keep friends. If you know a person who doesn't

have any friends, although he may have money, I believe that you would think twice before agreeing to step into his shoes. Without friends, life is not worth much and business does not progress very far without friendships.

A successful businessman relates the following observation:

Why do you like your dog? Because your dog likes you. Does that sound like an inane statement? Let me assure you that it is a most profound thought. I have a little dog. When I come home at night, I do not have to whistle for him because he is waiting for me, and he comes running to me like greased lightning. He wiggles his whole body and tail with pleasure. I get down so he can lick me a bit. He thinks that I am a wonderful fellow - he thinks that I am a big shot. In fact, he is the only one at home who makes a fuss over me. He likes me and I can't help but like him.

If anything should happen to him, I would feel terrible. He has worked his way into my heart because he makes a fuss over me.

Here is the point: If you want to make friends with people (customers), make a fuss over them. Pay them unusual attention. You can be sure that many of your competitors are too busy - they are too interested in other things - to make a fuss over their customers. With this approach, you win hands down every time!

We have to understand human nature before we can understand people. Let us delve into the human mind and find out what makes the human being do what they do. When we discover that secret, we shall know exactly how to deal successfully with people in order to produce the most harmonious human relations.

The most fundamental and far-reaching influence in human life is ego, which is the Latin word for "I." I have a good opinion of myself, you have a good opinion of yourself and customers have a good opinion of themselves. Remember this when dealing with people. Generally speaking, a human being has a high opinion of himself; if you want to make a hit with him, do something that will raise his opinion of himself. Make customers feel important by making a fuss over them and they will like you.

Address Customers by Their Nickname, If Any: The first requirement of successfully handling people is: Call people by name. When you call a customer by name, you say to him, "You are important. I like you. You are somebody." When you don't call a customer by name, after he has been in your place of business several times, you are really saying to him, "You are not so important. You are just another customer."

There are, for example bank tellers who never call customers by name although this is one of the best ways to make friends. Even though they know the customer's name, because it is on the passbook, back goes the passbook without name-recognition, and their attitude is: "Just another customer. Don't expect me to put myself out for you."

The latter method is the horse-and buggy method and any business that is employing such representatives need not be surprised if the public gravitates to competitors who know more about handling people successfully.
Cheerfulness: Give every customer, no matter what the transaction a smile; and this applies to our relatives and associates likewise. This is now standard practice in many stores, banks, public utilities and other institutions that serve the public. A smile is standard equipment in any first-class institution. However, a little shopping trip on your part will, no doubt, result in your discovering several horse-and-buggy business establishments in your community where this practice is not followed.
Salesmen who do not understand how to handle people try to sell their troubles to their customers. But they don't succeed because troubles have no market value; they are a liability when worn on the face. A frown really says to the customer: "You're not so important. Your business doesn't mean much to us." A smile says: 'I like you. We value your business."
When you smile among your associates and in your family circle, you raise the ego of those around you. They feel that you value them highly. You bind them to you and make them want to serve you. They like you because you like them. Remember the dog story. If the expression on your face shows indifference to them, they will probably be indifferent to you. In such a circumstance, you would not be a salesman

because you would not be selling yourself.

Now, when you are happy, you naturally smile, don't you? The big problem in business is to smile when you are not happy. Nobody can be happy all the time; lots of disheartening things happen each day. Yours hoes may pinch; you may have indigestion; you may have a domestic difficulty; you may have made a bad investment. They are your affair; make sure that you don't unload them on other people who are not interested in them: other people are interested in their own problems. Try this method: When you are not happy and don't feel like smiling, just show your teeth. Check your expression in a mirror. It looks something like a smile, doesn't it? Customers may notice an artificial quality in that expression, but they are sympathetic because they know that you are doing your best to be friendly. You can be sure that they like it much better than a frown or an attitude of indifference.

Show Appreciation & Be Gracious - It costs nothing to simply say, "thank you." No matter what the transaction with the customer, a "thank you" is in order. It is only necessary for you to shop in several business establishments to find representatives who don't know this law of human relations. These people, in most cases, really don't mean to be unfriendly; they have just not learned how to handle people.
A "thank you" makes patrons feel good; it makes people feel important and friendly toward you; it makes them like you; it enables you to sell yourself to them and make friends of them. You never lose when you make an investment in successful human relations.
Listen to people when they talk. This raises their ego and makes them feel more important. Since this is a very pleasant feeling, these people like you much better because you have made them feel happy. In other words, they are now more friendly to you and anxious to do favors for you.
Some people apparently listen to others when they talk but their eyes show lack of interest. They fool nobody but themselves. Others look around and seem bored, as if to say, "I wish you would shut up." If you want to hurt a person's feelings (ego), don't show any patience when he explains something to you. And don't pay undivided attention to him when he is talking. The importance of knowing how to handle people is shown in this story:

Several years ago, I knew a certain bank officer who always seemed abstracted when I talked to him. He always irritated me because his lack of attention made me feel that I was of no importance to him. One day I gave him 200 shares of stock with instructions to sell them at market on the Chicago Stock Exchange. When I received my next monthly statement, I found that he had sold the shares on the New York Curb where, on that particular day, the price of this stock was nearly a point lower than on the Chicago Stock Exchange. This meant a loss of $180, which the bank finally refunded to me on the basis of my representation.

That bank officer not only irritated me but everybody else with whom he dealt and when he was finally demoted to a position where he didn't have to deal with the public, he had considerable ability was qualified to deal only with things-not people. It requires considerably greater skill to deal with people than it does to deal with things.

Show a Sincere Interest in Their Personal Life: It is surprising how many friends you can make, even among people who don't look inviting. Everyone is interested in himself. All you have to do is encourage people to talk about themselves and they find you interesting.

The best way to be unpopular is to talk continually about you. That chases people away from you. People are only mildly interested in you; they are profoundly interested in themselves and their possessions. If you want to win at the game of human relations, draw people out and listen to them talk. Then, they think that you are wonderful. They like you. They want to see you again soon. You suddenly become popular.

You may say: "That is all right for their ego, but where do I come in? How about satisfying my ego?" Well, here's where your ego is satisfied. When you learn to control others by following the laws of successfully handling people, you get the satisfaction of accomplishment. You feel the thrill of the master who understands

people and draws them toward him. Your increased ability to deal successfully with people should be a satisfactory return to your ego.

Never Show Superiority over Someone Else: Do you know that a person can high-hat another and never know that he is doing it? Do you feel superior to a customer who is poorly dressed? If so, you will probably high-hat him and never know it. Any condescending attitude on your part will be quickly detected by him and resented. High-hating hurts people's ego. It makes them feel less important. Several years ago, a large stock brokerage firm retained a specialist in order to increase business. Toward this end, he sent out letters to all former customers in order to ascertain why they no longer did business with this broker. Some of the replies received were startling.

One letter from a Chinese said, "I'll tell you why I no longer do business with you. I go to your Mr. Birch and ask him to buy some stock. He says, "O.K., boy, I fix you up." I am 62 years old. I have saved $20,000. I know Dow-Jones. I read the Wall Street Journal. I do not like to be called boy."

Twenty thousand dollars' worth of business thrown out the window because a superior-acting customers' man thought he could patronize a customer. Numerous other letters were received which showed how customers had been lost at that branch office. Yet that branch manager complained that he had not been advanced as far as he thought he should be. He thought that his story was very convincing, but to the expert it was simply wishful thinking. He was a "babe in the woods" as far as human relations were concerned.

Suppose that branch manager had shaken hands with the Chinese and said, "Thanks for the order. We are glad to have your business, Mr. Wong." That Chinese would have told other Chinese, who would have been in with their money to open accounts. It is a fact that people from other countries respond to good salesmanship just as much as the people of the United States. Their money is just as good as ours. They deserve our respect and they respond favorable to all of the laws of successfully handling people.

Gain Acceptance by Raising Their Ego: When William Wrigley, Jr., famous chewing gum magnate was a young man he sold soap among French-Canadian merchants. He found them cold and suspicious until he discovered how to raise their ego. This is how he did it.

He learned two words of French and when he entered a store he would wave his hand which held a bar of soap and exclaim "Savon mineral," which means mineral soap.

Invariably, the salesman's foreign pronunciation and obvious effort to learn a language dear to their hearts produced smiles even among otherwise suspicious and aloof customers. Their egos were raised by his avoiding all possibility of high-hat and air of superiority. He made these merchants feel more important and they liked him for it.

In dealing with foreigners, an effort to learn a few words of their language is a big factor in breaking down sales resistance. Likewise, in talking to any class of people, a use of the terms they use tends to put both you and the other person on common grounds and avoids any feeling of high-hating.

Be Constructive In Arguing: Never argue! When you argue, you argue to win and, if you win, the other person has to lose. People don't feel as important when they lose as when they win. You injure people's feelings if you make them lose in an argument.

Arguments antagonize people because their opinions are being attacked - and their opinions are as dear to them as their names. In arguing, people oppose each other; they take opposite sides. You can't win people to your way of thinking by opposing them. Opposition produces resistance instead of assistance.

The arguer is usually a self-centered person who likes to hear himself talk; who likes to expand his own ego at the expense of the ego of other people. If you encounter an arguer, listen to him. He likes listeners who can "take" what he has to give. The arguer wants the center of the stage and resents any attempt to crowd him off.

If you feel that it is necessary to disagree with another person, you can avoid an argument by apparently agreeing, and then, in a roundabout way, disagreeing. This technique protects his ego or pride and through using it, you can retain his good will and friendship. For example: "That is an interesting idea you just explained but have you ever looked at it from this angle-? "I am glad to get your viewpoint: however- "It does look that way, doesn't it?

An Unnecessary Argument: A depositor tells of this experience at a bank:

I had two accounts in a certain bank: one a Trustee account that had to be signed with the word "Trustee," and the other a personal account that needed only my signature. My monthly statement showed that both accounts had wrong balances, and when I complained to the bank officer he replied, "You must have failed to put the word "Trustee" on some of the checks which you wrote on the "Trustee" account." I replied, "I did not," and glared at him. I continued, "I insist that you produce all the canceled checks and find out whose mistake it is since you have accused me of making the error." He said that it was not necessary but my ego was hurt and I insisted that it was necessary. He dug up the records and found that the bank had made the mistake.

Instead of following the horse-and-buggy method of human relations that this banker used, why didn't he say, "I'm sorry this mistake has happened. We shall look up the cause of the error, make the necessary corrections in the passbooks and mail them to you." Why didn't he do this? Because he didn't understand this seventh law on successfully handling people.

It is so easy to handle people correctly when you know how. The difference between having trouble with people and not having trouble with them is a hairbreadth. It hurts people's ego to impute errors to them, even if they have made them.

People like other people who make them feel important. That is the keynote of human relations. Invariably follow this principle when you are dealing with people and you will invariably sell yourself and your products to them, because it is easy to sell your products to a customer who is sold on you. A customer is sold on you when he is friendly toward you because you have raised his ego.

In conclusion, it should be emphasized that the end product in the outcome of any situation is the result of personalities in action. Therefore, the more versatile a person is in his or her ability to handle different types of people, the higher degree of success is in the final outcome of a given circumstance.

We encourage you to develop your skills to the maximum - stay alert to what is happening; study how people react; use good common sense and judgment in your actions and/or reactions towards people.

From our viewpoint, we have noted the different types of personalities that have to be dealt with in a diplomatic way. Of course, your judgment and personality have to do the rest in order to engage into productive communication with each individual.

REVALATION
#10
PERSONALITY

What is Personality: By the personality of a man, we mean those qualities which, singly or in combination, distinguish him as an individual and separate him from the crowd. In a way that no science has explained, a man's personality is stamped not merely upon his face, but on his speech, his walk, and his manners. Every one of us carries a personality trade-mark. No matter how we try to hide or disguise it, men of experience will always discern it and what it stands for. Personality, at bottom, is the man himself, although it has an external as well as an internal aspect. The physical and surface traits of a man are very important in our estimate of his personality; however, grounded they may be in something deeper. It is a question, in fact, whether the surface traits do not constitute the overwhelming influence in shaping a man's personality, or shall we say, in shaping the visible pattern thereof? Certainly, the surface traits are the ones that most people see and comment upon.

Everyone admires almost to the point of envy, the person that has a magnetic personality. The quality is also referred to as "charisma." It is almost magical as to what one possessing charisma can accomplish, especially in the field of business and sales.

Some people have a more natural tendency towards this type personality than others, yet anyone can develop a better personality. The method is not easy, because it takes study practices and application. The end results are always worth the effort in this pursuit.

A professional personality is necessary in order to sell, and is something definitely more than one's natural personality. It is in effect the result of self-confidence possessing a thorough knowledge of one's profession or field of endeavor.

The lack of an attractive natural personality, however, is not a handicap to the prospective salesman. It is the professional sales personality that sells merchandise, and this can be cultivated to the point of highest expertise. First impressions are of great importance in salesmanship, and a successful sales personality results from the cultivation of the personal factors that produce first impressions.

These factors are: Smile, physical carriage, actions, tone of voice, voice inflections, pronunciation, shaking hands, poise, body tone, clothing, appearance, manners and mannerisms. A study of yourself will constitute an analysis of your sales personality,

which may be viewed as "everything about you which makes an impression upon the customer." Everything about you that distinguishes you from other salesmen becomes your unique sales personality. It has often been said that a salesman's personality is the only factor in making him successful in his profession, but we must also recognize that it embraces his ability to manage the presentation of his merchandise and his skill in managing customers.

It is more realistic, however, to look at the salesman's personality as one of the three equally important legs on which his success must stand. No matter how desirable a personality a salesman has, he will lose many sales unless it is supported by a thorough knowledge of his merchandise and customers.

Meaning of "Professional Personality"- Everyone has two personalities: native and cultivated. Our native personality makes friends, but it is our cultivated or self- acquired personality that sells goods. This principle of personality explains what otherwise seems a paradox: a salesman with a pleasing personality who is a failure. In other words, it takes more than a smile and sociable qualities to sell goods, the same as it takes more than these pleasing qualities to make a man a successful lawyer, doctor or engineer. It is the "professional personality" that makes a person a success in his profession, and this comprises not only the ability to make friends but also a certain impressiveness which a person acquires when he is conscious of his own professional knowledge and skill.

A salesman develops this professional personality, or effective selling personality, when he is equipped with a complete knowledge of scientific salesmanship and is confident that he can successfully handle any sales situation that may arise.

The salesmen who are failures are those who haven't developed an impressive professional personality. Their personalities are weak because they lack confidence in themselves, and this lack of confidence is due to lack of knowledge and training. If someone grossly insulted you, how you would act would depend on your knowledge, training, and self-defense equipment. If you had mastered boxing, your ordinary personality would instantly change into an effective boxing personality. This would be impressive before you struck a blow, because of your confidence in your ability to handle the situation successfully; and an apology might be forthcoming without resort to force.

If you felt inadequate to respond as you would like to, you're ineffective, apprehensive, unprofessional personality might lead to further insults. Don't think that there is anything mysterious about "strong personalities." They are what they are because they have been made strong through scientific training.
People who know what they are doing show self -confidence in every move they make in their eyes, facial expression, gestures, carriage, and bearing.

In other words, personality is in the mind, because self-confidence is a mental attitude. The big thing is to sell yourself to yourself; then you will have no difficulty in selling yourself to others. Be sure what you can do. When a customer resents your interruption, throws obstacles in the path of the sale, stalls, or does a hundred and one things to avoid buying, you must be equipped with sure-fire strategy and tactics which you know will successfully meet the situation.

Is The Lack of an Attractive Natural Personality a Handicap? Some salesmen lament the fact that they lack the natural personality endowments possessed by others. They believe that they are handicapped because they are not naturally so handsome, so big, so vivacious, such good mixers, or something else that other salesmen are.

They don't realize that just the opposite may be the case: that the salesman who has been born with all the attractive graces and virtues of personality may be the one who is handicapped. Unfortunately, there are some salesmen who have natural engaging personalities but who also have the early conviction that they are superior, and that it is therefore unnecessary for them to work as hard as those with less favored natural personalities. Here then is their fatal handicap.

On the other hand, there are many salesmen who have early realized that their natural personality was inferior to others, and have determined to improve and cultivate it. Through acquiring early habits of work and perseverance, they have ultimately acquired a tougher, more aggressive, and more effective sales personality than other salesmen who were their superiors in natural endowments.

Does Natural Personality Reveal Sales Ability? One sales trainer has illustrated this important point in the following report:

My first experience in hiring salesmen was as general agent for a company that sold its products through house-to-house salesmen, mostly college boys. In the first college that I visited, I had had good success in securing a group of boys that I considered of high caliber. One boy in particular I felt fortunate in signing up. He was known as a "college leader" and had been voted the most popular man on the campus. He was handsome, affable, a good mixer, and an all-around good fellow.

I needed one more boy to fill my quota but he seemed hard to find, for the available human material had been pretty thoroughly worked over by other general agents as well as me. Finally, my attention was called to a young farmer boy who was working his way through college.

I was disappointed when I saw him. He was lean, gaunt and cadaverous looking, with a blank expression as solemn as an owl, and slouched along as if he were behind a plow. I said to myself, "He will never make a salesman; his personality is against him." But to get the matter over with as soon as possible, I asked him if he would like to be a salesman.

Suddenly his blank expression vanished, for when he opened his mouth his face disappeared. It was such a generous smile that it warmed me all over as he drawled, "I don't think I could sell anything."

I terminated the interview quickly with the firm intention to drop his consideration, but I couldn't forget how his good nature and generous spirit warmed me up. Besides, I needed another salesman and prospects were scarce. So, I sold him the idea that he could sell and put him in my training class with the rest of the boys. Then I sent them all out into their territories.

When the first weekly report arrived, I hopefully picked up the one from the college leader. No sales. "Well, I thought, "That is all right. I didn't make a sale the first week I worked either."

Finally, I came to the report of my farmer boy. One sale. I said to myself, "Looks like a miracle, but I suppose somebody took pity on him because he looks so hungry."

There was no second weekly report from my college leader, and I wondered what had happened to him. But I was greatly cheered by a report of three sales from my farmer. A few days later, I received a letter from my prize choice saying that he had gone home to mamma. This was one of the biggest shocks of my life. I had banked on his attractive natural personality and had lost my investment. This was the first inkling I ever had that a successful sales personality was something more than a pleasing natural personality.

My farmer boy beat out the whole group in sales, completed college, also a professional school, and is now a very successful businessman. I had been such a failure in judging prospective salesmen, and my mind was so confused regarding the personal qualities to look for in prospective salesmen, that I decided to go into the farmer boy's territory and find out why he had made a big success.

The different housewives who had bought from him answered my inquiries in many different ways, but they all simmered down to the fact that he had developed two outstanding qualities of a successful sales personality. As one woman stated it, "You couldn't make him sore and you couldn't drive him away."

Don't think that he would force his way into a home. He would retire with a smile if he was refused an interview, but he would be back and at what hours! I found that he even called on customers before breakfast and in the evening.

After he had become an outstanding success, one day I joked with him about getting

customers out of bed in the morning to sell them, he replied solemnly, "Well I was brought up on a farm, and it is awfully hard for me to sleep after 5:30." Then his mouth opened and his face disappeared.

You Can't Keep A Man Down Who Believes In Systematic Work And Is Uniformly Good-Natured About It. The point to be made here is that this farmer boy looked as if he were handicapped by his natural personality as compared with the college leader, whereas just the reverse was the case.

The college leader had found the going through life so easy that he folded up when the going got tough, while the farmer boy had evidently realized his lack of natural personality endowments and had more than made up for this lack by developing a "working" personality which not only sold lots of merchandise but which made him popular with his customers.

So, don't worry if your natural personality is not all that you desire. It is the cultivated personality that counts in selling. Certain personality qualities are necessary in selling, and the only way to get them is through the proper training. Few people are born with all of them - only one in a hundred. These are so-called "born" salesmen who just naturally sell but don't know how they do it. Such geniuses are found in all professions.

But these born salesmen are so rare that we seldom meet them. Your competitors for a prospect's business in any kind of merchandise or service will be average salesmen with average capacity.

Some will make more use of their opportunities than others and therefore will develop a considerably larger income. Some will develop more successful personalities through training than others. But they have no more natural mental capacity than you have and no opportunity for development that you do not possess.

Program To Create A Sales Personality: The main thing for you to do then, if you are determined to develop a sales personality, is to: (1) ascertain what qualities of personality are necessary in selling; (2) know why they are considered necessary equipment; (3) know how they can be acquired; and (4) practice the rules for acquiring them.

The following will disclose the first three operations; only you can perform the last. Practicing the correct principles of personality development will give you a "skilled selling personality" if you maintain self-discipline over both your body and mind.

In other words, you have to manage yourself. Your conscious mind has to be developed to the point where it will control your easy-gong, lazy, instinctive subconscious mind. When you have learned to manage yourself, then you have made a big step toward successfully managing customers, managing merchandise, and managing the sale.

SELLINGYOURSELF: If you have a sales personality, you sell yourself to customers. When you meet a customer, the first thing he sees is you, yourself, your personality. If he likes your personality, he will listen to your story; if he doesn't,he won't. You have to sell yourself to customers before you sell your merchandise, and if you succeed in the former, the latter is easy.

Too many salesmen irritate customers by their crude personalities and then wonder why customers don't appear interested in their sales presentations. They have failed to sell themselves but somehow believe that they can still sell their merchandise. Selling yourself on the instant you meet the customer develops customer assistance instead of customer resistance. It makes selling easier, more pleasant, and more profitable.

You can thus understand why it is necessary to analyze thoroughly the development of a sales personality. Salesmen who find it difficult to close sales have usually made a bad impression in opening sales. They make an unfavorable first impression, fail to gain the customer's confidence, and therefore, have an uphill struggle from the start.

A favorable first impression from the customer's viewpoint is determined by what he can see and hear. The customer can see the salesman's actions (facial express, physical carriage, gestures, and manners) and his clothing; and he can hear the salesman's words and tone of voice.

WHAT IMPRESSION DO YOU MAKE? Walk up to a full-length mirror and study your physical attitude and appearance, your facial expression, your bearing, your posture, your poise, your carriage, your clothing. Ask yourself whether you would be favorably impressed if this person in the mirror called on you. Would you buy from yourself? Do you look important enough for a busy buyer to lay aside his many pressing duties and grant you an interview? Would you impress buyers as having something very important to tell them?

When selling from house to house, after ringing the doorbell, a salesman can often see through the corner of his eye a curtain pulled gently aside, and he knows that his fate is silently being decided. He learns that a dignified, deliberate bearing, with shoulders thrown back, gives an air of importance that gets more audiences than an impatient, nervous, hurried manner with shoulders forward and chin thrust out.

PRIME FACTORS IN CREATING A GOOD FIRST IMPRESSION: There are eleven factors which have a considerable bearing on producing good first impressions and enable you to sell yourself.

Smile

Physical carriage

Actions

Tone of voice

Voice inflections

Pronunciation
Shaking hands
Poise (lack of nervousness)
Body tone
Clothing - appearance - and manners
Mannerisms

YOUR SMILE: The first factor in producing a good first impression is the habit of greeting the customer with a smile. Simple and self-explanatory as that may seem, there are nevertheless important considerations involved.
Almost everyone quickly detects an artificial smile. You yourself have undoubtedly had more than one experience along these lines. Someone who has a cause to plead, or an axe to grind, has flashed a smile at you which you instantly rejected as being a mere pose - a practiced and studied sham. Resentment automatically followed the detection. "Does he think I'm so stupid," you said to yourself, "that he expects me to fall for that?"

Then you've had the opposite experience, too. Someone, whether friend or complete stranger, has smiled at you in genuine and sincere pleasure when your paths crossed. Perhaps it was nothing more significant than the fact that this person likes people; perhaps, on the other hand, it was as personal as the fact that he liked you. The reason is much less important than might be supposed. The important ingredient is the element of sincerity. If that was present, the smile, even if both brief and impersonal, assuredly "warmed" you to that chap, to the point at least where you were glad to give him a hearing.
Translated into the actualities of salesmanship, this means that if you cannot work up sufficient interest and enthusiasm in your next interview to produce a pleasing expression in your face, you are not in condition to undertake the interview itself. A person who dislikes others, or who is indifferent to them, carries a heavy handicap in selling. A person who, for whatever reason, wishes he were elsewhere rather than making that next call will reveal his aversion or preoccupation, whether he realizes it or not. A genuine smile is always a reflection of a state of mind. It is at times necessary to "dig deep" to equip oneself to possess one.
PHYSICAL ATTITUDE SPEAKS LOUDER THAN WORDS: There is an old saying that "actions speak louder than words." Some salesmen make a statement and then contradict that statement by their actions. For example, what would you say if you saw a traveling salesman slouch over onto the counter in a physical attitude of utter indifference, and at the same time say positively to the dealer, "You are bound to make more money carrying our line because of the superior consumer acceptance that has been developed by our extensive advertising." It is bad enough for a customer to contradict you, but to contradict yourself is

absurd. Yet stores are doing this right along. In them one can often see salespeople leaning against the fixtures and so blending into the store scenery that customers hesitate to disturb them.

The store advertising and windows welcome and solicit the customer's visit, but the physical attitude of indifference exhibited by the salespeople contradicts this welcome. Back up what you say with the right physical attitude. Then your effectiveness will be doubled instead of cut in half. Your sales talk may be the nail that will pierce the customer's resistance, but your physical is the force that drives it home.

DEVELOP A BLENDED PERSONALITY: You can't blend oil and water; you can stir them up but they will always be two distinct, separate substances. Similarly, some salesmen's personalities are a combination of different qualities but not a blend. Their personalities are faulty; that is, they have a fault or line of cleavage which makes them ineffective because they exhibit clashing characteristics. Instead of being one person they are two.

Their words say one thing and their actions another. They confuse instead of convince. They slouch around and at the same time tell you that the superiority of their goods is universally recognized. Develop a blended personality. Make your sales talk you. Make them one and the same thing. Proceed with all forces of your personality moving in one direction - toward conviction and the sale. Permit no jarring contradictions that would make your efforts futile.

DAMAGING THE CUSTOMER BY YOUR ACTIONS: The third factor in producing a good first impression is to make your actions support your words. Since actions speak louder than words, study carefully the actions that accompany your words. Do they aid your words in convincing customers? Are they neutral? Are they negative?

If you sit back in your chair during the interview with your hands in your lap, you are in a receiving attitude. You can't give if you are all set to receive. Hence this posture is negative because it nullifies or contradicts your speech.

If you sit straight up with your hands on your knees, you are in a neutral attitude from which you can proceed forward or backward. When you lean forward and extend your hand towards the customer, you are in a positive, giving attitude which harmonizes with your speech and makes it convincing.

The most forceful and convincing salesmen energize their speech. They back up their words with physical vitality. They make customers feel what they are saying as well as merely think it. They thus arouse the powerful emotions of the subconscious mind and enlist their instinctive support.

A shopper reports: I recently saw a retail furniture salesman use this strategy effectively. He was showing a large davenport. Instead of merely standing beside it

in a receptive attitude and portraying its advantages, he caught hold of it and moved
it so the back could more easily be seen. Then he tilted it so the underneath construction could be observed.

ADAPT YOUR TONE OF VOICE TO DIFFERENT TYPES: Another factor in producing a good first impression is to use your tone of voice effectively. In managing customers and treating them the way they want to be treated, the tone of voice is of prime consideration. The voice, if properly handled, may often control others where words alone fail. In managing a refined man or woman, a low precise tone is more effective, whereas with a rough, uncouth prospect, a loud, hearty, full-throated tone will be more influential.

A high, penetrating tone has been found to be effective with a thick -skinned surly customer; a smooth, oily, ingratiating tone with a pompous, conceded, positive customer; and a sad quavering tone with an unfriendly customer who is trying to break down the price structure. Your tone of voice is controlled by your mind and faithfully reflects your mental attitude. By analyzing your different tones of voice under different circumstances, you will often be able to detect mental attitudes that should be adjusted more accurately to meet adequately conditions that need control.

VOICE INFLECTIONS EXPRESS IDEAS: The fifth factor in producing a good first impression is to develop effective voice inflections. Ideas are expressed by words, tone of voice, voice inflection, facial expression, and other bodily movements. These are all vehicles for getting your ideas across to the customer's mind. Be sure that they are as carefully thought out and planned as the modern automobile is, and they will be as efficient in transportation.

It is impossible to say when you should have a rising or a falling inflection in your sales presentations, but if you rehearse your sales talks aloud, you can check the nature of your main inflections and then by experimentation determine which is the most effective.

Never say anything to a customer unless you understand fully what you are saying and feel its full import. Then you will in turn make the customer understand and feel it is by the correct inflection of your voice. Check this rule against the definition of salesmanship, and you will see that it is one and the same thing. You have to think accurately, to tell intensely what you are saying, and your listener will act the way you want him to act.

SHAKING HANDS: Another important factor in producing a good first impression is to be able to shake hands. It has been said repeatedly that salesmanship is a mental science. Well, even a hand shake is mental. Whether or not you should attempt to shake the buyer's hand depends on your mental attitude.

Are you confident that you can help the buyer and that you do not merely want the commission on the sale? Do you expect him to respond wholeheartedly? Then offer your hand, and seldom will it be refused. The buyer will be glad to make your acquaintance. Are you afraid of the buyer? Do you feel inferior to him? Is the commission on the order the prominent idea in your mind? Do you fear that the buyer may refuse your hand? Then don't offer your hand, because many refusals may only make your work more difficult.

So, you see-self-confidence is the key to the situation. In fact, it is the key to success.

Get this quality above all else.

DEVELOP POISE - OVERCOME NERVOUSNESS: Even experienced salesmen have an attack of nerves before calling on important prospects, or when kept waiting in the outer office of the buyer. Since this difficulty is of mental origin, its remedy must be sought in the mind.

Divert the mind from thinking about the outcome of the interview - think of something else. If you have made a complete preparation for the interview, there is no sense in getting your mind into turmoil by last minute apprehensions and forebodings. When the moment comes to see the buyer, you will do the right thing if you have trained your mind and body to do it.

A popular and prominent speaker states: Some people say that nervousness results from lack of preparation, but I know better from experience. For many years, I have been giving addresses before large sales conventions, and although I am always thoroughly prepared in advance, I get increasingly nervous as the time for the meeting approaches unless I divert my mind from its contemplation. This I do in several ways depending upon what the situation permits. If I can be alone for an hour directly preceding my appearance, I read an exciting story (several of which I always keep on hand) which will permit of no mind wandering or worrying.

If I am to speak at a banquet, I ascertain the special interests of my neighbors and keep them in a conversation to which I closely attend. When I was a traveling salesman, I opened the day by reading short success stories and biographies, not letting my mind speculate on the day's calls, all preparations regarding which I had made the previous evening.

When waiting in the outer office for the buyer, I have read booklets or articles which I have torn out of magazines. Besides keeping my mind and body fresh for the interview, this scheme has made productive many thousands of hours which otherwise would have been wasted.

CLOTHING, APPEARANCE, AND MANNERS: An up-to-date company cannot afford to have any sloppy or slouchy representatives. Many of your customers never see any other representative of your company; thus, you are the company to these customers. A salesman who is dressed neatly and inconspicuously and is well groomed and clean always gets a more favorable reception than the salesman with greasy hands, last month's haircut, baggy trousers, run-down heels, soiled collar and cuffs, and yesterday's shave.

The salesman's manners are equally important, since they either add to or detract from his personality. No feature of our personalities is neutral; each either helps us or puts a question mark in the minds of the people we meet.

For example, the salesman who swings a pencil when he talks until it becomes conspicuous and makes you think of what he is doing rather than what he is saying. Another salesman has a chain of keys which he keeps winding and unwinding around his fingers.

I have heard salesmen say "Huh" at intervals during an interview until it became annoying. Some salesmen have developed the habit of clearing their throat, scratching their heads, leaning against something handy when they are talking, or drumming their fingers, thereby in each case injuring their sales personality. Repeated actions become disgusting mannerisms.

Says another customer: Impressions are all against the salesman if his manner of approach is hesitant or his suit is mussed, his tie crooked, his shirt soiled, and he smelled like a tobacco shop.

Never wear anything or do anything that will divert the customer's attention from the picture you are attempting to paint on his mind. Make your personality assist you in painting this picture; don't permit it to make the sale more difficult.

Make your personality an asset - not a liability.

Never allow an opportunity pass by that will enhance your image and impression with others. Become a recognized personality. People have become famous simply because of their charisma. This is evident all around us, on television, radio, and in business and politics.

People Skills Can Be Learned: One crucial fact is implied in everything we've said: people skills can be learned. They're not innate or inherited; nobody brings them into the world at birth. They're acquired by men and women willing to expend the necessary time and energy.

This means there's nothing mysterious about people skills. They're not vague, indefinable qualities like "charm" or "magnetism" or "charisma." They're techniques which have been learned-and mastered-by thousands of people. Nobody can say, "I don't have what it takes to size up people" or "I'm not the sort of person who can motivate others." "What it takes" is not a special sort of person; what it takes is learning the necessary skills, practicing them, getting feedback, and then using the skills until they become "second nature."

REVALATION #11
Observation

Seeing believes is a withered adage that ought to be given a decent burial. Far too many of us "see" in much the same way as the fabled blind men who "saw" the elephant-part by part, with almost no realization of what we see. To form beliefs on the basis of such observations is sheer folly. To act on the basis of such "seeing" is sometimes disastrous.

The art of accurate observation, of truly seeing, is very nearly a lost art. Television, which has been called "the opiate of the asses," is partly to blame. We no longer see; we look or we watch. Yet accurate observation is one of the essential steps to power thinking, and it deserves to be revived. If your experience is to have meaning, you must be able to observe accurately and generalize from what you have seen. Conversely, however, before you can learn by observing, you must learn to observe.

Professor Abraham Bernstein of Brooklyn College tells the story of the girl who complimented him on his necktie at the beginning of class. Halfway through the class-which, incidentally, concerned the techniques of careful observation-he, turned his back and asked members of the class to describe his tie? Not one student could do it, not even the girl who had complimented him on the tie. In fact, she could not tell him the color of it.

Many such examples could easily be demonstrated, but the point is clear: You do not always see what you look at. If you doubt the truth of this statement, close your eyes and try to describe in detail the clothes you are wearing. Can you do it? Some people can, of course, but many more cannot. A few men, I am told, do not even know the color of their wives' eyes, but that situation must surely be unusual. In a psychology class recently, a teacher held up a large playing card that was a red four of spades. (Spades, of course, are supposed to be black.) Then the teacher laid the card face down on his desk and asked the students to describe it. Twenty- seven out of twenty-eight called it either a black four of spades or a red four of hearts.

Only one student actually saw the card for what it was: a visual trick.

If such visual tricks were restricted to psychology classrooms, you could laugh about the experiment and forget it. Unfortunately, there are similar visual tricks played on you in business and industry, on television, and in books, magazines, and newspapers. Some of these tricks are consciously planned to mislead you, as for example a movie advertisement that quotes a reviewer as having said,

... great....colossal," when the reviewer actually said, "This movie is a great waste of time and a colossal failure." Those ellipses(...) are the visual trick. You should

notice them. You should know that they indicate omissions, in this case some very important omissions.

Some visual tricks are not necessarily meant to mislead you, but they can be dangerous nonetheless. When a company's annual report is printed on slick paper

with four-color illustrations, you should still read the figures in the report. However impressive the report may be as a high-quality printing job-and however substantial the company may therefore appear-you had better make sure that sales and profits are still what they ought to be. A beautiful package can hide some pretty ugly facts.

When you look at something, you should do so with an open mind but not with a vacant mind. Let's say you are a salesman who has asked to evaluate the sales potential of a new product your company is introducing. You will remember that any such evaluation will proceed from partial ignorance. However, you can lessen that ignorance substantially by making some careful observations. You can look at the product and compare it with previous products or the products of competing companies. Does the past experience of your own or competing companies indicate that buyers are looking for something approximately like this. Are there similarities in design, size, color, price, and so on? If so, it may be safe to conclude that there will be some similarity in sales potential. At any rate, you should not disregard the similarities between the new product and older ones. These similarities can be extremely significant, for people's needs and wants do not change overnight.

A person who notices similarities has a tremendously valuable tool for repeating past success, his own or someone else's. It has been said that the musical scores in Rodgers & Hammer stein plays all follow a certain pattern. The implication is that Rodgers & Hammer stein carefully analyzed Oklahoma, their first hit, as a guide to future productions. "Why did Oklahoma succeed?" they asked. "What blend of ingredients made it popular?" Would a similar, but not precisely the same, blend produce another hit?" Their answer to the last question was that it might - and it certainly did. Thus, it is possible to "match" songs from, say, Oklahoma, South Pacific, and The King and I, and to see the successful pattern, or formula, within which Rodgers and Hammerstein worked. These men were masters at observing similarities and then putting them to use. You should acquire the same habit.

If you are reading carefully, you will have noticed that the preceding advice on noticing similarities seems to be in direct conflict with Ford's experiences with the Edsel. The Edsel was similar to competing American cars in design, size, color, price, and so on. And that was precisely the trouble. The Edsel had no significant differences that would sell it. It was just another car. It was altogether too similar to most American autos.

If you were trying to estimate the sales potential of a product, therefore, you would look for both significant similarities (desirable ones) and for significant differences (also desirable ones). The desirable differences are often called "gimmicks," though the word "gimmicks" has undeservedly offensive connotations. The difference, or gimmick, may be important, or it may be trivial. If it is important, it can lead to fantastic sales success and widespread acceptance. Witness the automatic transmission, the aerosol can, the filter cigarette.

A classic example of such observation, and the creative use of it, can be seen in the advertising campaign for the Volkswagen. The VW, unlike the Edsel, is different from other cars in a number of major ways. It has an air-cooled engine. Its design does not change from year to year. It is a very small car. It gets unusually good gas mileage. By observing these differences and capitalizing on them, the VW advertisers managed to make their car seem very attractive. Volkswagens have continued to sell despite the introduction of American compacts and despite the efforts of other European auto makers.

No matter how accurately you observe and how brilliantly you draw conclusions from your observations, you will not be entirely objective. This is an important point to remember, because most people seem to think that complete objectivity is easily attainable. Nothing could be more untrue, for complete objectivity is beyond the reach of anyone. A New York Times reporter is not wholly objective, nor is a justice of the Supreme Court, nor a research chemist, nor a teacher, nor a sales manager, nor a saint.

A power thinker can only approach objectivity; he cannot perfectly achieve it, there are obvious reasons for this. When you observe, you observe with all your being and all your senses. What you are, what you have been, and what you hope to be-all of these inevitably color your observations. To a poor child, a half dollar actually looks physically bigger than it does to a rich child. This has been experimentally proved many times. The moral of this: You can observe accurately only within your limitations-and everyone has certain limitations. These limitations include your hopes, your fears, your likes, and your dislikes. It is impossible to discount such factors, for they are built into your mind and heart.

What does this mean in terms of power thinking? It means: (a) that you should recognize your own prejudices and, insofar as possible, take them into account when reaching conclusions or making decisions, and (b) that you should recognize the motives, prejudices, and limitations of the people with whom you come into contact. You can, and must, take these limitations into account if you are to become a power thinker.

To illustrate one failure of objectivity: I know a former high school English teacher who refused to have his students study grammar, because, he said, "It's a useless subject." He was fired after one year, and rightly so, for his conclusion about English grammar was an emotional one entirely. He overlooked the fact that thousands of school administrators have for years considered English grammar a necessary subject, and more important, alas, he ignored the fact that the state in which he taught demanded the teaching of grammar. As he later confided in me, this teacher did think that English grammar was necessary-but he didn't like the

subject, he didn't know it well, and he didn't feel competent to teach it. Instead of admitting this and doing something about it, he constructed a wild realization, to wit, that the subject ought not to be taught, by him or presumably by anyone else. An accurate observer would have taken his emotions into account. He would have realized that even a modicum of objectivity indicated, under the circumstances, the necessity of teaching English grammar.

In addition to recognizing your own limitations when it comes to observing and drawing sensible conclusions, you should recognize the limitations of other people in this respect. A true Marxist, for instance, cannot see the fallacies of dialectical materialism, even when these fallacies stand in concrete form before his very eyes. "No doubt," said a friend of mine, "there are some Russian visitors to the United States who think that New York City is paper-mache miracle, thrown up on a few hours notice especially for their visit. An all these cars! No doubt drives from every point in the country expressly to make an impression on the foreign visitors." An exaggeration, of course, but there are a great many people who literally will not credit their own eyes and ears if observations conflict with prejudices or predilections.

Objective observation-that is, absolutely objective-is impossible. But a power thinker will credit his eyes and ears even if their evidence seems to conflict with his beliefs. Power thinking requires at least an approach to objectivity.

In the field of gemology, observation is the soul in the nature of the business. The gemologist has to determine from sheer observation the value of the diamond or the gem.

As we know, every diamond has value, depending upon the clarity, the size which is often referred to as the carat, the shape, the imperfections and the observation which includes the mood of the market for such gems and of course it is very important to mention that fake diamonds have been misjudged by the public and even the jewelers and gemologist.

The conclusive value is really a matter of expert opinion based on observation of all the factors. No two diamonds are exactly the same which is another complication to the evaluation process. Many other industries have to be as critical in their observation in order to avoid mistakes and mainly to make a fair profit.

The purchase of real estate, for example, has so many contingencies as to its intended use that this has to be observed and explored over a long period of time to determine its value and what it could be used for so observation is a critical factor whenever an investment is to be made.

REVALATION #12
LISTENING

Listening and hearing are two different things. Hearing is more of a mechanical process whereby you casually hear unimportant things that the brain tells you only to get your attention so that you can react. Listening is a mental process of which you absorb important statements that are analyzed and digested. An intensive listener almost injects one's own thinking into what is heard and subconsciously analyzes the content and importance. Listening also embeds a thought process which causes the mind to remember with more clarity the meaning of what is heard.

On the evening of October 30, 1938, several million Americans milled about the streets, in mortal fear for their lives. They clung sobbingly to one another or drove wildly in all directions to avoid asphyxiation and flaming death at the hands of "Martians with foul leathery heads that are as tall as skyscrapers."

Behind this mass hysteria was an hour-long ratio adaptation of H. G. Wells' the War of the Worlds. Presented by Orson Wells as an on-the spot description of a Martian landing in New Jersey, the program was clearly identified as fiction at the start. Half an hour later, two announcements to the same effect were made. Another announcement ended the show. Four times the listeners were told that they were tuned to a dramatization. Yet···

* The National Guards of several states were alerted for possible duty. Clergymen of all faiths were swamped with calls from people who wished the protection of prayer.

A sorority meeting at a distinguished eastern university broke up as the girls rushed hysterically for telephones, automobiles, and police protection.

A woman in California broke her arm when she fell down the stairs in a dash for safety.

Everywhere, people telephoned tearful farewells to loved ones.

Why should millions of intelligent men and women have been so completely "taken in" by Mr. Wells' program?

The reason is simple: they were not listening. Undoubtedly most of them heard the announcements, but they did not listen to them. The difference between hearing and listening will be clear as we go on.

The High Cost of Defective Listening: While little real damage was done by the "invasion from Mars" broadcast, bad listening is one of the most costly habits in the world - in terms of money, time, energy, and injured personal relationships. Take the salesman for a floral wholesaler who received an order for fifteen gross

117

of roses and relayed it orally to his shipping department. The person in charge wrote down "50" gross instead of "15". Two days later, in response to a panicky call, the wholesaler had to make good the error. He not only paid for forwarding and returning thirty-five gross of roses, but also lost money because of spoilage.

A prominent Ohio physician recently faced the unpleasant task of posting bail for his sixteen-year-old son after the boy had been arrested with a friend for housebreaking. Later, asked why-with a substantial allowance, a good home, and loving parents-he had forced his way into the house, the boy replied that he wanted to feel important. "At home, nobody would listen to me. I'd tell Mom or Dad about what I was doing at school or my plans for the future and all they'd do was grunt. They made me feel as if I didn't count." Is listening important? You bet it is! Career Benefits: Because modern business and industry rely so heavily on rapid communications, the ability to listen well has become particularly important to personal success in the 21st century. Interviews, conferences, marketing and production meetings, telephone calls, closed-circuit TV addresses-all are integral parts of today's business complex.

And tomorrow, when some lucky men are tapped to guide their firms in the 22nd century, you can be certain that the real plums will go to those who listened, understood-and learned.

The man who "catches on fast" has an inside track to success. That's for sure. How Good A Listener Are You Now? Right now, get a pencil. In the left-hand column jot down as much as you can remember about the very last conversation you held before reading this. Perhaps you were chatting with your wife, or a pal, or the elevator man, or your colleagues. No matter. Get down as much of what the other person said as you possibly can. Take your time and don't give up until you feel sure you have it all.

Now check yourself. Ask the person to tell you what he said and write that down in the column next to your version. You may have to make a phone call or run next door to find out, but do it. Now.

Any discrepancies? Did you omit-or add-anything of importance that wasn't said? Do either of you disagree on details?

It's not enough to shake your head and say, "By golly, I'm not as good a listener as I thought." You must do something about it. And even if your performance just now was good, you can become superb.

The "45/50" Club: Some years ago, the director of research for a metropolitan school system conducted a unique experiment.

He asked sixty-eight adults of various occupations to take notes, every fifteen minutes, on the amount of time they spent reading, writing, talking, and listening. After two months of acting as their own Boswells, all sixty-eight filed their reports. The research directory discovered that over two-thirds of their waking hours were spent in verbal communication. A breakdown of the figures indicated that the

average subject spent 16 per cent of his "communicating time" in reading, * percent in writing, 30 per cent in talking-and a whopping 45 per cent in listening!

In short, if your day is merely average, you spend about five hours just listening to your associates, customers, suppliers, employees, wife, children, friends and neighbors; to instructions, information, suggestions, advice, criticism, and complaints.

Yet, experts agree that most of us only listen to half of what is said to us. In other words, although we spend 45 per cent of our communicating time in listening, we only "get" 50 per cent of what we hear (the "45/50 Club" is probably the biggest nonprofit organization in the world).
This means that for two and a half hours every day of our lives, we live in a vacuum, as completely cut off from civilization as if we were on a desert island!
You can miss a lot of opportunities that way.
The Five Profits of "HI-FI Listening" Fortunately, there is nothing compulsory about membership in the "45/50 Club." All it takes to drop out is an awareness of the problems every listener faces and a knowledge of the tested, proven solutions to them.
What can withdrawal from the "Club" do for you? It can help you to:
Increase your knowledge. Whether you're a banker or bookkeeper, doctor or detective, mailman or machinist, you can learn something from almost everyone. It may be money-making news, a labor-saving idea, the one clue you've been searching for to help you solve a personal dilemma. It may be mentioned casually, as a conversational "aside," but if you don't listen to it, you'll never learn what it is. Socrates, reputed to be the wisest man of his time, spent almost all of his time in for he knew what all good listeners know-that people "open up" when they have a receptive audience. A skilled listener inspires even a mediocre conversationalist to give his best; a poor one can dampen the spirits-and performance-of a consummate orator.

Improve your business performance. The man who tunes out instructions as soon as he thinks he knows what they are who lets old ideas straight-arm new ones...• who permits his attention to wander while being addressed••.who won't take the trouble to ask questions when in doubt-each is setting the stage for slipshod performance and costly backtracking. But understand what's said to you the first time around and you will virtually eliminate missed appointments, overdue reports, unmet deadlines, undelivered shipments, contractual errors, and personal misunderstandings. You will save time, work, and money. It's hard not to promote a man like that.

Become a more persuasive, influential person. Every automobile company maintains a customer relations staff whole job is to soothe the ruffled feathers of irate customers. Usually, a car owner is so burned up over his real or imagined

grievances that the c.r. man serves as little more than a verbal punching bag-at first. By the time ninety-nine out of a hundred interviews end, however, the customer is completely satisfied, a loyal fan of the firm. How do the C.R. men do it? "Mostly," explains one, "we listen. Sometimes it's just to a lot of nonsense; sometimes, it's to a legitimate gripe. But no matter which classification a complaint falls under, it gets after he's convinced that we know where he stands, he's willing to hear our side."

The moral is clear. Intelligent listening can be a convincing, disarming technique of persuasion.

When you listen-really listen to someone, you are paying him the ultimate compliment. You are saying, ''I recognize your importance and value your thoughts." Wouldn't you like someone who said that to you?

Develop language facility. Long before you were strong enough to pick up a dictionary, much less read it, you spoke English. How come? Simple. You listened, and then imitated what you heard. It was swift, effortless, and permanent. To a very large extent, that process is still going on. You hear a strange word at a lecture whose meaning you can guess from its context, a new pronunciation by a television announcer, a beautiful tum of phrase in a sermon at church. Unconsciously, you say to yourself, "I must remember that." Pretty soon, it's become part of your vocabulary or diction. Improve your listening ability and it is bound to show in your speech and writing.

In a nutshell: master the rules of good listening and you will increase your knowledge, do your work more efficiently, be a more persuasive and popular person and express yourself more effectively than you ever dreamed possible. Know a better recipe for success?

The Four Rules For 20/20 Listening: Hearing and listening is not the same thing. One is a purely physical experience; the other, physical and mental. You can't help but hear the sounds that fall within earshot, but whether or not you listen to them depends on you.

Listening is a process of understanding and acting upon what you hear. The act may be no more than weighing what you hear or changing your mind or making a decision, but when you truly listen, you do something. For example, suppose you are in a department store around Christmas time. A child cries. More than likely, you go about your business. You've simply heard a child cry.

But suppose you are bedding down for the night in the Wisconsin woods after a day's hunting. Its ten p.m. and pitch-dark. The nearest town is 20 miles away. A child cries. Almost certainly, you will grab your flashlight and look for what you assume a lost, frightened kid. You've listened to a child cry.

Notice. When you hear, you neither think nor act. When you listen, you put facts together (the dark woods, the distant town, a child's voice), judge the situation ("A lost child!") and act (switching on the flashlight, searching for the child). You might say that hearing is like staring blankly at a distant object. You see something, but it doesn't really register. Listening is a process of focusing on what is actually out there.

To help you get a crystal-clear image every time, here are the four simple rules for 20/20 listening Consider the source.
Hear what he really says.
Listen actively.
Make sure you understand. In that order.
Consider the Source: "A four-eyed green monster over seven feet tall walked toward me."
If your five-year-old son told you that, you would smile. If a character in a science-fiction movie said that, you'd keep a straight face. If a renowned scientist, just back from a government-sponsored expedition to the Brazilian jungle, reported that to you, you'd probably be thrilled and ask, "What was it?"
Different Speakers, Different Listening. In each instance, you would weigh the statement in the light of what you knew about the speaker. In the t1rst case, you
would doubtlessly attribute the statement to your son's overactive imagination and forget it. In the second you would willingly enter into the spirit of the story and temporarily suspend your critical faculties because you realize that the actor is merely repeating the lines of a fiction writer. In the third, you would probably accept the statement because of the scientist's reputation for-and dedication to-truth.
Different people merit different degrees of belief. You wouldn't dream of putting a down payment on a new car just because the office boy said, "You're going to be promoted." But hear the same sentence from your employer's personal secretary and you will at least start talking about a new car to your wife. Let the boss himself pronounce those magic words and you will probably make the rounds of showrooms.
Unconsciously, you attach a "credence quotient" to many of the people you know. You may, for example, trust your brother implicitly. But from experience you have learned to discount about 40 per cent of what your neighbor says. Of course, people's "credence quotients" vary according to what they're talking about. If your brother is a stockbroker, you are apt to believe what he says about the national economy. You may be more wary about what he tells you are going on

behind Kremlin walls. Even though you take your neighbor's words with several grains of salt, if he is an automobile mechanic you will probably accept his judgment of the new cars.

How to "Case" A Speaker: Ideally, a good listener keeps in mind three facts about every person who speaks to him:

The speaker's identity. Your clergyman, business partner, physician, lawyer, accountant-each, because of who he is, has your confidence. But what about others? Customers may bring up certain points in order to obtain a concession of some kind.

A salesman obviously will not mention-or at least will soft-pedal-the drawbacks of his product. A Republican may not see things in the same way as a Democrat-and vice versa. Before listening to anyone, ask yourself, "Who is he?"

His qualifications. Your colleague may know heating equipment inside out-that's his business-but don't let his unquestioned authority in that one field cast a halo over everything he says. He may know no more about traffic management than little Orphan Annie. Your insurance man may be a whiz at helping you plan your financial future, but as a hi-fi expert he could be a dud. Before accepting what, you hear as gospel, as yourself, "Does this man know what he's talking about? What's his education, his background, his experience, his authority?"

His vested interests. A salesman talks to you because he wants you to buy something from him. A politician addresses you because he wants your political support for himself or his party. A debater says what he says in order to influence your opinion. Daily, you are bombarded with statements geared to "sell" you on a product or a view-point, to get you to do something-change your mind, support a project, part with money, approve a course of action, sign your name. The object of all that talk is not always your best interests. Therefore, as you listen to someone, ask yourself, "Has he any special, personal reasons for saying that?"

The first general rule for good listening, then, is:

Consider the source.

"Who is he?"

"What are his qualifications?"

"Has he a vested interest in what he says?"

Practice this moment to drive the point home to yourself. Think back to the last time you were listening rather seriously to someone-half an hour ago or several hours ago. Maybe your wife or a friend was telling you about a new product you should buy, or someone who works for you was suggesting hiring another person, or your boss was asking you to think about a change in procedure.

Whatever and whoever, consider the source right here. Answer each of these questions in writing:

Who is he?

What are his qualifications?

Had he a vested interest in what he said?

A major barrier to good listening is prejudice. You don't like the speaker's appearance, delivery, point of view, political affiliation, economic status, or the way he pronounces your name. You transfer this disapproval to his speech, assuming that he can't possibly have anything of value to say. Therefore, why listen to him? But a man who wears a soiled shirt could be a brilliant engineer. Because someone stammers when he talks, it doesn't necessarily follow that his thinking is impaired. A Republican, bachelor, or bald man might be able to tell you a lot you don't know about buying a house. A man currently out of work may know. far more about mutual funds than you.

The point is: distinguish, between the speaker and his message. Does this contradict rule No. 1, consider the source? Not at all! Consider the source by all means, but don't judge a man solely by externals.

Ideally, you should listen without any prejudices whatsoever. Since we all have biases of one kind or another, this is practically impossible. But you can do the next best thing: recognize what your prejudices are and make allowances for them.

To help you discount your own leanings in the future, bring them out in the open. Write down as many types of people and mannerisms that tend to influence your opinion as you can think of. Perhaps you dislike short people, people who say "err" when they talk, rich men, women who wear open-toed shoes. Maybe you are unreasoningly partial to Swedes, college graduates, and girls who wear glasses. No matter how absurd your prejudices put them down here. In fact, seeing them on paper may rid you of them. But that's unimportant right now. Your main purpose is simply to identify them so that you may be aware of their influence on your ability to listen without any chips on your shoulder.

Look Out For "Trigger Words:" Closely allied to "chip-on-the-shoulder listening" is emotional listening- unreasoning reaction to "trigger words." And because many of these words work at the subconscious level, they are particularly apt to interfere with listening to what is really said.

You're an employer. One of your men comes to see you and begins, "We were talking things over at the union... " Immediately, you see red. "That blasted union," you think, "if those men think they're going to bleed another penny out of me•.." While your mind is busy cataloguing what you consider union abuses, your employee has told you what the men actually discussed. Maybe you hear it; maybe you don't.

There are certain words that produce temporary deafness in each of us. Let some people hear words like radical, labor, Negro, Catholic, Jew, Russian, intellectual and they automatically set their minds on disapproval. Others react equally strongly to conservative, management, English, Arab, Irish, and Puerto Rican, uneducated.

In either case, when "trigger words" are allowed to cast their spell, judgment and logic go out the window; only emotions remain. And that means the end of effective listening. Again, the only way to combat the effects of "trigger words" is to become consciously aware of them.

Learn To Concentrate: Many people throw in the towel at the first sign of a message that will take some effort to understand. Others are the victims of

persistent daydreaming. Still others allow themselves to be easily distracted. In every case, the remedy is the same; concentration. But first, a rundown of the characteristics and causes of each.

Throw-in-the-towel listeners. Spoiled by exposure to simple, catchy phrases in radio jingles, the rapid-fire gags of comedians, the simple level of routine remarks, they have unwittingly downgraded their demands on their listening ability. This insidious habit tends to create a vicious downward spiral, for you ask less and less of yourself until you lose patience with everything except the most elementary statements. "Too tough," you say; "let it go." It goes, all right-right past you.

Daydreamers. They stare glassy-eyed at the speaker, nodding from time to time, and thoughts a million miles away. Somehow, they have confused physical presence with listening. Daydreaming may result from the soothing, almost hypnotizing, tones of the speaker hearing a "trigger word" that sets up a train of thought totally unrelated to what the speaker is saying simple fatigue.

"What's-that?" listeners. They permit themselves to be thrown off the track by any other sounds, sights, or sensations in their vicinity. If a dog barks in the distance, they stop listening. If their seats are uncomfortable, they stop listening. If the speaker is wearing an eye-catching tie, they stop listening. If the man next to them coughs, they stop listening. They may never tune in the speaker again. If they do, they have at best only a fuzzy notion of what he's talking about. Their basic trouble is that consciously or unconsciously they have no real desire to hear what is said; consequently, they are most alert for excuses to stop listening. Recognize yourself in any of these capsule portraits? If you do, it's time to turn over a new leaf. How? By consciously loading the dice in your favor. By nipping in the bud the three attention-robbers that are most often responsible for lackadaisical listening. These are:

Fatigue: In a combination publicity stunt-scientific experiment in 1959, New York disc jockey Peter Tripp went without sleep for more than 200 hours. During his ordeal, a battery of doctors and skilled technicians put him through exhaustive tests in an attempt to pinpoint the precise effects of fatigue. Among other things, Mr. Tripp's ability to understand oral directions nose-dived. This was expected, for its known that listening is not a passive affair. It requires real effort to get every point a speaker is making, all the while relating his comments to known facts and reasonable logic. Good listening takes energy-lots of it. If you are tired to begin with, you cannot possibly listen on all cylinders. So be sure you get enough rest. Lack of incentive: Frequently, we avoid listening because we have not sold ourselves on the importance of what we are about to hear. If your doctor gave you several bottles of colored pills and told you that your life depended on taking a green pill every 22 minutes, a red pill every 47 minutes and a yellow pill every 58 minutes, you would listen to his instructions with complete attention and, in all

probability, write them down too. If an employee of yours said, "I think I know a way you can increase your business and gain a lot of valuable good will besides," you would drop whatever you were doing and listen-really listen.

It's natural to be most interested in those things that affect our health, fortune, security, and loved ones. Why not take advantage of this built-in selfishness by bringing a "What's-in-it-for-me?" attitude to everything you hear? Sure, you may have to wade through a carload of baloney before you find a few cuts of real beefsteak, but that's the only way to do it.

Once you develop the habit of listening for profit, you will acquire the kind of miserly affection for the spoken word that only the very best listeners possess.

Insufficient Practice: Like any art, listening to difficult material takes practice. The more of it you do, the better you become at it. A lot of people have simply forgotten how, through neglect. Solution: purposely expose yourself to "hard listening." Go out of your way to attend lectures, listen to radio and TV interviews. Sunday afternoons are particularly rich in thought-provoking panel shows. Tune them in. Listen. The further removed the topic is from your own interests, the more challenging-and effective-your practice sessions will be.

Listening isn't remembering; it's understanding. If the two were identical, those people who have been gifted with so-called "perfect" memories would be the best listeners in the world. But they aren't. Understanding is the ability to see relationships between different facts and grasp the fundamental ideas behind them.

If you are going to be a good listener, you must be able to appraise the speaker as to expertness, and, in doing so, determine how much weight should be given to his words. You must grasp the speaker's main idea. In addition, you must pay attention to the words used, noticing whether they are concrete, abstract, meaningless, or "loaded."

As a good listener, you must know whether the speaker is seeking the truth or merely trying to push a pet theory. You cannot make the mistake of reacting too fast or of drawing conclusions too quickly. In group discussions, you must know how to encourage the non-speaker and how to silence the compulsive talker. All in all, effective listening is a real challenge.

Thus, suppose your boss calls a meeting and says, "We've studied the results of the last quarter and found that sales have slipped badly. In Cleveland, Brown reports a 22 per cent dip; Smith in Chicago says they're down 8 percent; in Dallas, Rogers has a 12 per cent loss; our San Francisco branch is off 14 per cent. In other words, overall sales are down almost 15 per cent. We're pinning our hopes on the new washing machine-dryer combination and when I unveil it, I think you will all agree that there is reason for optimism. Here it is, and Mr. Collins, of engineering, is going to tell you exactly how it works.''

An unskilled listener, hearing the above, says to himself, "Sales down badly in the last quarter, sales down badly in the last quarter. Remember that." While he's talking to himself, he hears-not quite so clearly-that Brown, in Cleveland, has reported a 22 per cent dip in sales. So now he thinks, "Sales down badly in the last quarter. Brown in Cleveland reports..." By this time, however, the boss is talking about Chicago-a fact the unskilled listener probably won't even hear. And so it goes.

When Mr. Collins gets around to explaining how the new machine works, the listener will be so rattled by his inability to remember the boss's introductory remarks that he will probably give up completely. Even if he doesn't, the chances are overwhelmingly against his understanding the directions.

A good listener abstracts the basic idea behind all those figures and simply says to himself, "Sales for last quarter down about 15 per cent." He hears the corroborating facts but makes no attempt to commit them to memory. Unburdened by trivia, his mind remains alert for the next idea. The strange thing is that when you do grasp an idea, your understanding of it helps you-almost unconsciously-to remember the supporting facts.

Sometimes, a speaker gives definite clues to an idea. He may begin with "My thesis is... ," "I think... ," or "My purpose in talking to you is... " then give facts to back up his idea. Or, after a series of facts, he may wind up with such phrases as: "Therefore, it seems fair to say... ," "In short....,""To summarize... ," "In other words... " Listen for the clues and you will seldom miss the idea.

Listen Actively: Listening is the other half of talking. Just as an effective speaker uses more than words to put across his ideas, so does an efficient listener use more than his ears to hear what is said. If a speaker may employ gestures, facial expressions, pauses, and inflection to enhance his message, a listener has hidden assets to draw from, too: his mind, eyes, hands, and voice. The trick is to learn how to use them.

Anticipate the Speaker: No matter who is talking to you, you can bet it's for one of four reasons: to give you information; to persuade you to do something; to "get it off his chest;" or to entertain you. No matter what his reason, though, every speaker has a central idea that he would like you to grasp. To bolster that idea, he makes one or more points.

The skilled listener not only hears what is said, but uses his supersonic thought processes to guess what these points will be before they are made. Between words, so to speak, he asks himself, "What's this fellow driving at?" As often as possible, he tries to apply logic to what he has already heard and anticipate the next point. Logic failing, he makes an educated guess.

If he is right, he has heard the point twice-from the speaker's lips and from his own inner understanding. Consequently, his retention of the point is strengthened. And even if he is wrong, he has learned something: by comparing his erroneous conclusion with the one finally drawn by the speaker, he has sharpened his own thinking ability. But there is still a lot of time left between the spoken word and the fleet-footed thought. So, the effective listener begins to--

Weigh what's been said: Just because your guess was wrong when you tried to anticipate the speaker, that doesn't mean that you are the poorer thinker. You may be a far superior logician, more objective in your views and in possession of information unknown to the speaker. In short, your conclusion may have been the correct one after all.

Therefore, you must use some of that precious time lag to judge what the speaker has said and the conclusions he has drawn. Is his point really illustrated by his examples? Are the examples one-sided? Is he over-generalizing? Is there too much emotionalism in his presentation? Is his evidence based on fact-or hearsay? Is he arguing from a half-truth? Is he drawing false analogies? Is his logic valid? Could his information be out-of-date? Has he overlooked any pertinent facts that would alter his conclusions?

Any discrepancies that the listener notices are filed in his mind for instant reference against the time when he must make a decision-agree, or disagree, or verbally commit him to a course of action.

Usually, when a person talks to you, he watches for a reaction to what he's said. A raised eyebrow may make him pile up more evidence in support of his case. A smile may cause him to ask a question. A quizzical look may jar him into recasting his thoughts in different language.

In other words, he checks from time to time to see whether you are keeping up with him. To help you tick off his points with him, he may pause and utter transitional phrases like "Another thing.·.," "Then, too·.," "Furthermore..."

As the speaker takes time getting into his next point, the accomplished listener seizes the opportunity to review what has already been said. Mentally, he repeats every point that has been made, stopping momentarily at each to see whether he has it right.

This review not only improves comprehension and retention, it also helps the listener to judge the general direction of what he is hearing. Even while all this is going on, a good listener has enough additional time in which to --
Listen "Between the Lines" You already do this, for example, when you ask your child to look you straight in the eye and repeat what sounds like a king-size fib. All

the technique requires is a little more conscious effort. Sometimes, after all, what a person does not say is more important than what he says.
To illustrate: a salesman was having a tough time selling a particular prospect on his product, a new duplicating machine. The purchasing agent readily admitted that it would undoubtedly save the firm thousands of man-hours and dollars-but he kept repeating, "We just can't buy at this time." "Whenever the salesman took out his order book, the prospect would shy back and say, "We're not interested." Every time the salesman tried to get the prospect to talk about large items he had bought in the past, the man hastily changed the subject, apparently preferring to speak of the failures of a previous purchasing agent. In despair, the salesman left. Then, playing a hunch, he phoned the firm's purchasing department and asked a few questions. Sure enough, it turned out that had been talking to the wrong man! His "prospect" simply lacked the authority to buy anything n that price range.
The experienced listener uses part of his "time lag" to search for-and consider-all the possible meanings in what is not said. He asks himself a host of questions: Why does the speaker skip certain types of examples while lingering over others? Does the speaker's silence on a particular subject indicate that it is a sore point with him? Why does he studiously avoid using Mr. Wilson's name? Does he gloss over facts that obviously challenge his conclusions? How come he blushes a little whenever he quotes that price? What's the real meaning behind all that desk-pounding? Why does his voice rise in pitch whenever he tries to explain his reasons for wanting to leave?

The answers to questions like these can provide a skilled listener with new insights into a speaker's motives, character, and integrity. It's almost like having a third ear.
Because the ability to listen "between the lines" is so important, yet so seldom cultivated, perfecting your own skill in this area will give you a tremendous listening edge over everyone in your circle.
Many listeners leave an interview or conference with only the haziest notion of what they've heard, simply because they didn't take the trouble to draw out the speaker - or tried to draw him out in the wrong way.

The best way to find out whether or not you understand what you hear, of course, is to ask questions. But you must know why, how, and when to ask them. And this is precisely where many otherwise accomplished listeners fail badly.

There are really just two reasons for asking questions: clarification and specification.

In the first case, clarification, the listener simply wants the speaker to repeat or rephrase his remarks. Thus, he might say: Would you expand a little bit on the

alloy's tensile strength?" or "What's your exact recommendation again?" or "Would you repeat that argument against working overtime?

In the second case, specification, the listener wants to make sure that he isn't misinterpreting or projecting unintended meanings into a message. So, he might ask: ''What kind of truck did you use there?" or "Do your remarks apply to men under thirty, too?" or "Exactly when in November does the new policy start?" No speaker dislikes intelligent questions, for a pertinent query is a compliment. It indicates interest. But be sure your question is purposeful.

If your question is asked in a spirit of challenge, hostility, or skepticism, you risk snapping the delicate thread of rapport that ideally exists between speaker and listener. Throw out a question like, "I suppose you want me to believe all that malarkey?" - And you instantly put the speaker on the defensive. He's apt to answer in a similar vein and before you know it, communication has turned into a verbal free-for-all. Or, insulted, he may cut his remarks short and never get to say the things that would profit you most. The word: politeness.

Even if your question is purposeful and polite, it will be largely self-defeating if it is badly timed. Unless the speaker is exceptionally experienced (and few are}, a question suddenly hurled at him will throw him off center. It may break his train of thought. Possibly, it anticipates something he is about to say. Or, it may prevent others-if there are others-from listening to him.

You owe it to the speaker, the rest of his audience, and yourself to hold your questions until the end of his talk. At the very least, force yourself to wait until he has completely developed a thought and paused before going on to another.

There are few relationships more delicate than the one between a psychiatrist and his patient. At stake is the psychic welfare of a human being, often the peace of mind of an entire family, sometimes the safety of a community.

The doctor must not only get to know his patient, to understand him, as no one else does; he must also let the patient know that he understands. And what takes up most of the time of a psychiatric session? Listening!

How does the psychiatrist make certain that he understands what he hears? By restating in his own words what the patient has told him and asking, "Is that right?"

Take a tip from the psychiatrist. If you are at all unsure that you understand a speaker, briefly restate what you think he's said and ask, "Is that what you mean?" If it isn't, he'll be glad to set you straight. If it is, you can compliment yourself on really having listened.

Most poor listening results because the listener does not even try to share the speaker's thought. He isn't interested enough. He finds the subject dull. But as

G.K. Chesterton once said, "There is no such thing as an uninteresting subject; there are only uninterested people."

To be an effective listener, you must be interested in what is being said, this means you must abandon your prejudices about certain subjects, and then make a special effort to listen, and listen aggressively, when these "uninteresting" subjects are discussed. Look for something of real value to you in all speeches and discussions. You will usually find it. Also, ask questions. Pretend you are interested- and soon you will be.

When Albert Einstein talked about physics, even the President of the United States listened. But when he talked about politics, the seediest ward heeler in town was likely to walk away. Why? Because Einstein was an expert in physics; he knew what he was talking about. In politics, however, he was no more knowledgeable than the next man; in fact, many thought he was a bit duller than the average citizen.

Everyone has areas of competence and areas of ignorance. When a listener makes the mistake of assuming that a man who knows the ins and outs of the stock market also knows how to pick the ponies at Aqueduct, he is flirting with disaster. Yet people make this mistake every day. Otherwise sane men accept medical advice from their favorite mechanic and automotive tips from the family doctor. Don't you do it?

Very well, you say. But how does one decide whether the speaker is an expert? In most cases you don't have to decide, for it is already quite clearly established. An M.D. is presumed to know something about medicine. An auto mechanic is supposed to know something about your car's engine. A nuclear physicist should know quite a bit about the nature of atoms. Listen to those men speaking on their own subjects and you will not waste your time.

In addition to being an active participant and judging the expertness of the speaker, you must listen carefully to what is said. Just listen carefully... That sounds like an easy rule, doesn't it? But how many people do you know who listen with their hearts instead of their minds? Too many people make the error of assuming that eloquence equals intelligence and that a smooth style of delivery guarantees truthfulness of content.

Remember - A speaker may have a tongue of silver, but a heart and brain of tin. Unless you judge a speaker by what is actually said, rather than by the manner of delivery, you will fall victim to a good many smooth-talking charlatans. You are not likely to agree to saw off Manhattan Island, or even to buy the Brooklyn Bridge, but you may do things almost as foolish.

An effective listener hears precisely what is being said. He pays much less attention to the way it is being said.

Ten Pointers for Effective Listening:

Don't say a subject is uninteresting, for all subjects are interesting. There are, however, uninterested listeners.

Gauge the speaker's expertness on the subject under discussion. Listen carefully to the man who knows what he is talking about.

Don't equate eloquence with intelligence. A very poor speaker may say a great deal, while a brilliant speaker may say nothing.

Make every effort to understand the big words used by a speaker. Demand understandable English of people addicted to gobbledygook.

Require concrete statements in place of emotion-laden clichés.

Determine the speaker's motive before you try to evaluate what he is saying.

Don't draw conclusions too quickly. Give the speaker a chance to make his point before trying to contradict him. Evaluate only when comprehension is complete.

Learn how to get the non-speaker into a group discussion.

Use every possible method to silence the haranguer and teller of tall tales.

Retain your composure and sense of humor. Effective listening demands real effort, and such effort is impossible in an atmosphere highly charged with emotion.

REVELATION #13
NEGOTIATION

Negotiation came about in early times even before money was the main media of trade. In fact, the Island of Manhattan in New York City was negotiated by Peter Stuyvesant of the Netherlands with the Indians on the island. The trade is the most famous negotiation in history. The fact is that Peter Stuyvesant was a shrewd trader. He knew that the Indians wanted something they did not have and so he offered them a box of beads worth at that time about $28.00. That is said to be the greatest trade and negotiation in history. It boils down to satisfying a seller with a buyer by virtue of appeasing all parties.

We have come a long way when gold and real currency came into existence and started to value all goods.

Whether or not we like it, we all must negotiate. Therefore, becoming skilled in the negotiating process is going to determine the quality of our lives to a great degree. Most of us are engaged in some kind of negotiation nearly all the time, few of us recognize it for what it is.

Whenever two people exchange ideas with the intention of changing relationships, however they confer for agreement, they are negotiating. For many people, this definition changes the framework for negotiation.

Negotiation is an important part of our daily interaction with others. With some planning and research, negotiations in all areas of life can be more successful and fulfilling. As with other managerial skills, it can be learned, practiced and mastered, with the rewards great.

Most negotiations are made by compromise. The seller wants to get as much as possible and the buyer wants to procure the goods at the lowest cost feasible. The result of satisfying the buyer and the seller is by means of both parties compromising at a point that is acceptable to them. Of course, most negotiations are in matters of where large sums of money are involved such as real estate, or the thousands of contracts made daily between businesses. In today's world, most items are recognized as to a set range of value and there is no negotiation involved excepting that the educated buyer knows what he has to pay and the range of value as competition establishes the value.

Nothing could be simpler in definition or broader in scope than negotiation. Every desire that demands satisfaction-and every need to be met-is at least potentially an occasion for people to initiate the negotiating process. Whenever people exchange ideas with the intention of changing relationships, whenever they confer for agreement, they are negotiating.

Negotiation depends on communication. It occurs between individuals acting either for themselves or as representatives of organized groups. Therefore, negotiation can be considered an element of human behavior. Aspects of it have been dealt with by both the traditional and the new behavioral sciences, from history, jurisprudence, economics, sociology, and psychology to cybernetics, general semantics, game and decision-making theory, and general systems.

Yet the full scope of negotiation is too broad to be confined to one or even a group of the existing behavioral sciences.

Every day, the New York Times reports hundreds of negotiations. At the United Nations and in capitals around the world attempts are made to settle the "small" wars. Government agencies negotiate with the United States Congress for appropriations. A utility company confers with a regulatory agency on rates. A strike is settled. Two companies agree to merge but must obtain the consent of the Justice Department. A small but valuable piece of real estate changes hands. These are the types of negotiations that the Times might describe any day of the week. Occasionally there may be a spectacular agreement, such as the nuclear test ban treaty, to attract worldwide attention. But even more important, at least to the people that participated in them, are the countless negotiations that are not mentioned in the Times or in any other newspaper.

Even that age-old negotiating situation, subject matrimony, is but slightly influenced by the vaunted computer. The computer may take over the role of matchmaker-but it is merely predicting that two particular negotiators have the best chance of reaching a satisfactory agreement.

Up to the present time, no general theories were available to guide an individual in his day-to-day negotiating activities. All too frequently we have had to learn to negotiate the same way we learned such things as sex-by trial and error. The man who claimed to have thirty years' experience in negotiation might simply be making the same mistakes every year for thirty years.

Thus, most of our knowledge about negotiation, unfortunately, has had to come from our limited personal experience. And most people impose further restrictions on the negotiation process. Here, for example, is an excerpt from a study by the Committee for the Judiciary of the U.S. Senate released a few years ago:

To an American, negotiation is the least troublesome method of settling disputes. Negotiation may be exploratory and serve to formulate viewpoints and delineate areas of agreement or contention. Or it may aim at working out practical arrangements. The success of negotiation depends upon whether (a) the issue is

negotiable (that is, you can sell your car but not your child); (b) the negotiators interested not only in taking but also in giving are able to exchange value for value, and are willing to compromise; or (c) negotiating parties trust each other to some extent-if they didn't, a plethora of safety provisions would render the "agreement" unworkable.

The Committee's three requirements for successful negotiation drastically limit the area of possible action. Children are sold, even in America, as the occasional revelation of a black-market baby ring clearly indicates. And a parent whose child is kidnapped would not hesitate to negotiate for its release. All issues must be considered negotiable whenever there are human needs to be met.

As for the second requirement, it is impossible to foresee in any negotiation what the outcome is going to be. Therefore, it is impossible to anticipate in advance that either party will be "willing to compromise." Compromise is usually arrived at during the normal course of bargaining. It develops naturally as a result of a thorough examination of the facts and the opposing and also the common interests of the negotiators involved. Although compromises may be worked out as a result of a negotiation, the parties should not enter into discussions with the sole intent of compromising. Even in a "simple" negotiation, a number of issues are involved. It would scarcely be to anyone's advantage to compromise on each of them. The old saying, "The wheels of diplomacy often turn on the grease of ambiguity," is applicable here. It is better to enter into a negotiation without self-imposed limitations, ready to seize any advantage that is offered.

The Committee's third stipulation is almost impossible to meet. Generally, the parties involved in a negotiation do not "trust" each other. Indeed, the handling of other people's mistrust is the skilled negotiator's stock in trade. To summarize, I doubt whether there would be negotiations if the Committee's three conditions were the prerequisites to success.

Today many businesses have begun to recognize the broad scope and importance of effective negotiating techniques. Some progressive sales organizations attempt to provide their salesmen with these techniques along with selling kits. The business of selling franchises, for example, has been very successful along these lines. Almost every conceivable product and service is sold through franchise distributors. Prices for these franchises can run from hundreds to hundreds of thousands of dollars. Although, the prospective franchise purchasers usually have had sufficient business experience to raise the funds necessary to go into the venture, they are rarely skilled negotiators. And their preconceptions about negotiating techniques often keep them from obtaining all the concessions they could get.

If you know that within one month, you will find yourself across the table from your negotiating opponents, how do you prepare for this face-to-face encounter? Bow can you foresee the strategy of the opposite side, and how can you prepare to cope with it? The answer is not a simple one. It may be summed up, however, in a phrase reminiscent of school days: do your homework. There is any number of life situations for which preparation is necessary. Negotiation is one of these. For successful results it requires the most intensive type of long and short-range preparation.

This preparation requires, first of all, intimate knowledge of yourself. If you can be easily goaded to anger, you are very apt to be tricked into an unfavorable settlement because of your emotional state. People in an emotional state do not want to think, and they are particularly susceptible to the power of suggestion from a clever opponent. The angry person cannot instantly change direction, even if he finds that he has just made a ridiculous blunder. The excitable person is putty in the hands of calm, even-tempered negotiator, a negotiator who has learned how to use emotions only for effect.

How do you go about examining yourself? You must have the courage to ask yourself many disturbing questions, perhaps beginning: What, in general, do you seek in life? What do you want out of your business career? What do you want from this particular situation? Going from the general to the specific is by no means an easy task. As Lincoln Barnett has stated: you will be trying to transcend yourself and perceive yourself in the act of perception.

Other long-range training for negotiation calls for the exercise of a variety of skills. You must have the patience and accuracy of a scientist in searching the literature of past experiments. You must combine the scientific attitude with the cunning of a detective in digging up facts and figures about your opposition. You should be able to apply the current teachings of psychology to predict what the other fellow will try to do. To solve a problem, it sometimes becomes necessary and important to learn many new long-range skills, an important one being the art of listening.

After you have completed your research, you must keep an open mind and always be ready to make changes in your appraisal of the situation. It is possible that some of the facts may require modification or that your approach must be changed. Lapse of time alone often tends to call for a change in strategy. Therefore, it is important to be constantly on the alert for new developments.

It has been said that one never loses until one gives up. An important phase of short-range preparation for negotiation is research. Research should be objective; objective not in the quality of the evidence you gather but in your attitude toward such evidence. There is a positive reason for amassing information. It amasses a wealth of material in your mind so that you may take advantage of any new de elopement in the negotiation.

You should be prepared with every possible kind of information about the people with whom you are going to negotiate. When President Kennedy was preparing to go to Vienna for his first meeting with Khrushchev, he made it a point to study all of

Khrushchev's speeches and public statements. He also studied all the other material available relating to the Premier, even including his preference in breakfast food and his tastes in music. It is doubtful if such intensive research would be required in most negotiating situations, but the extreme importance of President Kennedy's conference warranted this meticulous search for every detail concerning his protagonist.

To utilize the information you obtain from research, you must rely upon your general fund of knowledge and experience. It is essential to examine the opponent's past history, inquire into previous transactions he was connected with, and look into every business venture or deal he has consummated. Also investigate any deals he has failed to conclude successfully. Frequently you will learn as much, or more, about people from their failures as from their successes. If you carefully analyze the reasons that a certain deal fell through or a negotiation failed, you will probably get a good understanding of how the opponent thinks, his method of operating, and his psychological approach. All this will give you clues to his needs and prepare you to negotiate with him more advantageously. Consider what proposals he made, what counter-proposals he rejected and why, how flexible he was in the bargaining, how emotional his approach was.

Suppose you are studying an opponent's previous deal that involves the purchase or sale of real estate. The value of the tax stamps that were affixed to the recorded deed will tell the price at which the property was sold. Bear in mind, however, that there have been instances where an excess amount in tax stamps has purposely been used to attempt to hide the actual price of the property. Do not rely on one source. There are other agencies that will assist you in getting a fairly close idea of how much the property was sold for. Try to use more than one source for verification.

Merely by investigating a previous real estate sale, you can get an idea of what kind of man you are going to deal with. You can find out how long he held the property before he decided to sell it and how much profit he was satisfied to take. All these factors are useful in sizing up a prospective opponent. You can never know too much about the person with whom you will negotiate.

These days, some of the most rigorous negotiation takes place within a corporation-between one department and another. No business is altogether frictionless. The executive who is trying to maximize the effectiveness of his own part of the operation sooner or later runs into conflict with other departments-

and other executives who are also trying to be effective and look good in the process. When this happens, skill at negotiations is essential to the manager. It can mean life or death for his career.

Let's take a typical case. Mantee, Inc. is a medium-sized company manufacturing a line of office equipment. The episode essentially concerns two men: Fred Jones, vice-president for engineering and design, and Lee Parker, vice-president for sales.

Mantee has begun to market a new machine, called the "500." It is not important to specify its exact function. The "500" was developed by Jones's department, which also maintains the responsibility for inspection and quality control. Parker's job is to sell the "500," along with the other products that Mantee manufacturer. He is also responsible for the servicing of the equipment after it is sold.

When Jones agreed that the "500" was ready for marketing, he specified that it was not to be run at more than 1.300 units per hour. His staff was still working on modifications that could possibly double that output.

However, Jones has found out that a number of customers are running the machine at a much higher capacity. Subjected to this kind of stress, the "500" seems to have held up pretty well, but there have been some breakdowns in use.

Jones confronts Parker with this, and with other information he has learned. While Parker's salesmen are not guaranteeing the higher output, they also are not emphasizing that the equipment should not be run above 1,300. Parker feels that he must take full advantage of the potential of this new machine while he has an edge over competition. It isn't just a matter of selling the "500"; with the "500" as a "leader," Parker is better able to sell the whole Mantee line. Furthermore, Parker adds, breakdowns in service have not reached anything near an intolerable rate.

Parker is willing to take the responsibility, but Jones, thinking realistically, realizes that a widespread product failure would have an extremely bad effect on the company's position. It would also reflect upon Jones's reputation and certainly not enhance his career.

Mantee's president, in meaningful tones, has told Jones and Parker, "I am most anxious that you work it out between yourselves." In other words, if at all possible there is to be a negotiated settlement. A meeting has been scheduled a week hence at which the two department heads are supposed to ''work it out."

When we have thoroughly prepared-when we have probed the assumptions existing on all sides-and, most particularly, when we have translated our knowledge into an understanding of needs, then we have mastered the "pieces" in negotiation.

How we deploy them on the board is a matter of technique-strategy and tactics. These two words-strategy and tactics-are clearly differentiated in definition. In practice, however, it is often hard to tell whether a particular move is a bit of strategy or a tactic. In fact, the work "stratagem" seems to combine the idea of strategy and tactic.

We will consider strategy as comprising the techniques used in the actual process of negotiation and tactics as devices used to implement the strategy. Many of life's situations may be likened to the technique we use when we dance in a crowded ballroom. When we move, where we go, how fast we go-all are determined by certain def1nite conditions: the tempo of the dance music, the partner, the other couples, our mental state, the presumed mental state of the other people, subconscious adherence to traff1c rules and regulations, and so on.

Our strategy, for example, may be to circle the outside of the floor or it may be to penetrate to the center. The tactics we use -a particular step or change of direction-are governed by that strategy and also by the conditions around us at that moment.

In studying the techniques of successful negotiation, we may think of them as so many tools which we learn to use. The Encyclopedia Britannica defines a tool as "an implement or appliance used by a worker in the treatment of the substances used in his handicraft, whether in the preliminary operations of setting out and measuring the materials, in reducing his work to the required form by cutting or otherwise, in gauging it and testing its accuracy, or in duly securing it while thus being treated."

The inexperienced negotiator's strategy will be limited to a few simple and obvious devices. The expert negotiator, however, will employ a variety of means to accomplish his objectives. These means will involve "when" strategy or "how and where" strategy. They may involve the use of an agent as well.

Selling automobiles is a highly competitive business. Many potential buyers try to take advantage of this by going from dealer to dealer with the request, "Just give me the price." Sooner or later the buyer will be hit with a "low-ball price, one that is too low to be realistic and may even be below the dealer's cost. After the buyer has completed his appointed rounds, he will return to the low-ball dealer. He will expect that since he has completed his negotiation, there is nothing more to talk about. But the negotiations have just begun. The salesman will assail him with "extras" and high-priced f1nancing. He may take the order and never deliver or switch to another car. The low-ball price will be blown to bits.

On the corporate level, the roles can be reversed. This time the seller is the victim. but the strategy is essentially the same. It is used when a business is in dire straits and must be sold immediately. The potential buyer offers a price or a deal that he knows is unrealistically good. He stalls but continues to offer the lure until all other potential buyers have lost interest. Then he offers his real price on a take-it-or-leave-it basis that the seller must accept.

On the international level, "dumping" of surplus goods is an "honest" form of low-balling. The selling price is low, so low that it drives the competing industries in another nation out of business. Then the rival nation enjoys a monopoly position and charges monopoly prices.

"When" strategy can be separated into several of the following: forbearance, surprise, fait accompli, bland withdrawal, apparent withdrawal, reversal, limits, and feinting. Here are a few examples of these types of strategy.

Forbearance ("waiting in haste"). Age is a great teacher of this strategy. It is seldom used by the young or the insecure. Circumstances that warrant this strategy usually have elements that would ordinarily tempt or provoke one to anger and impetuous action. However, forbearance, or the withholding of such action, will be used when it offers a great reward. The reverse of forbearance is the "rash act." Your judgment and values determine whether forbearance or acting immediately would be warranted.

Knowing when to stop is another element of forbearance. The salesman must know when to stop talking. The attorney must know when he has sufficiently cross-examined the witness. Next to knowing when to seize an advantage, the most important thing in life is to know when to forego an advantage.

Surprise. This strategy involves a sudden shift in method, argument, or approach. The change usually is drastic and dramatic, although it need not always be so. Sometimes, in fact, the change can be ushered in by as insignificant a sign as the alteration of the tone of voice during a negotiation. Where you have carried on the entire negotiation in a calm, even voice, one blowup can effectively make the point. Winston Churchill illustrates this when he states: "I have often tried to set down the strategic truths I have comprehended in the form of simple anecdotes, and they rank this way in my mind. One of them is the celebrated tale of the man who gave powder to the bear. He mixed the powder with the greatest care, making sure that not only the ingredients but the proportions were absolutely correct. He rolled it up in a large paper spill, and was about to blow it down the bear's throat, but the bear blew first."

Fait accompli ("Now what can you do?") This is a risky strategy but it is often a temptation to use it. It demands that you act, achieve your goal against the opposition, and then see what the other side will do about it. Those who employ this strategy must make an appraisal of the consequences in case it should prove to be a failure. An illustration of the unsuccessful application of this strategy was the attack by England, France, and Israel upon Egypt during the Suez crisis. They acted without prior consultation with the United States and hoped to present the world with a fait accompli. The United States intervened, however, and forced them to abandon the attack and to withdraw.

Bland withdrawal ("Who, me?") An example of this strategy is the person who is caught red-handed but who turns and says, "Who, me?" The following illustration, while not directly related to negotiation, is in essence similar to maneuvers that are frequently encountered at the bargaining table. During the 1964 Presidential campaign, the press would attack Senator Goldwater for some statement he was alleged to have made. But Goldwater would say that he had been misquoted, or that he never had said anything of the kind, or that what he was accused of saying had been taken out of context, which altered the meaning altogether. However, the very frequency of his use of this strategy made it ineffective to all but his most ardent admirers. The newspapers just couldn't be wrong all the time-or so a majority of the voters thought.

Apparent withdrawal ("the man who wasn't there"). This strategy is made up of a mixture of forbearance, self-discipline, and a little deception. The aim is to convince your opponent that you have withdrawn, but without his knowing it, you are still in control of the situation.

Reversal ("You can go forward, backward"). In this strategy, you act in opposition to what may be considered to be the popular trend or goal. Bernard Baruch once said that people who make money in the stock market are those who are the first in and the first out. By this he meant that you should buy when everyone was pessimistic and sell when the prevailing atmosphere was optimistic. This strategy may sound easy to execute, but in reality, it is exceedingly difficult. Were it not so, we could all immediately become rich and powerful.

Limits ("This is the absolute end"). The French have become famous for using the time limit as a strategic method. Restricted agenda is also a form of limit; that is, you will not negotiate on more than one subject or you will negotiate only in one particular manner. Restrictions on communication are also a use of this strategy; you will deal only through your agent, or you restrict the communication coming out of a negotiation.

When this approach is carried to an extreme, we have what is known as the "silent barter." Some tribes in Central Africa engage in a unique form of negotiation. The tribe desiring an exchange leaves its good on the bank of a river. A neighboring tribe takes these goods, leaving other goods which they consider of equal value. If the first tribe is not satisfied, they leave the pile there until it is added to, In the event that no additions are made, the first tribe doesn't show up to do business again.

Feinting ("Look to the right, go to the left"). This involves an apparent move in one direction to divert attention from the real goal or object. It can also involve a situation in which you give your opponent a false impression that you have more information or knowledge than you really possess. This strategy has been successfully used in criminal trials. The district attorney is duty bound to tell the court all of the information and facts that he has in his possession. He may not withhold from the court any evidence that may be pertinent to the case, even though it may not help the prosecution. He does not always do this Feinting strategy by defense counsel may lead the district attorney to believe that counsel is in possession of "all" the information and, therefore, the district attorney may feel the obligation now to tell the court all rather than continue to withhold pertinent facts.

At this point, we are no longer negotiating but using sales strategy and so it is important to learn the different techniques of accomplishing a successful sale. The negotiator really becomes a salesman therefore, it is important to learn the psychology involved in selling. The next Revelation will outline the key factors involved in influencing by soft persuasion how to consummate a successful transaction. Persuasion is a matter of enlightening the buyer or seller as the case may be on the benefits that would be received from making the decision to act upon closing the deal that is being offered.

REVELATION #14

PERSUASION

Everybody has to be a
salesman even though
they don't consider
themselves selling a
particular product.
Persuasion is
developing confidence
whether it is a doctor,
lawyer, mechanic,
teacher, and
policeman.

There are basic rules that should be learned and used in the pursuit of selling yourself to others.

Reviewing your selling performance from time to time can mean the difference between fairly good sales and maximum sales possibly in hundreds of thousands of dollars. A daily accounting of sales income, less expenditures and fixed overhead, can be the directional index charting the need for correction and adjustment. It is recognition of the fact that you should recheck techniques in the field, alter your sales presentation from top to bottom, and revamp your tactics to match variable financial and social conditions.

Stress the novelty angle. If your product lends itself to such a tactic, be sure to build on this interest by piling up irresistible benefits to stimulate desire. Base the presentation on factual information instead of exaggerations that do not ring true. Credibility can be shaken in the decision-making process when you stretch the truth as a hook or inducement and the line will nap. Once you capture the prospect's attention, hold it with an offer of gilt-edge benefits backed up with valid evidence. You can use case histories, testimonial letters, published articles from trade journals, laboratory reports, etc. Possibly the best closing ammunition to bring into range is an unconditional guarantee that proves the manufacturer will repair without charge or replace any defective purchase with a new item.

Establish a reputation . You can't buy the kind of word-of-mouth advertising that locates prospects and gets referrals but your service between sales can generate good will and satisfaction of inestimable value. Checking back with customers at regular intervals serves a triple purpose. First, you may be able to write up repeat orders on items purchased in the past. Secondly, you can handle before they fester any possible complaints on problems that may arise. Thirdly, you can fulfil the demand for new needs due to fluid situations and other changes in your customer's requirements.

Ask for the prospect's opinion. You usually explain the multiple advantages of owning your product and quote a price and perhaps set him to thinking about what you have to offer. But the rush to complete the job often prevents you from listening to any feedback. He may really have something important to say.

Remember, the prospect can simply influence his own's buying decision by this strategy. So, make the prospect an expert. Ask him frankly what he thinks of the product after you have enumerated its chief benefits. Some features will have special value that justifies a purchase, while other aspects you presented may not have been so classified. Here's your chance to explain how these points meet his specific needs.

Now he can openly admit the named benefits appeal to him. The admission is vital, leading to the next step - a definite purchase. Let the prospect "speak his piece" as the foremost participant in making a decision. Put him on a pedestal and let him be the expert, truly a persuasive sales maneuver that can pave the way to open-minded selling.

A more obvious device is to include a multiple-choice question in the closing minutes of the sales pitch, preferably narrowing the choice down to a selection between two items: "Do you prefer the standard beige color or the new metallic brown harmonizing with your desk?" The idea is to allow the prospect a voice in making a decision, actually a final commitment to buy.
You are also a show person and you have the aptitude for staging a powerful demonstration. But first, you must arouse interest in possessing the product, a desire to enjoy the benefits you describe. Then you can concentrate this attention on a see-for-yourself demo that covers one or two principal points and get him excited about the pending purchase. Active participation makes it difficult for him to ignore this direct form of person-to-person selling. He will not be inclined to postpone buying action if you follow through now with your best close.
Make appointments to control time. You can account for an eight hour day by planning your workday for more productive time devoted to selling. If you can

144

schedule appointments, less time will be lost between calls in coffee breaks, driving around, goofing off, personal errands, etc.

Phoning ahead lets you organize the itinerary with priority on promoting your product or service. Both prospect and regular customer will appreciate the courtesy you show in arriving promptly and confirming that you value his time. Anticipate questions and objections. Answer them in the presentation before the prospect proposes them. How? Keep a record of what happened in previous interviews, which particular features attracted customers, which product benefits were most appealing, which single sentences in the close induced buying action. Note that in most cases you convinced him how he could save time, money and effort, all directed toward personal satisfaction. Secondly, give your sales efforts a personal touch. Personalized selling implies an individualized service. How can you provide improved service without efficiency and know-how? By identifying and servicing specific needs, you can help the prospect confront a daily problem.

Each new promotion is a challenge. Be alert to opportunities in newly developed sales programs and check the possibilities in your area. You know what your market will buy in time- saving supplies and convenience devices, in energy conversation

equipment for do-it-yourself homeowners, in a variety of lines appealing to kids, etc.

Product diversification will help you upgrade your selling efforts by capitalizing on response from satisfied customers. They have the wherewithal to spend and will be most receptive to your offers. Replenish your lines with imagination and creativity to tap this continuing market. Yes, change is the name of the game in direct selling. Look for product improvements, add-on lines of related products and new sales programs to set up your earning power.

While we have used the scientific method in discovering the principles of salesmanship, it should be borne in mind constantly that a sale is not a coldly scientific process. It is a friendly, red-blooded, man-to-man transaction. It cannot be accomplished by any scientific formula that neglects the human element. If one were to take the trouble to investigate, he would no doubt discover that certain definite principles might be followed by an aspirant for social position, but it is at the same time true that no one would expect to become a social lion merely by adhering to a set of coldly calculated rules. The same principle holds true in selling. In fact, there is a great deal of the social in successful selling.

There are certain definite methods of securing a prospect's friendly consideration, however, and there are a number of fundamental purchasing motives to which appeal may be made. These can be used effectively by the salesman who is sincere in his methods.

Securing Prospect's Respect and Admiration. The attitude of the average businessman when a caller is announced tends toward indifference. His resolve is not to give more time than is necessary but he is not antagonistic. On the other hand, unless there is some definite reason for it, he is not over-friendly. The moment a salesman appears, therefore, he sways the balance for or against himself. There are some men who are easy to turn down - to shut off without a hearing.

They seem to belittle their propositions, no matter how important these may be. There are others to who even the confirmed "grouch" accords a courteous reception. They dignify their propositions. What is the reason for the difference? We must give here the same answers that we have given previously in a different connection: caliber, personality. We shall assume that the salesman is clean-shaven, well dressed and well groomed. The development of a man's intellect and his tastes, and the things, to which he devotes himself outside of business, do much to determine his manner, expression, voice and actions. The surest way for a man to improve his salesmanship is to improve himself.

Once the approach has been made and the interview secured, there should be something in the poise, evident culture, well-modulated voice, thoughtful and courteous manner and well-groomed appearance of the salesman that will excite the admiration of the prospect. The salesman who would sell his goods to the prospect must first sell himself.

Securing the Prospect's Friendship. The salesman is not satisfied merely with gaining the respect and admiration of the prospect. A man may be respected, and even admired, and still be disliked. He wants an atmosphere of warm friendliness to pervade the entire interview. So much has been said of courage as a requisite of successful salesmanship that the natural inclination on the part of the salesman, especially the young salesman, is to set his mouth in a grim, straight line and prepare to fight his prospect for an interview. Instead of doing this, he should ask himself when approaching his prospect, "Now what is there about this man that I can sincerely like and admire?"

The Sincere Compliment. If we stop to think, we shall realize that in many instances the chief reason for our liking some people is that they like us. If we recall the foremost characteristics of men - salesmen and others - who have won our confidence and friendship in business, we shall discover that their chief characteristic was interest in us - interest in us and in our business. While the compliment, however sincere, that comes early in the interview may arouse suspicion, the fact remains that pride in himself, in his business, in is achievements and in the opinion that others hold of him, is inherent in every man. Why not then, in the course of the interview, compliment your prospect sincerely on his firmness, his affability or his judgment, as the case may be? Why not remark admiringly upon the individual touches that make his business stand out from others? Why not congratulate him upon his achievements in business and in other lines? Why not mention the high regard in which he is held by his townspeople?

We like to hear such things about ourselves. We are convinced that there is that about us which can be sincerely liked and admired. It is perfectly evident, then, that the same must be true of the other man - of the prospect. We recognize these good qualities in others, but somehow fail to mention them. The good salesman is a student of human nature; he understands these virtues and manages to mention them in the interview. One of the biggest elements of success in salesmanship is the ability to see and tactfully to acknowledge the good qualities of the prospective customer.

Appealing to self-esteem-The exclusive-agency man who asks the dealer's opinion of his plan is merely making a very subtle appeal to his prospect's self-esteem. The story is told of a man who came out of the Southwest a few years ago to promote and secure financial backing for a development company, the profits of which would be large and almost certain. He felt that if he could get the name of just one big

man, in Wall Street as a subscriber to his stock, the rest would be easy. He was not known in the financial district, however, and he knew that he would never get beyond his introductory remarks if it became apparent that he was trying to sell stock in a new promotion.

One evening; at an exclusive club where he had been a guest for some time, he managed to sit beside a big financer to whom he had been introduced some time previously, and with whom he had associated on several occasions. "Mr. Brown," he said, "I am going to ask a favor of you. I have rather a large proposition that I wish to submit. The trouble is that I am chiefly a practical man. I can swing the operating end after a company has been organized, but I am rather green about the financial end. Now, I don't know any of the big men down in the Street, but I have read and heard much about you and your enterprises. I wonder if you would give me a little advice." The big man leaned forward, smoothed out a scowl that had begun to form, and prepared to listen. Give him advice? Why, of course he would.

He had thought at first, though, that this man had intended trying to get him to subscribe to some stock. Simply discussing the thing as one man of business might with another was entirely different. The promoter unfolded his story, casually producing maps and reading here and there from the reports of experts. The financier showed more and more interest as the talk proceeded asked a number of questions, and examined minutely the several documents produced. "Why, man alive," he broke in, "that's a first-rate proposition. Anyone will listen to you on that. Of course, what you need first of all is money. I'll tell you what I'll do. Just put me down for a $25,000 block of that stock now. You don't need much advice on how to handle this thing. Just use my name to get in to see some of the fellows and tell them your story just as you told it to me."

Calling upon a man merely to get his advice or his friendship and cooperation, or for some other such motive, is an excellent way of paying him a compliment that will put the interview on a friendly footing.

Acquisitiveness and desire for profit.-The necessity of taking the "you" attitude, of appealing to the prospect's self-interest, of showing him clearly how he will be benefited, has been emphasized previously in these pages. The salesman who thinks principally of himself and his house during the interview probably will not make the sale; he will do well to forget his interests and think of the prospect's interests. In the last analysis, we are all selfish and self-centered; we buy from selfish motives, and the salesman who can satisfy this desire for gain on the part of his prospect is appealing successfully to the most deep-seated of all buying motives. This motive rests not alone upon the desire to get but also upon the desire to keep. Many years ago, a collection of battle pictures of the Civil War, reproduced from famous paintings, was put on the market. The price for the series was fixed at ten dollars. At the end of six months, close to sixty thousand dollars had been spent for advertising and the receipts amounted to less than one thousand dollars. It was decided to cut the price to five dollars in order to sell out the edition and recover part of the loss. The plan was to spend no more money but simply to announce the reduction to the trade. But a clever advertising man who was called into consultation, conceived the plan of sending circular letters to the members of the Grand Army of the Republic and to the Sons and grandsons of Veterans, enclosing a receipt for three dollars, made out in the name of the member and signed by the publishers, to apply on the purchase of the pictures. The price of the pictures, the circular stated, was ten dollars, but the publishers wanted every member of these organizations to have them-hence the receipt which, accompanied by two dollars, would entitle the member to the pictures.

Here was something of value with which it was difficult to part. A signed receipt for three dollars is not easily thrown away. The result was that a great many of these men used their receipts either to get the pictures for themselves or to secure them for a friend, as a special favor.

This same appeal to acquisitiveness can be made in personal salesmanship. The dealer who is offered an exclusive agency feels that he has within his grasp something of value which he must relinquish if he does not sign up; the special price that will not be offered again is a strong incentive to immediate purchase. The offer of a limited supply which necessitates restricting the special opportunity to a favored few, prompts that favored few to take advantage of the unusual conditions. The special arrangement of a wide assortment in small lots, which the salesman will make for today only, is tempting. Acquisitiveness may be de1med as that quality in the human being which makes it difficult for him to relinquish anything of potential value.

Closely allied with this characteristic is the tendency of the average person to reach out eagerly for anything that is held back. The salesman who can create the impression that he is not especially anxious to sell can create in the prospect an anxiety to buy. There is something in human nature that makes us want what is not easy to get.

Love of home and family. Business men may calculate to the last penny where their business is concerned, but ninety-nine out of every hundred are generous when it comes to the home and the comforts of the family circle. The average man will make all sorts of sacrifices, put forth extra effort and spend much time on trains, to provide a suburban home which he himself rarely has an opportunity to enjoy by daylight, solely in order that his wife and children may be comfortable. The piano salesman, when he learns that the prospect has a daughter, does not tell of the

high- grade 1mish or the fact that this instrument is thirty dollars cheaper than a competitor's but points out how, with a piano in the home, the daughter will be happy and contented. The automobile dealer talks to the husband and father in terms of health and enjoyment for his wife and children and the prospect will buy if it is at all possible. The retail salesman's suggestion that one does not want to be anything but generous in the home is often sufficient to affect the sale of high-priced clothing or furniture of the finest quality. The love of family and the desire to do everything possible for their comfort and happiness in the home are innate in every man.

Some fundamental human instincts .-Besides the motives which have been discussed there are others to which an appeal may be made. A prominent psychologist says:
The generally recognized instincts in man are as follows: fear, anger, shyness, curiosity, affection, sexual love, jealousy and envy, rivalry, sociability, sympathy, modesty, play, imitation, constructiveness, secretiveness and acquisitiveness.
Some of these have been already considered; all are powerful motives impelling men to act. The salesman, consequently, as a skilled workman, should consider them his tools, employing first one, then another, or combining them according to the particular situation at hand.
Two avenues of appeal.-There are two distinct avenues by which a salesman may approach the prospect for a favorable decision. He may, by pure logic and sound argument, appeal to the prospect's reason-to his intellect. Or he may, by positive suggestion and vivid word pictures, appeal to the prospect's imagination-to his emotions.

Are we moved by reason or suggestions?- We are prone to look upon man as a purely reasoning creature who comes to a decision by carefully weighing all arguments pro and con and deliberately deciding whether to do, or not to do, the thing under consideration. We are inclined to explain our own actions according to this theory, either because we thoroughly believe it or because we try to hide what we consider to have been our weakness in coming to a decision without having gone thru a reasoning process. For, until recently at least, to allow the emotions to sway one even in an unimportant decision was considered either childish or hysterical. If this were true, the logical appeal to the intellect would be the only one to use as a means of influencing intelligent people.

As a matter of fact, most of us seldom decide things by the reasoning process alone. The man who makes even a majority of his decisions solely by reason is indeed rare. Nor is it true that the ablest men are the most logical men. In fact, the logical individual is likely to be rather cold and austere. The imaginative man, who is ruled by his emotions rather than by his intellect, is usually most successful in handling men and inspiring enthusiasm and loyalty in those about him. In the crisis, the emotional appeal is most potent. "England expects every man to do his duty," was the appeal from Nelson's lips that won the battle of Trafalgar. "The gold guard dies but never surrenders" was the slogan that gave every man in that glorious company the strength of ten. There is dynamic power in the thought that appeals to the emotions and translated into action it accomplishes a result that often seems superhuman.

It is by no means our intention, of course, to intimate that logic, argument and sound reasoning are not essential and even vital in most, if not in all. sales talks. The best sale talks are, as a rule, a skillful blending of intellectual and emotional appeals.

Appeal to the intellect.-Arguing or reasoning with a prospect-that is, appealing to his intellect alone-causes deliberation and consequently delay. He considers the advisability of buying or not buying-whether to give in to the salesman's arguments or to resist them. He will weigh pro and con the qualities of the salesman's goods as compared with others. The possibility of not buying is always kept in mind. If by cold logic and direct argument the salesman has convinced the prospect, against his inclination, that he ought to buy, it is possible that he will have created an antagonism which will render the closing of the sale impossible. Yet here again, we do not want to get the impression that the intellectual appeal has no place in selling. The salesman, who has not studied his article until he can produce reason after reason why a logical man should buy it, is not likely to succeed. The professional purchasing agent and the department store buyer have competitors' goods in mind and will buy from the salesman, not because his proposition is a good one, but because it is a better one. Hence argument is necessary in selling to trained buyers. In the sale of scientific goods, the ability of those goods to do the work for which they are designed, and to do it well, must be demonstrated.

Even in these cases, however, suggestion and the imaginative appeal are used at the close. The department store buyer must imagine the goods moving rapidly. The scientific man must picture himself using the article. As salesmen we should realize that, while the appeal to the intellect has its place, cold logic and abstract arguments of themselves close few sales. They must be accompanied by some imaginative appeal that will create in the prospect's mind a mental picture of his condition and needs and convert conviction into an impulse to buy.

The imaginative appeal.-A prominent and well-to-do lawyer in a New England town had in his office a veritable rattle-trap of a typewriter whose type was badly broken and out of alignment. A typewriter salesman had made several ineffectual attempts to get him to buy a new machine. The salesman pointed out that the old machine would not last much longer anyhow, and that its appearance was not in keeping with the dignity of the office, but all to no avail. The lawyer clung to the old machine. Then one day the salesman sat down in his own office and typed a page of legal cap on a disreputable old machine that he had taken in exchange; the typing was blotchy, broken and out of alignment. Next, he typed a similar page with one of the newest and best machines in stock. With this material in hand, he called upon the lawyer.

"Mr. Lawyer," he began, "when you go before a jury you are particular as to your dress. You make sure that your clothes are carefully pressed; that your shoes are polished; that your linen is immaculate-and you would never think of appearing in court with your face unshaven. Why? You would be just as good a lawyer, no matter what your appearance. Your arguments would be just as forceful. But you are afraid that a poor appearance might lessen others' opinion of your ability-create a bad impression, in other words. Mr. Lawyer, you don't always get an opportunity to present your cases in person. Sometimes you are asked to submit briefs. How do you get up your briefs? Like this (showing the poorly typed sheet), so that their slovenly appearance detracts from the forcefulness of their arguments? Or like this (showing the neatly typed sheet), immaculate and pleasing in dress so that they produce a favorable impression even before that are read?"

This appeal to the imagination put the whole matter in a new light. The lawyer in his mind's eye saw the judge pick up his slovenly brief and frown as he glanced at it. He doubtless recalled close decisions where he had lost when, to his mind, his masterly brief had entitled him to win. The sale was made.

By the imaginative appeal is meant the introduction into the prospect's mind of some suggestion around which the prospect constructs a mental picture, with him as the central figure. The result of the appeal to the intellect is analytical in its nature. the result of the imaginative appeal, on the other hand, is synthetic-it involves the relating of one thought to another and the building of the picture in the mind of the prospect. The salesman who furnishes a stimulus for this synthesis is said to be appealing to the imagination.

An examination of selling talks will reveal the fact that many of them are aimed at the emotions. The vacuum cleaner salesman previously referred to caused one of his prospects to picture her going to the matinee. The telephone man whose work has been described painted for the merchant a vivid picture of clerks wasting time, and a more pleasant one of employees giving efficient service to customers. There is in New York a builder of suburban homes who goes to considerable expense in furnishing one of his newly constructed houses with fine rugs, period furniture, tapestry and expensive pictures. All prospects are taken first into this model home so that they may imagine themselves living there. Then, and not until then, they are

shown the other houses; and they picture everyone furnished like the model. This same man has instructed his salesmen never to use the word "houses," but always "homes," because the latter then holds the greater and more pleasurable appeal to the imagination.

In the great achievements of history, in the progress of invention and scientific discovery, we find imagination to have been the great stimulus to action. In selling, the imaginative appeal is effective because it stirs at once into action.

Positive suggestion.-The imaginative appeal is made by introducing into the prospect's mind suggestions calculated to form associations, or associated ideas. An order blank spread squarely in front of the prospect is a positive suggestion to him to sign. For this reason, most salesmen, if their business requires a contract, place it before the prospect before they start their closing tactics. They also hand a pen to the prospect. Some salesmen prefer to reach for the prospect's pen, dip it into the ink and hand it to him. Either procedure is a positive suggestion to write-to sign.

That these suggestions can have any appreciable effect is difficult to believe until one recalls some of the marked results of positive suggestion. Someone coughing in an assemblage starts countless other coughs. A person sitting opposite another in a street car yawns, and lo! The observer is yawning, too. This will nearly always be so, even though the observer has consciously and firmly set his mind against accepting the suggestion to yawn. One person looking intently upward will cause everyone who sees him to follow his gaze. If the person who stares perseveres, it will be but a few minutes before he is surrounded by a curious crowd, gazing intently upward.

Positive versus negative suggestions.-A salesman who can remain in a happy mood and maintain a cheerful, smiling countenance before a prospect that is inclined to be cranky and crabbed, will eventually suggest cheerfulness and a happy mood to the customer, before long, will get an answering smile because of the power of positive suggestion.

The form of a question can be made to suggest the answer. "This is a great proposition, don't you think so?" is a positive suggestion which will often bring an affirmative answer. "Do you think this is a good proposition?" is neutral and may be answered in either the affirmative or in the negative. You don't think this is a good proposition?" is a negative suggestion that will bring a negative answer. In retail selling, "We have just secured some new neckwear that will harmonize with that shirt you have just purchased; I am sure you will be interested in looking at it," is a positive suggestion; while, "Is there nothing else I can do for you today?" suggests the answer, "Nothing else, thank you."

A garment salesman picking up his sample, scrutinizing one of the seams closely, and putting it down without a word, will cause his prospect to imitate the action. The prospect will discover nothing but a remarkably well-finished seam, which is exactly what the salesman wants him to discover. Throughout the selling talk the salesman says: "You will get this," and "You will get that," and "These goods will start to move off your shelves the moment you get them in," instead of prefixing his remarks with "If you buy," because the positive assertion creates a positive suggestion that the prospect is going to buy.

Use of motives and appeals.-A great pianist running his fingers over the keyboard strikes a key here and a key there and creates a beautiful melody, and then, with sureness born of a thorough knowledge of his instrument, strikes the keys for a grand harmonious chord. He must not only master the technique of his profession but, actuated by a keen interest and a sincere love of humanity, he acquires a knowledge of human nature that enables him with sure strokes to touch upon the motives that move men to action, to reach their intellects with sound logic or to stir their emotions with forceful images. Here, then, is the real difference between the young salesman who, starting out with a thorough knowledge of the theory of selling, gets a few orders, and a big, regularly producing star of the sales force-a knowledge of human nature.

We are prone to look upon man as a purely reasoning creature who comes to a decision by carefully weighing all arguments pro and con and deliberately deciding whether to do, or not to do, the thing under consideration. We are inclined to explain our own actions according to this theory, either because we thoroughly believe it or because we try to hide what we consider to have been our weakness in coming to a decision without having gone through a reasoning process. For, until recently at least, to allow the emotions to sway one even in an unimportant decision was considered either childish or hysterical. If this were true, the logical appeal to The intellect would be the only one to use as a means of influencing intelligent people.

As a matter of fact, most of us seldom decide things by the reasoning process alone. The man who makes even a majority of his decisions solely by reason is indeed rare. Nor is it true that the ablest men are the most logical men. In fact, the logical individual is likely to be rather cold and austere. The imaginative man, who is ruled by his emotions rather than by his intellect, is usually most successful in handling men and inspiring enthusiasm and loyalty in those about him. In the crisis, the emotional appeal is most potent.

An examination of selling talks will reveal the fact that many of them are aimed at the emotions. The vacuum cleaner salesman previously referred to caused one of his prospects to picture himself going to the matinee. The telephone man whose work has been described painted for the merchant a vivid picture of clerks wasting time, and a more pleasant one of employees giving efficient service to customers. There is in New York a builder of suburban homes who goes to considerable expense in furnishing one of his new constructed houses with fine rugs, period furniture, tapestry and expensive pictures. All prospects are taken first into this model home so that they may imagine themselves living there. Then, and not until then, they are shown the other houses; and they picture everyone furnished like the model. This same man has instructed his salesmen never to use the word "houses," but always "homes," because the latter term holds the greater and more pleasurable appeal to the imagination.

By "sales call," we mean any call made on a prospect or customer to advance a sale - either now or in the future. A sales call might be a fact-finding or prospecting call (to explore a customer needs in preparation for a presentation at a later date), or a presentation call (to confirm what was learned on the fact-finding call, present the product, and close the sale), or a post-sale call (to provide follow-up service) or a complaint-handling call (to settle a sales-related

problem) or a call-back call (to correct an earlier failure).
Set the right tone- make the customer feel confident and at ease.
Arouse interest and attention-explain the purpose of the call and persuade the customer that it's worth her while to concentrate on it.

Get the customer involved-set a pattern of active participation (with the customer speaking up and contributing) instead of passive participation (with the customer merely sitting back and listening). Check the customer's receptivity-find out if she's ready to cooperate in making the call pay off for both of you.
Extend an appropriate greeting. An appropriate greeting is confident (if you don't feel confident about what you're doing, why should the customer?) and cordial (friendly but businesslike). A firm handshake, a clear statement of identification (your name, title, and company) and a "social probe" ("How are you?") will usually do it-provided you get the customer's name right. This is so important that it's worth a little research; if you can, check the pronunciation of the customer's name· before the call. You should have an air of pride about yourself on the fact that you can remember names from one day to the next. As a consequence, to not pronouncing or remembering a person's name correctly or the town he lives in, his chances for a successful promotion automatically becomes annoying to the point of being rejected completely. It cannot be over emphasized how important remembering names and pronunciation. There is one sure way to remember names. It works for almost everybody and pays big dividends.

Ten Pointers for Learning and Remembering Names:
Decide now to begin learning and remembering the name of each person you meet.
Listen carefully to a person's name when you are introduced to him.
Ask the person to repeat his name if you fail to get it the first time. Ask him to spell it if it is an unusual name.
Repeat the person's name immediately, at the same time you acknowledge the introduction.
Keep repeating the name throughout your conversation. Use the name once again at the very end of the conversation.
Try to associate the name of every person you meet with some outstanding physical or personality trait.
Become acquainted with the distinctive names of people of different national origins.
Write down the names of people you meet. Make sure you know how to spell these names.

be genuinely interested in people- their looks, personalities, jobs, and so on.

10. Try to learn at least one new name a day by meeting as many people as possible. Most of all, meanwhile in the interview it is well to leave something to the imagination of the prospect in order that he may discover selling points for himself. Very often, a cleverly constructed, sketchy and incomplete presentation will cause the prospect to fill in the gaps by using his imagination and by asking questions until he has completely sold himself. Or, if this is not easy, he should at least be encouraged to ask questions which will bring about a full statement of all points. Most salesmen talk too much and do not allow their prospects to talk enough. There can be no more effective way to secure the true interest of the prospect than by getting him to participate in the presentation. It is a good opportunity to hear the objections and to overcome them.

Explain why you're there. Once past the small talk, tell the customer what your purpose is -and be explicit: "I was in the neighborhood and just thought I'd drop by" is not a statement of purpose; it's a way of saying you have no purpose. The customer's entitled to know what the call is all about. Spell it out.

Explain what the customer stands to gain. As soon as you explain why you're there, she's likely to wonder: "So what? Why should I care about that? Why should I give up some of my valuable time for that purpose?" To head off these questions- and to raise receptivity- couple your statement of purpose with a tentative benefit statement. Tell her why you're there (purpose) and what she's likely to get out of it (tentative benefit).

Probe receptivity. The opening is supposed to lead into the exploration of needs. But how do you know the customer's ready to work with you in exploring her

needs? You don't-unless you ask. So, right after explaining your purpose and the tentative benefit, probe her receptivity. An open-end probe will usually do the job ("How does that sound?"). If you get a positive answer, fine. Go on to the next step. If you get a negative answer ("I don't really think I'm interested"), probe to find out why and then try to raise receptivity before going on.

Explore the Customer's Needs.

Confirm (or disprove) your existing ideas-the assumptions about the customer's needs that you started out with.

Uncover new needs -needs you know nothing about, and may not even suspect. Get the customer to acknowledge her needs-say out loud that they exist and that's aware of them.

Establish your expertise-prove, by skillful, intelligent probing, that you know what you're doing.

In a word, the purpose of this second step is to give you the information and the credibility you'll need to develop benefit statements that will pay off.

How it's done: (a) probe the customer's needs (b) summarize them, and (c) probe receptivity before going on.

Open-end. These are ideal for starting the customer talking about her needs ("What are you presently doing to provide retirement benefits for your administrative people?")

Neutral. Once the customer gets started, keep her going with neutral probes so you get full-not superficial-insight into her needs ("Fill me in on that profit-sharing feature").

Reflective. If the discussion gets sticky-and discussion of needs can get sticky-clear the air with reflective statements ("You're obviously not very happy with the treatment you got").

Summary. Whatever the customer tells you summarizes it from time to time to make sure you've got it right ("As I understand it, you now have a partly-contributory retirement plan.")

Closed-end. You'll need some closed -end probes to pin down details. But use them sparingly; otherwise, you may choke off discussion ("How many years of employment are needed to get full-vested rights?").

Deliver a benefit statement. To recap: restate the customer's needs, prove that your product or service can fill it, and personalize the benefit by focusing on the word you-the customer. If the proof is long or complicated, space it out-don't bunch it together. Follow the guidelines for building trust, understanding and commitment.

Probe for the customer's acceptance: Don't move to the next benefit until she understands and accepts the first one. Try an open-end probe ("How does that strike you?", "What's your reaction?"). If her answer shows she doesn't understand ("Well, I'm still not clear on how that prepayment feature works") or accept ("I don't see how that's going to help me"), go back and straighten things out.

Check the customer's receptivity. Before going on to the next benefit, make sure the customer's ready: "Can we move on to the cash-reserve feature... and see how it'll cut your costs?" If she's reluctant, probe to find out why, and straighten it out.

Deliver another benefit statement: Once the customer's ready for the next benefit, repeat the cycle. Keep on until you've completely proven all the benefits your product or service can deliver to her. Don't waste time on product information that has nothing to do with her needs. She's not interested in what your product might do for other people; she's interested only in what it will do for her.

Summarize the benefits and check for omissions. Once you've told the whole story, summarize the benefits ("Okay, let me recap what this plan will do for you ..."). Then, check to see if you've omitted anything the customer wants to know ("Have I overlooked any of your requirements?").

Prove net gain. Now that you've told the benefit story, you still have a big job on your hands: to prove net gain. Remember: you want to generate understanding and commitment, and, while the customer may understand you perfectly, her commitment may be weak or non-existent if she thinks: "Sounds like a good deal-but not nearly as good as what I can get from Company X," Or, "That's an impressive list of benefits, but it still doesn't add up to what I've already got." Or, "I like the idea, but I wonder if I wouldn't be even better off by going with Company Z." So, now is the time to do some comparison selling; stack up your benefits against those she's considering getting elsewhere. Show that your total package of benefits will deliver more satisfaction-more need fulfillment-than any other package of benefits.

Manage Objections: Objections can arise at any time. All we're saying is that they're most likely to arise now -after you've presented your product or service. If they don't arise spontaneously, if the customer doesn't bring them up on her own, then now is the time to probe for them. If you don't if you take for granted that silence means agreement, you may be in for a shock when you try to close and the customer refuses to buy.

Shows you're willing to face up to objections. This is important. It bolsters your standing with the customer by saying: "I'm confident of my product and my ability to explain it. I have nothing to hide, nothing I'm unwilling to talk about. Feel free to say anything; whatever you say, I'll discuss it to your satisfaction."

Uncovers the real objection Many so-called "objections" cover up real objections the customer would rather not talk about. Time spent on those phony objections is time wasted. Only the real objection is worth managing.

Generates commitment. Objections either prevent or dilute commitment. Commitment means: "I'm fully convinced." An objection means "I'm not fully convinced." Obviously, the only way to get commitment is to get rid of the objection.

Answer the real objection. Once you've uncovered what seems to be the real objection, summarize it, answer it, and, if possible, convert your answer into a benefit statement:

Okay... as I get it, you're concerned because the permanently-sealed drive unit is the only part warranted for five years... while the other parts are covered for only a year. You're right... but actually that's a plus for you. You've said your number-one need is low initial cost- equipment for the lowest possible capital outlay. That's what you'll get with this model. One way we've managed to price this machine below anybody else is by trimming back our warranty.

HUMAN APPEALS THAT SELL:

Warm friendship versus cold service. - While we have used the scientific method in discovering the principles of salesmanship, it should be borne in mind constantly that a sale is not a coldly scientific process. It is a friendly, red-blooded, man-to-man transaction. It cannot be accomplished by a scientific formula that neglects the human element. If one were to take the trouble to investigate, he would no doubt discover that certain definite principles might be followed by an aspirant for social position, but it is at the same time true that no one would expect to become a social lion merely by adhering to a set of coldly calculated rules. The same principle holds true in selling. In fact, there is a great deal of the social in successful selling.

There are certain definite methods of securing a prospect's friendly consideration, however, and there are a number of fundamental purchasing motives to which appeal may be made. These can be used effectively by the salesman who is sincere in his methods.

Securing prospect's respect and admiration.-The attitude of the average business man when a caller is announced, tends toward indifference. His resolve is not to give more time than is necessary, but he is not antagonistic. On the other hand, unless there is some definite reason for it, he is not over-friendly. The moment a salesman appears, therefore, he sways the balance for or against himself. There are some men who are easy to turn down-to shut off without a hearing. They seem to belittle their propositions, no matter how important these may be. There are others to who even the confirmed "grouch" accords a courteous reception. They

dignify their propositions. What is the reason for the difference? We must give here the same answers that we have given previously in a different connection: caliber, personality. We shall assume that the salesman is clean shaven, well dressed and well groomed. The development of a man's intellect and his tastes, and the things, to which he devotes himself outside of business, do much to determine his manner, expression, voice and actions. The surest way for a man to improve his salesmanship is to improve him.

Once the approach has been made and the interview secured, there should be something in the poise, evident culture, well-modulated voice, thoughtful and courteous manner and well-groomed appearance of the salesman that will excite the admiration of the prospect. The salesman who would sell his goods to the prospect must first sell himself.

Securing the prospect's friendship.-The sales person is not satisfied merely with gaining the respect and admiration of the prospect. A man may be respected, and even admired, and still be disliked. He wants an atmosphere of warm friendliness to pervade the entire interview. So much has been said of courage as a requisite of successful salesmanship, that the natural inclination on the part of the salesman, especially the young salesman, is to set his mouth in a grim, straight line and prepare to fight his prospect for an interview. Instead of doing this, he should ask himself when approaching his prospect, "Now what is there about this man that I can sincerely like and admire?"

The austerity with which most men meet salesmen is usually a shell beneath which there is a smiling good nature. The crustiest individual improves upon acquaintance, and usually gives evidence of good qualities. There is no prospect so grouchy that he is not loved by some people and sincerely liked by a great many others. Cheerfulness begets cheerfulness, and if the salesman has a sincere liking for the prospect though nothing may be said, it will manifest itself and enable the salesman to "get under the prospect's skin," so to speak. The only way to handle men, to influence men, to sell to men, is to love them; and that love must be sincere; it cannot be successfully counterfeited. The real salesman likes people, both collectively and individually.

This same principle applies as regards the town in which the salesman is working. The young salesman out on his first trip is apt to find himself of an evening in a small town in an ill-kept hotel. He is likely to yield to the impulse to write long letters to friends, telling them what an awful town he has struck, and concluding that he sees small chance of doing business in such a "one-horse burgh." The star salesman who has grown gray in the business can tell you the good points of every town he has been in. If its citizens are the least bit progressive, you may be sure

he knows it and praises them for the ambition they show. If the town is small, he will be able to point out that at least it is growing and that it has more paved streets and a better lighting system than most towns of its kind. If its industries are small, nevertheless they are efficient. He is not at all surprised that able business men have picked the town to live and work in, and he does not wonder how they ever manage to remain there. It is absolutely essential that the salesman get in harmony with his environment and learn to like the town and appreciate the spirit of its citizens if he is to do business there.

The sincere compliment.-If we stop to think, we shall realize that in many instances the chief reason for our liking some people is that they like us. If we recall the foremost characteristics of men -salesmen and others-who have won our confidence and friendship in business, we shall discover that their chief characteristic was interest in us-interest in us and in our business. While the compliment, however sincere, that comes early in the interview may arouse suspicion, the fact remains that pride in him, in his business, in his achievements, and in the opinion that others hold of him is inherent in every man. Why not, then, in the course of the interview, compliment your prospect sincerely on his firmness, his affability or his judgment, as the case may be? Why not remark admiringly upon the individual touches that make his business stand out from others? Why not congratulate him upon his achievements in business and in other lines? Why not mention the high regard in which he is held by his townspeople?

We like to hear such things about ourselves. We are convinced that there is that about us which can be sincerely liked and admired. It is perfectly evident, then, that the same must be true of the other man- of the prospect. We recognize these good qualities in others, but somehow fail to mention them. The good salesman is a student of human nature; he understands these virtues and manages to mention them in the interview. One of the biggest elements of success in salesmanship is the ability to see and tactfully to acknowledge the good qualities of the prospective customer.

We would like to emphasize that salesmanship is a tool that everyone uses daily, whether or not one realizes that fact. The more you learn about selling, the more one comes to recognize that selling is an endless study of human nature itself. With this view, selling becomes a fascinating endeavor.

We wish you fun and profit!

REVELATION 15:

LEADERSHIP

Success means many wonderful, positive things. Success means personal prosperity: a fine home, vacations, travel, new things, financial security, giving your children maximum advantages. Success means winning admiration, leadership, being looked up to by people in your business and social life. Success means freedom: freedom from worries, fears, frustrations, and failure. Success means self-respect,

continually finding more real happiness and satisfaction from life, being able to do more for those who depend on you.

Success means winning.

Success-achievement-is the goal of life!

Every human being wants success. Everybody wants the best this life can deliver. Nobody enjoys crawling, living in mediocrity. No one likes feeling second-class and feeling forced to go that way. Some of the most practical success-building wisdom is found in that Biblical quotation stating that faith can move mountains.

Believe, really believe, you can move a mountain and you can. Not many people believe that they can move mountains. So, as a result, not many people do.

On some occasion, you've probably heard someone say something like, "it's nonsense to think you can make a mountain move away just by saying 'Mountain, move away.' It's simply impossible."

People who think this way have belief confused with wishful thinking. And true enough, you can't wish away a mountain. You can't wish yourself into an executive suite. Nor can you wish yourself into a five-bedroom, three -bath house or the high- income brackets. You can't wish yourself into a position of leadership. But you can move a mountain with belief. You can win success by believing you can succeed.

There is nothing magical nor mystical about the power of belief. Belief works this way. Belief, the "I'm-positive-I -can" attitude, generates the power, skill, and energy needed to do. When you believe I-can-do-it, the how-to-do-it develops.

But a small number of these young people really believe they will succeed. They approach their work with the "I-m-going-to-the-top" attitude. And with substantial belief they reach the top. Believing they will succeed-and that it's not impossible-these folks study and observe the behavior of senior executives. They learn how successful people approach problems and make decisions. They observe the attitudes of successful people. Belief in great results is the driving force, the power behind all great books, plays, scientific discoveries. Belief in success is behind every successful business, church, and political organization. Belief in success is the one basic, absolutely essential ingredient in successful people. Over the years we talked with many people who have failed in business ventures and in various careers. We have heard a lot of reasons and excuses for failure. Something especially significant unfolds as conversations with failures to develop. In a casual sort of way, the failure drops a remark like "To tell the truth, I didn't think it would work" or "I had my misgivings before I even started out" or "Actually, I wasn't too surprised that it didn't work out." Disbelief is negative power. When the mind disbelieves or doubts, the mind attracts "reasons" to support the disbelief. Doubt, disbelief, the subconscious will to fail, the not really wanted to succeed, is responsible for most failures.

Remind yourself once again that you are not pulled to high levels of success. Rather, you are lifted there by those working beside and below you. Achieving high-level success requires the support and the cooperation of others. And gaining this support and cooperation of others requires leadership ability. Success and the ability to lead others-that is, getting them to do things they wouldn't do if they were not led-go hand-in-hand. The success-producing principles are valuable equipment in helping you develop your leadership capacity. At this point, we want to master four special leadership rules or principles that can cause others to do things for us in the executive suite, in business, in social clubs, in the home, anywhere we find people. These four leadership rules or principles are: Trade minds with the people you want to influence. Think: What is the human way to handle this? Think progress, believe in progress, push for progress. Take time out to confer with yourself. Discuss the subject with others who are knowledgeable on the subject matter Using the rules, you have learned in everyday situations takes the mystery out of that gold-plated word, leadership. Leadership Rule Number 1: Trade minds with the people you want to influence. Trading minds with the people you want to influence is a magic way to get orders-friends, associates, customers, employees-to act the way you want them to act. Not too long ago, the citizens of the United States and of the world became witnesses to a political drama that had all the ingredients of a first-class Greek tragedy. Were it not for the fact that the episode revealed some sense of the nature of power conflicts among influential men, one could safely have stopped reflections on the event at the point where its human interest ended and its deeper significance for leadership began. I am referring, of course, to the Adlai Stevenson episode that exploded on the public scene with an article in the Saturday Evening Post.

We do not intend to go into a commentary on this article but, rather, we want to use this episode to launch my reflections on the human dilemmas of leadership as they affect every person who works in a position of authority and responsibility. In the course of the Stevenson affair, we became privy to backstage rivalry among subordinates close to the President. We saw attempts at political homicide and character assassination through the use of "the leak" of so-called secret positions in the deliberations of high councils of government. We saw the President of the United States drop his guard, if only momentarily, to show us how difficult it is to make or hold friends while in the Presidency. And throughout the revelations, charges, and countercharges, we learned just what the medium of exchange can be in power conflicts; namely, prestige, personal integrity, friendship and loyalty, jealousy and egotism-all typical human sentiments likely to be found in any human encounter where people care about what they are doing.

Most of us are accustomed by virtue of our training and inclinations to externalize conflicts and dilemmas. If an executive finds himself immobilized in the face of a difficult problem, he is apt to look to the outside for an explanation. He might perhaps say to himself that he is unable to act because he has inadequate authority delegated to him. Or he might hesitate because he feels subordinates are holding out on him by providing too little information, confused positions, and mixed signals. In this case, he is likely to vent his frustrations on their incompetence.

When an individual begins to achieve some success and recognition in his work, he may suddenly realize that a change has occurred within himself and in his relations with associates. From a position of being the bright young man who receives much encouragement and supports him, almost overnight, finds himself viewed as a contender by those who formerly acted as mentors. A similar change takes place in his relations with persons who were his peers. They appear cautious with him, somewhat distant, and constrained in their approach, where once he may have enjoyed the easy give-and-take of their friendship. He becomes torn between the responsibilities of a newly acquired authority and the strong need to be liked.

If in your experience, you have encountered an executive who seemed unable to take a stand on a problem, who seemed to equivocate or talk out of two sides of his mouth at once, then the chances are reasonably good that you have come upon a man in the throes of status anxiety. Sometimes this will appear in the form of hyper- activity-the case of the executive who flies from problem to problem or from work project to work project without really seeing an activity through to completion. In this case, the executive is utilizing the tactic of providing a shifting target so that other persons have difficulty in taking aim at him.

During a person's lifetime as they become more important, are called upon to make a speech. Especially that of one that is a leader or about to become a leader. Here are a few hints to help you organize and have a mind's set of the salient points. Think of yourself as being brave. You have already begun to develop courage simply knowing that you can do it. You have already taken a bold and courageous step forward.

By desiring to prepare you. First of all, you want to make an outline of the subject matter that you want to express, and then organize your mind as to what the most interesting beginning will be to obtain the immediate interest of your audience. Then follow through leading up to the point that you want to make most impressive. Use your mind to organize the sequence of knowledge you intend to express. Write out the entire speech in composition form.-double space so that you can make

changes, additions and deletions, then re-write the composition form in a clear concise writing that you can study over several times. Not necessarily does this have to be remembered word by word, but it will give you a format mentally of how to present your message with words to the same effect.

Having courage will show up in your voice and posture and mannerism. Practice the speech a few times a couple of days prior, if possible and then once again before the actual time. Making changes as you see fit is perfect and will relax you from the fact of forgetting exactly the way you originally intended to say it, as you will begin to talk more naturally without having to refer to your past memory.

Think progress, believe in progress, and push for progress.

One of the most complimentary things anyone can say about you is, "He stands for progress. He's the man for the job."

Promotions in all fields go to individuals who believe in- and push for-progress.

Leaders, real leaders, are in short supply. Status quo-errs (the everything's-all-right-let's-don't-upset-the-apple-cart folks) far outnumber the progressives (the there's - lots-of-room-for-improvement-let's-get-to-work-and-do-it-better people). Join the leadership elite. Develop a forward look.

There are two special things you can do to develop your progressive outlook:

Think improvement in everything you do.

Think high standards in everything you do.

Having a small note card of the highlights intended to cover is not necessary but can be helpful, and perhaps make you feel more comfortable.

The fact of the matter is that public speaking actually becomes easier the more times

that you are called upon and you will actually relax and enjoy it more and more so get busy and the fear will vanish automatically. If you are afraid, simply go right on in spite of your fear and your fear will begin to vanish. Every speaker, actor and politician, has the same fear in the beginning, so you now belong to a big club. The fear diminishes and the pendulum will swing all the way to the joy that is received from capturing the audiences' attention and influencing them with control of the subject matter with the purpose you originally intended.

If there are names you wish to mention, it is suggested that you write them on a card and study them to the point that you may not even have to refer to the card while making the speech.

The following pointers are suggested: Introduce yourself at the beginning of the speech, possibly where you live, where you work, what your professional title is and why you are making this presentation and that you are happy to be here and hopeful that your information is helpful to you and possibly mention at the end of the speech that you are happy to answer any and all questions pertaining to the subject matter you have just spoken about.

In order to make your speech more impressive, it is necessary to act enthusiastically about whatever you are talking about. Enthusiasm as General Dwight D. Eisenhower would have described in his lectures on leadership would be as follows: If you push a string, it will not follow you, but if you pull a string and have enthusiasm as to where you are going, the string will follow you. Enthusiasm is the key to leadership to get everybody on board to head in the same direction. Therefore, from the very beginning of your speech, you have to demonstrate in your speech and in your mannerism enthusiasm of the subject matter to have everybody follow you with the same attitude.

The exercise of leadership requires a strong sense of identity-knowing who one is and who one is not. The myth of the value of being an "all-around guy" is damaging to the strivings of an individual to locate himself from within and then to place himself in relation to others. This active location and placement of one's self prevents the individual from being defined by others in uncongenial terms. It prevents him also from being buffeted around the sea of opinions he must live within. A sense of autonomy, separateness, or identity permits a freedom of action and   thinking so necessary for leadership.

Not the least significant part of achieving a sense of identity is the creative integration of one's past. There is no tailor who can convert a hayseed into a big-city-boy - any more than a dude can become a cowboy for all the hours he spends on the range. Coming to terms with being a hayseed or a dude permits the development of a unique person who goes beyond the stereotypes offered to him as models.

Closely related to the need for a sense of identity is constancy in how one represents and presents him to others. Constant alterations of one are confusing to work associates. These shifts are particularly damaging to ordinates that are entitled to the sense of security that comes from a feeling of reasonable continuity in the responses of their boss. For instance:

We knew of one group of executives, many of whom had the practice of taking tranquilizers before a meeting with the president of the company. They claimed that they needed the tranquilizers to help them withstand the angry reactions the president demonstrated when people acted as though they had not thought through the ideas they were presenting. We think they were mistaken. They used the tranquilizers because they were very unsure as to just what he would get angry about or when. If they had had some sense of the standards of performance to which he reacted kindly or harshly, they would have been able to spend less time worrying and more time working.

Most executives believe that gregariousness and participation in many activities at work and in the community, are of great value in their life. In a sense, this belief is true. But we would urge that greater attention needs to be paid to selectivity. Without carefully selecting the matters he gets involved in, the executive faces a drain on his emotional energy that can become quite costly. Selectivity implies the capacity to say "no" without the sense that one has lost esteem. The capacity to say "no" also implies that one is so constituted that he does not need esteem from diffuse persons and activities to enhance his self-worth.

Training one to act and react in the ways discussed may sound like a formidable task. Formidable it is, but perhaps the basic necessity is to overcome the sense of inertia to which we are all susceptible from time to time. While it sounds puritanical, the most elementary step necessary for achieving a mature orientation as an executive is to assume responsibility for one's own development. Basic to this responsibility is the experiencing of one's self in the active mode. As soon as an executive is able to assume responsibility for his own experience and in the course of doing so overcomes the sense of inertia, he is on the road toward experiencing leadership as an adventure in learning.

Fortunately, increasing recognition by executives of the importance of their continuing development has made it possible for them, in conjunction with universities and institute, to examine the dilemmas of leadership and to experiment with new approaches for their resolution.

There are usually different approaches to different problems. Every group or organization needs leadership to make progress with the best answers to correct or mitigate the problems. Therefore, many factions or groups of people become cohesive with the person they admire respecting and wishing to have their concepts adopted in the best interest of their lives.

Such examples in all politics ranging from small businesses, large businesses, local governments to state governments and federal governments are involved to resolve the dissatisfactions that exist. The world continues to change along with the people's thinking and that is what makes the theater of political life.

Different approaches to satisfying the problems are usually in the scheme of a

politician's objective. A politician is the best representative of leadership, for he has to promote and campaign with his plan of action. Thusly, in order for his political career to be successful, he must win the favoritism of the majority of voters. In so doing, he is competing to be the leader of his constituents.
The candidate for a position of leadership has to be admired and respected for all of his past performances and achievements in order to win the office he or she is seeking.

Therefore, a leader has to convince the populous of the value of his platform of ideas, intentions and methods. This requires a life long study to learn a lot of things from psychology to mathematics.

REVELATION #16
INFLATION

This report could possibly be worth hundreds of thousands of dollars to you. All things are possible and some things are more probable than others. It takes an open mind to set a goal to attain wealth. Of course, wealth has a different meaning to various categories of the financial strata they are starting from. For the most part, people simply want to attain more, whether it be bigger incomes, or a large score in capital gains.

It is a fact that some industries will flourish in the next few decades while others will decline in product and growth. No doubt that a deep study of economic factors will result in much confusion because of the complexities involved and the many constantly changing variables that effect changes in our economy.

There are some long-range trends that can be relied upon in spite of the intermediate short-term swings and changes in the economy. One of the long-term trends is that of continued inflation. Nowadays everybody basically conditions themselves to accept the fact that things will continue to become more expensive. If you believe that long term inflation will be the result of our continuing economic system, then you can have definite reason for making certain types of investments, and engaging in particular businesses that will grow in value with the economy and hedge inflation. In short, you can profit from the inflation to protect wealth. All that is required is the knowledge of what type of investments and businesses to engage in that has proven to be extraordinarily profitable during the past years of inflation. This report intends to highlight such information. There are three reasons why higher inflation is inevitable:

Inflation is the government's only way out. The truth is our government is in financial difficulty and the whole world knows it. The debt is so large that raising taxes would not even solve the problem. Since the debt is so huge that the only answer is to reduce its debt through inflation. That means printing up more money. The result of this added money supply reduces the purchasing power value of the dollar, thereby requiring more dollars to buy those same goods.

This inflationary change produces a situation where certain types of investments can benefit while others are disastrous. It is now believed that the inflation rate

169

has a tendency to grow as firmly as any trend can be. This means that America's five most popular "safe" investments are guaranteed losers to inflation. These are CD's, Money Market Funds. Bonds. Treasury Notes. and Mortgage Investments. It is anticipated that the inflation rate will range about four to seven percent a year during the decades to come. This changes everything about investing in these interest-bearing debt instruments. Here is why - If all you get is six or seven percent interest in a "safe" interest bearing investment, you will wind up with only four to five percent after taxes. If inflation is running five to seven percent, it means you are already losing ground. The higher the inflation rate, the more you lose. Just like that in the past a small but significant portion of your wealth is eroded away by virtue of the reduced purchasing power of the dollar. Every month this erosion continues, it multiplies your losses like a "financial cancer" consuming its host. To understand just how costly this can be at only four percent inflation or

the higher purchasing power is slashed by one-third in only ten years at seven percent inflation (where we are heading). You lose half of the value of this accumulated wealth within ten years. Instead of earning money on the money that you have scrimped and saved, it is now diminishing. This trend on this type of investment is to be.

Here is how to immunize you against this loss due to long term inflation. One should realize this and adjust their investment portfolio as they sensibly determine. This does not mean that we advocate withdrawing all your CDs and cash in all the treasuries and money markets. Not quite, for there is some sense to moderate diversification. All the foregoing investments do not represent ownership, only indebtedness by others to you. This is the wrong side of the fence to be standing. In order to profit from inflation, you must place some of your funds into the ownership type of investments, such as common stocks, real estate, precious metals such as coins and gold, and business ownership. We believe the timing is right for this investment concept to stay ahead of inflation over the next decade. It seems as though there were the times in recent history that offer the opportunity to profit from inflation if your investment decisions were well made and will continue to do so.

Higher prices growing slowly even higher become invisible to most as they are expected, but if you study the year-to-year increases, you will realize the galloping cost of living trend. This may afford you a classic chance of a lifetime opportunity, once you realize how to position yourself before a major shift in public perception, one of the great keys to amassing investment wealth.
Corporate bonds are a graveyard. The takeover fever has made it common to see companies deeply in debt takeover fiscally sound companies, resulting in Triple Bonds of a good rated company, exposing themselves to the jeopardy of having

their good bonds turned into "junk bonds" overnight! Be cautious and limit anything where your interest is low and fixed for a long term.

Gold is considered by many to be the world's leading premiere inflation hedge. The most exciting gold bull market will be in gold stocks, not gold bullion or coins. These stocks will be expected to triple during the next decade. It can be viewed as an indirect taxation of your accumulated wealth. There is a definite correlation between the price of oil and gold, as oil prices rise - so does gold or vice versa. It is observed that gold stocks offer an extremely leveraged way to profit from the rise in gold. For example, if bullion increases by just 20 percent, the gold stocks seem to dramatically sour. Some gold stocks can escalate rapidly by 100 percent to 500 percent or possibly more. Advances in mining techniques now allow the best mines to produce a greater output than ever before. It is prudent to stay clear of gold stocks in South Africa or terrorist countries.

The best way to own gold is to have them in your possession (not in stock or a broker's account). Gold coins that are minted in South Africa are 24 carats and one ounce each. They are referred to as bullion coins. They are not legal tender in the

U.S. but that is not the intention to own them. The other popular bullion coin is from Canada called the Maple Leaf also one ounce-24 carat. These should be part of your overall asset inventory portfolio. Gold bars or bullions are not as practical as coins. There are other precious metals such as high silver content that are considered too difficult in volume to store.

If you buy gold coins you have to ascertain that they are solid gold and not clad which is simply fake plating.

Rising inflation can be extremely bullish for some stocks, while a disaster for others. Volatility will reign supreme, with wild gyrations up, down and across various industries. Examine carefully the labor-intensive Dow stocks that could be hit hard by rising wages and inflation. The best strategy is to study the best investments that will get a big boost from inflation, and those special situations that are so inevitable in their own right that profits are virtually locked in.

TAKEOVER SITUATIONS

Takeover stocks can be the winners. The reason is a low dollar makes U.S. companies cheap to the tremendous influx of foreign investors, as well as domestic raiders. With inflation being perpetual and heading higher, the U.S. dollar will be viewed as weak against foreign currencies, like the Japanese yen and German mark. Thus, adding fuel to continue the takeover craze. This can mean a bonanza for you because shares in such firms rise 50 percent to 100 percent or more within months of a takeover announcement. If one will keep abreast of this segment of the securities market, then a windfall can result as you hang onto the coat-tails of the big boys gaining wealth with this technique.

SAFE PROSPECTS.

The Best Opportunity of the Decade for Conservative Investors: Doubling your money in just three to five years sounds too good to be true, especially with a group of safe blue chips. It is exceptional when you consider that most money market funds and CDs are now yielding a mere six to eight percent per year. This is as sure as just about anything you can find in the investment world. And you may earn a lot more than a 100 percent capital gain. It is wise to have a stock broker account with the most creditable firm that you can determine.

REAL ESTATE

If someone advocates that real estate is a bad investment in today's economic climate, you can rest assured that they are short-sighted. The fact is that real estate has always been and always will be the best investment for the long term. During these slow times, one of the best capital gain is simply good farm land. Today, hundreds of thousands of acres of prime farm land across the country are currently severely undervalued - many of them are actually selling for half, or less, of their intrinsic productive values.

The opportunity is enormous in scope. Good buys can double within five years and quadruple within ten years. It is timely to buy such land now, if one is inclined or able to. The reasoning is simple and logical. Due to the combination of advantageous factors, such as relatively low interest rates from anxious sellers, who will accommodate sales with seller financing, and the decline in prices due to a relatively sluggish confused market. Large tracts of farm land are available. Land can almost immediately become productive to cover expenses and there are tax breaks as well as government subsidies now and in the future. You can even lease the land to an outside farming contractor.

Most people do not realize it, but everything we see neatly packaged in the grocery store has come from the farm. It is so basic to the fundamental of survival, not only to the U.S., but the starving world as well. We see the probability of farm land values advancing at least 200 percent faster than the rate of inflation. The farm investment can realistically quadruple the original investment with a five-year period, not to mention the amenities and enjoying the production income additionally received. A study shows that this is the first time in more than 50 years that this kind of situation exists in farm land. In fact, this is the same situation that occurred during the great depression of the early 1930s, when fortunes were amassed in undervalued real estate.

Inflation may be lying dormant at the five percent level, but with world pressures and financial circumstances, it is quite possible to have a ten percent to 15 percent true inflation rate during the 1990s, realizing too that the government will try to present statistics that may reflect less inflation than actual for political reasons. Perhaps the true inflation rate is already suppressed with the claimed five percent or six percent.

Our taxes are increasing, the money supply is continually growing, the national debt is staggering, the U.S. dollar is being forced downward by foreign currencies and markets, and the foreign trade deficit is becoming bigger. Also, these combined factors will cause the price of goods, services and food to rise again and again during the coming future. Note, too, food farm products must rise. The only counterbalance to inflation as far as the individual is concerned, is to offset the burden with properly investing to counter balance in your favor to protect your wealth.

PLATINUM

Inflation and demand for the metal will accelerate platinum prices at a disproportionately higher rate than other precious metals. Industries around the world require this metal, such as electronics and automotive and even dentistry. There is simply no substitute that is as reliable for certain needed applications. And platinum can demand top dollar abreast with inflation. Since 70 percent of the world's share of platinum comes from South Africa, there exists a threat with ever increasing possibilities of supply being cut off. This fact alone can greatly enhance the platinum from other sources. It is a metal product derived from and along with gold mining - so there is a valid reason to explore gold mining stocks. The second largest supplier of platinum is the Soviet Union, and they are taking advantage of keeping the market stable and high whenever the markets command the metal. They let the prices surge and then trickle their supplies into the market at high prices. There is an increased demand in platinum by investors. The British have coined the "British Nobel" which contains one full ounce. This is the first platinum investor coin (to our knowledge) in history. Investors are adding this coin to their portfolio. All factors combined point to the probability of a huge bull market for platinum and possible unprecedented. The upward thrust can prove to reach levels of $3,000 to $4,000 per ounce from the present level.

SILVER

It is predicted that the silver reserves of the world will be largely depleted as time goes on. Industries worldwide will scramble to buy every ounce available, causing the largest silver bull market beyond anything before seen in silver. Russia and China are both striving to produce as large a silver production as possible to capitalize on the anticipated demand. Yet this will not change the shortage. Silver will dramatically double or possibly triple during inflation. The technological eraand revolution will lead to thousands of new electronic products that will require the consumption of millions of ounces of silver. China alone will probably use 500 to 700 million ounces of silver every year for the next decade. This yearly consumption is greater than the amount of silver mined worldwide each year.

Fortunately, and unfortunately, there are a few substitutes for silver. Industries continue to search to no avail. The metal is unique, pure and simple. Regardless, silver will not be replaced in the production of TVs, computers, electric parts, or in photography, and very little can be reclaimed.

COLLECTOR'S COINS

It is now recognized that coins originally printed for numismatic currency purposes have achieved a numismatic value for greater than the face value, strictly based upon the quantity in circulation and originally coined. The dramatic appreciation of the past ten years should convince anybody of the great advantage to deal in coins. There are reputable dealers around the country. An independent investigation should be made of each you may choose to do business with, as we can only report on who is a dealer. Most people are unaware that U.S. rare coins have outperformed every other category of investment over the past 30 years between 1950 to present. Coins of numismatic value outperformed greater than the DOW,

fixed interest-bearing instruments and real estate, including gold bullion. Many coins virtually exploded in value, marking gains of nearly 2000 percent.

BANK FAILURES

U.S. banks are in trouble suffering from hundreds of billions in poor judgment loans made over the years. Other poor judgment lending practices led to domestic defaults on commercial loans and real estate mortgages where conservatism was disregarded. Major Banks now show more liabilities than assets and are burdened additionally with nonproductive foreclosed properties. This kind of imbalance will have to be corrected by the U.S. Government, which cannot allow the banking failures to collapse the whole economy. Therefore, their only way out is to pay off the imbalances with new cash, which means more printed money that, in turn, equates to more fueled inflation. This further clarifies where we are headed with more inflation.

Due to the fast-changing world, in many aspects the U.S. tries to help the needs of different countries. This results to an additional burden to our monetary obligations which in turn requires additional money supply. Due to printing more money, the inflationary problems are worsened because additional paper currency reduces the purchasing power of all existing currency by diluting the value of the dollar. To explain the effect of printing additional money would be taunt amount to adding more water to good soup. The taste may remain acceptable but the nourishment is inadequate and more soup has to be ingested.

WORLD HOT SPOTS

Wars cost money too! Even if fighting has not erupted, a ready military has to be paid for, and in the event of a battle conflict, the costs of fighting a war drain heavily on the chances of any country, especially a super power like the U.S., a policeman for the whole world. At times, war seems inevitable to occur and hard to avoid during the 1990s, considering the circumstances of oil in the Middle East and the unsettled conditions in Central and South Americas. The cost of U.S. protection is paid for by the inflated money supply for more inflation.

OIL STOCKS

Oil may be the highlight of investments for attaining wealth until a substitute is discovered.

MORE SALIENT FACTS OF REINFORCEMENT

There is on the horizon what is now called the beginning of a Mega Bull Market in Gold. Even before the Middle East crisis the signs became indicative. There are several other significant factors that will drive gold to new highs:

1. The fragile banking system in the U.S.

The bias Federal Reserve policy to expand the money supply with less conservatism.

3. The U.S. dollar is headed sharply lower, as worldwide bankers hear the cracks in U.S. financial situations.

The U.S. is becoming a world class debtor for the very first time in history, with an imminent recession on the horizon.

The U.S. foreign debt amounts to $800 billion and continuing to grow at an increase of $100 billion or more per year. This means that accumulated wealth will be leaving the control of this country.

Real estate market has been depressed across the nation; the junk bond market has virtually collapsed from the $200 billion high; savings and loans, commercial banks, insurance companies, large brokerage firms are in financial stress.

Oil prices are soaring and gold prices are usually affected to more parallel with oil. The U.S. in moving closer to the edge of debt liquidation.

Japan is experiencing a stock market reversal similar to the U.S. 1929 stock market crash. They may be tempted to inflate the money supply and expand credit. When an ordinary country inflates the money supply, it confines the problem to that country. However, when the U.S. inflates the money supply, with having the world's largest economy and reserves, it causes a loss of confidence worldwide and shatters the dollar value. The reaction to this happening causes investors, business men, and institutional banks worldwide to seek gold and flee into other currencies.

EMERGING TRENDS

Working mothers will be a continued and growing trend. It is conceivable that greater than 65 percent of mothers will be employed outside the house. This trend was noted in 1976 when 31 percent of mothers were working, and by mid 80s more than 50 percent were working mothers.

Time saving and convenience oriented products and services will be necessary to fit into their busy lifestyles. Just to start to stimulate your ideas, think about services such as day care, catering, grocery deliveries, and so on. Shopping by mail and TVs via the telephone and home computers will be used more extensively than ever before. The advent of credit card ordering will be the norm in spite of interest and lack of deductions on credit cards. The rapid increase of credit card use is indicative of this popular trend. Also, there will be more family households, but smaller families. Research has projected that new family households will be increasing at a faster rate than single households, and the average age of first marriages is becoming younger. The new family unit is expected to be smaller, perhaps with only one or two children. During the ensuing decade, these new families will place a great emphasis on leisure activities, such as entertainment, exercise equipment, and will be health minded. Eating out and quality shopping will be apriority.

Two income families will become the norm and not the exception. The cost of luxuries will be met by two incomes. Vacation, home security systems and luxury cars seem to be within the desired choosing.

We will experience an unprecedented time in history. The aging population wills an impact on many different industries. The Baby Boomers of the post war period (1946 and 1964) are now reaching middle age and the parents are living longer while retiring earlier. The interesting statistics are that during the 1990s the population of 18 to 25 years old will decrease by nearly 12 percent while the number of those over 85 years of age will increase by 50 percent. The 45 to 54 age group will increase by nearly 45 percent and the 75 to 84 age group will increase by some 20 percent.

The impact of statistics will cause the upper middle age and older to control a larger amount of the nation's discretionary income. They will have the financial ability and means to travel, concentrate on health and be active in more activities due to having achieved better health and education. By planning ahead after analyzing these facts and trends, you can fulfill the needs.

THE FEDERAL GOVERNMENT DILEMMA

The Federal Government is in the position where taxing our incomes 90 percent would not be nearly enough to cover the avalanching obligations that are mounting, especially with the Middle East oil problem unsettled and conflict in the winds. In conjunction with the Social Security imbalance, rising military pensions, and pensions of all civil service employees, along with the veteran's disabilities and benefits, these are all unfounded liabilities, yet mandated by law.

Unfortunately, there are only two choices for the politicians, either default on our debts and obligations or secondly, with no other alternative - pay the debt in devalued or inflated dollars created on the printing press. Of the two evils - the politicians will find the inflated money supply the more palatable and avoid political suicide. Hence, inevitably more inflation ahead.

The question then is - will you let this erosion diminish your wealth, or use strategy to enhance your wealth.

THE INFORMATION AGE

Knowledge is Power is a truism that applied especially well to the 1990s, for it is the technological breakthrough that will produce some of the greatest profit opportunities in history quickly approaching a cure for baldness and impotence, regrowth of vital organs, inexpensive solar power, cars made of tough nonmetallic materials, ceramic engines, factory foods, Alaskan peaches, and computer innovations that will dwarf everything accomplished to date. Knowledge will undoubtedly be the tools for greater success. The company or individual knows the greater the size and abundance of opportunities, one can take advantage of. We are on the verge of seeing the conversion of all Europe in a United Europe, the complete collapse of Communism, perhaps legalized drugs, high tech terrorists, major changes in business, unions, socialized medicine and revolutionary changes in every facet of industry and living conditions, both domestically and worldwide.

We can expect to see declining wealth and prestige for many parts of the United States, compared to the Far East and Western Europe. An aging work force and a darker skinned population. It is a new century and the beginning of a new way of life... perhaps very different. The decade of the 90s threatens to be the most fast moving, chaotic unsettled ten years yet witnessed, with pitfalls, traps, and unique wealth opportunities. Knowledge and awareness can keep you from becoming the unfitted victim of change and channel you to attain wealth.

A significant influence in change may come from the weather. Over the past several thousand years, average temperatures around the world have varied only by about two degrees. It is predicted that a warming trend will begin that will raise world temperatures by an average of three times that amount by the next century. If this happens, then farmland value can plunge, but on the other hand commodities can skyrocket. It is interesting to note that this won't be bad everywhere. Alaska and Siberia, for example, can thrive from such a change; the increase of 30 degrees in temperature can create a million and a half acres of fertile cropland in an agreeable climate. Alaskan real estate will skyrocket in such an event. Perhaps parts of Russia and China, which are now dry and barren wastelands, can become as thriving as California's San Joaquin Valley farmland.

New gold mining methods is revitalizing old gold mines with exploratory drilling. Geologists are optimistic about finding the biggest and richest gold field ever discovered in mining history. A new method of gold mining call "block caving" will enable a much less costly system for extracting gold from the earth. It would be like an open pit as far down as 1,000 feet below the surface.

These prospects are real, which will cause the U.S. gold mines to be more powerful and important than those in South Africa or Russia. Such a situation may put the U.S. back on the gold-based currency system.

The wild gyrations of gold prices will result from such a gold strike, which could easily be more than 30 million ounces according to a geologist's study of certain areas near Carlin, Nevada. If one is to invest into buying shares of stock in the gold mining companies in this area, they would realize a large profit upon such a discovery. This type of investment, however, must be realized as speculative and prudence should be exercised when investing in this field. There are about five old mining companies operating in the Carlin, Nevada area. These companies represent the largest profit potential possibly in the last 100 years. Profit is more assured by the fact that even if gold declines, these companies with an advantage of less costlier gold production can cut their prices to meet the market easier than other competition.

The research in computer technology performed in the 70s and 80s is getting ready for the future, for example, a new type of "pacemaker," an anti-intoxication vaccine to prevent drug and alcohol addiction, defeat lung cancer and certain leukemia conditions, and dozens of other medical breakthroughs including voice controlled computers with artificial intelligence.

GEOGRAPHICAL MIGRATIONS

Demographic studies indicate the beginning of a new mass migration. Fifty years ago, a trend started of people moving from the cities to the suburbs. Now, there is a trend of migration from the cities and suburbs to a few selected well-chosen small towns and rural areas. Educated and successful people will live where they want. The factors causing this migration are due to crime-ridden confected, air and water polluted cities, with high taxes and costs of living. Many cities have deteriorated to the point of disgust and they will be abandoned before they will be improved or rebuilt.

Wealthy and substantial people will choose up-and-coming communities with culture, clean industry, and natural beauty where high-tech prosperous companies will locate to places like Pitkin, Colorado; San Juan County, Washington and Albemarle County, Virginia.

Lucrative real estate opportunities will exist ready for pickings for those that choose right and get there first. The higher quality life will be the community asset far from the drug scene, criminals, and pollution.

INVESTING IN THE FUTURE

In the future, we are going to see more global investing. Events such as United Europe and the Far East political changes will cause effects on our importing and exporting markets, strength of the U.S. dollar and fluctuation of interest rates reacting to the financial climate, thusly affecting the returns on our capital investments.

Huge European multinationals will compete with huge U.S. companies. Another development is that the Far Eastern Nations, Japan and the "little dragons," will form a cooperative of their own. With the help of the Chinese, the Far Eastern combine will be very powerful and economically unstoppable. A greater portion of the world's manufacturing will be accomplished in the Far East. Huge fortunes will be made and invested there. More wealth will be created there than anywhere else in the world. Buying shares now in multinationals could be the winning trend from significant profits in the next decade that follows. It is interesting to explore, investing in IBM, Whirlpool, International Paper Co., Shear son Lehman Hutton Inc., Coca Cola Co, and Dow Chemical USA. Many of these companies have paid good dividends - but they should now be viewed for the prospects of stock value appreciation and growth for capital gains. There are many other U.S. companies that will be dealing with the Orient. Already, Taiwan and Japan are becoming the world's leading buyers of gold, stockpiling about ten million ounces a year, about one fourth of the entire world's production. Much of this gold buying is from the U.S. which is somewhat welcomed as an effort to disguise the imbalance of trade between the two countries. Smart investors do not ignore these trends.

Many Americans have already and are continuing to make fortunes out of the "miracle economies" of the Orient. Many more will participate in these fortunes over the next decade. Mutual funds make it relatively easy to profit from these events happening half way around the world, without ever leaving their hometown. Tremendous profits have been made investing in Japanese stocks over the past decade. They have performed magnificently and the Japanese Stock Market is considered one of the best places to invest. There have been low points, but overall it has good future prospects. The growing financial clout of these high growth economies, combined with the U.S. indebtedness, will eventually force the dollar lower as compared to other currencies, thusly an inflationary dollar by a debasement of the dollar.

If you are looking for a growth area in the U.S., think about California. It is the closest Pacific Rim economy growing by leaps and bounds. By all measures, it is able to complete successfully against most foreign producers. If California was a country by itself, it would be one of the richest nations on earth, and getting richer with time. If one is looking to relocate in one of the more productive states, consider looking into California.

THE INFORMATION AGE

The world is truly shrinking. It is now possible to get real time stock market quotes from Europe and the Far East on a screen at a desk in New York or Chicago or Los Angeles. And this is, likewise, simply done by investors in Tokyo or Frankfurt. Real time news from the west affects investment in the east and vice versa. This means that investing globally is not that remote in this new era of time. It means, too, that the choice for diversity is increasing and, therefore, the opportunities are greater as well. It also means that the risks previously associated with foreign investing is reduced, particularly, the lack of timely information. Indeed, the risk now may only be the "missed opportunity.

The attitude of the U.S. consumer was to forget about thrift and the U.S. budget deficit grew faster and larger than the trade deficit. It is these factors that caused the dollar to further erode in purchasing power, inflating the money supply.

As a suggestion, explore the Mutual Funds that are investing into foreign companies as well as the U.S. companies conducting business off shore.

May you have good fortune from your acquired knowledge.

REVELATION #17
CHALLENGE

Every business has many challenges to overcome. It requires a business philosophy of thinking ways to buy pass the obstacles by either going under, thru or above. The answer is to have the determination to think out the different strategies that do exist. Putting your brain power to work is how to proceed. You must have the will to find the best answer and know that you have tried your best. In so doing, it is a good idea to develop a backup plan of action. Winning at challenges is the formula for making progress.

If one is just starting out to venture into the business world, it becomes a prudent act to learn the basics. The challenge of business is as great as the unlimited potential that exists.

In everyday speech, the word "business" does not possess a clear- cut meaning. It is applied rather vaguely to trading and manufacturing occupations as distinguished from the arts and professions.

For the purpose of this report, business may be defined as follows:

"Any occupation in which men, at the risk of loss, seek to make money by producing commodities for sale, or by buying and selling commodities, or by hiring the services of others for utilization at a profit."

Or, more concisely:

"Business is any gainful occupation of which profit is the goal and in which there is risk of loss."

This definition, like most others, fits some cases rather loosely. The farmer, for example, can be said to be in business only in so far as he hires labor and markets his products. As he enlarges his operations and hires more men to work for him, he becomes more and more a businessman because he is more and more concerned with the typically business problems involved in accounting, management, salesmanship and credits. More evidently, the rural storekeeper is in business, for he buys goods in the hope of selling them at a profit and takes the risk of not being able to do so. The clerk in his employ on a salary takes no business risk and is not thinking about profits; hence, strictly speaking, he is not a business man. But he is part of a business machine and is learning how to do business, and so is commonly Thought of as being in business.

The owner of a factory who buys raw materials and hires labor is taking risks and is in business. Some of his employees are workers with tools and machines; they are not directly concerned with business problems, and are not thought of as being in business. Other employees, such as those connected with the purchasing or the sales department may have to assume distinctly business responsibilities; we think of them as being in business.

The bookkeeper, who keeps the records of purchases, sales, output, costs, etc., stands on the border line between business and manual labor. As a mere bookkeeper, he is little more than a machine, but as a potential accountant, able to

improve his employer's system of bookkeeping and to warn him against the danger of increasing costs, he steps into the ranks of businessmen.

In general, the great mass of laborers in manufacturing establishments and on our railroads, whose work is mainly with their hands, are not thought of as businessmen although they are connected with business enterprises. They have no part in the solution of problems involving risk and profit, and are not being trained for such efforts. They have "jobs" in business concerns, but they assume no business responsibilities. On the other hand, every business enterprise employs men upon whom the employer unloads some of his responsibilities. Such men, from cashiers to department managers, are in direct contact with business problems and are regarded as business men even thought their own money is not at risk.

PROFIT AND RISK ARE ESSENTIAL ELEMENTS:

It is not important to decide whether this or that man is in business, but it is important to understand that the work "business" necessarily implies a financial statement upon which the two most important words are profit and loss. If profit is not the goal, then the enterprise is not a business one.

By the profit of a business enterprise is meant the income left over after all the costs and expenses have been paid. A small storekeeper doing a cash business must sell his goods at such prices and in such volume as will enable him to pay the wages of his employees, a fair wage to himself, rent to his landlord, interest on capital invested, and all other expenses. If, at the end of a year, his inventory shows that his stock of goods has not shrunk in value and his outstanding debts are no greater, the increase or decrease of his bank balance during the year will disclose his profit of loss.

PROFIT IS THE GOAL OF BUSINESS:

Later in this report, we shall make a closer study of profit and endeavor to show how profits are earned and against what odds. We shall also see that the struggle for profits which we call business has been a tremendous force in the development of human capacity and in the advancement of civilization.

IMPORTANCE OF MONEY AND PRICE:

At the present time, almost all goods are made to be sold. Specialization and the subdivision of labor have been carried so far that few men produce the things which they themselves consume. Old people recall the days when farmers had little need for cash, for they bought little at the stores. Their own farms produced most of their food and the material for some of their clothing. Today the average farmer in the United States and Canada devotes his energies to the raising of a few crops. He sells these for money and buys much of his food and all his clothes.

So, it happens that money and prices have become very important matters. What men really want are goods or commodities, things which possess what we call value. To get these is the ultimate object of work, but under modern conditions the immediate reward of work is money - with money the things wanted can be purchased. By the price of a thing is meant the amount of money it sells for. Evidently the subject of money and its purchasing power is of great importance to all people.

Since businessmen must figure their profits in money and cannot make a profit unless they sell at a price higher than they bought, it is evident that the forces which control the purchasing power of money must not be ignored by the wide-awake businessman. That is why the subjects of money and prices and credit are so fully treated in modern business texts.

BUSINESS MUST SATISFY HUMAN WANTS:

Although the businessman is seeking to make a profit for himself, he must nevertheless think more of others than of himself. He can earn his profit only through his ability to please others. If he is a trader, he must buy and sell things that people want. He is not a dictator and cannot make people buy his goods merely because he himself thinks they are better than the goods people call for. So, the businessman must study human wants and caprices. He may not approve of their tastes or of their judgment, but if he wishes to make a profit, he must be ruled by them. He may be a manufacturer of shoes and know very well that high heels make walking painful, but he will not let what he knows about physiology and anatomy shape the model of any woman's hoe - unless possibly his wife's.

P. D. Armour once said that he chose to deal in pork because it was an article of food that nearly everybody wanted in some form or other. A business dealing in a commodity that is in universal demand, such as wheat, flour, or cotton cloth, is capable of tremendous development. The profit on each barrel of flour or each gallon of oil may be small, yet the gross profits may run into the millions because of the large sales.

NEW WANTS ARE CONSTANTLY APPEARING:

A remarkable development of machine production characterizes our century. Invention after invention has lowered the costs of production and made possible a great increase in the output of commodities. One man with the aid of modem machinery is able to produce many times what is grandfather could produce fifty or sixty years ago, or his father thirty years ago.

Nevertheless, the efficiency of the machine has not pleased everybody. Some pessimistic souls have seen in its tireless output only the bogey of overproduction, with goods of every description piled high in the manufacturers' warehouses for want of buyers. Such pessimism is based upon a fallacy, namely, the assumption that man has a definite number of wants and that when these are satisfied he will be content.

As a matter of fact, man is a bundle of an infinite number of potential wants. This is one of the important characteristics which distinguish man from all other animals. The wants of all the lower animals are fixed in number, and when these are gratified, the animal is ready for sleep.

But man is insatiable. As his power over nature grows or as his wealth increases, his wants multiply. When poor and half-nourished, his idea of heaven is a place where there is an abundance of roast beef and vegetables. A poor and ignorant Yankee farmer was once asked what he was working for. "Salt pork and sundown," was his illuminating reply. He wanted the day to end so that he might get something to eat and go to bed. If that farmer should inherit a fortune and go to New York City to live, it needs no prophet to foretell what would happen to his taste for salt pork, or that sundown might become a signal for something more exciting than going to bed.

THE OVERPRODUCTION BOGEY:

Fortunately for the business producer, as well as for the man who wishes to sell his services, there is not the slightest possibility that the world will ever be overstocked with the things that men desire. General overproduction is impossible. The word overproduction has no significance in business except when it is applied to a single commodity. The introduction of the automobile brought about a temporary overproduction of horses, wagons and harnesses. The increasing use of gas and electricity led to a glut in the kerosene lamp market. Some people prefer rice to potatoes, both having substantially the same value as food; if this taste for rice should spread rapidly throughout the country, then there might be an overproduction of potatoes.

Since the businessman is striving to make a profit, he must constantly be on his guard, whether he be manufacturer or trader, against overproduction or overstocking in special lines, and seek to anticipate the changes of demand to which the market is susceptible. He need have no fear that any increase in the

production of goods will so satiate the human race that there will be no desire for his services. As production increases, wealth will increase, and the demand for goods will not
only be greater but will also be more varied.

IMPORTANCE OF SALESMANSHIP ANDADVERTISING:

The reader has gathered from the two preceding sections not only how necessary it is for the businessman to study the wants of his customers, but also how important it is that he be able to give them just what they want. To sell a man anything, you must first know what he wants and then be able to convince him that

you can supply it at a reasonable price. In the old days of so-called community production and marketing, when there were no railways or steamships, both production and trading were usually on a small scale and the businessman knew most of his customers personally. Now, however, production and marketing are world affairs. A manufacturer in a Massachusetts village may sell in all the continents of the globe. Thus, it happens that marketing has become one of the most important of business problems. No man can succeed in business if he ignores its difficulties and its perils.

Advertising and salesmanship, which are vital parts of the marketing process, have special importance in any business which deals in something new. The salesman and the advertisement must rouse in people a desire for that new thing. The manufacturer cannot afford to wait for the slow development of his industry that will ensue if he lets the advantages of his product be discovered gradually as a result of its use amount a small number of customers. Hence he makes it known in every possible way, and for that purpose spends money in a fashion which is grandfather fifty years ago would have regarded as astounding extravagance. Salesmanship and advertising are in great part responsible for the spectacular development of all our leading industries, and will continue to open up markets for the new products of tomorrow.

THREE GREAT CLASSES OF BUSINESS:
For our present purpose, it seems proper to divide business into the following three classes:

First - The production and sale of goods. This kind of business is commonly known as "industry," and embraces, besides manufacturing, the extractive industries: mining, agriculture and lumbering. The individual farmer may not be classed as a businessman because of the small scale on which he operates, yet agriculture as a whole is properly regarded as an industry.

Second - The purchase and sale of commodities. By "commodity" is meant anything which has value and is therefore salable. This kind of business embraces all activities of trade and merchandising.

Third - The purchase and sale of services, whether the services of human beings or the uses of material things. This class embraces many different kinds of human activity. The banker may be regarded as a dealer in that valuable but immaterial thing called credit, or we may say, without splitting hairs, that the charge he makes when he discounts a promissory note is for the service the bank renders. A theatrical manager who hires the services of players is a businessman, butthe

players are not. The railroad, steamship, telegraph and telephone companies sell services. The city landlord sells to his tenant the right to use an apartment; strictly speaking, he is selling a service.

This use of the word "service" may seem technical to the reader, but it is not difficult to understand. A man renders you a service whenever he aids you in getting what you want. Any man, who makes a "business" of rendering services to others and is looking for a profit and taking a risk, is in business.

THE PROFESSIONS:

There are many gainful occupations that are not classed as business for the reason that profit-making is not their primary aim. The most important of these are the professions and the arts. The three best known professions are law, medicine and theology, often referred to as the learned professions. In recent years, other callings have acquired a claim to rank as professions, as for example, engineering and architecture.

A professional man finds his reward not merely in the money he earns, which comes to him usually in fees and retainers, but in his love of the work and his sense of its dignity and importance, in his personal independence, in the distinction he achieves because of his skill and intelligence and the respect he commands from his colleagues.

The professions differ from business occupations in that they have definite codes of ethics which prescribe and limit the conduct of practitioners in the various contingencies likely to arise. It was considered at one time in the past for a professional man to advertise, however business world has changed because of the global communication is now a common practice to advertise and does not have to depend upon notoriety or word of mouth.

Members of some of the professions, however, are wise if they make a study of business problems. Many of our most successful lawyers, for example, are constantly occupied with cases which cannot be thoroughly understood by one who is ignorant of business principles and customs. The engineer or the architect who knows nothing of corporation finance or business law, or cost finding will never rise to the highest rank in his profession.

IS BUSINESS A PROFESSION?

If we analyze the so- called learned professions, we find them distinguished by these two characteristics: first, in their practice, brains are far more important than technique or manual skill; second, education in certain sciences is essential to success. No calling deserves to be called a profession if its tasks and problems are so simple as to be within the grasp of any man of ordinary ability and education.

The problems of a profession can be correctly solved only by a man who has had thorough training in science.

The physician, for example, apart from is knowledge of "material media," must be well grounded in anatomy, physiology, chemistry and bacteriology. Psychology should be added to this list. The well-trained lawyer should be disciplined in the sciences of pure logic and of jurisprudence, in ethics, in the evolution of law and in the theories that explain and justify legal doctrines. When the physician or lawyer is not thus trained, the young lawyer merely knowing the statutes and procedure of his jurisdiction, and the young physician knowing only drugs and symptoms, both are empiricists and do not deserve to be called professional men.

Certain business callings in recent years have risen into the professional ranks. Some years ago, few public accountants would have claimed that their occupation was professional in character. The accountant was then often referred to as a "bookkeeper out of a job." But the really expert accountants knew very well that their tasks cannot be performed by the ordinary bookkeeper, that the accountant cannot do his best work unless he knows a great deal about the business man's problems.

It has been largely because of the accountant's belief in the high character of their work that University Schools of Commerce train men in all the sciences underlying business as well as in the theory and practice of accounting. For the same reason, many states have passed laws providing that no man shall style himself a "certified public accountant" until he has successfully passed examinations conducted by the state authorities. In view of these conditions, the accountant may fairly claim that his calling has acquired professional standing.

Other business occupations, notably advertising and the work of the credit man are rapidly moving in the same upward direction. Entrance into these callings is not yet guarded by statute, but many of the leaders already realize the need for superior training, and Schools of Commerce are doing their best to supply it.

WHAT CONSTITUTES SUCCESS IN BUSINESS?

Since profit is admittedly the aim of business, it would logically follow that a businessman's success can be measured only by the amount of money he makes. As a general statement this is perfectly true, yet erroneous inferences and implications are quite possible.

The manager of a New York City bank may raise the net earnings of his bank by one million dollars a year and yet not really be as successful as a small country banker who increases his bank's revenue by only ten thousand dollars a year. In the same way, the business of a city merchant may annually expand by a million dollars, and yet he may be properly regarded as less successful than a small country merchant whose volume of business is increasing at the rate of only ten thousand dollars a year. The city banker and merchant have practically unlimited opportunities of expansion, while the country banker and merchant are hemmed in by a narrow environment. The latter may have done all that could be done to increase business, keep down costs, and increase net revenues.

Suppose that two brothers go into business, one going to the city, the other preferring to remain in the home town. The one in the city has a fortune of a million dollars at the end of twenty years, while the country brother has accumulated only fifty thousand dollars. It would be unfair to conclude that one is twenty times more successful than the other. We must not forget that while profit is the aim of business, men are influenced by many other motives when they choose a business or a location. Money is the tangible reward of successful business, but money is not everything worthwhile in life.

To judge wisely, therefore of a man's success in business, we must know: First, has he accomplished what he set out to do? Second, has the volume of his business been as large as was warranted by its location? And, third, has its management been so sound that profits have been as large as could reasonably be expected?

DIGNITY AND IMPORTANCE OF BUSINESS:

To people who are not well -read in history, it may seem strange that no author should think it necessary to prove that business is an important and worthy occupation. To them it will seem perfectly obvious that business is both important and worthy. Only a generation ago, however, if a boy chose to be a lawyer or a doctor or a preacher, his parents took pride in the fact, and viewed with more or less unconscious pity those friends whose sons had gone into business.

In Europe many years ago, business was thought something altogether too vulgar to engage the attention of the nobility, and two thousand years ago, when business was comparatively simple, especially among the Greeks and Romans, business matters were attended to either by slaves or by a class of citizens much despised. To devote one's life merely to the making of money was deemed ignoble and unworthy. How much finer to be an orator, a warrior, a poet, a painter or a sculptor!

It would be a waste of time to make comparisons and try to determine whether one calling is nobler than another. Men are born into the world with different capacities, and it should be the duty and ambition of each to do that work which he can do best, and to put all his soul into it, whether he write poetry, paint pictures, play the violin, or buy and sell groceries. Then each will deserve respect and honor since each is rendering a community service.

When we consider that the rendering of services to humanity is an essential element of business, and that no business can long be successful if it fails to render such service, we must admit that a great businessman deserves honor and respect just as does a great lawyer or physician. The adjective "commercial" cannot be justly used to imply reproach or contempt. To be sure, business may be done in dishonorable fashion. There may be lying, cheating, misrepresentation. But these evils are also founding the professions. In the long run, both in the professions and in business, they work against great success. Business as a calling cannot be indicted because some grocer uses loaded scales or some broker deceives trusting investors.

Business has made our civilization possible. If we should return to the methods of business in vogue even a few centuries ago, our national wealth would dwindle and disappear. The farmers' great markets would vanish and production would come to a standstill. The debt society owes to business is so obvious and so great that there should be no excuse for an author to devote a page to a discussion of this sort. But there is an excuse. It is the ignorant and often vicious hostility to business frequently manifested, and the untrue assumption that our wealth is wholly the creation of farmers and factory workers.

HOW BUSINESS CREATES WEALTH:

History shows that nations grow rich and their peoples enjoy a high degree of comfort and culture only where the principal occupations are manufacturing and trade. No principally pastoral or agricultural nation has accumulated great wealth or distributed the conveniences of civilization widely among its people. The reason for this state of affairs is a simple one - agriculture does not produce savings in the large amounts needed to provide capital.

Without the large amounts of capital savings accumulated are a manufacturing or trading nation, the really notable technological advances do not get made. It takes money, and a lot of it, to perfect new machines and processes - to take the discoveries of science or the happy inspiration of inventive genius, and from these to perfect the process which gives a new product to the world, or which converts a former luxury into a common article of convenience. Even where it is a simple matter of bringing a widely desired product from another land, it takes capital to build ships, to hire and maintain crews, and to develop the instruments and machines for making navigation safer and swifter.

As a humble example of what capital and machines can accomplish, take the familiar table companion, black pepper - unobtrusively present in the household, free on the counter of the cheapest restaurant. Most people would be surprised to learn that not too long-ago pepper was so rare that bitter wars were fought for the possession of the pepper lands. Pepper was high on the list of objectives that lured Columbus to set his course for the Indies. The pepper carried back to Europe on the only surviving ship of Magellan's fleet paid for all the lost ships and yielded a profit besides. Men with capital to invest launched more ships, developed steamships to replace the slower clippers, and established the network of wholesale importers and retail outlets that have made pepper as plentiful and inexpensive as anything grown in the local community.

INVENTIONS AND THEIR ECONOMIC TIMING:
The world rightly reveres its great inventors and discoverers. Too much honor can scarcely be paid to these men of genius. Nevertheless, the inventor is helpless unless
the   times are ripe to receive his discoveries, and unless other men are ready to risk the funds necessary to exploit his ideas and promote their acceptance. That is why so many important inventions have had to be discovered and rediscovered, not once, but many times. It may take decades or even centuries to bring an invention to its commercial fruition.
The case of Hero of Alexandria, who lived in the second century before Christ, will illustrate the point. Here invented not only one but two steam engines - a primitive model of a steam reaction turbine and an equally primitive pressure engine.
Alexandria was a great city, wealthy and enterprising, and a center for scientific research, but the inventions of Hero went unrecognized. Men were not looking for steam power in an age of abundant slave labor.
Neither was the world ready for the steam engine in 1601, when Giovanni Della Porta published his plan for one. Just before the century ended, however, an Englishman, Thomas Savery, obtained a patent for a water-raising engine, powered by steam. England, unlike Egypt and Italy, had coal mines from which unwanted water had to be pumped, necessity once again mothered invention. Still, acceptance was slow; less than a half-dozen steam engines were in actual service in England prior to 1790. It took the genius of James Watt to show England how efficiently

the machine could replace hand tools. Once the demonstration was understood, England changed from an agricultural to an industrial nation, from handicrafts to mass production and worldwide commerce.

BUSINESS LIMITATIONS UPON INVENTION:
Not only does the inventor stand in need of other men's capital savings for the funds required to develop and promote his discovery, but he must also consider the full picture of what his invention may involve as a business venture. If he sets up his own company to produce and market his discovery, it will need capital for plant, personnel and equipment. If he sells his patent to an existing company, that company must decide whether it can supply the demand which the invention will create, or whether it must expand, and how much. If the company decides against expansion, and the invention is wanted by more customers than the company can take care of with its present plant and capitalization, competitors will soon be in the field, with "improved" models to sell.

This matter of considering public demand for an invention can be very serious. It must be kept in view when an investor or a research department is estimating the cost of promoting a new idea. Research creates wealth, but experience shows that a capital investment is required larger than the wealth created. Customers must be taken care of - this is a major law of business; but meeting their demand calls for a capital investment that may mount high. Actually, under present conditions, it is a rare inventor who is able to finance the development of his invention and then finance the company that must be set up to supply the demand his invention may create. Nor can any company manufacture and market all the products and product improvements that an alert research department is able to devise; to try to do so, would hopelessly dissipate its energies and capital. It must concentrate on a few.

OPPORTUNITIES FOR THE BUSINESS EXECUTIVE:
None of the many changes taking place in the world's economic life appears likely to diminish the opportunities open to the man gifted with executive ability and trained in business administration. He is wanted everywhere - in communistic Russia, in socialistic Sweden, in democratic America. The complexities of machine production have only increased the demand for his services.

What is important is the attitude of the young man in business and the vision that animates his efforts. Is his present work merely a "job" to him - a disagreeable routine in which he sees no future? The typical man with a "job" is very much given to thinking that he is overworked and underpaid, and to complaining about the big salaries paid to the men above him.

The trouble with men of this kind (unfortunately, they are numerous), is that they do not know what business means, cannot see the possibilities in their work nor how to make it help their progress upward. There is a sense in which every business

191

"job" is a gold mine. The man, who works for the gold in the job rather than for the money in the pay envelope, is the fellow who gets on. He knows that he is learning the A, B, C's of business, no matter how humble his work.

But the man who starts low down the ladder need not be a drudge all his days. Business is much more than a "job"; it is, in reality, a fascinating game. Analyze any popular game - baseball, tennis or golf - and you will f*md that there is a great deal of downright work performed in each. It would be called work if performed outside the game. What turns all this effort into a pleasure? Three circumstances appear to explain the change: First, the number of obstacles in the way of successful play; second, the joy the human animal takes in triumphing over obstacles, particularly if at the same time he proves himself the better fellow; third, the freakish behavior of the goddess of chance, which adds surprise to the game at every tum.

All these game elements are found in business, and your real businessman, if he is in good health, gets as much pleasure out of his day's "work" as he ever did out of any game he played as a boy. That is why he is so often tempted to stay in active business too long, when the need for staying has passed.

Add to these considerations the fact that business, if rightly pursued, not only makes for personal happiness but mightily aids the progress of society. It conceives most of the ideas which make for better living and puts these ideas into practical form.

Business supplies the needs and comforts of peacetime and the munitions to defend the nation in time of war. Pursued with intelligence and integrity, business is worthy of the best talents of any man.

Put your talent to work with our best wishes!

REVELATION #18

CAPITAL

Capital is the heart of any business. After establishing the amount required whether it is starting capital of a new business or expansion of an existing business, or capital for increased inventory, there are many approaches to raising business capital.

In this Revelation, we are attempting to introduce a few basic approaches. More detailed information should be sort out from specialist in the field of finance or you can obtain a copy of our published folio originally written and copyrighted in 1956. This publication is kept updated. It is available from our Wealth Society. The purpose of Capital is to make money with money and to learn the in depth information.

WHERE DOES BUSINESS GET ITS CAPITAL?

Capital comes either from the savings of others, as made available through lending institutions, or it comes from the profits accumulated by a going concern. Thus, profit is actually the life-blood of business and of business expansion. In the words of Webster, capital is "an aggregation of economic goods used to promote the production of other goods, instead of being valuable solely for purposes of immediate enjoyment." Capital savings, borrowed from others or accumulated from operating profits, fathers new enterprises or expands old ones, and so creates ever-widening employment and wealth.

In a democracy, where enterprise may be regulated but is essentially free, capital savings are voluntary. Business companies set aside a part of their operating profits as "surplus", other parts for "depreciation" and "maintenance." The precise amounts are at their own discretion. In countries where business enterprise is not free but is wholly directed by the government, capital savings may be forced not only on business but also on the population as a whole.

WHY BUSINESS NEEDS MORE CAPITAL, AND STILL MORE:

It is the advent of the machine that has compelled business to seek larger amounts of capital than were ever thought necessary before. The Age of the machine was only in its infancy when the thirteen colonies formed the United States of America.

There were few factories, few good roads, no railroads nor steamships, very little machinery of any sort. Newspapers were broadsheets printed on hand presses and read by candle light. It was still true, as men had always believed, that "labor is the source of all wealth."

The progress of the Machine Age changed all that. Economists estimate that the electric power now generated in the United States does the work of half a billion men working eight hours a day - many times the entire working population of the nation. Machines do almost anything, from carrying a message across the seven seas at incredible speed to building a battleship in the fewest possible operations. Machines, and the science back of them, are now the true source of wealth.

But machines cost money, can be had only if the business has the necessary capital. At one point in time, a neighborhood grocery store could be equipped with simple shelving and counters, and stocked on a relatively small capital investment. Today, even the small store must be equipped with refrigerators, frozen food bins, and preferably, modern display cases of several types. Electric grinders improved weighing machines and cash registers are other items that must be bought. Papa and Mama, with the aid of the kids, may still run the store as of before but the store is considerably different - and more expensive. Stocks are more varied.

BUT CAPITAL IS NOT EVERYTHING:

In and of itself, capital is inert and sterile. It may be an indispensable means, but it remains only a means, requiring the direction of human intelligence and enterprise. Two business men may start out with the same amounts of capital, but one may fritter his away in unprofitable by paths, missing the main highway of success. That is why, despite the large amounts of capital needed in many industries, there is always room for the man imbued with the spirit of enterprise. New machines and new applications of science may close some doors because of their initial expensiveness, but they open other doors through the by-products and accessories they create.

The truth that capital without enterprise is dead may be illustrated from the curious case of India, much of whose capital is in the primitive form of cattle. As every schoolboy wrestling with Latin knows, the word "capital" is derived from the Latin "caput," meaning head, and referring especially to heads of cattle. In earlier ages, cattle were wealth and used as money. To know how wealthy a man was you merely counted cattle.

At one point in time, India, according to this primitive standard, should be wealthy, for it has more cattle than the next five or six cattle- holding countries - more than three times as many as the United States, more than ten times as many as its neighbor to the east, China. One would expect to find a most profitable dairy and meat industry in India. But no, the Hindu religion makes the cow a sacred animal, to be venerated but not butchered. The cattle are left undeveloped and produce little milk, and that low in fat content. The result is that Indian consumption, both of milk and of beef, is the lowest of any large population, and the Indus of India are perhaps the most poorly nourished of any people in the world. Moreover, the expense of maintaining their useless herds of cattle is keeping the Indians poor. Most people, who have tried to raise capital, have failed. I will tell you that for openers they failed because they were selling profit and loss statements, break even projections and tax benefits. They were selling something the risk capital investor (and particularly the small one) is not really interested in. Every book, article and report we have ever seen about raising capital talks about preparing a prospectus. Presenting the potential investor with an arm full of facts, figures, statistics and numbers, numbers, numbers till they are coming out of the prospect's ears. We never used a formal prospectus, never had break even charts, used no five-year projections, and, above all, stayed away from pages full of numbers and statistics, yet I've always been successful. In raising capital. My business was selling dream fulfillment. We were selling something that the prospective investor could understand. Action, excitement, and the potential for fabulous returns on his investment. This is the dream of the small investor. Be wants to be part of something that is moving and growing, to get in the game and play, not sit on the sidelines and read box scores.

So, when you decide it is time to rise from $5,000 to $50,000 for your new business, remember that above all you will be selling participation in a dream, a way to the top, with excitement and action along the way. If you present your offer in those terms, you can raise the money you need at once and even have investors competing to put up their money.

ANSWER SOME ADS YOURSELF:

The first thing you should do, if you have never tried to raise capital, is to answer some local ads seeking capital. See how they approach you; what they offer as an inducement to invest; what type of close they use to get the money. Ask them questions, and see how well prepared they are to answer them (this will prepare you for the questions you will be asked); see what kind of contracts or agreements they offer you, etc. First, answer ads from individuals seeking capital. Then after you have seen how they do it, answer some ads offering franchises. Here you will find a different and more tempting approach. You will see and understand the difference in raising capital between the amateurs and experts.

MY SYSTEM IS BASED ON IMMEDIATE PARTICIPATION:

My system, like that of franchise offers, is based on action and immediate participation. The reason that I was able to meet a total stranger and have him writing a check for $50,000 in a few hours, is that we developed my presentation so he or she is participating in the business venture, even before they have invested a dime.

By using this method, we convinced the potential investor that he is not investing in a property that may or may not contain gold; he is convinced he is in on the ground floor of an operating gold mine. And, that with or without him, the gold is going to come out of the ground. Thus, he sees his dream before him, in operation, and all he has to do is climb on the bandwagon. This is the key to raising capital from small investors. Give them excitement, involvement, and let them smell the gold... they will do the rest themselves.

I'M NOT DISCUSSING SWINDLES:

In case you think that this is the system that is used to swindle people, you are right, it often is. But we are assuming that you have a legitimate proposition that only requires capital to get it into operation. There is nothing wrong with selling it to investors as an exciting and potentially fortune building opportunity, rather than as a set of figures on some pieces of paper.

People who have invested in my offers have made millions from them. Sure, some have lost money, but the fault was in their perceptions and operations, not in the proposition. Keep in mind that U.S. Steel was almost 100% blue sky stock when it was formed, that J. Paul Getty got his first lease by having a banker bid for him to scare away the other bidders on the lease; that Lord Thompson of Fleet Street who recently died as one of the world's richest men got his start by conning a radio station in Canada out of a $50 radio tube he needed to get a one lung station on the air··.his first property, and he died with communications holdings all over the earth.

Business is risk, and if you don't want to gamble, don't invest in business. The first people who backed Henry Ford, Coca Cola, the Wright Brothers, Thomas Edison, Sears and Roebuck, Xerox all made millions. Those who thought the basic ideas behind these business endeavors were not viable lost the millions others made.

So, go into your business with the knowledge that the first investors have the opportunity to make thousands on every initial dollar they invest if you are successful, and, in essence, you are doing them the biggest favor anyone will ever offer them by letting them in on the action.

Remember, Colonel Sanders was giving away franchises for a few dollars when he started. McDonalds and Burger King started with one hamburger stand and you could have gotten a franchise for peanuts at the start. Your one-horse wagon can also turn into a super-jet if you are successful. So, don't be bashful or unsure about offering people opportunity. It's what made this country.

PREPARING YOUR OFFERING PACKAGE:

The first step in raising capital is to prepare an offer, and put it in a saleable package. The package should consist of the following:

A. The Business Structure

The Marketing Plan

The Operating Plan

The Financial Plan

These four segments make up your package, and give the potential investor everything he needs to make a decision.

THE BUSINESS STRUCTURE:

The best, and really only suitable business structure for raising capital is the corporation. It offers many advantages to you as the entrepreneur and to the potential investor as well. In your case, it offers you the opportunity to have a company put into existence for a modest investment. You incorporate and test the papers, and you have a business entity. You have stock to offer the investor at once. You can see and feel the stock certificates and read the charter and by-laws. This gives you a feeling of getting something for your money at once. Everyone knows that stock can go way up in value, and even make one rich. You don't have to say this, they already know this.

It offers the investor protection against losses of anything other than what he invests. He does not risk his other assets as he would in a partnership. It offers tax advantages with the use of Sub-Chapter S, and Rule 1244 corporations. He can get medical and pension benefits that are deductible to the corporation as business expenses, but not taxable to him as income.

It is not my purpose here to give a lesson in corporation structure and benefits; you can get this information from a good CPA and you should have one before you set out to raise capital.

FLOATING A SMALL STOCK ISSUE:

The trickiest part of capital rising is the selling of stock in a company that has no business history. You must first clear your offering with the Securities and Exchange Commission, and then with the states you intend to offer the stock for sale in, and finally comply with any local regulations regarding such sales.

It is not easy nor is it particularly an efficient way to raise capital, since sales and promotion costs are invariably quite high, and results are often disappointing. But it can be, and has been done. Jimmy Ling, who started as an electrical contractor working out of a truck, incorporated in Texas, and cleared a stock offering, and sold shares in a booth at the State Fair. The result of this initial offering was Ling- Tempco-Vought, one of the 50 largest corporations in the United States, so it can be done.

When you decide to float a small stock or security issue to raise capital, your first decision has to be what kind of stock or security are you going to offer. In general, there are three types: common stock (the ownership and basic risk of the business); preferred stock (guaranteed return; can participate in profits and has superior rights to assets in case of liquidation); debenture or indentured bonds (can be issued in various manners; debentures are without security other than company potential income; indentures are secured by physical assets of the company).

Most people understand common stock. It needs no explaining to the average investor; he's buying a share of ownership in the company, and expects to share in the profits, if any. This is the simplest form of equity to market because it is so common. In floating a small issue, this needs less detailed explanation, particularly if you are going after relatively unsophisticated investors. Preferred stock is the widows and orphans gamble. It usually carries a set of percentage of return, is cumulative (that is, if dividends on preferred are passed over because business is bad, they accumulate and no dividend can be paid on common stock until all accumulations are cleared on the preferred). They can be participating or non-participating, which means they can get an extra dividend along with the common (usually after a maximum dividend has been paid common; i.e., if the common dividend is $2 a share, then everything over $2 would be share and share alike with preferred, anything under $2 would not be shared), and they can be voting or non-voting (usually non-voting unless there is a missed dividend, then voting rights may be granted).

The bonds (debentures or indentures) can also take several forms. They have the advantage of obtaining capital without dilution of earnings by issuing more stock. They give the buyer a fixed return on his investment. Indenture bonds are secured by real estate (called mortgage bonds) or by equipment and fixtures (secured by trust certificates on the equipment), while debentures are only secured by the general credit of the company. In starting a new company, unless you plan to use proceeds to purchase real estate and major items of equipment, the indenture bond is not practical.

The sweetener to a bond offering can be a convertibility option. The holder can collect his fixed interest while he sees how the company is doing, and then at a future time (usually a limit stated on the bond), he can convert the bond into common or preferred stock. This in effect gives him some security in the initial phases of the operation, and also gives him the chance to participate in eventual success.
Another sweetener for a bond buyer can be warrants attached to each bond. There are simply options to buy common stock at a stated figure, usually within a given time limit (although some warrants are issued in perpetuity). This, in general, gives him the same right as a convertible; but he must pay extra for the stock, and his bond cannot be converted.

The techniques of the various securities and what the best-selling type would be is a matter of serious investigation. You should discuss the problem with your banker, attorney, and accountant, and get some advice from a mortgage banker if possible. If you are going to market the issue yourself, you'll want the type of security or stock that wills less with the least resistance. The problems of bond issues are ever greater, and suffice it to say that the new business planning to float its own stock issue should stay with straight common stock. It is what people understand, and when selling it, you don't have to explain some trick esoteric financing scheme that will only confuse your prospects.

When you decide to proceed with floating your own stock issue, you will immediately have to contact the Securities and Exchange Commission in your area (by checking the phone book of the nearest big city) about notification or filing of your offer. For the new enterprise or small business attempting to float and sell their own stock issues there are four courses open which make sense. They are the intra-state offer, which involves selling up to $500,000 worth of stock in your company to residents of your state only. This offer does not require filing, but only notification of the SEC of intended sale.

The major problem with intra-state offers is that if any buyers of the stock were to sell that stock to someone outside that state within a year of purchase date, the offer no longer qualifies as intra-state, but becomes an inter-state offer which requires filing with the SEC. Therefore, an intra-state offer needs some sort of escrow agreement from stock buyers that they will hold their stock for at least 12 months before they sell it to someone outside their domicile state.

The second method of selling stock yourself is under the so-called Rule 257, which limits an offer to $50,000 that is usually sold locally. This requires only a notification to the SEC and does not require filing a prospectus the seller intends to use in selling his stock. However, Rule 257 is not open to new enterprises. It is only available to established businesses with an earnings record. Obviously, Rule 257 is a rather simple way to raise $50,000 if you have an operating business with an earnings history.

The third method of floating your own stock issue is to go what is termed the Regulation a route. Regulation issues are limited to $500,000. You fill out a set of forms telling the SEC who you are and what you intend to sell, and then file this as a notification of intended sale. This is to be filed at least 10 days prior to making the offering. If the SEC does not challenge the offer, the usual proceeding is to get a "no action letter" from the regional office of the SEC where your materials were filed. This is simply a letter stating the SEC will not stop sales at the present time, but they reserve the right to do so in the future, and that buyers of the stock will have the right to challenge the validity of the Reg. An offering and demand their money back on the basis the offering required a full filing.

The sticky point in filing a Regulation a notification with the SEC will be with your prospectus. In your prospectus, you will have to tell them the truth, the whole truth, and nothing but the truth or the SEC will refuse to let you go ahead with the stock sale. In general, this means in a new enterprise, you must state emphatically that there are no earnings that you are doing no business, that there is risk involved, etc. There is little harm in saying this and the sale of stock in a new enterprise is a "ground floor syndrome proposition." People like to get in on the ground floor and are aware there is risk involved. So, by stating this in the prospectus you are doing little to harm your chances of sale. The main thing to avoid is any promises of great return in a short period of time by purchasing this stock or any unrealistic statements that the prospect can't lose, and so forth.

PREPARING A STOCK SALES CAMPAIGN:

Our first step is to be sure you are on firm legal ground. Have your attorney clear your proposed offering with the SEC, or do it yourself. You can contact the nearest regional office, and find out what avenues are open to you. They will tell you what you have to do and what must be filed. Rules for small stock issues are changing all the time, becoming more liberal in some cases, so find out all you can from them, then pick the best way to go and launch your campaign.

Selling stock, like selling any other product, requires careful preparation, market analysis, a sales pitch, publicity, advertising, training, a time schedule, and a sales goal. When you sit down to decide how you are going to sell this stock, you must first analyze your available manpower. Remember this; the only people entitled to sell stock in a corporation are officers of the corporation or licensed security dealers. You can't hire salesmen off the street or have housewives going door-to-door selling stock. If you line up some licensed security salesmen to help, well and good. If not, you will have to divide the sales work up among the officers of the corporation.

In order to set realistic goals for each individual who will be selling stock, it will be necessary to sit down and figure out the approximate size of the prospect list you are going to need in order to realistically reach the goal you have set. As a rule of thumb, experienced security salesmen will tell you that you need approximately twenty suspects to equal one prospect, and four prospects to equal one customer. And this is selling recognized security of well-known companies on major exchanges. To sell stock in a new company with no earnings record and no national reputation, it should require something larger of a prospect list than what the average stock salesman uses. But, you have an advantage starting, in that you and your associates can sit down and make a list of people that you know who would be potential buyers of stock in your company simply through personal contact. This then will be your first step. You and your associates sit down and make out what

will be called a F.A.R. list. This means friends, acquaintances, and relatives. This is the list used by all insurance salesmen, security salesmen, and others who are starting out in the field and it is used as their initial prospect list. The length and potential of the
F.A.R. Will tell you approximately how much larger a prospect list you are going to need in order to complete your projected sales goal.

If your stock issue is $500,000, and this is your sales goal, then you figure your F.A.R. list will absorb half of that amount, this leaves $ 250,000 to sell to a general suspect list. If you consider $2500 as your average unit of sales, then this means you will need approximately 100 customers in order to complete your sales goal. Working backward from the formula security salesmen use, you need 400 prospects (a prospect is somebody who will submit to an interview and hear your sales pitch), and to obtain the 400 prospects, you will need a suspect list of twenty times that amount or $8,000 names. These names can be obtained in several ways. First, you make a list of business and professional men in your own community or your own general area and total that up as your suspect list. As a rule, these people are investors in stock in one kind or another; and they have the available funds to invest in others. Next, you can contact a mailing list broker and get lists (costs of list of names) of known stockholders, investors, and speculators in your area. These will be obtained from compiled lists of subscribers to stock market information services, magazines such as Forbes, Baron's and other financial publications, buyers of books on investing and other such logical sources.

ORGANIZING YOUR LISTS:
When you have all your lists on hand, organize them into communities and neighborhoods so that when you start your telephone sales campaign, you will be setting up appointments in small areas. This will make calls on prospects much easier.

DEVELOPING THE SALES PITCH:
When you obtain an interview with a prospect, you will have to have a definite, organized sales presentation in order to interest him in participating in your stock offering. In doing this, you will have to recognize that you will be talking to the stock trader. He is well informed about stock investing, recognizes risk potential, and his interest is simply in the growth factor of your company. In other words, he's interested in speculating in stock, not investing in it. In presenting your case to the trader, you will have to convince him that there is a good growth factor in your company. In other words, he's interested in speculating in stock, not investing in it. In presenting your case to the trader, you will have to convince him

that there is a good growth factor in your company and that the stock will be worth considerably more than he is going to pay for it in a relatively short time. You should recognize at the outset, he knows more about the market than you do and, therefore, you should stick strictly to the growth potential of your company, its market, and the methods of operation that are going to make it grow. Stay away from any discussion with him about further types of financing issuing convertibles, warrants, letter stock, etc. He will chunk in a pretty fair size of money if he is convinced the growth factor is there.

GETTING FAVORABLE PUBLICITY:
The first step is to hire a competent man or woman who will help you plan and promote a public relations campaign that will coincide with your stock selling effort. Keep in mind that advertising is strictly limited to the name of your company, the amount you are offering, and that a prospectus is available. This is the rule of the SEC, and any flamboyant type of advertising where you are promising huge profits, get rich quick or anything of that nature, or even inferring that your company is in a great growth situation and a highly profitable investment will bring the SEC down on you like a ton of bricks. So, advertising is simply done to spread the word in the financial community that the stock is available, and serves little useful purpose in selling stock to the public at large. Therefore, your public relations campaign is really your only advertising campaign.
In getting media exposure, the first logical step is to hold an open house, grand opening or other type of function that will bring the press, cameramen and city dignitaries to your new factory, offices, headquarters, etc. This is usually in the form of a combined press and cocktail party in which invited guests can participate in the freebees and in so doing more or less obligate themselves to give you a generous amount of publicity.

Your major publicity campaign efforts would tie in precisely with the opening of your stock selling campaign. This puts your company name in front of the suspects of prospects you have listed, and makes it a good deal easier to obtain interviews for the purposes of selling stock. A skillful public relations campaign can really be the difference of a successful and unsuccessful effort in reaching your ultimate stock sales goal. So, work very carefully on the plans and see to it that they are followed through to the letter.
THE SHELL CORPORATION:
Our system was to form a shell corporation. One that was duly incorporated by the state, and entitled to do business, but no specific type of business was named. We spent a good deal of time working up impressive names for my corporations. Things like Packard- Sterling; Prince & Barons; International Security Funding and the like. This was to give the investor something to write home about. He was a

director or Vice-President of Prince and Barons, Ltd.; Packard Sterling. It's part of the dream. If you offer him stock in Greasy Spoon, Inc., instead of International Halls of Leicester (a fish and chips parlor), you lose something of the dream. So, don't stand short on the name. Even if you don't raise capital on your first go, you've still got a corporation with an impressive name to try again.

We used a simple system to develop impressive names for the companies. We took words that sounded impressive and put them on a list. Then when we needed a name, we would make combinations of the words and pick one that sounded right for what we wanted.

USE PROFESSIONAL HELP:

Always try to use professional help in developing your offer. A good accountant and an attorney are going to save you much more than they cost. We always used them to form my corporations, making each of them a shareholder, and this assured me that I, they and the investor would have the best set up possible for the program we were developing.

A WORD ABOUT PARTNERSHIPS:

Partnerships are seldom good business structures for a new enterprise. There are too many intangibles ahead, and where you have two decision makers, you have problems. Even in the best run businesses, partnerships are difficult, and for new businesses they are almost suicide. It invites participation of wives or husbands of partners, their relatives, and almost constant friction about how the operation should be run.

In corporations, fifty one percent, or majority stock holdings make you king. Disputes are solved by the majority stock holder, and you can't run a new enterprise with a committee has to be a boss who makes the decisions, and keeps things moving.

My advice is to avoid any kind of partnership arrangement (even limited partnerships) as you will only have troubles you don't need in getting underway.

THE MARKETING PLAN:

The real excitement in your offer comes in the marketing plan. Here is where you show the investor where the gold is and how you are going to get it. The potential investor can see how the money is going to be made, and can visualize the dollars rolling in.

Most marketing plans we have seen are so dry and dull that they put you to sleep. They show graphs of market share; competitive dollar volumes; inventory turnover ratios; advertising budgets without any advertising to look at. We consider this stuff a lot of nonsense and have never used it. Now, this doesn't mean you should not know these things, you should and must. You must know how this product, store or service is going to get business and income, and what the potentials are for doing it. But, you must present it as an exciting reality, not graphs and figures.

ADVERTISING, THE EXCITING SHOW:

The most exciting part of your marketing plan is your advertising, and promotion of the business. It is something a prospective investor understands and can relate to. We have always been able to get a good deal of advertising material together at little or no cost to me. First, we contacted some ad agencies, and as Packard Sterling, Inc., offered them a chance to get my account. We went over my ideas for advertising and promotion (showing them the possibilities that we were a six-figure potential account) and asked for a presentation of some ideas (at their risk). The results vary from stupendous to zilch. But if you contact five or six smaller agencies, you'll get some good material back. When it arrives, you tell them how great you think it is and that you will present it to the board of directors for approval and implementation (and the stuff is good, when you get going you use it).

If you want more ideas and material to show (and there is never too much),contact some commercial artists to design logos, packages, etc. Have them submit roughs on speculation that you can show your board. Some will and some won't but you will get enough who will present some well-designed ideas to the investors.

GETTING ADVANCE PUBLICITY:

Another facet of making your first contact with the Chamber of Commerce is to have the manager get you an appointment with the editor of a local paper. You give him information about the new business you are starting, and always have a narrative book for him to bang the story on.

NOW, WHAT HAVE WE DONE HERE?

We have taken an idea for a business and made it seem like it was going business. That things were already in motion, that operations had already begun is the impression created. In reality, there is still nothing but the idea. No income is coming in, no sales have really been made, but there is the appearance they have. There is action, excitement, motivation and proven potential in existence and that is what you are trying to sell.

THE OPERATING PLAN:

This is the plan that shows how the business will operate. This is the program we pay the least attention to, and simply summarize. Basic business is the same. You buy something, or do something, and sell it for more than it costs. All business operates like that. The method of doing it differs only in respect to what is bought; raw materials that are processed into a product; a product that is resold; a service that is given in one way or another, etc.

We figure how the business will operate. What will be needed to produce what we sell, and project that into a cash flow, and profit picture. We use charts to show how the product or service is created and delivered. We show costs, and sales prices, and project profits. As a rule, we use material from the association or books to develop this, and, using the percentages provided by the association, show how much is needed for each segment of the operation. We found a chart that gets it all down in one place and we simply fill in the figures.

IS YOUR CASH SUPPLY ADEQUATE?

"How much cash does my business need?" is a question which often troubles owner-managers of small manufacturing companies? And rightly so because cash is the fuel which is necessary for operating the business.

The amount of cash which a company needs for profitable operation depends on the company itself because cash requirements vary according to the type of business. The amount which would be an adequate cash supply for one company may well be too small for another.

In thinking about cash needs, many managers use an old rule of thumb. It says that usually a company's cash balance should be equal to at least one- fourth of the company's current debts. However, if you operate blindly on this rule you may run into trouble.

Another method for determining cash needs is to compare industry ratios and statement studies, offered by trade publications, with your company's finances. But keep in mind that these ratios and statement studies are averages and should not be relied on solely when determining your own company's needs. Companies have individual requirements and goals which have to be considered in order to ensure profitable operation. You'll need to make your judgment on facts which you can get from your past financial records.

After you have these facts, you'll need to: (1) decide whether your cash supply adequate in the past, (2) estimate your future cash needs, and (3) take effective steps to control and conserve your cash for those future needs.

TWO KINDS OF CASH:

An adequate cash supply for your company should be one which enables you to pay your current operating costs on time and to provide for future expansion costs. Thus, you need to think about and provide cash for two kinds of costs.

First, you have to have WORKING CASH. Funds you use to buy raw materials, to pay wages, and to pay other day-to-day business expenses fall in this category. For most companies, they come from daily receipts-that is from cash sales and payments of accounts receivable.

Second, you have to have cash for CAPITAL expenditures-additions to, as well as replacements of, fixed assets such as your plant, equipment, and tools. Such cash may come from either a long-term loan or from daily receipts in excess of working cash requirements. If the latter source is used, it may be necessary to withhold the distribution of profits in the form of cash until enough cash is accumulated to meet the capital requirements.

An owner-manager should have a firm understanding of which portions of his cash he is going to use as capital cash and which as working cash. In his thinking, he should keep them separate. He should realize that cash on hand and in the bank, must first be set aside for outstanding obligations. The cash that remains may be used for new capital expenditures if the business warrants them.

A company's cash supply is the amount of money on deposit at the bank. (It also includes undeposited receipts and readily convertible securities such as U.S. bonds and notes). Except in highly seasonal businesses or in extraordinary situations, it should take care of requirements for working cash. But, a company's cash by itself is not profit because there may be large unpaid debts which can eat up a large checking account balance.

On the other hand, profit-a good net income --cannot be used for additional working cash if it has been distributed to its owners and is no longer available for expenditure. Profit is an important goal, and you should keep it in mind constantly. However, doesn't let preoccupation with profit block your vision so that capital cash is not available for growth and expansion?

In providing an adequate cash supply, you should also think of: (1) possible future increases in operating costs because expanded sales will mean bigger bills for labor and raw materials, for example, and (2) possible future increases in your capital expenditures when you have outgrown your present plant and equipment.

PLANNING YOUR CASH SUPPLY:

Your planning for an adequate cash supply should be done in three phases: (1) make a forecast, or estimate, of your future sales; (2) set up an operating budget based on your sales estimate; and (3) make a cash budget to show the amount of funds needed in order to carry on your operations.

Besides your basic books of account, the kinds of records you will actually need are:

sales records, (2) production cost records, and (3) monthly cash statements. These records help you determine the business (or cash} cycle in your company- how much money comes in from sales, how much goes out for raw materials, and so on. You use these records to provide you with information about your cash needs based on anticipated sales.

Estimate Sales: Sales are the starting point in forecasting the future needs of your business. You make a careful estimate of your sales expectations. You base this estimate on your company's past performance as described in your financial records. Keep in mind that the past is just a yardstick and does not take into account growth or any plans for expansion. So along with the facts from your records, take into consideration any expected changes in your business. For example, if your sales have increased by 5 percent each year for the past 3 or 4 years, you'd expect them to increase 5 percent next year if conditions stay the same. In making sales forecasts, you'll want to try to include some margin for unforeseeable events. For example, what happens if sales drop off 20 percent in the slack season rather than the 10 percent which is normal for your operation? When you have an estimate of your total sales volume for next year, break it down by months. You'll need monthly figures when you determine what an adequate cash supply is.

OPERATING BUDGETS:

Once you have an estimate of your sales volume, you can set up a production budget. This budget will project the selling, manufacturing, and overhead costs based on your estimated sales.

In developing an operating budget, you start with your estimated monthly sales figures for the next 6 or 12 months. Figure how much each activity of your business will cost in order to make your expected sales goal. Your records of past expenses will serve as a guide. For example, if you spent $40,000 last year for the raw materials necessary to do $100,000 in sales and expect to do $110,000 in sales this year, you would need to budget $44,000 for raw materials-an increase of 10 percent in both sales and raw materials.

You then set a figure for other cash needs, such as labor, overhead, and selling expenses. Some owner-managers find the advice of their key men and foremen valuable when they work up operating budgets. These supervisors, for example, help to see that details about their departments are not overlooked.

PREPARE A CASH BUDGET

After you have your operating budget, you are ready to work up a cash budget. It is a plan which shows the cash receipts you expect to take in during a certain period and the expenditures you expect to make during that time. These figures should be on a monthly basis. Prepare a detailed forecast of the amount of cash you expect to take in and spend month-by-month to cover 1 year.

Some owner-managers who have never budgeted find it easier to start with a 6-month budget. They use their experience from the first 6 months when developing the budget for the second 6 months. It is also a good idea to make a skeleton forecast for an additional 12 months. In this manner, you will have a plan for the next 2 years.

CONTROL AND CONSERVE:

After you have set up your cash budget, your task will be that of seeing that your company operates within it. If your budget estimates are good, the necessary amount of cash will be available at the right time.

One of the most obvious ways of safeguarding your company's money is the separation of your personal funds from those of your business. Let your company pay you a salary and show that amount as an administrative expense item in your company's budget and accounting records. Then use a separate bank account for your salary and personal expenses. In paying themselves a bonus, good managers wait until the end of the year and draw from the profits which are left after the needs of their businesses are taken care of.

If your need for cash is great around the first of the month, your credit policies should encourage customers to pay you near that time. Offering a discount for prompt payment, in many cases, enables a company to keep its money turning and thus operate with smaller cash balances.

OVERCOMING TEMPORARY DEFICIENCIES:

Even though you plan and control cash, there may be times when income from sales may not be great enough to cover your current bills. The problem: adjusting to a temporarily weak cash supply.

Sometimes you may be able to adjust by rearranging your billing cycle and by tightening your credit limits. At other times, you may need to arrange a short-term loan at your bank.

A BASIS FOR GROWTH:

Finally, maintaining an adequate cash supply is a basis for growth. Many owner-managers realize that it is good business not to distribute all their profits. They plow a large part of profits into expanding the business by using them for capital expenditures such as new machines and equipment.

In order to develop surplus cash which can be reinvested to provide additional profits, a company must, first of all, take in enough to pay its bills including periods when little, or no, money comes in from sales, for example, in a seasonal type of business. When such needs are provided for, the owner-manager can plan for growth.

Sometimes a business does not generate surplus cash fast enough so the owner-manager has to get his capital cash by long-term borrowing. He 1mds that it is easier to get such loans when he has maintained an adequate supply of working cash -one that enables him to build a reputation for paying his bills on time. Such a reputation makes a favorable impression with bankers, especially when they see that the owner-manager has built it by planning his cash supply.

THE FINANCIAL PLAN:

208

We call this the "greed report". Here is where you show the investor the true potential of his investment. You show him the benefits of being a seed capital investor as opposed to a buyer of stock after the company is operational and profitable.

In case you are not clear about this, here's the difference. A seed capital investor is, as a rule, a short-term investor. He puts up the money for the seeds, and reaps the rewards when the harvest comes in. The investor who comes along and buys stock when the company is solid and operating, is, in a sense, a long-term investor, because he is in it for both dividends and capital appreciation. You are offering your first investor the seed buying opportunity.

It works like this. The seed capital investor puts up his money and gets the business going. As soon as it turns the corner and makes profits, stock is made available to investors (the company, in effect, goes public), and they buy shares at a price based

on the market's estimate of the company's future performance. The seed capital investor can sell his stock at that time, and reap the harvest he planted. Often a dollar in seed capital can be worth a $1,000 in returns when the public buys in. Thus a $20,000 investment in seed capital could reap $20,000,000 in harvest income when the public buys in.

On the reverse side of the coin, if the investor is active in the corporation, and you from Sub Chapter S and/or Rule 12rr Corporations, losses can be passed through to stockholders to be deducted as losses from ordinary income. Thus, the investor has the opportunity of cutting Uncle Sam in on his losses as well as his gains.

In making your financial projection, include the target date for a public offering, so the investor can see where the pot of gold at the end of the rainbow lies.
Be sure to use your accountant in preparing your projection so it will stand up under scrutiny by other accountants. Don't make any foolish errors that will kill your deal if others look at it Put in all the tax saving options, shelters for income and other goodies you can develop to make it really exciting for your investor.
YOU ARE NOW 14 DAYS FROM THE MONEY:
When your package is ready to go, you will have your money in two weeks. Prepare an ad and place it through your real estate connection. There are two types of ads that you can use. First, the formal ad, which presents the facts without really trying to qualify the prospect. This type of ad would read something like this:
Corporation seeks associate to participate in immensely profitable new venture to be headquartered in your town. Active or passive involvement with secured investment of $25,000 required. Can prove six figure return in 18 months,
The second type of ad is for the less sophisticated investor, and one who is looking more for the big dream:

Are you looking for something better? Corporation seeks a local associate to participate in major new business venture. Your $25,000 fully secured investment, plus active role in company affairs will bring you a six-figure return in 18 months, with possible doubling of your original investment in six months.

You have presented an offer that has several important points to it. First you have promised a lot in return for relatively little. Second you have named a sum of money to keep out the shoe clerks. Third, you have mentioned fully secured. Fourth, you have provided an instant, free method of contact without having to write a letter, or delay in getting the ball rolling.

Another point; you will note this is a blind ad. There is nothing in it about what the business is, or even where it is at present. Many investors will not answer ads like this, and, frankly, you don't want the kind that won't anyway. You are looking for the person with the dream, not the one with the bookkeepers, how much return on my dollar, mentality.

If you have trouble composing an ad like this, then get copies of Sunday papers in metropolitan areas, look under business opportunities and salesman wanted categories and you will see many ads like this. It is easy to work up one of your own from what you will find there.

The key words in the sample ad we gave you are these: First, corporation. This indicates a business, not an individual. Corporation also co notates big business in most people's minds, so the ad indicates that a big business is looking for an associate.

Second, you have to use the term ''new business venture." Excitement, adventure are the connotation here. The shrewd investor wants nothing to do with new business; he's looking for established ones. But, the dreamer is turned on by new, so you have qualified your prospect again.

Third, fully secured. This connotation is without risk. This gives the reader sense of security, a feeling of little or no risk, and induces him to answer.

Fourth, you have a toll-free phone. He has visions of calling New York or Chicago or other major city and reaching corporate headquarters. It's a prestige move, and it costs him nothing. So, your ad has some power, and a lot of inducement for the dreamer to inquire. Ads like these get results.

When you are ready to see your prospects, rent a hotel or motel suite. Do not go to the home or office of a prospect. Meet them on your turf, and on your terms. By taking a suite you have two rooms, one for displaying your material and talking business and one for interviews and to be used as a waiting room.

This is important. Even if you live or have an office in the community, meet them in a hotel. This avoids any interruptions when you don't want them, gives you the time and setting you need to get your story across.

The first interview should be in the coffee shop or lounge over coffee or drinks. Never meet a stranger and sit down and start talking business. Use the first thirty minutes in a sociable atmosphere to become acquainted. Don't talk specifics about the business, just generalities. The great possibilities, and throw in some war stories about other successes in this field you are entering.

PRE-SCREENING THE RESPONSES:

Get back to your responses as soon as possible. Check with the toll-free number every hour or have them call you when something comes in. Get on the phone to the caller at once. Don't wait for inquires to pile up, do it right away or he may find something else more interesting. When you get a positive, affirmative response to your story and question, and then take the offensive. You become friendly, and talk to him about the area. Drop the name of the Chamber Manager, the senator who you have a letter from and any other local names you have accumulated, always telling how positive their response to your program has been. This is reinforcement for him, and allows you to make the next move.

THE WORKING INTERVIEW:

When the prospect calls back, and wants to hear more, you make this pitch:

"Glad you called, George. As I said, things are a little tight, but if you don't mind seeing me do some work while we talk, why don't you come over (and you set the specific time).

Now, you are ready for the big show. You call your real estate man, your insurance man, your employment agency, a printer, a supplier who will have things to sell the business, and anyone else you wish, and ask them over at forty-five intervals during your second interview. The purpose of this is simple. While you are showing your prospect the full picture, the real estate man shows up and you discuss location for the business. You draw the prospect into the picture, asking his opinion about this or that, and suddenly he is participating in a business venture. Do the same with the others. Have the employment agency send over secretaries, or other personnel you will be hiring, and include him in the interviews.

What is all this doing? It is proving to your prospect that this is a business in motion. It's taking off, and the money will soon be rolling in. You are exciting him, getting him involved and at the same time, between interviews, you are showing him all the goodies you have prepared. It's really powerful, and when you've gone through the entire program, talked to the people who came, he's either sold, or he's gone.

THE CLOSE:

The close is simple. When you are finished, you lean back and smile. "Well, George, are we in business?" If you've judged him correctly he will say yes. Okay, then here's what we'll do. You write me a check for $500 to bind me to the offer. We will give you two copies of the agreement, which I want you to take to your attorney. We will have my attorney get in touch with him, to go over anything that he feels is necessary, and then we'll sign at the attorney's office and we're in business.

If he writes the check, it's 90% sure that it will close. To ensure that it will, you give him some things to do at once. Arrange for a suitable location; hire the proper help, or anything you figure he would want to do. Get him going right away and he'll respond. There will be no question about going through with it.

The close is just that simple when you build your presentation correctly. If there is any hesitation on his part, jerk the deal away at once. If he says, "I'll have to discuss this with my attorney, wife, brother, etc." you look surprised and then say, "Okay, George." Get up, and say "Thanks for your help with the interviews. If you'll excuse me, I've got more people to see and things to do. Call me anytime, maybe we can get together on something else."

He will either be glad you let him off the hook, or he'll realize that he has to fish or cut bait, and he'll jump back in I've had more than one says, "Hey, I want in on this, I just meant that I had to tell them I was going in. I'll write the check now.

THAT IS THE SYSTEM: That is the 14-day system and it works. If you prepare properly, you can get the money, on your terms, in a few days by following the techniques we just outlined.

REVELATION #19
DECISIONS

In personal life and in
your professional
career, decision
making is necessary.
Making the right
decision, however, is a
lot harder because
you have to entertain
all aspects such as
repercussions that
could come about and
making no decision is a
decision in itself.
Sometimes, you may
decide that no action
would work out better
than forcing or
imposing a certain
direction. In other
words, let things
happen as they may.

If someone were to ask you what you do in your profession or job, you would probably answer that planning and organizing occupy a large portion of your time. You might mention that you spend time directing other employees and keeping a check on the various jobs in your jurisdiction. Hiring, firing, personnel problems, inventory control, resolving the various unexpected questions that arise, and always a stack of paperwork-the list could go on and on.

This description would no doubt apply to the activities of most managers. Planning, organizing, staffing, directing, and controlling are the five functions normally ascribed to managers, and most of your daily work falls into one of these categories. In the final analysis, however, one ability underlies all other managerial operations, and that is the capacity to make decisions. The job of managing is in essence the job of making decisions, and making sound decisions is the key to success in business. It's what you get paid to do.

DECISIONS-BASIC AND ROUTINE:

Decision-making comes naturally to all human beings. (It's sound decision-making that has to be learned.) From the time, you wake in the morning, you are constantly making decisions. What shall I wear? Should I stop for gas? Would a lobster roll be better than the blue-plate special? fortunately, most of our determinations are routine and require relatively little deliberation. Their effect is minor, and they often become patterns or habits. "I always fill the tank when it hits the $\frac{1}{4}$ mark." "I always have a lobster roll for lunch on payday." To the average person, routine or programmed decisions present no problem.

Basic or non-programmer decisions are another matter. These judgments are novel, unstructured, and consequential. We can see them in our daily life. Should we take that big vacation or put the money toward a new roof for the house? We can see them in business, too. Should we develop a new product line or wait until the competition makes a move? Should I move an old hand into a supervisory post, or push for someone from outside? These decisions matter. They involve commitment; large expenditures of funds, and a mistake could cause a setback for your department and jeopardize the successful running of the business.

HOW DO YOU DECIDE - HUNCHES AND INTUITION:

Ask yourself a question: As a manager, how do you make a decision? You may agree with Manager Ed Jeffers who says, "I know this company. I've been here 18 years. I know the equipment and the employees. I started out as a machine operator myself and worked up. So, when I need to make a decision, I have a feel for the problems, and I just follow my hunches. I don't always know why I decide a certain way, but it's always worked for me."

Call it a hunch or a gut feeling. Call it instinct or intuition. What it boils down to is long experience of trial and error, learning and observing. Jeffers is able to make decisions that work because he's had 18 years to build up an intimate knowledge of his company. He knows automatically the goals and objectives of his firm. He has a close acquaintance with the machines, the methods, and the people that produce the products in his department. Jeffers might call it instinct but, as Henry Ford said; instinct is "probably the essence of past experience and knowledge stored up for future use." If Jeffers were to change companies, his intuition might very well fail him.

We all get hunches. They may be good or they may be riddled with inconsistency, personal bias, and faulty logic. A manager may choose not to ignore his intuition if it has proved valuable in the past. But consider these. Would you buy a house on first sight because you had a hunch you'd be making a sound and happy investment for your family? It's more than likely that you would check the plumbing, count the closets, investigate the schools and the neighborhood, look into zoning ordinances, talk to bankers and, in short, examine every possible aspect before reaching your decision.

Do you owe your company any less? If you're faced with a decision and your intuition keeps prodding you toward a certain resolution, is it best then to ignore your hunch? Certainly not. It might prove to be the best solution available. If it is a good idea, however, there must be reasons for its merit. Think your hunches through. Be able to defend them, but don't ignore them. If your decision comes under attack, and the best defense you can muster is that you "had a feeling," then your managerial judgment will be the next thing questioned. For the manager, a hunch is only as sound as the roots which serve to support it. You can't be sure of a hunch if you aren't sure of the rationale that spawned it. Don't allow your intuition to work against you. Analyze your hunches and put them to work in your favor.

HOW SHOULD YOU DECIDE? AN ANALYTICAL APPROACH:

You originally asked yourself "How do I make a decision?" Now ask yourself "How should I make a decision?" Because this ability is as crucial to successful business practices and to your job as manager, it would be wise to consider the steps that lead to sound managerial judgments. The simplest approach to decision-making is borrowed from John Dewey's concepts of problem-solving. It's a formula worth repeating when faced with a decision.

First, state the problem.

Second, list the alternatives.

Third, select the best

alternative.

Using this simple approach, we can devise a blueprint, which can be adapted for use in most situations requiring your managerial judgments.

Determine Objectives

As you approach a decision, it is imperative to operate within a framework of objectives. Lacking these goals, you can hardly apply any direction to your thinking, for they are the pivotal point of any business operation. This is probably simpler than it sounds, because most organizations would agree that to "grow and prosper" is the company's cardinal purpose. To grow and prosper no doubt means to turn a profit, but such other values as the company's image, its views concerning human Relations and obligations to the consumer must also be considered. As we all know, they can affect profit, too. There are long-range goals and short-range goals, and you as a manager should be aware of them. If you're not, ask. A surprising number of managers never learn what the company's principal objectives are, have forgotten them, or have failed to keep up with them as they changed. Without this basic knowledge, you are handicapped in your capacity to do your job.

Identify the problem

"A problem defined is a problem half solved." As with many old adages, this contains more wisdom than is initially apparent. A problem must be defined before it can be dealt with. When treating patients, doctors are careful to discover and deal with the underlying ailment. Treating only the symptoms won't cure the disease.

The same applies to business. Get to the root of your trouble. Treating the symptoms won't solve the problem.

The following example demonstrates the importance of accurately stating both the objectives and the problem.

Ray Hall was having trouble meeting job deadlines. Orders were going out late, and he was worried about the large amount of overtime required to complete the work in his department. Because of this, the last job they'd rushed through had actually run at a loss. His people weren't slacking-he knew that wasn't the problem, but if profits were going down, it was sure to reflect on them all.

Hall's manager wasn't surprised when Hall presented his problems at their weekly meeting. He listened as Hall went into detail about how they were losing money. He nodded as Hall concluded that new equipment, especially a larger furnace was needed to meet the demands of the new orders that kept pouring in.

"You're right, Hall," he said. "But all your problems are symptoms of the growing pains we're going through. Don't worry too much because that Allied order ran at a loss. I guess we could have expected that but now we're pretty sure that we have all their future business. That amounts to quite a bundle." "It doesn't amount to much if I can't get the orders out," Hall interrupted. "We're swamped down there and we're running at full capacity on both shifts. What can I do if I don't have the equipment? We've got to get a larger furnace if you expect me to keep up to schedule."

"Hold on, Ray," his manager urged. "You'll be getting a new furnace and everything else you need but with all the business we're taking in, the real problem is going to be space. Our long-range goal is a new plant. I'm going out this week to look at four possible sites in this area. The problem mainly involves your department so I want you to come along. This will all take a while, of course. Your short-range goal should be to keep up as best you can and you're doing a good job at that."

Determine Possible Alternatives

You can and perhaps already have developed your own personal style in formulating alternatives. Depending on the time element and the pressure for a quick decision, this step encompasses the assimilation of data and the consideration of all possible or logical solutions, being careful not to rely on them as your only source of ideas.

Generate new alternatives, no matter how remote. Remember, one idea may trigger another. Do whatever helps you most-saturate yourself in data, spend a day on the production floor, keep a pad and pencil by your bed, and go fishing. If your ideas begin to sound stale, try talking to someone not directly involved. Another manager, for instance, can often see things in a fresh and novel way.

Evaluate the Impact of Alternatives

After you have exhausted your resources and generated all possible alternatives, take each alternative decision and mentally put it into effect. Visualize its impact on all facets of the operation. Here you must consider and weigh the value of all such applicable factors as new equipment, investment required, availability of materials and labor, effects on morale, government constraints, competitors' reactions, and so forth. Overlooking one factor or another could make an untenable alternative sound good and lead to a bad decision. Look for the bugs in your plans. Consider also any company policies or special circumstances that might come into play and affect your decision.

Manager Carol Leary is careful as she formulates and evaluates the alternatives open to her regarding a difficult decision. This care advances and supports her aim

to reach a practicable solution. As we observe the steps Leary employs, the value of methodical reasoning becomes clear.

Carol Leary is faced with an unpleasant decision. As manager of the Happy Cow Dairy Bar, she has noticed shortages in the day's receipts. At first the amounts were small and Leary attributed it to carelessness. She went over cash register procedures with the waitresses and ascertained that everyone could accurately make change.

The shortages have grown larger, however, and now Leary is sure that her problem is pilferage. By careful observation of cash register readings and cash- drawer counts, Leary learns that the money is disappearing between three and five o'clock. By comparing work schedules with the days on which thefts are noticed, Leary comes to realize that only three people could be responsible for the thefts. "I sincerely like all three of these people," Carol admits. I find it so hard to suspect any one of them, but I have to accept the facts, and I have to decide what to do to stop this." In determining her alternatives, Leary considers:

Firing all three.
Confronting each of them to see if one will give herself away.
Keeping all three as waitresses but forbidding them to use the cash register.
Scheduling one person to be responsible for running the cash register-in effect,

a full-time cashier.

Discreetly spying on them to see if she can catch one of them in the act of stealing.

Rearranging work schedules in such a way that any recurring loss will point more directly to one person.

Giving a talk on theft to all the waitresses and hoping that it hits home.

Following her hunch that the responsible party is Marilyn, since she was heard complaining about her high car payments.

What would you do? In evaluating her alternatives, Leary rejects number one immediately as unreasonable, unfair, and probably illegal. She rejects number two as rather useless and ineffectual. Number three, she reasons, would be demoralizing and would create additional problems, since it would be apparent to the entire staff that these three waitresses were under suspicion. She could appoint one persona as

permanent cashier, her fourth alternative, but this is contrary to the restaurant's policies. This job would not be enough work for one person, and the restaurant could not pay someone to stand idle for a good portion of the work shift. Number five seems a good alternative to Leary because she would feel best if she could catch the person red-banded. The possibility of this working, however, is uncertain. Number six would probably work, and Leary feels fairly safe with this decision.

Number seven might not be a bad idea in any case, but it is doubtful, Leary reasons, that it would solve her problem. Number eight Leary rejects as unfounded and biased.

Having evaluated her alternatives, Leary is now able to limit her options and to choose either number five or number six as her course of action. She has not reached a definite conclusion at this point, but the chances of her making a good decision are greatly strengthened by the analytical methods that she has applied to her job.

Choosing a Course of Action

It often seems like a large step from evaluating alternatives to formulating your decision. You may find after gathering and evaluating all the facts that your decision has been made for you. If that is not the case, then you, as the decision maker, must pass a value judgment on each alternative. These judgments could involve things about which you simply can't be sure. It cannot be denied that as you reach this point there is definite risk involved. The best advice you can follow at this juncture is to make use of a selection criterion that includes the objectives of your company, the desirability of the alternative, and the probability of the outcome.

Suppose you are faced with four alternative decisions. A is clearly the most desirable, but you can't be all sure of its outcome. B is almost equally desirable and the probability is clearly in your favor. It does not, however, encompass your firm's long-rage objectives. C is the next best alternative, and its probability is fairly certain. D is a mediocre alternative, but it's a sure thing. The decision is up to you.

Temperament-The Neglected Variable in Decision-Making
Certain singular variables remain to be considered regarding the decision- making process. One variable is you and the type of personal characteristics you bring to the job of managing. Are you impulsive, or do you tend to be cautious? Are you apt to rely on the opinions of others, or do you preferred to trust only your own judgment? Are you reflective, or naturally impetuous? Do you like to take chances, or do you prefer the safest route? Will you offer an opinion, or do you feel a need to be sure? Do you have any inclinations or biases that might affect your decision-making skills? There is no right or wrong answers to questions like these. The predominance of any of these traits becomes a handicap only when it operates to an
immoderate degree. Your responses should help to indicate to you any possible weaknesses in your style of decision-making.
For example, if you are the sort of person who is enthusiastic about new ideas, always anxious to get ideas into action, always eager to try something new, then being aware of these traits you should be careful to compensate for impetuosity when making important decisions. Force yourself into the habit of investing a fair minimum of time to each step in the decision -making process. List these steps and the alternative decisions you derive on paper in front of you. Enforce a short cooling-off period before putting your decision into action. In this way, you'll be less likely to cross the Rubicon only as a result of initial and short-lived zeal.

If you tend to be the reflective, cautious decision maker then you may have to employ quite divergent techniques. This will help in preventing you from becoming so preoccupied with data, details, and endless possibilities that your decisions become untimely and ineffectual. Ask yourself if the continual rehashing of alternatives serves any good purpose. Does it help you to reach a better decision, or do you work this way because you are excessively fearful of making a mistake? Like the rash decision maker, you too might profit by setting limits on the time spent on decision-making steps. In your case set maximum time limits, and when you've made your decision, act on it and go on with your other work. Extremes of disposition do not contribute to good decision-making. By becoming aware of these characteristics in your temperament, you can learn to compensate for them as the situation requires.

The temperament of the people who work for you also has a decided influence on the success of any new resolution. Directly or indirectly, your managerial decisions involve all of them. It is possible that neglecting this variable could undermine even your soundest verdict. This is not to suggest that you should eliminate any beneficial change or program on the grounds that your group might have apprehensions or difficulties in adjusting to your decision. You must, however, take into account the character of your group, so that you can best anticipate the repercussions of your planned course of action.

Taking this precaution, you will be in a better position to determine the most successful manner in which to implement your decision. It is a regrettable fact but, unless your decision is executed with care, your best laid plans can misfire.

What is the best way to disclose a decision? This will vary from group to group, situation to situation, and manager to manager. Some standard procedures are to post a notice, to make a general public announcement, to issue an edict, to speak individually to those directly affected, to alert key personnel and instruct them to disseminate your directive.

If you've accurately read the temperament and mood of your people, then your choice of method should follow naturally. Let's see how one manager handled this. Mary Riley is new in her job as manager of the Holiday Novelty and Card Company. Many of the employees have been with the company for more than 10 years and do their jobs comfortably and routinely. As a new manager, Riley has decided to institute certain changes but she's wise enough to foresee that, no matter how good her plans are, she's bound to meet opposition unless she proceeds slowly and tactfully.

The mood I sense around here is almost complacent, Mary thought to herself. Everyone's very satisfied with the way things are done. If I weren't so certain of my judgments, I'd be tempted to let things ride. But, I'm positive my innovations can

increase our profit over the Easter holiday. I've got to put my decisions into effect now.

If Riley issued a directive, or announced or posted her decisions, resentment and resistance to change would certainly have impeded her. She has gauged the temperament of her workers accurately, however, and decides that any new directives would be more favorably accepted if they did not come directly from her. In forming this conclusion, Riley had to override her own natural tendency to exert the authority of her new position. Instead she began to seek out allies. She spoke with two veteran supervisors. Riley led the discussion toward certain areas and casually mentioned her new ideas. "How do you think the rest of the crew would react if you suggested these changes? She asked. "I think they'd cooperate once they tried it. If they gave it a chance and saw that it worked, there'd be no trouble," one supervisor volunteered. "But would they give this a fair trial?" Riley asked. "Well," she was told, "they might if we talked to them and explained how it would make their jobs easier in the long run. It might be better if we started a week ahead in my department. I've got some newer employees -not so set in their ways." "Yeah," the first supervisor chimed in, "I'll bet when my people see what yours are doing, they'll keep their cool better when it's their turn."

Four weeks later Riley observed that her decided course of action had proven itself and was working. Her decisions turned out to be sound; and because she had not ignored the temperament of her workers, the benefits of her managerial judgment would soon be realized.

Consistently successful decisions are made by people who inform themselves. In effect, they purposely establish an up-to-the-minute program to keep informed. Making more right decisions than wrong ones is the key to success. It would be unrealistic to expect a 100% batting average. Nevertheless, we would venture to say that "the better informed, the better the decisions," thus achieving a higher success rate.

The businessman and executive are much depended upon for good and shrewd decisions. The financial welfare of many may be at stake. The decision maker is encumbered with the duty and obligation to choose or decide on many issues, from product selection to company policy

It is almost imperative for the executive to design and place into operation a well-thought out program to keep informed on all critical aspects of the economy, trends of the particular industry, competitive research programs and promotions as well as all in-house company problems and objectives.

THE EXECUTIVE'S NEED FOR INFORMATION:

The need for continuing, up-to-date information about the internal progress of a business is obviously a matter of the most urgent importance. It is met, as we have

seen, through a variety of methods: by tours of observation; by conferences with department heads, supervisors or foremen; by staff meetings at regular intervals; by a system of accounting and statistical reports, submitted on standard forms on an assigned schedule. The use of these devices of management enables the businessman to follow closely the progress of his department, his division, or the business as a whole.

Watching the rising or ebbing tide of activity within the business is not enough; there are tides outside the individual enterprise which the executive must also be informed about. "The day has gone," asserts a prominent advertising executive, "when it was enough for a business leader to think and act only in terms of his own company and his own industry. Every part of our economy now interacts so closely with other parts that responsible judgments by the businessman, in his own interest alone, call for a range of information not provided for in the past, and which we are only now beginning to span." What this executive had in mind was the interaction between industry and industry, between industry and agriculture, between production and distribution, between government and all of these. The individual enterprise does not operate in a vacuum, but rather in an increasingly complex industrial society, whose influence and ramifications often encircle the globe. What happens in that external economic world may spell life or death to the individual business.

When the officers of a wholesale grocery company saw that the increase of chain grocery stores in a certain metropolitan area was bound to react unfavorably on its sales to independent retailers, the company shifted its selling efforts from grocers to cafeterias for employees operated by industrial plants, public utilities, and other concerns. This amounted to changing the company's market, but the change worked out very well. The total number of accounts was smaller, but sales were larger. Moreover, the costs of making deliveries, of bookkeeping and of collecting accounts were radically reduced. By keeping informed of probable trends, the company's officers were able to direct their sales effort into green pastures before the old pastures began visibly to shrivel and dry up. It pays to know about pastures.

WHERE DOES INFORMATION COME FROM?
It would be interesting to know just how the officers of the wholesale grocery firm
obtained the trend data upon which they based their shift of market. Their facts about the growth of grocery chains in the metropolitan area may have been derived in part from observation, but doubtless their personal knowledge was confirmed by the reading of some survey reporting the complete statistics of chain growth. Such a survey may have been made by the Bureau of the Census, or by an association representing the chain stores, or by some advertising agency or other independent investigator. Somebody, certainly, must have collected the facts that the wholesalers used so effectively. They may have been made public in a newspaper, a trade journal, or a government bulletin.

These are all good sources of business information but sometimes the urgency is such that company officers cannot wait for private or government investigators to collect and publish the data they need. In that case, they may decide to finance their own survey, giving the job to some advertising agency or other organization equipped to conduct field research. The survey may prove to be simple or it may be fairly complicated, requiring the full-time labors of a staff of trained field workers. Results cannot be guaranteed, of course, but they are often good enough to repay the cost of the study several times over.

If sales keep slipping despite the introduction of every modern advertising and selling technique that expert advice can suggest, it may be that the fault lies not with the company but with the industry as a whole. When that possibility is suspected, an industry wide survey is in order, directed and financed by the leading trade association for the industry. At one point of time for example, cigar makers felt the need of investigating their sluggish sales. They set up a research institute, with a paid director and staff of investigators. What they discovered was most interesting.

The point of attack of the Cigar Institute was the cigar smoker. How numerous as he? Where was he located? What were his tastes and habits? It was found that he was surprisingly numerous - nearly fifteen million strong, to be exact. Still more surprising was the discovery that a full third or more of cigar smokers lived in suburban areas. There were other surprises, also, nearly all of them favorable to the industry. Fortified by the facts turned up by the survey, the cigar maker laid out an advertising and sales promotion campaign that put the emphasis where it would do the most good. The rural smoker, in particular, received more attention than he had ever had from any branch of the tobacco industry. Every member of the Cigar Institute was furnished with the 1mings of the survey, plus detailed plans for a sales promotion campaign.

TRADE ASSOCIATIONS AND CHAMBERS OF COMMERCE
It is not every year that a trade association 1mds it advisable to conduct a full-fledged survey, but investigations of one sort or another are going forward nearly all the time in most associations. The range of information gathered and passed along to association members is extensive. Data on new methods of production, sources of raw materials, sales and advertising ideas, pricing trends, credit ratings, pending or newly passed legislation, interpretations of court and commission decisions, collective bargaining procedures, and many other matters of importance to the operation of a business are made available to the association membership.

Meetings of trade associations, if national or regional are likely to be annual only, and the information available to their members is given chiefly through the medium of bulletins, newsletters or official trade journals. Local trade associations, serving the manufacturers, wholesalers or retailers of a single community (usually a metropolitan area), are able to hold more frequent meetings, and so need not rely as much of the printed word to reach their members.

RESOURCES OF TRADE ASSOCIATIONS:

Of the 1,000 or more trade associations in the United States, only about 2,000 are national or regional; the remaining 10,000 are state and local. As a general rule, the national and regional associations have larger resources than the state and local groups, and maintain more extensive headquarters manned by larger staffs of secretaries and research workers.

Sometimes the superior resources of a national association are derived through the affiliation of state and local associations with the national body. Affiliation creates a stronger organization, capable of exerting a wide influence. It is easy to see, for example, what influential power must be at the command of an organization such as the National Association of Retail Grocers, comprising about forty states and 300 local associations, with an underlying membership of 68,000 stores. The fund of profitable information that can be drawn from the experience of so large a membership is very great. The retail Grocers make a point of collecting data from their member stores, and of relaying what is most timely and valuable to the entire membership, making use for that purpose of a monthly trade journal and occasional bulletins on special problems.

When needed information cannot be obtained by ordinary methods of canvassing the experience of trade association memberships, or when a question transcends that experience, the association leaders normally turn to professional research firms for assistance. The ending of World War II, for example, found the manufacturers of books in a quandary. Wartime demand for books had broken all records, but would this continue with the advent of peace? How much, if any, should book manufacturing plants be expanded? Research and discussion within the industry got nowhere, and the officers of the Book Manufacturers Institute, trade association of the industry, decided to get expert help.

MAKING USE OF THE GOVERNMENT:

Although membership in a trade association will nearly always yield valuable information to any executive, there will be some problems peculiar to one's own company that will not be considered by the trade association, or, if considered, not with the precision or fullness of detail that is desired. Many such problems will not warrant referring to a professional agency or research consultant; yet the executive wants more information than he can gather locally, without spending too much money.

The solution may be to consult with the various agencies maintained by state and federal governments to assist business men, and especially the smaller concerns. A growing number of states now operate departments of commerce or the equivalent under another title, and these departments collect statistical and other economic data which they are willing to place at the disposal of the inquiring executive.

State departments of labor, banking, or insurance, and the various bureaus and commissions set up to supervise specialized areas of government, are often in a position to give information on those problems falling outside the scope of a state department of commerce but still of genuine concern to business operations.

The alert business man will provide himself with a list of the agencies of his state that might be of help to him - the correct title of each agency, the administrative heads to see, the scope of the agency's work, and the sort of information it can give. The computer and internet might be of considerable service in making these sources quickly discoverable.

So, in conclusion one can feasibly design a program of being well-informed thusly making more successful decisions.

The other advantage of being informed is that the stress or burden of making a decision is greatly reduced. The confidence level of one's decision-making is greatly enhanced, creating a special feeling in making a well-informed decision. It is similar to a jockey on a horse, knowing intimately just what the horse is capable of. We hope you acquire that special feeling of confident decision-making.

REVELATION #20
HEALTH IS WEALTH

This report is intended to enlighten any reader, but emphasis is placed upon the importance of good health for the business person. This includes anyone who runs their own business, or a corporate executive with extensive responsibilities.

PHYSICAL DEMANDS OF BUSINESS:

Few people, except physicians, realize the physical demands which modern business places upon executives and employees alike. Both work under the double load of pressure from above to secure results and the mental and physical exactions of the tasks which they, respectively, are performing. Today, the nervous strain of high-speed production is intense, and the physical drains upon human energy to turn out large quantities of work per day have been appreciably increased. Physical unfitness, unless guarded against, or remedied if it has developed, may lead eventually to a serious and sometimes permanent break-down.

WHAT IS A STRONG BODY?

To the average person the term "bodily strength" is probably more or less synonymous with "muscular strength," and complacently regards the bulging of his flexed biceps and overlooks the sagging bulge of his abdominal muscles in taking an incomplete and even dangerous inventory of his physical assets - and liabilities. Balanced and coordinated development of the entire muscular system is essential to perfect health, while heavy over development of any part in an otherwise poorly developed individual is likely to be detrimental to health. Women are usually more health-conscious than men and they realize that good habits and proper dieting is more essential than muscles. It is evident by the fact that aerobics is one of the best health routines, and more women engage in this than men! The activity and efficiency of the vital organs of the body are in large degree dependent upon the activity and efficiency of the supporting muscular system.

The abdominal muscles are perhaps the most important, as well as the most abused and neglected in the body of the average person. The combination of sedentary occupation punctuated by spasmodic outbursts of exercise and overeating is one not calculated to secure balanced coordination and strength. Too much food, too infrequent and then too violent exercise, constipation and autointoxication - these are the pitfalls into which many a strong man stumbles. The bay window is an unnecessary and dangerous addition to the business person's architecture.

The muscles of the back, from one end to the other, including the neck, are important to your well-being and efficiency. The person with chronically weak back muscles and a poorly trussed spine sits uneasily in their chair. The body sags, their stomach bulges, their neck hurts and their headaches. The strong mind and the weak back may be a less undesirable combination than the reverse, but it is scarcely more likely to lead to real business success, and far more likely to lead to ill health and misery. Chronic backache is one of the common complaints of the day and is ascribed by the victim to a variety of causes any one of which may be correct for the moment. Essentially, however, the fault (when not due to injury or congenital defect) is to be found in weak and poorly developed back muscles.

The muscles of the lower leg and foot are too often neglected. The arch of the foot is a flexible bridge supported by elastic muscular trusses which go as high as the knee. Other small muscles in the foot itself form a dynamic network of support and strength. Weakness in these muscles, as in the back leads to pain, not only in the feet but in the knees, hips, back and even the head, with resulting nervous and physical instability of more or less consequence.

Injuries to bones and joints which impose long periods of rest and immobilization always result in weakened supporting structures, of which the muscles are the most important. Every physician understands that restoration of these muscles is essential in order to remove the distressing symptoms which follow these injuries. The symptoms of "chronic sacra-iliac" may be due in part if not entirely to weakened back muscles, initiated by the original injury and prolonged by undue inactivity and pampering. Many men and women suffer from a weird variety of symptoms which stem from weak muscles. In most cases there has been no originating injury, unless neglect or laziness can be called by that name.

A strong body is one in which all the muscles, because in daily use and adequately developed, perform their individual and collective functions properly.

SOUND NERVES:

There are many organic diseases of the nervous system, and most of them are difficult to treat. It is not necessary for a person to know anything about these diseases. All they need know that a man who keeps his body in good condition will maintain a sufficiently stable nervous system to cope with their environment and his business problems.

In our modem competitive, high-speed life, the businessman needs a sound nervous system. If one's nerves are in bad condition on account of autointoxication, headaches, backaches or foot aches, they will be irritable when they should be pleasant, restless when they should be in repose, unsteady and excitable when they should be calm. Bad nerves have shipwrecked many a business.

The health of the nervous system and the health of the body go hand in hand. Poisoning of the body by food or drugs, coupled with inadequate exercise and defective elimination, is by far the commonest cause of "jumpy" nerves. The pains and the aches of a poorly muscled body coupled with daily overeating, over drinking

227

and over smoking, are the natural preludes to irritability, bad temper, distrust, jealousy, discourtesy and all the other somber attributes of the neurasthenic. Radical and spasmodic attempts to recover by means of drastic abstinence or violent exercise are sometimes resorted to, usually leaving the victim more worn out and jumpy than ever.

The brain is the most important part of the nervous system, and the mind and will are its most important functions. A business person who thinks he can neglect his physical health and yet be as shrewd, far-seeing and resolute as ever, is the victim of a serious delusion. A perfectly well person easily finds his way out of difficulties that would floor them if they were sick or only half well. The person who is not in good physical condition seldom gives birth to a new idea in business. Not only does he lack imagination, but lacks also the grit and resolution necessary to carry a new idea into effect.

It should be obvious from what has been said that sound nerves, like sound muscles, will follow naturally upon any plan of living based upon moderation in habits, persistent and intelligent exercise, adequate rest, relaxation and play.
EXERCISE:
As a person grows older, their needs with respect to physical activity change. The strenuous games of youth become less and less desired and desirable. But the necessity for exercise, geared to the physical capacity, remains.
Exercise which is joined with pleasure and fun is of course best. It provides the necessary toning up of unused muscles and the equally necessary toning down or rest for the perhaps overused brain and nervous system. People past middle age should moderate their activity according to professional advice. In many instances, it would warrant a change of activity to perhaps highlight a program such as swimming, golfing, and fishing, unless one is in superb physical shape from earlier year's acclamation to a vigorous exercise schedule. Setting up exercises or moderate aerobics and or weight lifting under professional supervision can be beneficial to many persons while reaping the enjoyment. One has to listen to their body and avoid excessive workouts that can cause fatigue or harm instead of the benefit. Exercise to be effective must be undertaken with persistence and regularity.

If you have insomnia, try a bit of exercise as a hypnotic. If you get out of bed in the morning still tired, try a bit of exercise as a tonic. If you really want health, you must work for it! Educate yourself and act accordingly!
FOOD:

There are not many business people in the United States who suffer from under nutrition, or lack of sufficient food. There are many who suffer from over-nutrition-too much food. The tired person who follows the frayed dictum to "eat plenty of good food to keep their strength up" is literally digging himself an early grave. Good food, yes, but plenty? Let them first regard their mid-section, and make an honest inventory of their weight. There are very few exceptions to the rule

that too much weight means too much food and there are not many exceptions to the rule that too much weight means a shorter, but not necessarily a happier life. One of our large insurance companies spends considerable advertising money trying to teach the danger of excess weight. The company has sound business reasons for attempting this. If only partially successful, such an educational campaign will increase the company's profits by increasing the average life expectancy of its clients.

Excess weight is the one great shortened of life that you can do something about. No one else can do it for you. There is such an ailment as nervous indigestion, but to assume that such is the case without competent medical advice is folly. Self-diagnosis and self-medication in the face of persistent digestive disturbances is not good business. Some persons are naturally thin and under average weight, but enjoy excellent health. But the person who is unaccountably losing weight, and does not feel well, is in need of more expert attention than he can give himself. If he temporizes with food fads, vitamins, medicines, exercises and what not, he may well be heading for trouble. An early visit to the doctor is much less expensive than a late one.

DRUGS:
Practically all drugs, to be effective, must also be potentially dangerous. Self-medication is, therefore, a dangerous practice on two counts. An aspirin for the occasional ache or pain, or a mild laxative for the occasional overindulgence, may be forgiven. The habitual use of any drug without medical advice is either silly or dangerous or both.

Vitamins, of which we hear so much lately, are classed as food supplements rather than drugs, but the habitual and medically unadvised use of vitamins can be just as unwise as the indiscriminate use of drugs, if only by providing that false sense of security. Some people are naturally introspective and given to worry about their health. Their anxiety may or may not be justified, but self-medication and delay in seeing a competent physician is a fairly sure method of turning worry into dismal fact.

COOPERATING WITH THE DOCTOR:
Many people when consulting a physician, particularly a new physician, seem

reluctant or unable to tell the doctor the things he must know before he can make his diagnosis. Some exaggerate the trivial, others minimize the essential, and there are always the few who simply refuse to divulge any useful information whatsoever. Needless to say, the latter group will get scant attention from any doctor who has work to do. Much valuable time is thus wasted by patients who are unable or unwilling to give simple and direct answers to simple and direct questions. Several visits may be necessary before all the facts come out, and sometimes they never come out, to the patient's cost.

Occasionally the doctor, in his hurry and fatigue, forgets to ask the one important question. Some years ago, a man having vague digestive symptoms presented himself to a new physician who had a modest pride in his ability in the field of digestive ailments. After several weeks of fruitless questionings and expensive examinations, the exasperated doctor (looking at a vitamin advertisement) asked, "Do you take vitamins?" "Oh yes," said the patient. "I take plenty of them." This story has a happy ending, for the patient got well when he quit self-treatment. The doctor still laughs, but rather glumly, at the joke on himself.

Worry is bad medicine. If you feel sick, let your doctor share the burden. Tell him everything. He can worry for you scientifically and to much better purpose. Even though you are feeling perfectly well, let him look you over now and then. It will give him pleasure to examine and advise a healthy person, and it will give you renewed confidence to be assured that you are fit. It simply is not smart to worry about health and to fear a visit to the doctor. The truth, good or bad, will not be nearly as tough as the worry. Consider the words of the prophet who mourned, "That which I feared hath come upon me."

ALCOHOL AND OTHER HABIT-FORMING DRUGS:

The wise physician does not attempt to prohibit, but to restrain; not to coerce by threat or dire prediction, but to guide by reason and example. There has been much said and written, pro and con, about alcohol. After trying prohibition for thirteen years, the American people concluded that mass production and consumption of alcohol could not fully be prohibited.

Alcohol is a normal product of nature, its use and abuse have gone hand in hand with the use and abuse of food since the beginning of history, It is regarded by physiologists as similar to food on the ground that it is able to replace food by furnishing heat and energy for limited periods of time. Many physicians use it in the treatment of illness.

Excessive drinking, on the other hand, whether daily or occasional, is not to be classed with excessive eating, for aside from the immediately poisonous effect of massive quantities of alcohol, there is the danger of becoming habituated to a drug which steadily undermines the will to resist, ending finally in the tyranny of an appetite which too often brings mental incompetence and degradation in its train. Compared with this the purely physical effects of excessive alcohol are of minor importance.

The same general observations are true of the other habit-forming drugs of a dangerous type such as the many street drugs that are used for "social pleasures." Needless to say, that the word "dangerous" is too mild to describe the drug situation and the addiction that is so prevalent in today's world. As for tobacco, it would be proper to state that are definite health risks and one should avoid not only smoking, or even chewing, but to stay free of smoke-filled rooms wherever and whenever possible. In viewing the milder drugs such as tea and coffee, every man must be his own judge, for with respect to these drugs the doctors disagree. If a man does not use them, the presumption is certainly in his favor.

RIGHT MENTAL ATTITUDES:

Much has been written in recent years about the influence of the mind upon the body and some extremists go so far as to hold that all disease has its origin in the mind and can be healed by some process of right thinking. We need not here discuss the merits or demerits of any of the modern cults based upon the power of the mind over the body. It is enough for us to know that the mind and the body are intimately connected and that each in a mysterious way is dependent upon the other.

There was an interesting experiment made upon a cat. Fifteen minutes after the cat had eaten generously of raw beef, it was placed under the fluoroscope and its stomach was seen working vigorously and rhythmically while Tabby purred contentedly. Then a door was opened and a dog admitted into the room. Instantly the cat's stomach became rigid, and it did not resume its activities until ten minutes after the dog had been ejected. Here is an illustration of the effect of fear upon the unconscious and automatic activity of a most important organ.

It is certainly important for a person to get right mental attitudes not only toward his own work but toward the world in general. It is important for him to know and be master of them, and it is also important for him to know and be master of his work or business.

Work that is approached with some vision of its value and meaning will become a pleasure and a privilege, instead of drudgery. The person who comes to their job feeling apprehensive and half -sick is not going to enjoy it or be particularly successful at it. If one has not mastered the fundamentals of his work and fears the daily task that faces them, they will develop a mental attitude that sooner or later will affect him physically. They will have "nerves," sleep poorly, eat erratically, and smoke or drink unwisely. The result will be a continuing and increasing feeling of physical and mental inadequacy. The solution to such a state of affairs is first. to get into shape physically and second, to get busy and study the job.

RELAXATION:
Earlier in this report, we discussed the role of exercise in fostering physical and mental efficiency. The only kind of exercise that is suitable or safe for the businessman or office worker is that which results in relaxation of body and mind and turns worry and fatigue into poise and restfulness. Athletic competition and business efficiency are incompatibles. Games and hobbies, whether requiring much or little physical activity, that produce pleasure and forgetfulness of the day's worries are not only compatible with efficiency but are, indeed necessary to it. The right organization of one's work and working environment, as we have seen previously is in itself an easing of tension. Such organization may be acquired by anyone who is sufficiently interested in their work and in their future.
First, organize the day's work so that routine matters are disposed of as they come up, quietly and without pointless fussing or anger. Second, avoid the appearance of haste or excessive activity; learn to get at the problems at hand promptly, calmly and deliberately. Third, if you find yourself breaking either of the above rules, knock off and sit still for a few minutes, or take a short walk, or talk to an associate about anything but business.

Work handled in this way will be easier, and as it becomes easier it will be pleasanter, and any occupation that is pleasant can be relaxing. You can relax while you work.

One physician had this to say on the subject: "I suspect that neither the nature nor the amount of our work is accountable for the frequency and severity of our breakdowns, but that their cause lies rather in those absurd feelings of hurry and having no time, in that breathlessness and tension--by which with us the work is apt to be accompanied."

MODERATION:
This word is nearly synonymous with relaxation in that the latter implies moderation in the expenditure of our physical and intellectual assets. It is quite possible to relax immoderately and become lazy and shiftless. Some people do just that, because they "feel tired and need rest." It is quite likely that there is nothing about their fatigue that a little hard work would not remedy.

We are concerned here with moderation as it applies to busy people who have work to do. They seldom complain of fatigue, and when they do, it is not work that will be a remedy nor is it exercise, or play, or vitamins or what not. Until they learn to practice moderation in all things, they are quite as likely to be an s immoderate in their exercising and play as they are in their work.

Earlier we had suggested that moderation and control of the energy that goes into the daily job will result in an improved output and a happier worker. It is just as true that moderation and control of the energy in the form of food and drink that a person puts into them will result in improved efficiency and a happier individual. The rise in the mortality rates for certain types of heart disease during the past twenty-five years in disconcerting. Many of the victims of this disease are active and successful business and professional men in their late forties and fifties, and most of them in the prime of life and effectiveness at the time of death. These men have been laying the groundwork for their early passing during their active thirties. They have worked intensely, played hard and even violently, eaten and carelessly and heavily, and most of them have smoke incessantly. We do not know exactly what reasonable moderation might have accomplished in prolonging the useful lives of those who have gone, but the fact that people with such a background do tend to die early and suddenly should not let us forget that there is a word called "moderation."

From the foregoing information, it can be readily seen that moderation will keep the mind and body healthier. That means that better thinking can be done and better decisions will be made.
One should learn mediation and how to clear the mind to reduce the pressures of a fast-moving world. With these objectives in mind, we suggest that your studies encompass learning and practicing a routine of yoga. Practically every City has such facilities to be taught yoga or, it is suggested to join a Health Club that can give you a routine of body exercises. Smart people stay looking young simply because these programs will reduce the stress in your body and mind.
Thinking clearly without being distracted from ailments or aches and pains will allow you to make life easier and more enjoyable. People are under the impression that in today's advanced medical world there is an answer for anything and all you need is money to solve the problem. We are emphasizing right now that if you have a problem, as described in the foregoing information, it is up to you and not only the doctor to help you. The lifestyle you lead should be in accordance with the good practices you have learned and eliminate from your life the harmful ways that you may be in the habit of doing.

You can't do a good job if you don't have the strength and stamina to cope with the many problems you face every day. Your mind won't work better than your body in the long run.

Scientific and medical research long ago documented the linkages between daily habits and lifetime health, and the evidence is irrefutable: People who exercise live longer.

This conclusion is further supported by the ongoing College Alumni Study begun in 1962 and led by epidemiologist Dr. Ralph S. Paffenbarger, Jr., of the University of

California at San Francisco. The study shows that individuals who walk an average of five city blocks a day, climb five flights of stairs daily, or engage in 30 minutes of vigorous sports play a day are significantly less likely to suffer a heart attack or sudden death than their more sedentary counterparts. Even more important, by the time these individuals reach their seventies, they live an average of two years longer than non-exercisers.

A wealth of anecdotal experience demonstrates that exercisers enjoy a higher quality and quantity of life; the College Alumni Study adds proof that physical activity also extends the quantity of life. Equally strong evidence underscores the negative impact of poor health practices. Cigarette smokers, for example, is 30 times more likely than nonsmokers to develop lung cancer and three times as likely to incur heart disease. Elevated cholesterol and blood pressure independently expose the individual to twice the risk of heart disease. Even more alarming is evidence that risk factors multiply-rather than simply add to-each other. An individual with high cholesterol and elevated blood pressure who smokes is 8 times more likely to develop heart disease than an individual with none of these risk factors.

While the impact of personal habits on health is self-evident, the relationship between exercise and job performance is not so obvious. Executives often ask what happens to their bodies when they exercise. Physical activity triggers a number of physiologic processes, some immediately, some within a minute or so, and stills others within 5 to 10 minutes. This is because the body has two major systems for generating the energy required for exercise and all other daily activity. The systems are called "aerobic" and "anaerobic."

Aerobic literally means "in the presence of air." This system combines carbon-containing fuels in the body, such as glucose, with oxygen carried in the bloodstream to generate the molecules needed to supply energy. The aerobic energy system is the body's primary energy producer. It is responsible for virtually all of the energy that maintains the body at rest and more than 90$ of the energy produced during exercise-except during short bursts of intense exertion.

The anaerobic system generates energy in the absence of oxygen. Even at rest, a small portion of energy comes from this source. Its major roles, however, occur during the first minute of exercise, before an increased amount of oxygen-rich blood

can reach the exercising muscles and during short bursts of high -intensity exercise when the demand for energy briefly overwhelms the capacity of the aerobic system.

If you consider the body analogous to an automobile, the aerobic system is like the regular carbonization system for the engine. The anaerobic system serves as a kind of fail-safe system for the engine. The anaerobic system serves as a kind of fail-safe system or booster pump to allow short bursts of intense energy. The aerobic output is by far the most efficient. When the anaerobic system kicks in, it allows increased energy production, but it also generates a lot of waste products because it is so much less efficient.

What happens, then, when you begin exercising? Let's say you are about to spend 20 minutes jogging, fitness walking, or working out on a stationary cycle. As you take your first step or perform the first pedal revolution, the exercising muscles immediately begin to expend energy to contract and call on the heart and lungs to deliver more oxygen-rich blood. It takes 45 to 90 seconds for the increased quantities of oxygenated blood pumped out by the heart to reach the exercising muscles. During this time, your muscles rely on local energy supplies while your body slowly shifts from anaerobic to aerobic energy production.

By the time you reach the two-to three-minute mark (about a quarter mile for most joggers), energy production stabilizes with more than 90% coming from the aerobic processes. As long as you maintain a steady pace and exercise within your appropriate capacity, energy production will be very stable and your workout will remain comfortable.

At the end of your exercise, as you taper off, energy production declines slowly; however, energy consumption remains somewhat elevated for several minutes after you stop. This time period is sometimes called "oxygen debt" to suggest that you are "paying back" some of the initial anaerobic metabolism used at the beginning of your exercise and, to a much smaller degree, throughout your workout.

Besides providing insights into your energy levels, understanding the physiology of exercise will also help you appreciate the importance of gradual warm-up and cool-down periods, During the first few minutes of exercise, your heart and lungs are struggling to catch up with the needs of the exercising muscles. Sudden strenuous exercise, without proper warm-up, will, at the least, be very uncomfortable, since you force your body to become deeply anaerobic and generate large amounts of waste. Sudden strenuous exercise can even be dangerous, since you force your heart to jump from its normal resting state to intense activity without proper warm-up.

Cooling down is no less important. During peak exercise, subtle changes occur in the blood vessels. For example, many of the vessels to the muscles dilate to facilitate blood flow to areas where it is needed most. After the workout, your heart and cardiovascular system are easing back into the resting state. A gradual cool-down allows vessels to constrict, blood flow to be redirected, and normal, slower rhythm to resume. At the same time, proper cool-down also helps your body rid itself of wastes that have accumulated during exercise.

Whether for competitive athletes or competitive executives, certain types of activities and sports are classified as "aerobic," since they are ideal for conditioning and improving the aerobic energy production system. The most common aerobic exercises, and the ones we recommend, are fitness walking, jogging or running, swimming, and cycling (outdoor or stationary). Rowing (outdoors or on an indoor machine), cross-country skiing (outdoors or on a simulator), and aerobic dance are also excellent aerobic exercises. The underlying similarity among all of these forms of exercise is the use of large muscle groups in repetitive fashion.

When an inactive executive initiates an aerobic exercise program, or increases an existing one, important physiological changes occur. These changes, which reliably occur during an 8-12 week period, include an increase in work capacity, less fatigue at any level of work, and a decrease in resting heart rate. Together, these changes are called the "training effect." Hundreds of scientific studies have demonstrated that these changes occur in men and women of any age, providing they follow an appropriately high level of exercise on a regular basis for 8 to 12 weeks.

There are four criteria for achieving a training effect. The exercise must be:
Aerobic
Consistent (We generally recommend 3 to 5 times per week)
Intense (enough to elevate the heart rate to 60% to 85% of predicted maximum)
Continuous (20 to 60 minutes per session)

These four guidelines have been adopted by the American Heart Association and the American College of Sports Medicine as a prescription for aerobic exercise. Some exercise physiologists summarize the last three guidelines as FIT: Frequency 3 to 5 times per week, Intensity (60% to 85% of maximum heart rate), and Time (20 to 60 minutes).

As you develop a consistent pattern of aerobic exercise, you begin to establish regular times when you call on your heart and exercising muscles to work harder. Over an 8 to 12-week period, both become more efficient. The heart becomes more productive in terms of pumping larger volumes of oxygenated blood (in medical parlance, the "cardiac output" increases).

One manifestation of this increased efficiency is the decrease in resting heart rate that individuals experience shortly after starting an exercise program. Since the more efficient heart pumps out more oxygenated blood per beat, fewer beats are required per minute. As Dr. Paul Dudley White, the father of American cardiology, said, "Every human heart is programmed at birth for a certain number of beats."

Most cardiologists agree that it is healthier to take those beats with a trained heart at 55 beats per minute than at an untrained rate of 80 beats per minute. Another physiological change that occurs with training is the increased efficiency with which exercising muscles extract oxygen from the blood. Thus, while the heart muscle is growing stronger, the exercising muscles are growing more efficient, reducing the load on the heart since more oxygen can be extracted per unit of blood pumped out. While this adaptation to exercise is important to anyone who wants to improve cardiovascular endurance, it is critical to patients with coronary heart disease who have angina or have suffered a heart attack. The load that is taken off the heart by the increased efficiency of exercised muscles is often the key to resuming an active life.

While exercise physiology may seem a bit arcane, it underlies the improved energy levels and sense of well-being you experience once you launch an aerobic exercise program and stick with it.

The predictable training effects, which represent increased cardiovascular endurance reliably begin to occur within 8 to 12 weeks of starting an aerobic exercise program and are highly adaptive for hard-charging executives. The greater endurance, increased feelings of well-being, and control over one's body, as well as the reduced sense of stress, all contribute directly to the needs that top executives typically express.

You probably think better but not notice it right away but having more stamina and being more alert is certainly a good place to start. If lower stress, greater stamina, and an enhanced sense of well-being were the only benefits of improved cardiovascular fitness, they would easily justify prescribing aerobic exercise for every executive in America. However, there's an even greater justification or incentive, and that's the role that consistent aerobic exercise and cardiovascular health is far more than a matter of productivity; it is an issue of life and death.

REVELATION #21
ORGANIZE

Almost everyone is endowed at birth with a capital of half a million - not in actual coin-of-the-realm dollars-but in precious hours, A half a million of hours of life! Time is money. These hours represent a great asset, especially if you use them to do things that make money.

How much of your capital in time have you now used efficiently towards the goal you covet? You may still have a quarter of a million hours left that you can channel into a program for winning financial independence as a badge of success, to enjoy the fruits of your success during your later life, or to leave an estate to your loved ones.

The time is now-not next month or next year -to put your fortune-building plan into effect, before Father Time starts to clip your wings.

Will power is the guiding force of human destiny. Power of will lifts man past physical handicaps; a giant will has put a crippled body in the executive seat of one of the greatest properties in America.

Consider the will power of Napoleon-the one thing that carried him past obstacles that seemed insurmountable. In the face of defeat, disgrace, exile, and imprisonment, his giant will have struck off iron chains and brought him back a conqueror.

Willpower is a commercial asset, the value of which is far beyond human reckoning. One of the world's greatest generals once observed: "For everything you must have a plan." Plan, according to Webster, is "an arrangement step by step; a procedure; a method of action."

John R. Sauer, the mastermind behind the prestigious firm of Success Associates International, Inc., maintains that it was a definite plan of action that he formulated, backed of course by motivation, that catapulted him into the magic circle of wealth.

That company's outstanding training text, "Bow to Become Financially Independent," stresses the need for a plan-a complete business program-for acquiring fortunes; the course then outlines with precision all steps necessary and offers a formula to follow. The training text reveals failure-proof methods of successful millionaires who have put the capital hours of their life to work to earn precious dividends in accumulated wealth.

In this day and age, you can start a business with little or no money capital. Credit itself is an asset. There are ways that you can tap the public purse to obtain working capital for worthy enterprises. The public purse is also called O.P.M. - Other People's Money. The course mentioned above shows how credit can be developed and how the O.P.M. factor can be used.

Everyone knows about the population explosion today. Another important explosion occurred during the late 60s and continues into the 70s. Possibly this explosion is far more important for the welfare and future of everyone. It is called the Knowledge Explosion.

From the start of the Age of Science in the middle of the Seventeenth Century to the present, Professor Solomon Diamond-in his book The World of Probability-estimates that the fund of human knowledge has doubled every fifteen years. "Today," he says, ''we know about two million times as much about the universe we live in and the creatures, which include man, that inhabit it as was known shortly after the death of Galileo."

In the field of human achievement, motivation, self-advancement and self-improvement, more specific, scientific, useful information and ideas have been developed in the past ten years than in the two hundred years before it.

The man who is really serious about becoming financially independent can no longer plead ignorance of the ways and means of becoming successful. The facts are available. What he needs is the grit and the motivation to start a fortune-building program.

You-and every other red-blooded, ambitious man in this country-are virtually on the threshold of liberation-liberation from monetary worries. Opportunity is the vehicle that will provide the escape from poverty and the rewards of wealth.

In this great land of America there is no scarcity of opportunity. Hardly a service or a product cannot be improved. The men who recognize and initiate these improvements by using their imaginations will reap their rewards in fortunes.

Never forget Grover Cleveland who said: "Seeing opportunity and seizing it are two different relations." The man who sits in a poker game all evening and never makes a bet will eventually ate away all his chips. Life is like that, too. You must make an occasional bet. You must take a calculated risk now and then as you go along if you ever hope to get anywhere. "Nothing ventured, nothing gained," is a law of life. You must be willing to back your abilities with your capital hours, using them as your stake. If you don't believe in yourself, how can you expect anyone else to believe in you?

It is a law of nature also that if you want to receive, you must be prepared to give. There's no getting around this rule of the game. You must make some bets-bets on yourself-or be left jogging along in the same old routine rut.

If you want to get rich, the secret is simple: Supply a need. Find a product or service that people really need. Merchandise it better than anyone else. Offer it at the lowest price you can, and pocket the profits. Put some of the profits into investment channels. That's all there is to it. The man who tries to get more than he gives is riding for a fall.

The entire world loves a winner. The instinct of hero-worship is inherent in everyone. The man who fights a good clean battle and comes out on top can count on the crowd's sympathy. "We want you to win!" Look at the reception the astronauts were given on their return from the moon. Look at the applause sports champions and entertainment stars receive. The principle of the winner applies not only to spectacular achievement but to humbler victories as well.

Are you a salesman? The boss wants you to win. He gets a glow of satisfaction in seeing you batter down obstacles, and it isn't solely a matter of profits. If you are going to make a speech, the audience wants you to succeed. Are you a scientist working in some remote laboratory? A thousand learned voices will be ready with accolades if you succeed. The world wants you to win. It needs more successes.

No one can lick you but you yourself. In the long run, you are the only one who can keep yourself from getting ahead. If you stubbornly refuse to be downed by disasters, obstacles and reverses, the world will not count you out.

Not only are you the fighter, but you are the referee himself. The decision is really yours to make. It is only when you say, "I'm licked!" that the fight is over. Many a fight has been won in the last tough round.

Everyone is talking about the pollution of the earth these days. Not too many are aware of another form of pollution-pollution of thought and mind-thoughts tinged with skepticism, pessimism, self-recrimination, doubts and fears. These are the invisible impurities that can disease and cripple the power of the mind, and can haunt your future.

Self-motivation is one sure remedy for mind pollution. If you hold tenaciously to positive thoughts of your goal there will be no room in your mind for negative thoughts.

ORGANIZE YOUR TIME:

You won't find it in your wallet or your bank account. You can't borrow it. You can't work harder and earn more of it; and certainly you can't hoard it. In fact, all you can do with it is spending it. It's Time, of course, the universal coin of achievement, equally available to all.

Robert Ripley, the "Believe It or Not" man, once pointed out: "A plain bar of iron is worth $5. This same bar of iron, when made into horseshoes, is worth $10.50. If made into needles, it is worth $355. If made into pen knife blades, it is worth $3,285, and if turned into balance springs for watches, that identical bar of iron becomes worth $250,000." The same is true of time.

Some people can turn an hour into horseshoes; others can turn it into needles. A smaller number know how to change it into knife blades. But only a few of us have learned how to transform a golden hour into true-tempered watch springs!

Think of the man you most admire. Perhaps he is a high-ranking government official, a man with awesome responsibilities, and one whose decisions affect millions. Perhaps he is the president of a giant corporation, the moving force behind a far-flung industrial empire who must be up to date on a thousand crucial facts. Perhaps he is a world-renowned scientist whose experiments have resulted in a better world for all. Perhaps he is a next-door neighbor who somehow manages to be successful at everything he tries-the sort of man who gets things done with an apparent minimum of effort.

Whoever the man-regardless of his age, economic status, or family background-he has not one second more of time at his disposal than you!
HE SPENDS HIS CAPITAL:
He has merely learned how to spend his share of available time to best advantage, to pack every working minute of his life with meaningful, productive accomplishment. If you knew what he knows-*how to eliminate the needless steps in every job, the proper way to start a day, what not to have around when working, the simplest way of reaching a decision, the easy road to self-discipline-success in your job and all other activities would virtually be assured.
There are not many like him, for few people have mastered the art of getting things done efficiently. Most of us coast haphazardly through our days, relying on "inspiration," chance, and scrambled last-minute activity to do our jobs. We dissipate our time capital with a recklessness we would never permit in our handling of money matters. Can you honestly say that you are using your time in the most fulfilling, profitable way? At day's end, can you look back with satisfaction to a succession of accomplishments? Do you regularly get the things done that you want and hope to do-and still have time to pursue your hobbies or to find new ones, to do all the reading you want, get acquainted with your family, make new friends, join in civic activities?

If your answer to these questions is a blanket yes, congratulations! You are well on your way to success. If, however, you find yourself shaking your head and admitting that your capital of minutes, hours, and days seem to glide wastefully past you-what follows can literally change your life.
For while there is no way of trapping a minute and saving it for future use, there are hundreds of ways to use each passing minute so effectively that it does the

work of two.

A double-duty minute here, another there and you will soon find the extra hours for which you've searched so long. By mastering the following techniques and tips for out-witting the clock, you can increase your working time capital by 500 hours-or more than twelve forty-hour weeks-annually.

Just think! What could you do with three extra months each year? Perhaps that question should be rephrased: What couldn't you do with three extra months each year? Think about it! Even more important to your Personal Success Program, of course, is the fact that your greater efficiency will have a big effect on your job and its future.

You wouldn't dream of building a house before you had floor plans to work from. You wouldn't hop into your car for a transcontinental trip without first consulting a map. Then why expect your use of time to take care of it?

Behind every achievement, large and small, lies a plan. And if you are determined to getting things done, the sooner you learn how to plan, the better.

It's really possible. All you have to do is:

Define your goals.

Work out a definite program.

Set up timetables.

Concentrate on essentials.

Let us take them one at a time.

DEFINE YOUR DAILY GOALS:

You'll get wherever you're going a lot faster if you know where you are going. Basic stuff! Perhaps. But most people bumble along ineffectually simply because they've never pinpointed in their own minds precisely what they want out of life. Lacking targets to aim at, they play each day "by ear." But if you spell out your goals you will have not only the direction but also the incentive for getting things done.

It is important that you keep those goals as vivid as possible. Thus, a picture of your "dream home" in your wallet can be just the thing to pump that extra bit of drive into your system. A "thermometer" chart of savings for a business of your own can make thrift into a thrilling game.

Want to lose weight? Don't torture yourself with "what's-the-use?" thinking. Instead, dig up a photograph of yourself in your slender days, tape it to the refrigerator, and watch your will power turn to iron!

Does this vivid-goal technique work? Ask any size-sixteen gal who blows two weeks' salary on a size-twelve evening gown, then diets her way into it. Or ask the young salesman who always dreamed of visiting far-off lands. A so-so performer during his first two years with a gardening equipment firm, he suddenly opened up with a spurt of sales that dazzled his sales manager. In six months, he matched his previous year's record. By the end of his third year, he was top man in his district. The secret? Be had plastered his bedroom with travel posters. The first thing he saw upon waking in the morning was an aerial view of the Eiffel Tower; the last thing to meet his eyes at night was a tantalizing senorita in a lace mantilla.

If you stop and think for a moment, however, you will discover that you have more than one goal in life. Each can be a powerful ally in your success.

BUSINESS AND PROFESSIONAL GOALS:

First, there probably is your work goal. Perhaps your aim is to increase the amount of correspondence you turn out each day. Then take a tip from the large-company executive who devised this simple way of boosting his output. In his own words, "I found myself turning out only eight or ten letters a day when I knew I should be producing twice that number. So, I decided to try a little experiment. Before coming to the office one day, I put twenty beans in my right pocket. I promised myself to transfer a bean to my left pocket every time I dictated a letter-and took a solemn oath not to leave my office until every bean had been transferred. I stayed overtime the first day, but when I left the office, every bean was in my left pocket. The second day, I did better, the third still better. By the second week, I was turning out twenty letters a day with time to spare. My little game had paid off."

Perhaps your long-range goal is a specific income, say $15,000 a year. What do you associate with that figure? Two cars? A summer cottage in Maine? Long vacations? Then make that goal concrete with photos of the cars you'd like or hang the fish you caught last summer in Maine over your mantel or keep a me of travel folders in your library.

Want to be your own boss some day? Buy a name plate and place it on your bureau-a constant reminder of the day your employees will knock on a door to see you. No matter what the goal-better performance tomorrow or better life years from now-there is a way of dramatizing it to you? Find out what it is and you'll be on your way to achieving it.

PERSONAL GOALS:

You may entertain certain dreams for your family. These may include an extra TV set for the playroom, a trip across America next year, a fur coat for your wife, college education for the kids, financial security for all. Big or small, immediate or long-range, your dreams can be brought to earth and turned into concrete attainable goals. And once you can see them, you can aim for them.

SELF-IMPROVEMENT GOALS:

Finally, there is the goal of personal growth, which includes such aims as travel,

·widening the circle of your friendships, reading more books and magazines, enrolling in adult education courses, pursuing favorite hobby or sport, perhaps even learning a foreign language. Isolate the ones that mean most to you and give them top priority. By transforming your general desire for self-improvement into specific goals, you will have taken the first vital step toward their realization.

TAKE A SHOT!

Goals are not enough. You must fortify your determination to reach them. An effective form of insurance is-the boast! You commit yourself by announcing your

plans to those close to you-wife, sweetheart, friend, boss-people you'd hate to let down. The desire to "save face" is deeply ingrained in all of us. Why not make it work for you? On the other band, be sure you don't let your ambitions dissolve in talk. There is a great difference between a puff and a promise. Stick to the promises.

So, the first general rule for organizing your time is-

Define Your Goals

Having determined exactly what you want and committed yourself to success, you are ready to-

WORK OUT A DEFINITE PROGRAM:

Obviously, if you now earn $85 a week, it is not enough to sit down and say to your wife, "Mary, I'm going to double that amount someday." Such a goal, while certainly attainable, sounds discouragingly distant and indefinite.

The proper way to reach that goal-or any other-is to break it down into easy sections and approach it one step at a time.

Thus, a $200 weekly income becomes a good deal more than a pipe dream if visualized as an eight-rung latter: $170-$190-$220-$2S0-$280-$320-$360-$400.

Each ring, as a goal in itself, is attainable. In combination, they bridge what at first appears a yawning abyss between ambition and reality. Similarly, you may want to paint your house but 1md yourself shuddering at the prospect. The one-step-at-a-time approach whittles a major project down to achievement-size. By painting just one room a week, you can redo an eight-room house in two months-with, incidentally, a minimum of fuss and interference with household routine.

The point is: action breeds action, success breeds success. As you achieve each smaller goal, you will find your determination-and ability-to achieve the big goal gaining momentum.

REWARD YOURSELF:

To keep up this acceleration, reward yourself. Put a "price" on the successful completion of every task-and pay off without fail.

A successful magazine writer for example, always treats himself to a cigarette

244

after he has completed a page of text. It may take him fifteen minutes or two hours, but

he steadfastly refrains from smoking during the writing of a page. ''It may not sound like much of a reward," he explains, "but it gives me the necessary itch to get done."

Your reward may range from a cup of coffee for having mowed the lawn to a trip to Bermuda for landing the Wilson account. The important thing is to set a "price"

that you know you want-then aim for it. Sure, it's the old dangling-carrot routine, but it works.

PUT IT IN WRITING:

Once you know what your sub goals are, write them out in a business-like manner on the practice cards provided for that purpose. Make them realistic and detailed and arrange them in logical sequence. Next to each sub goal jot down whatever specific steps, special training, experience, practice, or contacts are necessary to their realization.

The accumulation of $1500 in cash, for instance, at the rate of $50 a month, will take 30 months. When 20 or 22 of those 30 months have passed, it will be time to start looking for a location that meets your requirements. A few months later you should enroll for that bookkeeping course. When would be a good time to start looking for employees? Finally, two or three months before the official opening of your station, you start planning your advertising campaign, to break about two weeks before you open your doors.

On the practice cards, you will notice a column headed "To be achieved by." In this column, set down your deadlines. It is vitally important, of course that you keep those dates realistic yet challenging.

Perhaps you can't expect, for example to save $1500 in six months. But with careful management, you can accumulate it in 30 months.

TURN YOUR PLAN INTO A PROGRAM:

The only way to reap the full benefits of planning is to turn this approach into a complete program for organizing your time. That means using the plan technique straight down the line, from getting tomorrow's chores done to realizing your personal "Five-Year-Plan."

Consider your daily and weekly goals as bricks. Piled on top of each other according to plan, they will, over a period of months, form walls. In a year, or two, or five, you will have the house you've always wanted.

SET UP TIMETABLES:

That house will go up a lot faster if you pour the foundation first; lay the bricks in order, then construct the roof. For the way to reach your goals, to get things done, is to work by a plan that makes sure each step is the right one to take.

One day, many years ago, efficiency expert Ivy Lee was interviewing Charles Schwab, President of Bethlehem Steel Company. Lee outlined his organization's service to Schwab and ended by saying, "With our service, you'll know how to manage better."

"Hell," said Schwab, "I'm not managing as well now as I know how to. We don't need more "knowing" but more "doing." If you can give us something to pep us up to do the things we already know we ought to do, I'll gladly listen to you and pay you anything within reason you ask."

"Fine," answered Lee, "I can give you something in twenty minutes that will step up your doing at least 50 percent. "Okay," said Schwab. "Let's have it. I've got just about that much time before I leave to catch a train."

Lee handed Schwab a blank sheet of note paper and said: "Write down the six most important tasks you have to do tomorrow and number them in order of their importance. Now, put this paper in your pocket and the first thing tomorrow morning look at item one and start working on it until it is finished. Then tackle item two in the same way; then item three, and so on. Do this until quitting time. Don't be concerned if you have only missed one or two. You'll be working on the most important ones. The others can wait. If you can't finish them all by this method, you couldn't have with any other method either; and without some system, you'd probably not even have decided which was the most important.

"Do this every working day. After you've convinced yourself of the value of this system, have your men try it. Try it as long as you wish, and then send me a check for what you think it is worth."

In a few weeks Schwab sent Lee a check for $25,000 with a letter saying the lesson was the most profitable he had ever learned. In five years, this plan was largely responsible for turning the unknown Bethlehem Steel Company into the biggest independent steel producer in the world. What worked for Charles Schwab can work for you.

The logic of this is simple. You can do only one thing at a time. If you try to do that one thing while worrying about the other jobs you can't do at the same time anyway, you'll take longer on the job you are doing and get still further behind the 8-ball.

So always list the jobs you have to do in order of their importance and tackle them one at a time. Forget the others until you've finished the one you're working on.

In the office or in your pocket, a daily calendar is essential-and not just for appointments. If a new job has to be started or followed up next Wednesday, note this on Wednesday's page and forget about it until Wednesday. If a letter has to be answered after you get some needed information, don't keep the letter on your desk while you wait a couple of days for the information. Slip it between your calendar pages or, if you have many such letters, into the Thursday folder. You'll find it Thursday and, if you still haven't received the information, it will remind you to follow up. Put everything you can on a timetable. Note it down and forget it until the right time comes.

TIME LIMITS GET THINGS DONE:

After you have decided the order of importance of the tasks before you, set time limits on their accomplishment. Tell yourself, for example, that you will write that long overdue letter by eight o'clock this evening, have that sinister rattle in the car attended to before driving to work tomorrow morning, read those reports before lunch; and clean out the garage before you tune in on your favorite TV show.

There are three good reasons for setting deadlines:

You challenge yourself. Everyone cherishes a certain image of him and will do anything to sustain that "self-image." Hence, a man who sees himself as a graceful dancer spends hours learning the latest steps in order to maintain his ideal of himself. Another. proud of his ability as an amateur photographer. surrounds himself with expensive cameras and equipment. Almost everyone's "self-image" includes a sense of honor. We like to believe that we can be counted on. By establishing a time limit in which to accomplish something, we are in a sense challenging our good opinion of ourselves. In order to meet that challenge, we summon all our capabilities. It amounts to "saving face" in front of you and it is an enormous incentive.

You alert your body. Sit in an easy chair and your muscles relax. You breathe slowly, your pulse beats at a normal rate. But get up with the intention of lifting that easy chair and your muscles, anticipating the job before them, flex and tighten; you breathe faster in order to deliver the extra oxygen your body needs for work; your pulse quickens as your heart pumps more blood to all parts of the body. Many other subtle physical changes take place.

In the same way, the knowledge that a certain task must be accomplished by a specified time alerts your body to prepare itself for the job at hand. Even if the assignment is mental, writing a report for example, your body responds by sending more blood and oxygen to the brain.

You are being affirmative. "If you think you can, you can," a wise man once said. When you say to yourself, "I will have my walk shoveled free of snow by 10 A.M.," you are really declaring your ability to shovel away the snow by that time. And it is always easier to do something when you know you can do it. Clearly, though, it is important that you be realistic about your deadlines.

HOW TO "CASE" A PROJECT.

Frequently, it is possible to estimate the time for a project from personal experience. Should you wish to read a 320-page novel, for example, you may know from past performance that you read novels at the rate of 40 pages an hour. You intend to read two hours a day. At 80 pages a day, it will take you four days to finish the book.

For projects that are outside your own experience, you can inquire among friends. You may never have drive to Montreal, but your neighbor took his family there last year. Because he is familiar with the roads, he is in a position to help you estimate how long the trip should take. Better still, you can check the exact mileage with your local automobile club and make your own estimate.

Some projects have built- in deadlines: paint must be allowed to dry, a basic course in merchandising lasts 16 weeks, trains run on schedules, offices close at 5 P.M., people go on vacations.

Simple arithmetic can help. If your long-range family goal is to move into a house of your own, you can judge pretty close to the wire exactly when you will have enough money for the down payment. Saving $40 a month and need $1500? You'll have the down payment in 37.5 months, or a little over three years. Allowances must he made for unforeseeable obstacles, interruptions, and necessary changes in plans. Getting things done on schedule calls for flexible tenacity, not bulldog obstinacy.

MAKE YOUR DEADLINES REALISTIC

Your deadlines, then, should be reasonable. If they are not, and you fail to meet them, you risk frustration and loss of confidence. To avoid either pitfall, bear in mind the following before you set your time limits:

Allow sufficient time for fact-gathering. Many tasks require specialized knowledge: reports must be read, people consulted, letters exchanged, phone calls made. Take these preliminary steps into consideration when establishing your deadline.

Don't forget the tools you will need. Whether your task calls for paper clips or power tools, remember the time it will take to beg, borrow, or buy the proper equipment.

Mishaps can upset schedules. Sure, you can save $1000 in a year-if no unexpected medical or dental bills pop up along the way. No reason why you shouldn't get to that appointment on time-unless there's a traffic jam. It's good planning to add 10 percent to any time limit-just in case. If those mishaps fail to materialize, it's so much gravy.

Interruption costs time. Phone calls, little emergencies, visitors, conferences-all can toss a deadline for a loss. Unless you've already found Shangri-La, make allowances for these petty time thieves.

Your supply of energy varies. Sometimes you feel you could lick Superman; other times you wonder how you can last through to 5 P.M. That's normal. We all experience bursts of energy and short circuits. On a day when you know you're clicking, you can shave your deadlines, confident that you will meet them. On "off" days, give yourself leeway.

By keeping your time limits realistic, you will avoid the "doing man's" archenemy, "deadline jitters," that unreasoning jumpiness that can paralyze your faculties and triple the difficulty of any job. A deadline, after all, is like a suit: too tight or too loose, it doesn't allow a man to show himself at his best. But carefully tailored, it flatters, builds confidence, and is supremely practical.

CONCENTRATE ON ESSENTIALS:
Ever have one of those days when you can't seem to get started? You spend your first half -hour sharpening pencils, rearranging papers, thumbing through old mail. Because you feel guilty about not being able to get down to work, you simulate work, going through the motions but accomplishing little or nothing.

The only antidote is to learn how to boss you. How To Gain An Extra Hour Every Day, Ray Josephs advises, "Develop the habit of self-starting, the frame of mind which says: "I shall never sit and brood for any length of time, questioning what I do. I'll begin on things I know can be started and from that beginning get the rest going." Self-discipline is based on three resolutions:
A. "I can." The knowledge that you have the ability for a job gives you the confidence to tackle it. Next time you find yourself shying away from a task remember how well you did it or something similar to it. Then dive in.
B. "I want to." What's your favorite sport? Golf? Skiing? Bowling? Whatever it is, you know that you can do it for hours without tiring. The reason is simple: you enjoy it, and you know what to do. The mind has extraordinary influence over the body. Expect to be bored by a job and chances are you will be. But whip up some old-fashioned enthusiasm for it and you'll be amazed.
C. "I must." In emergencies, men who never swam before have sliced their way through rivers. If you give yourself no alternatives to accomplishing a specific project, you will accomplish it. Those three statements-"! can," "I want to," "I must" are the keys to self-discipline.
ELIMINATE THE UNNECESSARY
Hard on the heels of the morning wind- up as a time killer are the many unnecessary steps we take in doing things. Common sense tells us that if we can simplify our work, we will save time and get more done.
Answer the following questions about the way you now do any job:
What are the separate steps I take in doing it? Actually, write them down here, for your most worrisome single job. Write them in order, so that you can study

them:

Can any of those steps be skipped without spoiling the result? Frequently, we become habit-bound and continue to do things simply because we have always done them. For example, before you drive to work, do you always sit in your car for a minute or two and warm up the engine? Except for the coldest days, you could probably just hop in and drive off in 30 seconds. (Save gas, too). Look over your steps to see if any can be skipped.

Can the order of the steps be changed? Just because you've always done ABCD doesn't mean that ACBD might not be a more efficient approach. If you always step into your trousers first thing in the morning. then slip on your shirt, try reversing the order. You'll find it's faster. Check your steps on the sample job again.

Are there any chores that can or ought to be done by someone else? One of the biggest stumbling blocks in the way of efficiency is the inability to delegate. Few have mastered the knack of separating the things that only they can do from the things that others can. If, for example, you are now looking up information, why not let someone else (if you have someone else working for you) do it? Let an ambitious neighborhood kid mow your lawn while you repair the hose. Have your assistant clean up your work bench. Look over your sample steps once more to see if you can delegate any of them.

DON'T SPEND DOLLAR TIME ON PENNY JOBS

Larry Shaw was a junior executive in an electronics firm. One day his department head called a top-level meeting to hammer out some fundamental points of company policy. The meeting, scheduled for 9 A.M. sharp, came to order precisely on time-but not a sign of Larry, who had a report to give. A hurried phone call to Larry's home brought forth this explanation from Mrs. Shaw: it was their son's birthday and Larry had dashed downtown to pick up some streamers for the party, to be held later in the day.

When Larry, somewhat breathless, arrived at the meeting at 9:20, he was stunned to find the conference room smothered under what seemed miles of streamers. "There is ten dollars worth of streamers here," his department head explained. "That's the amount of money you've cost the company by wasting your own time and the time of all the other men here. You earn $300 a week or $10.00 an hour. That's over 1.50 cents a minute. To buy $ 1.00 cents' worth of streamers for your boy's birthday, you spend $ 10.00 of your time. That's poor management." Larry Shaw came away from that meeting with a new respect for the value of time.

So, before you undertake any job, figure what the result will be worth. Then estimate your "time cost." Is the result worth it? If it isn't eliminate or delegate it. In order to drive this point home to yourself, jot down below how much your time is worth per hour.

Once you master the knack of looking at time as money, you will automatically be worth that much more to your company in terms of productivity and move that much higher on the list of those slated for future advancement.

DON'T GET IN DEBT TO YESTERDAY

You've seen them, people who, when Friday rolls around, are frantically working on Wednesday's chores. Panic stricken, they cannot do their best; in despair, they turn out slipshod work, hoping it will "get by."

If you have begun to practice the setting of time limits on your tasks, you know that these "traffic jams" can be side-stepped. If your day is planned to begin with, you can predict what you will be doing at any given hour. Your "mishap margin" takes care of minor setbacks. Everything is under control. But let's face it: sometimes things do go wrong and try as we may, comes 5 P.M. there are still things to be done. There is but one solution: do them!

The twenty or thirty extra minutes you spend in cleaning up a day's work will pay handsome dividends in self-discipline, peace of mind, and confidence. You will avoid that feeling of overwhelming defeat that greets those who must start each day by paying their debts to yesterday.

Many people even work overtime in order to start tomorrow's job the night before. In the morning, they get a psychological lift from finding a new task already begun. They can plunge right in and finish it.

Actually, they are taking advantage of a well-known psychological fact: our memory for incomplete tasks, sparked by the unresolved tensions they create, is 1000 per cent greater than our memory for completed ones. When you leave a job unfinished, your subconscious-that silent ally always on duty-goes to work on it. Later, when your return to the job, you are often amazed to discover that you have a whole new arsenal of ideas, approaches, and solutions to draw from.

Another method of avoiding backlogs is to dispose of minor morning decisions in advance. Hugh S. Bell, in his book How to Be a Winner in Selling, recalls a friend who dreaded mornings: "He said by the time he'd selected his suit, shirt, tie, and other wearing apparel for the day, and gathered up his papers and supplies, he was a nervous wreck. I told him I had once had the same problem, but that I'd learned to dispose of all these petty duties the night before.

"I suggested that he lay out his clothes ready to jump into, just like a fireman. Also, that he gets all his papers together and put them either in his car, his briefcase, or his pockets so that there would be no chance of forgetting them. Furthermore, that if he had some little chore that would take five or ten minutes, to do it before going to bed-that he'd sleep better. A few weeks later he told me that these suggestions had revolutionized his mental attitude."

RIDE YOUR ENERGY PEAKS

In the entertainment world, the general population is often separated into two categories: "day" people and "night" people. These designations refer to the fact that some of us are most alert during the morning, others in the afternoon or evening.

It's true. There are those who sizzle from 9 A.M. to noon and those who can't seem to get started till after lunch. These energy peaks, it has been determined, coincide with rises in body temperature. When your temperature is up, so is your efficiency.

That's the time to do your creative work and tackle skull-cracking problems. Temperature down? Do your less taxing chores.

Fortunately, these minor variations in your temperature are fairly consistent. So, if you can find out over a period of one day what your energy peaks are, you can adjust your work schedule accordingly.

So far, we have concerned ourselves with the four basic rules for getting things done.

They are, you will remember:

Determine your goals.

Work out a definite program.

Set up timetables.

Concentrate on essentials.

By now you know what your goals for the immediate and distant future are, how to reach them one step at a time, and how to establish - and meet - deadlines.

You are well on your way toward mastering the art of getting things done, but these techniques represent only half your battle. A hundred little villains can still nibble away at your efficiency.

ELIMINATE DISTRACTIONS IN YOUR WORK AREA

A cluttered desk or workbench cuts drastically into your productive time. Keep such temptations to idleness as newspaper, personal letters, puzzles, ornaments, and souvenirs out of sight. Once a job is done, get it out of the way. Otherwise, you may be seduced into lingering over it. Make sure your lighting is adequate for the job at hand. Investigate the possibilities of sound proofing your work area

ANTICIPATE THE TOOLS NEEDED

A lot of precious time can be salvaged simply by having the tools of your trade ready for action. This means that they are not only immediately available, but clean. Best time to set them up: the night before. Are small supplies handy enough? You can lose minutes a day-a whole week every year-if you must leave your work area every time you need paper clips, staples, rubber stamps, screws, nails, bolts. Monday, stock up on all the supplies you'll need for the week ahead. A simple rearrangement of equipment may be a step-saver. How about a pencil sharpener next to your desk? Any reason why those files you consult so often shouldn't be yards closer to you?

Among life's major frustrations are the well-intentioned interruptions of your work by friends, relatives, and co-workers. Some hints on making yourself less accessible when you really need to (always keeping in mind that you need to stay friends with your co-workers too!)

Try rearranging your lunch hour so that you are on your job when your co- workers are out eating. Sixty blissful minutes of golden silence!

Shift your furniture. You may look to inviting in your present set-up. Try facing the wall or working with your back toward others.

Be firm and let your co-workers, friends, and family know that at certain hours of the day you're strictly "off limits."

Find an inaccessible place to work-an attic room, an empty office, the public library.

Let your wife or secretary screen phone calls, intercepting those of little importance.

FINDING EXTRA TIME FOR EXTRA ACHIEVEMENT

It is one matter to do the things you must do more efficiently; it is another to do more things.

There are still just twenty-four hours in a day. Where is the additional time for self- improvement, hobbies, friends, and family to come from?

Ralph Thomas Reed, high-powered President of the American Express Company, is always at his desk by 8 A.M. Free from interruptions, he can plan his day, go over papers, and make the decisions that affect hundreds of American Express offices around the globe. By the time his vice-presidents arrive for work, a drift of yellow memos has usually settled over their desks. Mr. Reed is an outstanding example of the man who purposely rises earlier than absolutely necessary in order to get things done.

Why not emulate him? You needn't rise at the crack of dawn; merely set your alarm to ring fifteen minutes earlier than is your custom- and use the extra time for reading, attending to your garden, pursuing a course of study, listening to music, practicing your Personal Success Program.

Bow much time do you have from the moment you arrive home from work until bedtime? Four hours? Five? Six? How do you spend them?

You eat, of course. Read the paper. Watch TV. Bow about your family? Do you share some time with them? You should. Psychologists have charged the American male with neglecting his wife and children. Why not step out with your lady now and then- to a dance, a movie, a music recital, for a visit with friends? Bow about tossing around the football with Junior, or turning an approving ear to Sis' piano-playing?

Not counting your annual vacation, you have the incredible total of 107 days off each year - well over three months of your very own! Sure, sleep a little later now and then; it'll do you good. But put that treasure trove of time to use. In addition to home repairs, taking the family out on a picnic, joining in community enterprises, and indulging your taste for golf, fishing, or tennis, you have over three months to learn your business more thoroughly, develop new skills, and if you wish-earn money on the side.

Let's suppose that you had a bank that automatically credited your account each morning with $ 86,400 but never carried over the balance to the next day, and every evening totally canceled the remaining unused amount. What would you do? Spend every cent each day, of course! ACTUALLY - YOU HAVE SUCH A BANK every morning it credits you with 86,400 seconds of TIME. Every night it wipes out whatever balance of TIME you failed to use, never to be recovered.

Each day, TIME opens a new account with you. The loss or gain from use of TIME is solely yours, to either bear the loss or enjoy the accomplishments.

TIME wisely invested will pay off handsomely. Precious TIME invested today, will determine what your tomorrows will be. Don't waste your TIME. Review now - All the vital facts to obtain capital for profits.

MAKING AN AGENDA:

The manager makes it a practice procedure to make a schedule of things that have to be accomplished. This cuts down for each day usually done the night before. Naturally, it becomes impossible to accomplish all chores so what the manager did was place a star onto the most urgent items to be accomplished for that day. Whatever chores were undone was simply posted to the next day's agenda. It could honestly be stated that nothing was left undone and he did not have to keep everything in his head would increase his mental capacity.

There is a true story about a large corporate executive paying some efficiency export $25,000 for the same advice you are learning now.

DO YOU CONTROL YOUR TIME, OR DOES IT CONTROL YOU?

It often seems as though there's never enough time to accomplish everything. In fact, however, there's always enough time for everything important. The trick is to know how to use time intelligently - to learn to control your time, instead of letting time control you.

REVELATION #22
ENTREPRENEURSHIP

ENTREPRENEURS CREDO:

"I DO NOT CHOOSE TO BE A COMMON MAN. It is my right to be uncommon. If I can, I seek opportunity. Not security. I do not wish to be a kept citizen, humbled and dulled by having the state look after me. I want to take the calculated risk: to dream and to build, to fail and to succeed. I refuse to barter incentive for a dole; I prefer the challenges of life to the guaranteed existence; the thrill of fulfillment to the stale calm of Utopia. I will not trade freedom for beneficence or my dignity for a handout. I will never cower before any master nor bend to any threat.
It is my heritage to stand erect, proud and unafraid; to think and act for myself, enjoy the benefit of my creations and to face the world boldly and say; this, with God's help I have done. All this is what it means to be an entrepreneur."
Entrepreneur. Americans have fallen in love with this French noun, which the dictionary tells us, means "one who manages, and assumes the risks, of a business or enterprise."

The secret of the successful entrepreneur is in his or her ideas. To be more specific, the imagination and the vision one has in putting the idea into action and makes it a reality. It does not have to be a new idea either. Many fortunes have been made on the improvement of something existing.
Imagination is an underestimated power. Business men as a rule do not realize their indebtedness to imagination. That power is commonly thought of, not as a workhorse, but as a thoroughbred to be driven only by the poet, the artist, the storywriter. The imaginative man is often thought of as a dreamer. He may entertain us with the beautiful pictures his mind creates, but we do not expect him to be alert in practical affairs.

What is ironic about this current fascination is that the entrepreneur has occupied center state in the American economy from the very beginning. The first European settlements in North America were entrepreneurial ventures (and failures at that). Before Virginia and Massachusetts Bay were colonies, they were companies in which investors risked their incomes, and in some case their lives, in the hope of realizing a better life later on. From colonial times onward, entrepreneurs have sought opportunities, planned strategies, invented new products and services, taken risks, and found better ways to create industries and fortunes. Indeed, the American soil proved fertile ground for developing new businesses, based on minerals from aluminum to zinc, on manufactured goods from corn flakes to computers, and on services from small shops to financial supermarkets. Entrepreneurs are the unsung heroes of our past. These men and women saw challenges and opportunities where others saw nothing at all. Some were responsive, recognizing the opportunities arising out of changing circumstances; others actively created opportunities. In either case, they seized on ideas and worked tirelessly to overcome obstacles, sacrificing savings and sometimes their personal lives in the quest for new products and services. They took risks-though they often found creative ways to make the risks acceptable-and shaped how we live, from the way in which we earn our income to the ways we're likely to spend it. Risk involves losing valuable time, money and energy.

Can a busy housewife and mother of three run a successful home business? Linda S. Martin, a Specialty Merchandise Wholesaler proves that you can.
"My husband and I were talking about the business. I've been in business about one year now, but at the time, I had only been in business several months. I was proud of my achievements. I had established a large number of accounts and was making excellent profits.
"Don't you think I'm doing well?" I asked my husband, who has been in sales for many years.
"I think you can be doing better," he replied. "When your sales volume reaches $5,000 a week you can consider yourself a business success."
"I was angry at him. I started my business with virtually no investment. I never had any previous business experience. I had always stayed at home and taken care of my family. I was scared to death at first and wanted to quit. I got the needed help and encouragement from my supplier, the Specialty Merchandise Corporation (SMC), and stayed with it. I expected praise from my husband!
"The following week I called on my established accounts and prospects. I was mad! I didn't stop until my sales reached $5,000, I showed him! I did it and I was proud!
Most wealth is created by entrepreneurs understanding that creating a new business or expanding an existing business faces challenges. An entrepreneur realizes that a risk has to be confronted in order to obtain rewards. This, of course, requires a realistic view of having to face risks. This, of course, requires courage. You must have courage of your convictions in order to be an entrepreneur. There are thousands of cases that prove that at any age a man can get rich if he finds a widespread need and fills it. Here is one of the most remarkable case

histories. It demonstrates how technical skill can grow almost from nowhere, through concentration on a problem.

In one of our first case histories, the story of George Spitzer and his invention of the Rise aerated leather bomb, we saw one example of this. A man with no more than pharmacy school training learned to solve mechanical and scientific problems which first seemed impossibly beyond his powers. Elbert Hubbard once said that six months of concentrated study could make any man an expert. Most exciting is the story of the two musicians' sons who made a fortune out of Kodachrome color film.

The boys were only 15 years old when they first disclosed to each other their disappointment at the absence of color in photographs. From the age of ten both had been camera bugs, like thousands of other boys. The young are slaves to dreams; the old are servants of regrets. Only the middle-aged have all their five senses in the keeping of their wits.

In comparison with these lads, Neison Harris was an old man-he didn't begin until he had graduated from college, although the Toni Home Permanent made him a multimillionaire before he was 33.

Harris' "forebear" in the business was Charles Nessler, who invented the original permanent wave when he was a youngster in Germany. He had discovered he could curl hair by softening it with borax paste and heating it. He came to America, sold his method to hairdressers and made $3,000,000.

One entrepreneur at thirty-one, a husband, a father and broke decided to buy the money-losing Scudder's American Museum in New York. He bought the museum on credit and, drawing on his own impressive array of talents, paid for it in less than a year out of the profits earned.

If there was one dominant trait it was versatility. By the time he was thirty, he had clerked in a variety of stores, successfully running lotteries (a respected private business in his day), founded and edited a weekly newspaper, toured the South as an itinerant showman with a mediocre circus, manufactured shoe polish, sold Bibles, and written advertisements for a New York theatre.

None of these experiences was lost on him. Barnum learned something from everything he did.

From selling across a counter, he mastered the fine art of trading. From running lotteries, he came to understand, as no one had understood before, the value of advertising. Bis experience as an editor and writer gave him a deep respect for the magic of words. More important than all was what his career as a showman had taught him. "The greatest lesson I ever learned," he said, "was that everything depended on getting people to think and talk and become curious and excited about you." In short, he had stumbled upon the important secret of creating an image of himself in the public's eye.

You have to be a hard worker to achieve success? Not even this conventional assumption necessarily stands up. In the attempt to pinpoint the basic building blocks of success, the list grows longer and longer. But, in their boiled-down essence, three ingredients survive all the tests and defy exception. What are they?

Ability: You have never known a truly successful person who could not do at least one thing considerably better than most people.

Opportunity: The presence of a "showcase" for that ability.

Recognition: The acknowledgment of that ability 'by a third party of some importance.

Have you ever noticed the "ME, I CAN" in American before? It was pointed out to me years ago by my brother and it's something that has stuck with me ever since. The realization that being an American truly does give me the right that I can has made a great difference in my life. In fact, in my front yard, I have four gravestones that mark the burial of the words, 'If", Can't, Impossible, and Unfair'. It's helped our family, friends, and business associates to remind themselves not to put limitations on their lives. When Americans truly realize their potential and freedom to do great things, they accept the 'Me I can' attitude.

That is the attitude which helps one of our fundamental American rights, free enterprise, to flourish.

The only concern that I have is that many people going into business for them have no idea how to make a profit when they do start a business. The failure rate is quite high for small business ventures which scare some people from even trying. If you're a small business owner or thinking of going into business for yourself, apply the "Me, I can' attitude to yourself and everyone in your business.

One of the biggest problems for people working for themselves is that they were never trained for this. Most people that are trained or educated gain knowledge in some specific area in vocational school or college. Entrepreneurs also need specialized knowledge about how to work for them and make a profit.

Leopold Godowsky was the son of a famous pianist and composer. The father's composition Alt Wien has filled many a heart with nostalgic yearning for Vienna as it used to be. Leopold Mannes was the son of Clara and David Mannes, whose Sunday concerts in New York's Metropolitan Museum were beautiful reminders of a bygone day, Both Leopolds seemed destined to be musicians. Daily they practiced to that end.

One day, while they were still students at the Riverdale, New York, Country

School, Leo G. said to Leo M., or it might have been vice versa, "I have an idea how we might get color into pictures." "I have one too," said the other. They wrote their ideas on separate papers-found they both were the same: to make three plates, each sensitive to one of the three primary colors, then use three projectors to focus them onto one screen.

In the school lab the two boys actually produced a color picture. But they were not soon to learn their process wasn't new-nor was it too good. They graduated from Riverdale and went to college-three thousand miles apart. Summers, they worked together, perfected an improved three -nosed projector, and got a patent on it. But they came at last to the understanding that the real answer wasn't in the projecting device, but in the film itself.

It was not until they were 21 and had graduated from college that the boys went back to their project. By then they were earning their way in New York as music teachers and soloists. In the Mannes kitchen and bathroom they mixed emulsions and coated plates. Within a year these 22- year-old boys had produced a color picture integrated on one plate. It wasn't a good picture but it was an achievement that scientists had been seeking before the two Leopolds were born.

In the process of their mm development, it was not unnatural for the Leopolds to meet Dr. C. E. K. Mees, famous research director of the Eastman Kodak Company. He liked the boys and gave them a helping hand. Finally, they were invited to Rochester to complete their inventions at the great Eastman Laboratories and with a staff of specialist to help them.

A man named Richard Neison Harris was aware that women paid out millions of dollars for waves, called "permanent," and spent endless hours in beauty parlors. He saved these ladies much of their money with his Toni Home Permanent kit; have saved them time, he saved them the boredom of sitting under dryers, he saved them concern over their children at home and the roast in the oven. For this service women poured a fortune into the coffers of Wishbone Harris. At the age of 33 he sold his business to the Gillette Company for $20,000,000.

Life magazine has told the fabulous story of Wishbone Harris and his brother Irving, who joined him and created the slogan "Which twin has the Toni?" The chemical ingredient on which Toni is based is called ammonium thioglycolate. It is the same lotion that had been employed earlier in beauty shop cold waves, and Harris was not the first to offer it for home use. But he was most definitely the first to merchandise it successfully and is credited with creating today's tremendous home permanent wave industry.

Harris developed Toni after failing with a product called Rol-Wav- or perhaps because of it. In 1937, when he graduated from college, he borrowed $5,000 from his father and bought a little business called Noma, which supplied heating pads, curlers, wave lotions, and similar supplies to the beauty salon trade. He shaped this company into a neat if small operation purely on the strength of his likable personality-particularly his happy gift of gab.

One day Arnold Peterson's wife had trouble getting their baby carriage into the family car. Peterson was a machinist and he decided to make a collapsible stroller which could be transported more readily.

Peterson found he couldn't design a workable hinge. A religious man, he prayed for help. One night he saw the perfect collapsible hinge in his sleep. Next day he produced it and it proved practical. Arnold Peterson started making his Folda-Rolas in 1945. He began in a little building in Glendale, California. He had no experience in this field or any like it. Competition was tough. Stores wouldn't buy. He started selling his baby buggies house-to-house. Gradually they caught on and retailers came asking for Folda-Rolas. Today Peterson's annual volume is more than $2,000,000. He takes $60,000 a year for himself; he gives $100,000 to various churches.

If you study some of the great moguls of industry along with the small business man, you will soon get insight to the obstacles that have to be overcome. Actually, you will learn the enormity of obstacles that they had to overcome.

The following is a study of entrepreneurs that should be learned so that you can feel as though you are joining a large club. You will benefit by emulating their actions and maneuvers that were accomplished.

This study can give you an insight to the attitude of yesteryear. Mogul entrepreneurs. Perhaps you will be somewhat inspired by what you learn. The same principles that led them to success may be used today. Results may be even more dynamic if these principals are applied with modern-day technologies and marketing tools. If you like a challenge, then your oyster is waiting.

It doesn't matter if you haven't made your first million (yet): a true entrepreneur's in it for the challenge! So why not join their club? After all, most of them started off with less than you.

CAROL BARTZ, CEO of AutoDesk said "I have a simplistic philosophy: Surround yourself with good people, and the job gets done." And we all chime in "That's so true."

Carol Bartz is noted for knowledge that she has achieved and with that reputation, she is a person in demand and can earn far more than the average employee. In other words her wealth is in her knowledge.

Where are these good people, the high-achievers, those who earn promotions? Is it talent that distinguishes the employees that often are promoted? Just what are the skills which make high-achievers excel?

According to Michael W. Mercer, Ph.D., an industrial psychologist with Mercer

Group, Inc. there is six skills which make high-achievers excel:

Quickly making a great impression on anyone. "High achievers act much more charming and delightful than underachievers."
Negotiating, influencing, and persuading. This is non-stop salesmanship. Successful people do great at tactfully swaying others' ideas and actions."
Showmanship. "High-achievers act differently than underachievers in a variety of ways-from exuding more 'Can-Do' attitudes to call people by name in each encounter. In contrast, underachievers expect people to hand them opportunities, regardless of how they act."

Conducting highly productive meetings.

Delivering impressive presentations. Skills 4 & 5 go together. As a person moves up in his or her career, that person is the one conducting the meetings or giving the presentations. These high visibility actions help people form good or bad impressions of the person.

Crisp, clear business writing. Executives prefer to promote someone who writes memos, letters and reports in an articulate and interesting manner. Being competent in your work plus making a fantastic impression on executives can help you toward a promotion.

ASTOR: In 1783, a 21-year-old John Jacob Astor set foot on American soil. Among his possessions: the clothes he wore, $25 in his pocket, a thick German accent, and a driving ambition to be successful in his newly-adopted land. As limited as his inventory was, it was not unlike that of the thousands of other immigrants who arrived that year. The difference was the magnitude of his drive-for within three years of his arrival the stem-visage youth had begun to make his mark.
Building upon wise but modest investments in the fur business, Astor organized a trading company that reached from the Great Lakes to the Pacific and beyond. The largest portion of his wealth in those early years was derived from trading furs to Chinese and Japanese merchants in exchange for tea. Gradually, Astor turned his attention from trading to real estate-but not before his fur company was established as the first monopoly in the annals of American business.
Astor's wheeling and dealing in New York City real estate made him one of the richest men in America. He had parlayed that original $25 into a fortune estimated at the time of his death, in 1848, to be in excess of $25,000,000. Astor, however, was never satisfied. On his deathbed he said, "Could I begin life again I would buy every foot of Manhattan Island."

MORGAN: The career of financier J. Pierpont Morgan, Sr. spanned more than 55 years. Almost single-handedly, he formed U.S. Steel, General Electric and International Harvester. He had at his disposal liquid assets totaling $1.4 billion. And during the last 18 years of his life he wielded a prodigious influence on worldwide economic affairs.

Morgan's style of business was fast and direct. Much of his wealth, though, came at the expense of the nation's smaller industrial concerns. The ways in which he stifled his competitors were often questionable and, on occasion, blatantly illegal. Life, to him, was an endless chain of money making schemes concocted over brandy and cigars at the most fashionable New York City clubs.
An intense, determined man, Morgan looked, at least to one observer, "like a boiler about to explode." He and, to a large extent, the era in which he prospered both died in 1913. At the time of his death, Morgan's personal estate was valued at $70 million.

ROCKEFELLER: In 1860, a group of Cleveland businessmen sent their bookkeeper, John Davison Rockefeller, to assess the moneymaking potential of the then-infant petroleum industry. He reported: there's no future in it. The "Bloodless Baptist bookkeeper," as he was once described, was holding back information he sensed would one day be valuable.

And valuable it was-for, not too long after that report, Rockefeller invested his life savings ($2,000) in the refining business. It was a humble start for someone who through mergers and favorable railroad rates would soon control 95% of the nation's refining capacity. Eventually, the tremendous wealth generated by those refineries made Rockefeller the world's first billionaire.
An austere and, at times, ruthless man in his earlier years, Rockefeller mellowed after his retirement. He spent the greater part of his waning years supervising the charitable distribution of his fortune.
Yet the financial dynasty started by J.D. Rockefeller flourishes to this very day. Members of the clan occupy positions of power in government, finance and the arts.
Through them, the prescient Baptist bookkeeper from Ohio continues to influence world affairs.
MACARTHUR: Once, in the late 1920s, the assets of John D. MacArthur's insurance company were down to $10. But MacArthur's low-cost life insurance, custom- made for hard times, took off in the Great Depression. Some 40 years and a thriving $30-billion business after his all- time low, MacArthur retired to Florida. At least he intended to retire. In less than two years, he had purchased upwards of 100,000 acres of Florida, conservatively estimated to be worth more than $100

million. When asked about his newly-acquired real estate, MacArthur replied: "There are some men who can't walk by a crap game without wanting to get in; I find it hard to pass up a bargain investment."

Of course, MacArthur's tremendous success didn't come easy: he had to fight tooth and nail all the way up. He was a real scrapper in the early days, taking on such opponents as the FTC, the U.S. Post Office, and the American Hospital Association. And although he's somewhat less pugnacious now, he admits, "I have more enemies per square foot than any other man around."

Despite his immense wealth, MacArthur remains a man of simple taste. His home in Florida is more of a bungalow than a mansion. That's how it should be for a man who spends money only to make money. After all, why throw your money away when you can throw it around? The thrill is in playing-and winning-the big business game.

John D. MacArthur, entrepreneur extraordinaire, is one of the best players around.

Here are a few of the thousands of cases that prove that at any age a man can get rich if he finds a widespread need and fills it. Here is one of the most remarkable case histories. It demonstrates how technical skill can grow almost from nowhere, through concentration on a problem.

In one of our first case histories, the story of George Spitzer and his invention of the Rise aerated leather bomb, we saw one example

IBUKA: Masaru Ibuka, founder and honorary chairman of the Sony Electronics Corporation, is far from being the richest man in Japan. But he, perhaps more than any other Japanese corporate executive embodies the entrepreneurial flair that has made Japan's postwar economic resurgence possible. In 1933, after graduating with a degree in electrical engineering from a prestigious Japanese University, Ibuka looked forward to a comfortable career with the Toshiba Electric Company; his plans were upset, however, when he failed Toshiba's rigid entrance examination. So, for the next ten years, Ibuka ran the gamut of small electronics firms.

It was in the fall of 1945 that Ibuka set out on his own. He set up shop in a bombed- out Tokyo department store, where he manufactured just one product: a short-wave

converter for AM radios. The commercial success of his converters provided Ibuka with the working capital-a scant $525-to establish the company now known as Sony.

REVSON: Charles Revson had a framed needlepoint hanging on his dining room wall, until the day he died. It read: "O' lord, give me a bastard with talent." To the tough-minded, outspoken co-founder of Revlon, that was all one needed to find success in the corporate jungle-his career proved it.

The son of a dirt-poor Jewish cigar*-packer, Revson peddled nail polish on the streets of New York. He never stopped to ask himself what he was doing there. Revson wasn't kidding himself: he was going to make it in cosmetics.

With the help of his brother Joseph and chemist Charles Lachman, 26-year-old Charles Revson launched his own cosmetics company on an investment of $300. That investment, to put it mildly, was pitiful. For that reason, Revson and cohorts were forced to spend a great deal of their time splashing through loan-shark infested waters.

They had one thing to rely on, though: talent. It never failed them. Within a few years, the struggling company's determination and talent turned the trick-Revlon was underway to becoming the $600-million-a-year conglomerate it is today.

Few men in industrial history have been as domineering as Charles Revson, who, it was said, "chewed up executives the way some people chew vitamin pills." Yes, he ferociously demanded talent. But then, few men have been as rich: upon his death in 1975, Revson's personal wealth was estimated at about $100 million.

ONASSIS: The story of Aristotle Socrates Onassis reads like an implausible popular novel. The opening chapter was the same as that in the life of any other poor immigrant. At 17 he left Greece, alone, bound for Argentina. By the time he got there, he only had $60 to his name. He became a switchboard operator. It was as simple as that. But Onassis had bigger ideas. Using his father as a connection in Greece, Onassis began to import tobacco to Argentina. The business went so well that, by the time he was 25, it enabled him to earn his first million. There's more. With his first million and an appointment as Greek consul in Buenos Aires securely under his belt, Onassis turned his attention to the shipping industry. He traveled to Canada in 1932 and purchased for $20,000 a piece, the first six freighters of a fleet that would eventually encompass 76 vessels. When World War II erupted, these ships carried freight for the allies and reaped great profits for Onassis.

In the years after the war, the Onassis Empire grew to include his fleet of freighters and tankers, extensive land-holdings throughout the world, an airline and his beloved 325' yacht, Christina. When the "Golden Greek" died in 1974, he had accumulated a fortune variously estimated to be between 500 million and one billion dollars.

GILLETTE: Some entrepreneurs yearn to bring their products, services, or ideas to what they perceive to be a nation eager to enjoy and profit from them. Others see a gap in the market they hope to fill. Many are compelled by a vision of providing the

means to create a better society. King Camp Gillette, who in the late 19th century worked as a traveling salesman for hardware companies, was one of these; but to realize his ambition he first had to do something else-become wealthy. And to do this, he invented the safety razor.

Some entrepreneurs yearn to bring their products, services, or ideas to what they perceive to be a nation eager to enjoy and profit from them. Others see a gap in the market they hope to fill. Many are compelled by a vision of providing the means to create a better society. King Camp Gillette, who in the late 19th century worked as a traveling salesman for hardware companies, was one of these; but to realize his ambition he first had to do something else-become wealthy. And to do this, he invented the safety razor.

Born in Chicago to a businessman father who tinkered with inventions and a mother who wrote The White House Cookbook, Gillette was forced to leave school at 16 when the Great Fire of 1871 destroyed the family business. It was then he became a salesman. Among the companies he represented was one owned by William Painter, a manufacturer of a new kind of disposable bottle stopper. Painter was

doing quite well with his product, since America was on its way to becoming a "disposable society." Other products that could be discarded rather than recycled were also coming to market. Tin cans and cardboard collars were becoming common, and new items appeared regularly.

Painter spoke to Gillette about how a fortune might be reaped through the invention of "something that would be used and then thrown away" so that the customer would come back for more. The thought fell on fertile ground. Gillette had already worked on inventions and he later recalled that "some of them had merit and made money for others." From Painter's concepts, he hit on the idea of the safety razor.

It was really quite simple, though the execution presented problems. In this period, men shaved either with a straight razor or not at all, who helped explain the popularity of beards when Gillette was growing up.

The trouble was that the shaving ritual took time, and as the pace of life quickened, that presented problems. For reasons of safety, convenience, and economy, a faster method was needed. It is not known precisely when Gillette started experimenting with ways to create a new razor, but it was shortly before the turn of the century. The idea was obvious enough: A sharpened steel blade would be clamped between plates held together by a screw device that also served as a handle. Enough of the blade would protrude to present a proper edge to the face, but not so much as to nick a less-than- careful shaver. Gillette carved a model from a block of wood and, with the help of machinist William Nickerson, worked on several prototypes to show to prospective investors.

Working on the invention did not occupy all of Gillette's time. He continued working as a salesman to support his wife and young son and wrote (his second) social reform polemic, The Ballot Box, in 1897. Meanwhile, the processes of invention continued. Gillette had to work at fine degrees of tolerance. This meant perfecting the means of producing quantities of special steel, which then had to be drawn and honed to the proper degree of sharpness and cut to fit the razor.

All of this required money, certainly more than he was earning. But he did manage to convince friends to invest $5,000 to form the Gillette Safety Razor Company in 1901. Unable to resolve technical difficulties, his work progressed slowly. Gillette was close to bankruptcy when another group, who had no trouble perceiving the commercial possibilities of safety razors, came up with $60,000 more.

The first sales were made in 1903, when 51 razors were marketed, along with 168 blades. For a while Gillette feared blade sales would decline, as owners attempted to sharpen them on their stones. But the practice was soon abandoned: Gillette priced the blades so low that parsimony became unnecessary. Razor sales reached 90,000 in 1904, when a startling 12.4 million blades were sold. Now Gillette poured capital into advertising, and his razors swept the nation. Barber shop shaves didn't disappear, and many men clung to their straight razors, refusing to accept or even try Gillette's new contraption.

The turning point for Gillette came with World War I, an event that affected many established products. Soldiers and sailors had switched from cigars to cigarettes, from pocket watches to wrist watches. The convenience of safety razors (there was no room for a strop or stone in a kit bag, or time to shave with a straight razor) won the doughboys over, and they continued to use them after the war. In the 1920s Gillette ran many promotions, selling his razors in bulk to merchants who gave them away-once again boosting blade sales. Gillette plowed funds back into the business and established factories throughout the world. Gillette died in 1931, in the midst of the Great Depression, when his company had assets of slightly less than $60 million. Years earlier he had written that government had to provide work to the unemployed in hard times, something President Franklin Roosevelt would soon do. For most of his adult life, Gillette strove to bring to fruition his vision of a better world, and failed. What he accomplished was to revolutionize the way men shaved. His impact on the daily life of half the population was greater than that of most entrepreneurs of his time.

A lot of managers like to think of themselves as entrepreneurs. Although they've never started a business before, they believe it could be done if the conditions were right. Chances are they're fooling themselves.

Entrepreneurs are a special breed. It takes a certain blend of determination, persistence and guts to turn a dream into a going venture. There are thousands of accountants, clerks, plumbers, lawyers and executives who have fallen on their faces

trying. Yet others have found the way to succeed.

Courage is defined as a quality of mind or temperament that enables one to stand fast in the face of opposition, hardship or danger. It is synonymous with guts, dauntlessness, and heart mettle.

To be in the world of business it requires courage simply because there is a risk involved in every type of transaction that is intended to take place. First of all, it takes courage to make a decision to enter into negotiations. Then of course, it requires courage to execute an agreement simply because there is a fear of intentions not working out as intended. So, everything that we do encompasses a mental concern which of course, sounds bad. The truth is that by making a decision you have overcome many fears. There will be many obstacles along the way that you can meet with an appropriate answer.

With a positive attitude, you can overcome the obstacles therefore one must take chances. There is no business transaction without risk. The only way to reduce risk

is to understand and be able to calculate within the realm of your knowledge how small or bigger risk it is.

In order to move forward, you must accept the fact that you have self-confidence enough by virtue of your education, experience and background that there are answers to meet the challenge of obstacles. A calculated risk is related to all businesses. Many times, the risk is out of your control but never the less in the course of doing business, you must encounter risks. Without risk, there is no reward so it is definite that you have to resign yourself to the fact that you can handle risks simply because you are looking for the rewards. That is what courage is all about, accepting the truth even with calculated odds?

Entrepreneurship requires the most courage. The only way to reduce the risk and increase your chances of winning is your inestimable fortitude to overcome the fear. Starting a business takes courage. Running a business takes courage. Expanding a business takes courage. You can readily see that knowledge is the only way to reduce the fear of being an entrepreneur.

Many successful businessmen have known this through experience and observation of the fluctuating business climate that changes and fluctuates almost every day, One must be self-confident in conducting business and having the awareness that nothing is guaranteed or assured in order to protect themselves as best as possible regarding any decision or transaction that they are conducting.

In spite of the realization that we are dealing with risk in business, we must take the chance to do business. If you were to study the history of the famous wealthy moguls of our country, you will begin to realize all of the traumas and obstacles that had to be contended with in order to reach the heights that they did in business. They did not have the experience but they welcomed new challenges for example: At one-time John Rockefeller had only one oil well and the only reason he was able to do business is because he processed the oil to make kerosene. In so doing, he had a start and succeeded in filling a need because people nationwide required kerosene for lighting in their homes and in their factories. In processing the crude oil, the abundance of waste material was gasoline which had no value because there were no automobiles, no highways and there was no need for gasoline.

When Henry Ford decided to make automobiles, he had to choose either alcohol or gasoline to run his engines. The Ford engine could have been made to run on either alcohol or gasoline. Rockefeller was burdened by having the gasoline that could not be used in any way but an internal combustion engine.

Rockefeller had the problem to sell his burdensome buy product gasoline to Henry Ford's engine. As the automobile industry grew, the gasoline became the standard for every car made. As new roads and highways were created, more gasoline was· consumed than kerosene for lighting homes as electricity and bulbs took the place of kerosene. The point of this episode is to show that the evolution of change came about during Rockefeller's life time and his real wealth was made from gasoline rather than kerosene. The point is that he had the courage to start even though he did not know what obstacles or blessings were in his future.

We are sure that every entrepreneur goes through a similar or parallel experience. At one time, he had to change his entire operation and borrow capital to build a refinery and distributed gasoline throughout the country.

A lot of managers like to think of themselves as entrepreneurs. Although they've never started a business before, they believe it could be done if the conditions were rights. Chances are they're fooling themselves.

LOUIS R. KARPLES believed in being in business at an early age. His start was having a photography business while in High School. He did pictures for the school paper and was invited to many of the sweet sixteen parties to take pictures of the couples that attended. He had his own dark room and sold copies to the individuals. After he graduated, he published a few research projects and had a corporation called Advance Publishing catering to business men while going to night school to become a licensed building contractor which he accomplished at age 21. He performed small jobs like repairs and marine construction such as sea walls and docks and piers in Florida.

When the concept of condominium housing was popular in Puerto Rico, he went there to explore all aspects of condominium construction. At the age of 28, he built one of the first condominium townhouse projects in South Florida. Mr. Karples was the founder of Atlantic Construction Corporation and had a long career in housing development.

He proved that hard work along with honest treatment of people proved to be profitable for him.

There are tens of thousands of other entrepreneurs deserved mentioning. We only wanted to point out the examples of a few.

REVELATION #23
DECEPTION

Definition of Deception: The act of deceiving, trick meant to deceive; fraud; sham. Everybody is aware of the great effort that is made to save money which of course has a multi-faceted purpose. Unfortunately, there are con men (confidence men) to seek and devise ways of stealing your money without you even realizing that you are being conned and deceived.

The following stories are just a few of the many scams and schemes that crooks have been using in recent decades and probably as far back in time as business and trading started.

Of course, we all heard the warning that if it seems to be too good of a deal, it probably is a "fraud." In any case there is only one person that will look after your money honestly and that is you. Do not become a victim. This is not to say that everyone cannot be trusted but you have to make a scrutinizing determination to determine who you can trust. The fact is that in life we have to trust and depend upon others.

BERNARD MADOFF:

Bernard Madoff was born on April 29, 1938 in Queens, New York. He used $5,000 earned from a life guarding job to found his investment company. Madoff's firm offered reliable returns and his client list included celebrities like Steven Spielberg. Madoff's son reported him for securities fraud and Madoff pleaded guilty to 11 felony counts. In 2009, the 71-year-old was sentenced to 150 years in prison.

He was born to parents Ralph and Sylvia Madoff. Ralph, the child of Polish immigrants, worked for many years as a plumber. His wife, Sylvia, was a housewife and the daughter of Romanian and Austrian immigrants. Ralph and Sylvia married in 1932, at the height of the Great Depression. After struggling financially for many years, in the early 1950s, they became involved in finance.

Records of his Madoff's financial dealings show they were less than successful with the trade. His mother registered as a broker-dealer in the 1960s, listing the Madoffs home address in Queens as the office for a company called Gibraltar Securities. The SEC forced the closure of the business for failing to report their financial condition. The couple's house also had a more than $12,000 tax lien which went unpaid from 1956 until 1965. Many suggest that the company and the loans were all a front for Ralph's backhanded dealings.

But the young Madoff showed no interest in finance during this time; he was far more focused on girlfriend Ruth Alpern, who he met in junior high. The couple continued to date while they attended Far Rockaway High School in 1952. Madoff's other interest was the school swim team. When he wasn't competing in meets, his swim coach hired Bernie as a lifeguard at the Silver Point Beach Club in Atlantic Beach, Long Island. Madoff began saving money he made on the job for a later investment.

After graduating from high school in 1956, Madoff headed to University of Alabama, where he stayed for one year before transferring to Hofstra University. The next year, Madoff earned his bachelor's degree in political science from Hofstra. Bernard began to study law at Brooklyn Law School but quit later that year to begin his own investment firm. Using the $5,000 he earned from his summer life guarding job and a side gig installing sprinkler systems, Madoff and his wife founded Bernard L. Madoff Investment Securities, LLC.

With the help of Madoff's father-in-law, a retired C.P.A., the business attracted investors through word-of-mouth and amassed an impressive client list including stars such as Steven Spielberg, Kevin Bacon and Kyra Sedgewick. Madoff Investment Securities grew famous for its reliable annual returns of 10 percent or more and, by the 1980s, his firm handled up to 5 percent of the trading on the New York Stock Exchange.

CHARLES PONZI:

Charles Ponzi was best known for the financial crimes he committed when he conned investors into giving him millions of dollars, and paid those returns with other investors' money.

The details of the infamous swindler Charles Ponzi's early life are difficult to verify. It is believed, however, that he was born Carlo Ponzi in Parma, Italy, and attended the University of Rome La Sapienza.

Ponzi arrived in Boston in November 1903 aboard the S.S. Vancouver. He later told the New York Times that he gambled away most of his money on the voyage to America. "I landed in this country with $2.50 in cash and $1 million in hopes, and those hopes never left me." The young immigrant's charisma and confidence would help him pull off one of the greatest financial schemes in history.

Ponzi started out working odd jobs, including as a dishwasher in a restaurant. In 1907, he moved to Montreal, where he found a job as a teller at Bank Zarossi. The bank was formed to cater to the new Italian immigrant population, charging high-interest rates.

When Bank Zarossi went bankrupt because of bad loans, Ponzi was left penniless. He was sentenced to three years in a Quebec prison after he was caught forging a bad check. Rather than tell his mother in Italy that he was in prison, he wrote to her in a letter that he was working at a Canadian prison.

When he was released from jail, Ponzi got involved in yet another criminal venture, smuggling Italian immigrants across the border into the United States. This too landed him in jail. He spent two years behind bars in Atlanta.

Ponzi returned to Boston, where he married stenographer Rose Gnecco in 1918. He worked various jobs, including at his father-in-law's grocery store, but none of the jobs lasted long.

It was during this time that Ponzi got the idea for the great scheme that would earn his name a place in history. He received a letter in the mail from a company in Spain that contained in it an international reply coupon (IRC). An IRC is a coupon that can be exchanged for a number of priority airmail postage stamps from another country. Ponzi realized that he could turn a profit by buying IRCs in one country and exchanging them for more expensive stamps in another country. Ponzi's racket worked like this: he would send money to agents working for him in other countries, who would buy IRCs and send them, back to the United States, Ponzi would then exchange the IRC for stamps worth more than he paid for them, and sell the stamps. Ponzi reportedly made more than 400% on some of these sales. Not satisfied with running the profitable scheme on his own, Ponzi began to seek investors to turn even higher profits. He promised investors outrageous returns of 50% in 45 days, or 100% in 90 days. Ponzi paid these investors using money from other investors, rather than with actual profit - as in the criminal scheme of Bernie Madoff.

Although he did not invent the scheme that later came to bear his name, Charles Ponzi's scam was so extensive and initially lucrative that it brought national attention to the fraudulent operation for the first time. In 1919, The Italian immigrant promised investors they could yield considerable profits by purchasing international reply coupons from other countries and then redeeming them in the U.S. for postage stamps. To legitimize the scheme, Ponzi established the "Securities Exchange Company" based in Boston. A steady flow of new clients allowed him to pay existing investors, while pocketing millions of dollars himself. But soon enough, the scheme began to raise eyebrows, eventually collapsing and bringing six banks down with it. Collectively, his investors lost an estimated $20 million.

SCOTT W. ROTHSTEIN:

Scott W. Rothstein (born June 10,1962) is a disbarred lawyer and the former managing shareholder, chairman, and chief executive officer of the now-defunct Rothstein Rosenfeldt Adler law firm. He was accused of funding his philanthropy political contributions, law firm salaries, and an extravagant lifestyle with a massive 1.2 billion-dollar Ponzi scheme.

On December 1, 2009, Rothstein turned himself into authorities and was subsequently arrested on charges related to the Racketeer Influenced and Corrupt Organizations Act (RICO. Although his arraignment plea was not guilty, Rothstein cooperated with the Government and reversed his plea to guilty of five federal crimes on January 27, 2010. Rothstein was denied bond by U.S. Magistrate Judge Robin Rosenbaum, who ruled that due to his ability to forge documents, he was considered a flight risk.

On June 9, 2010, Rothstein received a 50-year prison sentence after a hearing in federal court in Fort Lauderdale, although federal prosecutors in 2011 filed a motion notifying the court they would be seeking a sentence reduction for Rothstein.

His firm had 70 lawyers and 150 employees, with offices in Boca Raton, West Palm Beach, Fort Lauderdale, Miami, Tallahassee, Florida, New York and Caracas, Venezuela. The firm focused on labor and employment matters, civil rights, intellectual property, internet law, corporate espionage, personal injury, wrongful death, commercial litigation, real estate, mergers and acquisitions, and governmental relations. His client list included: Citicorp, J. C. Penney, Ed Morse Automotive Group, National Beverage, Silversea Cruise Lines, Supra Telecom, and Wells Fargo. Until he was permanently disbarred by the Florida Supreme Court on November 25, 2009, Rothstein was a member of the Florida Bar and admitted by the United States Supreme Court. He had been given an "AV" peer review rating by Martindale-Hubbell.

Rothstein may have stolen millions of dollars from an investment side-business. A list of 259 persons or corporate entities entitled to $279 million in restitution has been sealed by the court.

ENRON:

The Enron scandal, revealed in October 2001, eventually led to the bankruptcy of the Enron Corporation, an American energy company based in Houston, Texas, and the de facto dissolution of Arthur Andersen, which was one of the five largest audit and accountancy partnerships in the world. In addition to being the largest bankruptcy reorganization in American history at that time, Enron was attributed as the biggest audit failure.

Enron was formed in 1985 by Kenneth Lay after merging Huston Natural Gas and Inter North. Several years later, when Jeffrey Skilling was hired, he developed a staff of executives that, by the use of accounting loopholes, special purpose entities, and poor financial reporting, were able to hide billions of dollars in debt

from failed deals and projects. Chief Financial Officer Andrew Fastow and other executives not only misled Enron's board of directors and audit committee on high-risk accounting practices, but also pressured Andersen to ignore the issues. Shareholders lost nearly $11 billion when Enron's stock price, which achieved a high of US $90 per share in mid-2000, plummeted to less than $1 by the end of November 2001. The U.S. Securities and Exchange Commission (SEC) began an investigation, and rival Houston competitor Dynegy offered to purchase the company at a very low price. The deal failed, and on December 2, 2001, Enron filed for bankruptcy under Chapter 11 of the United States Bankruptcy Code. Enron's
$63.4 billion in assets made it the largest corporate bankruptcy in U.S. history until WorldCom's bankruptcy the next year.

Many executives at Enron were indicted for a variety of charges and were later sentenced to prison. Enron's auditor, Arthur Anderesen, was found guilty in a United States District Court, but by the time the ruling was overturned at the US, Supreme Court, the company had lost the majority of its customers and had closed. Employees and shareholders received limited returns in lawsuits, despite losing billions in pensions and stock prices. As a consequence of the scandal, new regulations and legislation were enacted to expand the accuracy of financial reporting for public companies.

We all know that there are scams and schemes of all kinds and probably many variations of how money is stolen and how unscrupulous some people are about fleecing other people's money.
The only protection is to be open- minded and skeptical of everybody you do business with. That is not to say not to trust anybody, it is to emphasize the fact to verify as much as possible and use your judgment along with your gut feeling.

REVELATION #24
BUSINESS PHILOSOPHY

A "business philosophy" which is the subject matter of this Revelation is stated here to mean: "To adopt truthful principles with an underlying attitude for achieving the best results with a system or belief." If one believes that an efficient mind can lead to success and reaching an intended goal, then one should adopt the philosophy and attitude to strive in developing qualities that produce efficiency.

There are many-sided demands upon the businessman. One should readily realize the wide variety of tasks assumed by a business executive, either actually in his present position or, potentially, in the positions to which a successful business career is likely to lead him. The many-sided activities of management make heavy demands upon the executive's body and mind, often requiring a degree of physical stamina and intellectual alertness considerably above the average.

First among the demands made upon the business executives are those calling for knowledge and experience. The business man must know, or come to know, the particular field of operations in which he is working. His knowledge of this field must be exact and detailed. In addition, he must have a reliable familiarity with those related departments of the business which affect the success or failure of his own department or division.

Even with knowledge, however, an executive may fail to realize his opportunities through an inability to make the right use of what he knows. This inability usually stems from some defect of temperament or character, from some lack of vision, courage, initiative or perseverance. These larger traits of mind and personality limit the application of the business man's knowledge, setting a stage, so to speak, that maybe too large or too small for the operation of his skills and technical information.

Theodore Roosevelt was famous in his day as the apostle of the strenuous life. Few people realized, however, that his energetic handling of presidential duties was not a matter of temperament only, but was based on the most systematic organization of his working day.

Much has been written on the power of positive thinking and the conditioning of the mind in order to achieve success in life.

There are many modern-day Horatio Algers who have made millions in a short time by getting themselves into the right frame of mind.

It seems that this state of mind and attitude is what separates the successful person from the failure, the professional from the amateur.

While there is nothing wrong with reading for entertainment purposes, curiosity, or basic information, it is our hope that after reading the following information, you will be inspired to DO SOMETHING to achieve your goals. The old adage "nothing ventured, nothing gained" is still true today.

There are many successful men with only average intelligence. Nor is it the individual's talent or ability in much greater amounts than the successful person. Learning and doing, just not wishing and waiting.

Persistence is the common denominator. The willingness to spend time in accomplishing, the willingness to withstand obstacles, criticism, discomfort, and the ability to overcome seemingly impossible odds. Here is a guide to obtain greater confidence, self-assurance, recognition, success and money. You can acquire these only if you are willing to take specific actions.

Persistence can work like magic. Nothing in the world can take the place of persistence; talent will not. Nothing is more common than unsuccessful men and women with talent yet do not recognize their own genius. Un-rewarded genius is almost a proverb. The world is full of educated derelicts because they don't put their talents to use wisely. Persistence and determination alone will get the job done.

Self-Reliance: Self-reliance is initiative. Having initiative is to spontaneously respond to a confronting situation and deal with the demands of the situation without evasion. There is no anxiety in a self-reliant approach to problems; there is only the spirit of adventure and discovery. Emotions drive us toward our objectives. However, the nature and direction of our actions are determined, not by our emotions but by our basic degree of self-reliance. Therefore, self-reliance must be the starting point from which we work. Simply starting an adventure is most important.

One way to cultivate your potential inner tough-resistant quality is simply to hold a firm mental picture of yourself as possessing it. You should actually practice thinking of yourself as strong, controlled, and purposeful; not as wishy-washy, weak, and vacillating. Real strength and self-reliance is in you whether you know it or not.

In fact, you have within you all the strength you will ever need in order to handle anything you will ever have to face.

A more specific way to help you gain self-reliance is to make some special promise to yourself, then write it down, and carry it out for a definite predetermined length of time of your own choosing. By making and keeping such a promise, you quickly demonstrate that you can rely on yourself to do exactly what you said you would. This knowledge is the basis of self-reliance. If you feel weak and unsure of yourself, it is probably because from experience you know you tend to settle for the easy way out and refuse to see difficult situations to their finish. You cannot, or do not wish to sacrifice some momentary pleasure for a longer range greater good.

When you finally find that you do have the will power and are completely in control of yourself, you can indeed rely on yourself. In business, if you possess this steely

inner strength and rock-like self -assurance, it could make you one man in a million and fill others with admiration.

EVERYTHING STARTS WITH AN IDEA: Creative power of thought is the greatest power in the universe. You must first discover where your creative talents lie, and then begin to develop them. Try writing down anything you feel you have a talent for from past or present experiences. This may be in school, church, club work, business, social life, or at home. Then, you should follow-up on these talents. Every person can do something at which he's a natural, but this is often indicated only as little successes which hint of great capacity. By watching for these talents and taking decisive action upon them, you gain immediate self-confidence and multiply your success.

Thousands of people reach new millionaire status each year. We watch how the wealthy live on "Lifestyles of the Rich and Famous." For most this seems like nothing more than an imaginary fantasy. Money and the good life it brings seemingly are for other people, but not for oneself.

We can assure you- it doesn't need to be that way!

DECISION MAKING:

Making a decision about something often appears to you as a great impossible task that you would much rather avoid. The basic problem is that the mind will always tend to wander towards more pleasant and congenial thoughts, and does not want to concentrate on any problem for more than a very short period of time.

In business, there are a lot of critical decisions and procedures that must be performed. As mentioned in a previous Revelation, teamwork is a necessity. It cannot be over emphasized that the quality of people who are part of that team are amongst the best with their specialty. It is suggested that they be rewarded adequately for their contributions. If you are the Chief then you must look to employ the best Indians. Have the brain power to hire the best brain power that you can find.

Do not try to do everything yourself. In fact. delegate as many segments of your business as possible. Keep control of all aspects and keep on improving on your efforts to have your best input into each segment that you delegate.

For example, in legal matters such as forming a public corporation, you should seek to hire the best legal representation that specializes in that field. Accordingly, the same philosophy should be applied to engaging accountants and business consultants.

You continually must force yourself to think about it. In order to focus your attention on your problem and so be able to come to a decision, write down everything you can think of that can affect that decision. This simple technique will help you reach a wider decision than any other one thing can do. It encourages your thoughts along a single line, bringing about new factors which cause the mind to be even more attentive on the subject at hand. This technique gives you courage in making a decision, and dispels the anxiety of possibly making a mistake.

Perhaps you feel you would be much happier if you could break some bad habit. It is not possible to give up anything we regard as desirable by any amount of effort of willpower and discipline. You can do nothing about a habit unless you change its value judgment and put it in a highly undesirable context. To know yourself, you have to learn to look at your total behavior without any form of pride or humiliation about what you see condemning bad habits only serves to fasten the hour hold on them when you try to suppress them. Either do wrong or feel guilty, but don't do both; it is too much work.

Success is relative and individual and personal. It is your answer to the problem of making your minutes, hours, days, weeks, months, and years add up to a great life. To get the most out of life, you must take time to live as well as to make a living. You must practice the art of filling your moments with enriching experiences that will give new meaning and depth to your life.

We can assure you - it doesn't need to be that way! The world and especially America presents abundant opportunities. Ordinary people can and do become rich every day. That is a fact. Your fate is largely in your hands. No one can hold you back except yourself. Each of us has the gift of freedom to make whatever we want of our lives, with opportunity all around us.

Proven methods for achieving financial independence exist and have been used successfully by numerous people. They have acquired the know-how-the so-called wealth secrets!

The facts are simple and undeniable. If you learn the techniques for making money and place them into motion, you then can become successful, perhaps very wealthy. Where do you begin? How do you find money making techniques that are right for you?

There are basically two roads that can move you towards success. The first is by painstaking trial and error, the often referred to "school of hard knocks." You experiment, fail, and then try again, learning from your mistakes. The second is to obtain facts and information from others who have gained the knowledge and experience. One method is like trying to blaze a trail through a wooded wilderness. The other is like traveling down a six-lane highway. Taking advantage of the know and experience of others is a short cut to success. The important thing is to forge ahead, eliminating as many obstacles as possible.

Thinking about becoming successful or dreaming about gaining wealth is simply not enough. It is up to you to do what is required.

The foregoing material in this Bible will point you in the right direction to help achieve your goal.

The first step is to employ some courage. Unfortunately, few people just starting receive much encouragement from friends and family. They are more likely to be laughed at and ridiculed. This is human nature usually caused by a few reasons. There could be jealousy and "not wanting someone else to get ahead." Or otherwise, the person may want to protect you from being hurt or disappointed and, therefore, chooses to discourage you from taking any risk. They overlook the importance of achieving something worthwhile which means taking some risk.

The world is full of negative thinkers and skeptics. The financial failures around us are usually the wise guys and know-it-alls who criticize others who try to improve their lives.

Financial failures don't have the nerve or ambition to try to achieve a worthwhile goal. They are afraid that if they fail they will be ridiculed. Governed by fear they choose to embrace a life of failure rather than risk looking foolish.

Organization is a vital concern of any business, whether for the company as a whole or for each individual department. Good organization assigns activities and duties so that every department and every individual knows what responsibilities belong to him or to his department, how his department is related to other departments, and how the lines of authority run in the business.

But organization and operative efficiency, like charity, should begin at home. The earnest executive will investigate his self-organization. Is he planning and disposing of his own work with 100 percent efficiency? If self-examination tells him that his efficiency is below the standard he would set for himself, he should check up and start reorganizing.

Poor planning and organization create certain forms of wasted energy and time that are easily recognizable. One waste, for example, is a needless shifting from activity to activity during the business day. so that the executive is in the position of constantly stopping and starting, The human machine, like any other machine, loses momentum when it stops, takes time to regain momentum when it starts up after an interruption. Proper planning will group the major activities of the day or the week so that there will be a minimum of shifting from one line of action or study to another. Planning can reduce much unnecessary back-tracking.

One common fault in executives' self -organization is a habit of doing all the less important things first - a warming-up process intended to carry the executive along until he can really start pitching. What actually happens, as a consequence of this poor sequence of operations, is that the executive's most important tasks are postponed and bunched into the business hours of the day, when it is hardest to give adequate consideration to them and when their disposal becomes burdensome and fatiguing in the extreme. It is the little jobs that should take second place.

The first rule in becoming successful is adopt the positive optimistic attitudes common to all successful people. It makes good sense to look for opportunities with an open mind. You probably know more about what you are about to embark upon than any advice. By and large, what people predict for themselves generally comes true. The negative thinker who is of the opinion that he has no chance to become rich from anybody is almost always right. Having a negative outlook will no doubt affect all areas of his life-not only the financial. By the same token the optimist who feels confident that his dedicated efforts will make him wealthy will probably join the thousands of other people who have courage of their convictions following their own advice.

Does this mean that positive thinking can make you rich? No, but it helps! Positive thinking cannot make you rich. We wish it were that easy, but it requires perseverance. People who have the attitude that they are as good as the next guy act accordingly. If other people are taking advantage of the numerous money making opportunities that exist in America, why can't they?

Simply said, successful people are always looking for ways to make money! When they find logical and practical money-making systems they act on them because they know starting, trying and doing will allow them to succeed or fail. Therefore, if it does not succeed and fail then you are really falling forward. This allows you to put that experience under your belt and get ready for another opportunity.

If you try to make money one way, and it does not work, you must try something else, perhaps this time doing a little more research. Perhaps a slight adjustment is necessary or maybe it might call for an entirely different plan. Remember, to become successful you will have to learn from your mistakes. Or better yet, learn from someone else's mistakes. This is the winner's attitude to eventually hit a home run.

Instead of trying to figure out how to make money, why not let someone else figure it out first? After they have found the answers just have them teach you what they have learned.

It is amazing how many people want to reinvent the wheel. Many people are looking for some NEW way of making money. The last thing a person starting out should be looking for is a new way of making money. He should be searching for time-tested, basic proven methods of making money.

A major consideration in deciding to make the effort to become successful will be how you will live once you reach your goal. Most people who take steps toward financial success seem to have a vision of what their life will be like when they achieve their goal.
Think what it would feel like to get up each morning and decide for yourself how you fill your day. If you don't feel like working then you won't. Perhaps you would rather play golf or go to a movie. Maybe, if you really feel daring, you'd like to board a plane for some tropical island and bask in the sun for a few days. Getting away from it all will now be within your reach!

Being rich offers the benefit of not having to worry about your financial security. Personal freedom and true financial security is rarely if ever obtained by going to a job working for someone else. But this is something you already know. There may be no better reason to work towards making yourself rich than to bring yourself and your loved ones the peace of mind that comes from the security of being financially independent. We live in difficult times and things seem to be getting more complex. Having money helps getting over the hurdles.

Being rich starts in your mind. Of course, you can't become rich just thinking about it. Regardless, the first steps in achieving success always come from a person's thoughts. Visualization is a necessary step.

It is never too late or too early to begin the journey to success. History will show that people from all walks of life and every field of endeavor, no matter what their age or educational backgrounds were, and achieved their goals - no matter how great or small.

Many people are under the misconception that the way to get rich is to come up with a new idea. They believe you must find something original that nobody has ever
thought of before. This is wrong. Very few people get rich with a new idea or invention. The way for you to become wealthy is to study how other people achieved their success and then do the same thing. It is absolutely imperative that you learn the powerful money-making techniques that have proven themselves by

actually making ordinary people rich.

When you hear about a new money-making technique it is natural that you want to know the inside facts. It doesn't matter how smart you may think you are- or your educational background or how talented you are. It doesn't matter if you are a highly competent person with the ability to do very difficult things. When you are starting on your road to wealth you should begin with things that have worked for other people. There is no sense in making it harder than it needs to be.

How many times have you heard people recite the old saying "the rich get richer and the poor get poorer?" It is true; the rich continue to make more and more money while regular working people have to struggle just to get by. Wouldn't it be better to learn the secrets of wealth and the exciting techniques for making money? Wouldn't you rather be someone who is becoming richer?

The process of becoming wealthy means to continue to grow - going forward through the doors of life. Be ever vigilant and ever positive that doing the right thing at the right time is very important in the get rich formula.

You can begin those making money techniques immediately and be on your way to achieving total financial independence. But nothing will happen unless you act now. This is a brief summation and review of the information regarding secrets. It is strongly advised to read the entire Bible of Wealth Secrets again, perhaps in a few weeks or month to gain the more in-depth detail of how to greatly improve your life.

It is to be recognized that the scope of this information in is so broad that not all aspects related to the subject matter can be disclosed. It must be understood that all decisions that one makes is of their own conclusion after seeking professional advice to avoid pitfalls and liability. The costs of professional advice are a necessity to conducting any business and are tax deductible in most cases.

The information is intended to give you broad outlines for the purpose of ideas to be considered by you and cannot be solely relied upon for your final decisions. In the works of such a large scope, one must realize that it is never complete. An ambitious person must continue to build on their foundation of already acquired knowledge. With that mode of thinking in mind, continue to be aggressive and alert with an attitude of continuing to learn. No one person knows everything and for someone to have the knowledge of that fact, we would recommend the attitude to always be eager to learn more as if to say, the best qualification is that one realizes that one does not know everything, for if he thinks he does in reality he knows nothing.

REVALATIONS # 25
TURN IDEAS INTO
WEALTH

Did you ever say to yourself, "If I only knew how to put my idea into reality a fortune can be made!"

Ideas have made fortunes for many people. The trick is simple but requires work, patience and most importantly know-how.

The lady who invented Weight Watchers diet made millions and then sold the company for millions more.

The lady that invented white out became wealthy simply by bottling a white paint solution.

The non-scientist that saw the potential in Vick's Vapor Rub became a wealthy man,
by making that product.

Coca Cola Corporation started on a kitchen table by an enterprising man thinking of making a stomach ache remedy. Now it is the most popular beverage in the world. Fortunes are made continually from this product.

There are actually thousands of similar products that have made fortunes for entrepreneurs.

When turn an idea into satisfying a need, then you are on the right path to become rich. The ideas can be a product chemical formula, or a mechanical device, or a system of any kind that serves a need in business or private life. It can also be a design patent such as a logo. There is virtually no limit to an idea that will promise to generate wealth.

A business minded person can even seek out an existing formula and make it better. In fact, making it a better formula, produce a better product knowing that it is already a big success.

Ideas are not valuable when nothing is pursued to make them a reality. The idea may be very meritable but time passing without action will result in nothing.

Therefore, a good valuable idea is worth nothing unless acted upon and pursued to make it reality.

REVALATION # 26
GO FORWARD

Any action is a better than no action. There is no such thing as wasted effort.

Bernard Baruch wrote a book entitles "Falling Forward." The progress is achieved by Going Forward, even if it results in failure. We learn from our past mistakes. That is progress.

Samuel Johnson, who wrote the dictionary and a master of philosophy, said "if all obstacles must be overcome before anything is ever attempted, then nothing would ever be accomplished."

We must have a goal and courage of our convictions in order to solve the problems. Going Forward is progress. Even if it becomes a disappointment-nevertheless, that is progress.

Experimentation is "trial and error" but that is necessary to arrive at better answers. So – starting on a quest that does not guarantee a positive result becomes progress, just learning what does not work.

Every time an electric light is turned on you can relate to the work of Thomas Edison, certainly a most recognized inventor. His fame, of course, is the electric light bulb, but he had numerous inventions that were a product of genius thinking.

Edison while delving into the challenge of finding a filament that would not burn out asked why you are trying to find the impossible. You have already tried over 1000 filaments that don't work. Doesn't that convince you that it is a waste of time and effort? He replied it is not a waste of effort. "I now know 1000 filaments that do not work." This philosophy is by a genius and the world has benefited immensely. The only people that were hurt were the candle makers!

The planet we live on has encountered hundreds of wars in our history. As terrible as wars have been, they were responsible for tremendous progress in every field and endeavor from medicine to machines.

Nobody will deny it was all in vain and a wasted futile happening yet, there were gigantic benefits derived from the wars.

There are people that have attempted many business, simply on a quest, to find the business that is successful. Most likely they were aware that most businesses fail due to a host of reasons and many business problems were to be encountered and confronted with, yet they go forward to meet the challenges.

Entrepreneurs are optimistic, brave, ambitious, hopeful, and enthusiastic. They have courage of their convictions and go forward.

This mind set in philosophy has been the foundation of progress in our history. People have benefitted by those that make a commitment to achieve better things for mankind and themselves after evaluating the philosophy of "Going Forward."

It is logical and realistic to conclude there is no such thing as wasted time or effort.

REVALTIONS #27
RISK AND CHANCE

Risk is necessary if you are to win. You must assume risk and take chances. That is not to say doing things blindly. This is to mean that good decisions need to be calculated. The object is to control risks and proceed forward by having answers to the problems encountered. This of course requires a lot of knowledge as tools to solve problems and make progress towards your goals in quest for wealth. An abundance of thinking time must be employed to develop answers in dealing with obstacles. By overcoming obstacles with your business working Knowledge is the progress that you will make towards your goal. The better informed you are the better will be the results you will achieve for your efforts. The more you know the easier the better decisions will be the result. Your evaluations will be more accurate thusly you will be more effective with proper decisions.

The more knowledge you will have working for you, the more confidence you will gain. You will have better instincts to envision the problems before they happen. In a sense, you will have answers to solve the problems even before they begin.

Not having the advantage of a business education can be the costliest and riskiest part of any business undertaking. When you anticipate the risks, you are more than half way to find the solution. Having a background of knowledge will give you the answers to better control aspects of business decisions.

Right here now you have the opportunity to prepare yourself to meet the challenges of business in an educated way. If you are ambitious and wise you now can take advantage of the expert knowledge of others to help you seek wealth. Your decision now will determine what your tomorrows will be. You can join the few who are wealthy having the wealth knowledge or wind up in the majority of uneducated business people toiling through "trial and error" without ever making progress to be independent and wealthy.

Fear and hesitation to forge ahead is common place and you must avoid delays in your thinking as time going by is purely a loss of monetary gain. Your actions now, today, will determine what your tomorrows will be for you and your family.

You often hear people say I would have, could have, should have but didn't, having regrets of missing the boat and still wondering about looking for a magical opportunity to fall into their laps. Hopefully, you are at a point ready to make a decision now without hoping or waiting for a magical wand to be placed in your hands.

The world is full of mediocrity simply because most people do not have the vision or inclination to want to educate themselves in the field of higher learning of business methods, techniques and strategies and invest only a few dollars to learn the insiders know-how. They don't even know that such hard to find information is available inexpensively. They don't realize that they can invest in knowledge and work for them the rest of their life. They take seemingly the easy road and gamble their money in casinos, racetracks or the stock market. In fact, they are the pawns in the business world manipulated by the big investors who wind up stealing their money in the many ways that are conceived. When you own the knowledge of business nobody can take it from you, it is yours to keep and work for you the rest of their life.

Possession of the business insiders knowledge automatically offers you the advantage of being a business "insider." There is a theoretical wall that provides the professional from the layman. This will offer you the self-confidence you deserve, the courage of your convictions, and a great advantage over competition in regard to many aspects. More importantly, the knowledge will open up more opportunities by allowing you to recognize a fruitful opportunity from one that cannot work.

We all know that knowledge is power that is because you can justify having essential qualities of being a little bolder, smarter than your peers, more challenging knowing the risks and having an attitude to forge ahead with confidence. This is the formula for pursuing a goal of wealth.

REVELATIONS #28
BUSINESS CAPITAL

The world renown mogul of finance J P Morgan, often referred to as the greatest financier of our time always said' "finance people that have knowledge which is more important than basing decisions on their financial statement!"

Adequate business capital is the most important ingredient to the survival and progress of any and every business entity. All business failures can be attributed to the lack of capital. Therefore, it is vital and imperative that every entrepreneur and business manager be well informed and educated on the methods and market sources to raise capital. Not only is this knowledge necessary before starting a business, but rather more importantly a big advantage for a growing business. Expanding a business requires additional capital for new equipment and locations, etc.,etc.

There are two basic ways a business grows. One way is by its own momentum due to the need of the product and or services.

This growth pattern is by an expertly planned professional advertising campaign for introducing new products, improved services and new forms of sales media such as TV and internet campaigns. This of course requires unlimited sums of capital. Investment capital is always available, the secret is knowing how, where, and when to proceed.

Investors are abundant to put their savings to work earning interest and dividends, they have an insatiable appetite for good and varied business investments. It is intriguing to know that there is a large market of investors ready to take on high risk promising investments in order to receive the highest returns possible. This is often referred to as risk capitalists ready willing and able to gamble their money to make a big score. Often these investors are called "Angels" looking for the angle that produces the most profit.

So, it must be recognized that business capital is available for anybody. There are venture capital corporations that are looking for investments with a larger degree of risks simply *to* have a flowerfull story to sell their investors. This is what makes Wall Street and the Stock Exchanges dealing successfully in all types of investments ranging from established corporations to the new promising companies called IPO's initial public offerings. Some of these companies have no assets other than a new promising idea with a good potential.

When these IPO's do well they are then called "the·Darlings of Wall Street" meaning, that they are a growth corporation.

Many, many companies started small with just an idea and have grown into giants. That is the nature of the United States Stock Market phenomena. Good business ideas alone have grown into prominence.

If your ideas or inventions are merit worthy, there is no problem in obtaining investors as long as investors are invited in an organized way to invest. Wealth attainment is the Heratio Alger story that is feasible for anybody to accomplish.

It is very commonplace and often heard the statement of persons saying words to the effect, "If I only had the capital to take advantage of that opportunity, I would have, or I should have but could not". The regrettable fact is that they simply did not know how! This relates to the masses and majority of even educated people. This large segment of people is in a class of losers only because they were never confronted with the opportunity to be properly advised of the facts and information necessary, even if they had a yearning and a burning desire to be wealthy. In a sense, this is regrettable for many. It is a crime to one's self to lose out on a promising opportunity. You are lucky to be able to avail yourself for a small sum-valuable knowledge. Please realize that if the opportunity is lost to educate yourself the probability is you will never make it up again. This loss of opportunity maybe the biggest loss of a lifetime, and prove to be the most expensive by not having the wealth and still engaging fruitlessly in "trial and error". The secret of wealth can very well lie in enhancing your knowledge of "how and where to raise business capital". Nothing more can be said except that you are urged to act smartly.

REVALATIONS # 29
CONTROL PERSONAL
PROBLEMS

Everybody is confronted at various times of life with personal problems. Needless to say, that one's psyche becomes monopolized and overwhelmed with your thinking seeking to find solutions. This veil forms a cloud that interferes with the productive workings of the mind. Of course, in order to make progress in one's life, especially ambitious people that have a goal for success and wealth have to contend with finding the right answers.

Nobody has a magic wand, nevertheless, there are ways to control your thoughts as well as the abrasive situation of occupying your full capacity of thinking.

The world has a big problem of families that have internal relationship problems. To address the very common problem of marital dysfunction is to embark upon a widespread universal problem. A smart approach is to educate oneself as to the measures that can be taken to control the disharmony.

Most people having a marital problem are thinking of firstly a divorce. In most cases, a divorce is not the answer because it may eliminate a few problems but takes on many more problems at the same time. The best advice and you will probably come to the same conclusion after using prudent judgement is to stay married and implement measures to control and remedy the irritants that are causing disfavor with the relationship. It is very possible that happiness and harmony can be achieved with smart thinking. To implement such a plan, it makes sense to review the circumstances that could be remedied.

REVELATION # 30
INVESTING

The art and science of sound investing is to make investments that produce income. The income that will be earned will be commensurate with the risks. It is not wise to seek out the highest income available in an investment because the probability is that the risk would be more than is comfortable for the average investor.

In making a decision the risk factor must be taken into consideration when making a decision to invest your hard-earned money. Protecting the principle is considered a number one measure of consideration and therefore, the element of risk supersedes the attractiveness of an investment.

The importance of evaluating the safety is paramount and every other factor is of lesser importance. If they are paying interest or dividends. It should be determined what the history is to indicate how far back in time this has occurred, the capitalization of earning power when analyzed should determine the value of the investment. A prudent investor must have all the formulas in his mind to make good decisions. One cannot rely entirely upon a broker or solicitor of investments. Nobody is more concerned about the safety and value of the investment than the investors themselves. The broker or solicitor has a self-serving purpose in flowering up the product he is selling, therefore, the investor cannot rely on the sincerity and especially the knowledge to evaluate the merits of the investment.

Nobody should have greater concern about the investment than the person who is investing.

Basically, there are three types of investments, real estate, stocks, and bonds. Of course, there are many categories of how to invest in each of the three mentioned. For example, in real estate we can talk about equity in income property, mortgage investing, rehabbing rundown property, vacant land, country property, private houses and condos. In the stock market, there are numerous ways and categories of investing. There are many classes of common stock, options such as puts and calls, commodities, bank stocks, insurance stocks, public utility stocks, industrial stocks and IPO's which are initial public offerings. Then of course, bonds which is a specialty by itself has numerous classifications. These three categories, as you can see, are complicated with many variations. Then there are investments that should not be considered for many reasons unless one is in the business to begin with such as diamonds, gold, and other precious metals.

A person wanting to put his wealth to work must learn the "ins and outs" of the investment world.

Solutions research has solved the problem of providing the insiders information necessary for an investor to help determine what types of investment should be chosen to accomplish the best ways to invest. The advisory work contained in the CD entitled "Investing" will accomplish taking you by the hand and walking you through the maze of complications about investing. The information revealed is designed to cause you to feel comfortable and secure simply knowing that you have a good working knowledge of the scope of the market.

REVELATION # 31
HYPNOTIC MEDITATION

The study of hypnosis is amazing. These normal phenomena have a long history of proven accomplishments. Stories from ancient times to the present have reinforced the fact that we are influenced everyday by the power of suggestion whether it is eternally from hearing advertising or sales presentation and even doctor's advice or happening internally by our hearing suggestions from whomever speaks to us, or internal suggestions that we make to ourselves either positive or negative. Just thinking is a suggestion to our self and influences the conscious and subconscious mind. In effect, this in a scientific sense is referred to as hypnotism, self-hypnosis or autosuggestion.

It is referred to here as hypnotic meditation. **Many** people are using meditation in their lives everyday as a tool to relax, overcome pain, discipline themselves or just plain beneficial relaxation.

Hypnotic meditation can be practiced by anyone with normal intelligence. It is free and beneficial to the mind and body when employed in a purposeful way with the education of how and why it should be used. Hypnotic procedures have been used successfully over centuries to reduce pain, anesthetize body parts and areas to accommodate surgical operations, childbirth, and dental work instead of Novocain or anesthesia. Those procedures are amazing feats by themselves, yet only a small portion of the use that hypnotism can perform.

The subject of hypnotism has been unjustly ignored even by professionals because frankly it has a veil of mysticism and a cult impressions upon the layman's mind. The fact that it was used by charlatans, ancient doctors and entertainment it has been assumed by the unaware masses of people who are not educated to the facts of hypnotism. This by no means can justly condemn the recognition that the science of hypnotism should be labeled.

The most educated people of our day in business, medicine and the arts have been influenced by the powers of suggestion whether they realize it or not. When hypnotic meditation is recognized as a marvelous tool for living and making progress it then becomes more valuable as can be purposely directed to enhance a person's ability to accomplish more and enhance the gigantic power that their mind has but not readily utilized.

Once the power of hypnosis is learned and adopted by a person, the person becomes extraordinarily powerful in mind and body. We are not talking about walking on hot coals or weightlifting more than ordinary ability, we are talking about increasing one's business acuity to the point of becoming brilliant analytical and in everyway highly accomplished.

It is the pathway for a person to excel with every ambition that is desired to be realized. If your goal is to be independent and wealthy and highly regarded as successful, then you are a good candidate to make the study of hypnosis as the secret to your strength and success.

The staff of Wealth Achievers, Inc. has researched the hard to find information on hypnosis from interviews with professional hypnotists and users of this valuable phenomena. It is all in a book entitled "Hypnosis and Self-hypnosis Power" that you can begin using without delay. This precious information will change your life to make it easier, faster and more than perhaps you ever dreamed of.

REVALATION # 32
INVESTING SOUNDLY

The art and science of sound investing is to adopt the hard earned capital. Decisions are to be made to protect the capital from loss. Therefore, focusing on conservative investments.

Basically, there are three types of investments: Real Estate, Stocks, and Bonds. Of course, there are other forms less popular but have many drawbacks.

The object now after Wealth achievement is for protecting the Corpus Capital of your estate and develop income by receiving interest and dividends. The aim is to know how your wealth support you by providing income. Simply allow your money to make money!

If this is done in a prudent manner you will have the security of a lifetime and your estate will be intact for your family and future generations to come. Hopefully you can retire at an earlier than expected age.

Enjoying the fruits of your labor is the best part of life. Hopefully you will have good health and longevity.

Now the time tight for more leisure which means you can vacation, travel the world and do all the things that make life enjoyable. Now you can gloat in joy with all accomplishments. The work and sacrifices made are now appreciated more than ever before. It is a time when the love of life is real and you feel blessed. It is a feeling of appreciation, exhilaration, and security.

To protect your accomplished lifestyle to realize that knowledge that knowledge that brought you to this point was valuable. You are now convinced that new knowledge is needed to protect your wealth by investing shrewdly.

There are two CD's by Solutions Research that will give you the answers. The first one is "Beat Inflation and Protect Wealth" the second is "Stock Market Investing." The two CD's cost $20 each sold separately, purchased together the cost is $25.00. This knowledge will comfort you, satisfy your mind that your pointed in the right direction.

Unfortunately, there are scams to milk the people with money, wealthy people included as they are a special target. You will receive free from Solutions Research the CD entitled "Avoiding Scams and Thieves." This knowledge will give you peace of mind.

REVALATION # 33
KNOW THYSELF

You are now starting on the greatest adventure of your life-IF-yes, if you will read this revelation with a mind freed from previously formed opinions, skepticism, prejudices-and think while you read.

At this point I will not ask you to agree with me, any more than I would want you to disagree with what I am about to say.

The late John Wanamaker, the Merchant Prince as he was called by his contemporaries, seldom refused an audience to a salesman. He claimed that by listening to them he learned of new items coming on the market, but he prided himself in the thought: "I defy any man to sell me a thing I do not want." It is with this Wanamaker attitude I ask you to approach the thoughts you will find contained in this book. The enthusiasm which will result; the inspiration you will gain; the happiness you will find-and the success you will achieve will be of your own making-because your acceptance of the principles will come from your own reasoning, not that they were forced upon you.

Russell Conwell, in his world-famous book, "Acres of Diamonds," through countless illustrations, showed that human beings were constantly searching elsewhere for the very things they had at hand. Although he didn't say so, he could easily have meant the power which brings leadership; self-mastery; health and happiness.

Our outstanding leaders occupy their positions because of the power they have within. The heights to which you will climb will be the result of your use of the power you now possess.

You have lived with yourself all of your life, yet-unless you now have everything you want in life-you do not know yourself.

Ninety-five percent of all motorists are driving cars without anything but a vague understanding of that which is under the hood. They know that by feeding oil and gasoline into the car, and by manipulating buttons, pedals and steering wheel, the automobile will provide transportation. However, the driver with the understanding of the vehicle's complex mechanism, can operate with far greater efficiency. He will obtain more miles per gallon of gasoline; his tires will give increased mileage. And, his care will be giving good performance when other cars of the same age are being discarded as worthless.

Most of us are merely existing because we do nothing more than the obvious things; eat, drink and sleep. When we learn something about a human mechanism-and particularly the mind which controls it-there are no limits to the height we can climb.

On one occasion, I had an opportunity of visiting one of the country's finest laboratories. Room after room were filled with chemicals of every known description. Other rooms were replete with scientific instruments. I marveled as the chemist explained the purpose for which the multiplicity of devices were intended. After the tour was completed, and I had exhausted my vocabulary of adjectives and superlatives, the scientist concluded by saying: "With everything we have, and which represents the efforts of the world's greatest scientists, this laboratory, as great as it appears to be, does not compare with the laboratory each and every one has in his own physical being." "Right now," he continued, "the laboratory in your body is busily engaged digesting the food you ate at lunch, extracting from it the elements necessary for blood, bone, tissue, and energy. No laboratory in existence is equipped with the instruments or skill, to perform such a task."

In the field of photography, there is a new development in the form of a camera which will deliver finished prints in just a minute after the picture has been snapped. "Wonderful," you exclaim-but think of the human camera *we* have. We glance at an object and instantaneously the image is carried to the brain.

We marvel at sound recording. Through the use of electronics sound can be recorded on discs, wire or tape. This result, as interesting-and valuable-as it is, does not begin to prepare with our own human recording system. The ear-our microphone-receives the vibratory impressions which are at once recorded in the gray matter of the brain, and which can later be repeated through the voice.

Right now, you might be growing a bit suspicious. You may say to yourself: "Yes, perhaps I can gain a bit if I become a physiologist," and, you think, "it would take me years to learn all of that." Of course, this is not correct. We are constantly living through a series of habits. Success, happiness and well-being comes, not from added burdens, but by merely substituting right habits from wrong ones. The object of this opening chapter is to give you a slight idea of wonderful, amazing you.

Have you ever watched men and machinery evacuating for a new structure? Perhaps you, as I, have marveled at the humanlike operation of the giant steam shovel. You would see the boom lowered, the huge shovel digging into the earth and picking up hundreds of pounds of material; then easily swinging around and dump it into a waiting truck. Should you go into the cabin and watch the operator, you would see him surrounded by a myriad of levers. One lowers the boom, another presses it forward and raises it; another swings it around, and still another operates the jaws of the scoop of the shovel, permitting the earth or rock to drop into any receptacle which might be beneath it. Yes, it is astonishing-and seems almost alive. But what do we have within our human bodies? Think of the intricate network of cords and muscles brought into play each time we stoop over to pick up an object!

One time a man who thought he was about the poorest of the poor told me told me he did not have a single thing of financial value. That same morning, I had read in a Philadelphia paper an article to the effect that a man who had lost the sight in one of his eyes had offered the sum of $10,000 to

Anyone who would sell him an eye which could be transplanted. I asked this chap if he would sell one of his own. He indignantly told me he wouldn't, yet, just a few moments previously he had told me he absolutely nothing on which he could raise a dime.

So far, I have given you just a few illustrations regarding the physical portion of our being and how man has been unable to duplicate the functions of any part of the body notwithstanding unlimited financial resources which might be drawn upon in such an endeavor.

For a moment, consider the mental aspects of being. Man has been able to create instruments which would do certain things usually done by the mind. We have machines which can add, subtract, multiply, and divide; we have much automatic equipment which performs many operations mechanically. All of these, however, are the product of the mind. And, for each type of operation a specific machine or instrument is required. The human mind is capable of performing all of them.

By now, if you have been *thinking* while reading, you are beginning to sense that you do possess a body so amazing that a vast amount of study and research would be required in fully comprehending all that it does encompass. "So what?" you may proclaim. "Suppose I have a wonderful body," you think, "what has it done for me?" If such a question has come to your mind, it is a good indication, and, as you continue to read you will learn that you, as you are now, have all that is needed to enable you to acquire riches, better health, and, above all, happiness.

If you are a normal individual you have, at times, envied others for possessions they have and which you would like to have. They may have a better job, a business of their own, a fine home, a fabulous bank account. All right! Let us see if we can find the difference between the one who is highly successful and the one who is not.

Is the difference physical? You immediately agree it is not because the failure might even be better off physically, than the one who has acquired riches.

Is the difference education? At first you might feel inclined to think it is, but as you ponder you recall the names of many who have a fine educations and who are failures, while on the other side you know of those with but little education who have gone places.

And, while making comparisons, ask yourself what the real difference is-why is one a success, the other a failure? What does the success possess which is lacking in the failure? Each has the same type of marvelous body as we previously discussed, and, if both of them are normal, each has the same kind of mind. The real difference is one of Life's Golden Secrets, which will be revealed as you continue to read.

Some years ago, I recall visiting a large men's furnishing establishment with a friend of mine. He went in to do a bit of shopping, he said. My envy was certainly aroused to watch this man as he went from counter to counter. He stopped at the sport shirts department. Without once asking the price, he would look around and point to various shirts, saying: "I'll take that one, and this one, and you might include three of those, etc." When he reached sweaters, he did the same, selecting

three or four. At the necktie rack he picked them as nonchalantly as one would pick flowers in the garden, ending up with perhaps a hundred dollars' worth of ties. Several dozen pairs of socks were selected, as well as a large number of suits of underwear. All in all, he obligated himself for several hundred of dollars in a matter of about 10 minutes, doing so as casually as one might drop into a cigar store for a pack of cigarettes. At that time, my circumstances were such that I would have to think of my finances in order to buy as much as a single shirt. The contrast between me and this liberal spender was such that it seemed incredible that I would ever be able to do as much.

Have you ever watched a magician do a trick which baffled you completely? It seemed so mystifying that one would almost think the magician had some mystic help from the other side. Then, after the bit of magic had been exposed and explained, it appeared so simple, it seemed almost foolish.

I can now go on a spending spree like my friend, should I wish to do so, and as I look back to

301

the time when circumstances prevented me from doing it, the means of transition so simple, I almost feel apologetic for ever having been in a situation where I was forced to count pennies. A girl, in her early twenties, once came to me with a tale of woe. She had a good voice-and she knew she could sing-but she was sure she could never do anything with her talent. As we talked about singers of note, the look of dismay on her face plainly showed her certainty that such prominence was never meant for her. I spent several minutes in introducing this lady to herself, using practically the same words as you have read so far. Slowly a light dawned and she began to understand that, basically, there was little difference between her and those she had envied. This once discouraged miss has since appeared triumphantly, on the concert stage in most of the large cities in this country.

Have you ever rejoiced over a sleepless night? Perhaps not! There was one man, however, who considers a sleepless night as the turning point in his life. Upon retiring, his troubles did tend toward keeping him awake. He had obligations about to fall due, and, at the time, he could not see his way clear of meeting them. A question he asked himself caused him to completely change his trend of thought into channels which lead to a glorious life of security and contentment. The question? "What is the matter with me that I cannot take care of my obligations with the ease that so many others do?" The rest of the night he spent making a mental analysis of himself. He reached the same conclusions as are being drawn in this first revelation-that all men are born equal. During the long, dark hours of the night he compared himself with those he knew who were in comfortable circumstances and found in every case that they possessed nothing he did not possess-except, perhaps, the consciousness: "I can!"

Before the first rays of dawn started painting streaks of gold on the clouds, one of life's little golden secrets began seeping into this man's consciousness. Instead of arising drowsy and weary as might be expected after a sleepless night, he alighted with the verve of a child on Christmas morning. What happened to this man? Within a year he was in a position where he had a big income, was having a new home designed and built, and had plans for taking his family on a thrilling European vacation.

Although the results which may be obtained through the use of this book will sound like fiction, the book itself is not to be read as one of fiction. You are to think as you read it-and to properly do this, you should break up your reading time with sufficient pauses to allow for adequate mental digestion.

It would be possible to read this entire chapter in from twelve to twenty minutes. I would much prefer that you take at least an hour on these pages. Get yourself comfortable and fully relaxed. See to it that the lighting is sufficient to avoid eye strain. Then read the chapter paragraph by paragraph. Pause after each one and reflect; think about that which you read to make certain you fully comprehend the meaning intended. As you read the illustrations given, know the blessings which came to those mentioned can also come to you.

There is one more instance I would like to relate. A student who had been attending my course on Creative Psychology at a local college, in a plaintive tone of voice, asked me if he could talk to me for a few minutes after class. I granted his request. After a brief hesitation, he began "I believe everything you say is true, and that it is possible to succeed in life if he follows the right principles, but I can't see it for myself." I asked why. At first it was an effort to get him down to his basic trouble, then, as though forcing himself, he looked me in the eye and replied: "I'm not good enough. I've done lots of things of which I am deeply ashamed, and I can't feel that I am entitled to have the good things in life. It would seem unfair for me to make great headway while others who have lived cleaner lives would have to struggle along for a bare existence."

I asked this young man if he would try to make amends for his mistakes should he become an outstanding success. "Oh, yes, certainly!" he promptly replied. Then I brought up another query: "Wouldn't the world be a better place in which to live, then, should you take advantage of that which you already possess and make a great success in life?" He had to admit that the answer was yes.

Perhaps loss of self-respect is one of the main reasons why people are held back in life. They inwardly feel they are not entitled to success and happiness. Were they to stop to reason, they would find that with the right attitude, by gaining success, they could make up for many of the wrongs they might have done.

In this book, one dominant or major thought will be advanced in each revelation, and you are earnestly urged to stay with each revelation until you have thoroughly absorbed its main thought.

Right now, before reading further, ask yourself: "What is the dominant thought in the revelation?" If you have been seriously weighing each statement made, the correct answer will come to you. "I CAN-I can be a success!"

I would like you to burn those five words into your consciousness. Every time you think of it, say to yourself: "I can be a success." Make the statement several times upon arising in the morning; many during the day, and, without fail, repeat it again and again before retiring. And, as you say the words, do so with a note of elation. Back the words with gladness-and emphasis.

When you, as a child, wanted to go somewhere very badly, but doubted that you could, can you recall your tone of voice when you found you could go? "I can go," you sand aloud. That is the emotion you are to put behind the words, "I can be a success."

Your Pledge to Yourself!

"Put that in writing!" When two or more people enter into any kind of business arrangement of importance, a contract is usually entered into. This is done to provide a proper record of the obligation of the partners and to offer a means of prompting the parties thereto to live up to their written promises.

How about the promises on makes to oneself? Suppose you were to call upon a lawyer and ask him to draw up a contract between you and yourself. He would gaze upon you with suspicion, and wonder when your keeper would be after you. As ludicrous as this statement appears, we would be better off were we able to become obligated in some specific manner for the promises we make to ourselves.

If children did not obey their parents any better than human beings obey themselves, it would be a pathetic situation indeed. If you asked your child to do a certain thing the following day, you would expect him to do it, and if he didn't, you, most likely, would take him to task for having ignored your instruction. How many times do you tell yourself that on the following day you will do a certain thing-and then when the following day arrives, you do nothing about it? How many times have you promised yourself that you will overcome or modify certain habits-and then you fail to do so?

I might even refer to the annual New Year's resolutions. How many do you keep? With some people, I would be safe in asking, "Have you kept any of them?"

Some will impair their health through faulty living habits. They will promise themselves to correct the situation. Do they do it? Only in very rare instances.

The reason for our failure to keep promises we make to ourselves is obvious. In most cases, no one but ourselves knows of the promises, and we will not intentionally punish ourselves for breaking them.

I maintain that it is more important to keep those promises we make to ourselves than it is to keep those we make to others. We have to live with ourselves, and when we continually fail to do the things we intend to do, we lose our self-respect, and, if we cannot respect ourselves, it is expecting too much to look for respect from others.

Frequently a tinge of crimson will cross my face as I think of the hundreds, yes, perhaps thousands, of promises I have made to myself and never kept. And as I look back over those days, I recall that I didn't like myself as well as I might. Every time I learned of someone I knew making

strides, I would remember the many times I promised myself to do the things which would help me to climb.

One Monday evening I was preparing to retire and, while removing my clothing, my mind flitted over the things which had transpired that day. Nothing of importance happened. It was just another day. Then, with slight embarrassment, I remembered the promises I had made to myself over the weekend: I would start the week by organizing my desk and make plans for the entire week. I would tackle the tough assignments first. I would spend a certain amount of time for self-improvement, etc., etc. These, however, were merely promises but, as usual, the week had started and none of them were kept. The legend about the straw which broke the camel's back was quite apropos to the manner in which I felt that night. For some reason, and fortunately so, I was thoroughly disgusted with myself-so much so that I went to bed with a feeling that it would be a wakeful night. As I realized how undependable I was, and unusual though crossed my mind. "If a child continually disobeyed, I most likely would expect myself to find a remedy; yet I have never done anything to try to correct my disobedience to myself." An idea came! I decided that, for one week, I would keep every promise I made to myself. Before making it, however, I would carefully weigh it to make sure I could keep the pledge. This was not easy at first. Habit is a most powerful condition. I resolved to do certain things the following day, and when the next day arrived, was tempted to slide along and sidetrack the promise. But I stuck to my resolution. I actually forced myself to do the things I had laid out to do. By the end of the week I had made such strides-and felt so much more satisfied with myself-I determined to continue the routine of self-discipline.

Do I work harder than I did before making such a resolution? No. In fact, I don't think I work quite as hard as I did. To give a concrete example: It had always been an effort to keep my desk orderly. Mail comes in, and after reading it, it is laid aside for further reference. Something is piled on that, which makes it as good as lost. Papers of various kinds come to my desk for attention. I lay them aside until some future time. The result? My desk was always a pile of miscellaneous items-most of which had been neglected. Later I would always find myself in the position of taking time to explain why this and that had not been taken care of. And, incidentally, my mind never was at ease when at the desk, because all of the mass would appoint accusing fingers at me, reminding me that here were many things crying for attention.

One of the first promises I made to myself, after the burst of determination, was to get my desk properly organized. It would of have been easy to put that off, because when the time came I knew I would uncover a multitude of things I should attend to. But I kept that promise. I buckled down and removed everything, one by one, and in doing so, would either put it away properly, or take care of whatever was to be done. It was not an easy job-but it is amazing how pleasant it became. Before I was half through I found a song in my heart as I saw a bit of order coming to my desk.

Regarding the desk, I had made another promise to myself-and that was to keep it clean; to care for everything the moment it came to me for attention. Do you know that my work was much more simpler thereafter? And, best of all, my mind was more at ease. I could sit at my desk without the inner embarrassment.

Here is another little weakness of human nature I have discovered: many times, when starting a job, we will sit and think about it for many minutes before we start-sort of dreading the initial effort. And, of course, the longer we meditate about a job, the more difficult it becomes in our imagination. It reminds me of the days I was afraid of cold water. I would visit the beach and for a long time play around at the edge of the water trying to get the courage to jump in. Poking a toe in the surf, the sensation of coolness would make me withdraw in a hurry. I did such things until I got thoroughly disgusted with myself, and finally, in desperation, jumped in, merely to find how pleasant it was after the entire body had been submerged. With the tremendous satisfaction, I was getting by keeping promises made to myself, it was not difficult to form a habit of starting new jobs at once before even taking time to consider how easy or difficult they might be. Naturally, at the end of the week, there would be considerable pride in reviewing the great many things accomplished.

Up to this point, it may seem I am urging my readers to become like machines-to work, relentlessly, from the moment of arising to time of retirement. This would be very far from the truth. In fact, I think rest and recreation are just as essential to a well-balanced life as work. I will go so far as to say that unless you do allow sufficient times for restful recreation, the work you do will lack quality. So, another promise you should make to yourself, and which you should keep, is to arrange your day's work so that you can have time to relax and rest. And, here is a promise I will make to you! Living according to this new routine of self-discipline you will thoroughly enjoy your rest periods. You will enjoy them because your mind will be at peace and not confused with a myriad of promises you should of kept, but didn't.

So far, I have been talking about Self-promises in a general way; but right now, I want to bring up a promise you should make-and keep. It relates to the book in your hands this moment.

Undoubtedly your intentions were good when you obtained this book. You read or heard that it might prove of help to you, and you're reading it, perhaps in hope that it will help you. Your intentions are no doubt sincere and you intend to *try* the things suggested-to see what happens.

I have never forgotten the time when a very wise man gave me a bit of good advice. "I intend doing what you suggest," I told him. "Hell is paved with good intentions," he snapped, "start doing it now!"

We are all human and from childhood we fall into the pattern of following the lines of least resistance. We form-and live-according to habit patterns. Ant change-no matter how trivial-means the formation of a new habit. Therefore, it is so easy to think that you will do tomorrow the thing which you might-and should-be doing now.

The principles which will be covered in this book have been proved; not once or twice-but by thousands of people. Men and women in all walks of life have gained greater success, health and happiness through the application of these simple principles. Transformations which have taken

place in the lives of men and women seem almost unbelievable. The principles as you will find them are given in a manner so simple your intelligence will tell you in no unmistaken terms that you, too, can climb to pinnacles of great height. So certain will you be that you can duplicate what others have done you will *intend* to do everything suggested.

This intention on your part will not be one of those which will be applied towards the pavement in Hades. It will forecast success, because it will be *backed by action*.

The story is told of the lad who visited the sage in search of wisdom. "Come with me, my lad," said the wise man, and without conversation, walked slowly toward a nearby lake. Reaching the shore of the lake the sagacious man, without hesitation, continued walking into the lake. Deeper and deeper became the water until it reached the lad's neck. His frightened eyes meant little to the sage as he continued until, finally the water covered the boy's head. After a moment, the man of wisdom turned around and as informally walked to the shore.

After reaching dry land, the kindly old gentleman wryly asked the boy: "When under water, what did you want more than anything on earth?" Not a moment was required for the lad to answer this question. "Air was all I wanted, sir," he gulped. "Well, my son," mused the patriarch, "in order to gain wisdom, you must want it as badly as you wanted air, when under water."

Before attempting the next Revelation, whether that be a day, a week-or even longer-get yourself in the frame of mind whereby your determination is so great, you will not allow anything to stand between you and complete success so far as these principles are concerned.

It is not my intention to build within your mind a consciousness that hard labor will be involved in carrying through on the suggestions to be made. They will be simple, indeed, but since it is so easy to postpone the start of anything new, I want you to start right now in keeping all promises you make to yourself. There is something else I would like to say in connection with this new promise of yours. Along with your determination to keep the promise, build up an enthusiasm to go along with it.

There is a vast difference between the quality of work done as a duty and that which is done with enthusiasm. The enthusiasm is reflected in every phase of the job.

Passively reading this book will do a certain amount of good. To follow through on the suggestions in a matter-of-fact way will add to the good you will gain. But to *approach this work with unbounded enthusiasm* will bring a result far and beyond any concept of your present imagination.

The fine finish you admire on expensive furniture did not result from a mere application of a coat of varnish. Much preparatory work had to be done. The wood had to properly treated through sanding, filling, priming, etc., before any of the finishing coats were applied.

These revelations are preparatory steps, laying the proper foundation so that you will be ready to accept and absorb life's golden secrets as they are revealed to you.

As I write these lines, I am approaching my mid-sixties. I have not been successful all of my life by any means. I passed the age of fifty before I began to understand the principles as are now being revealed to you-and, at the time of the revelation, I was not only without money, but heavily in debt. During my fifties, I made greater progress-by following the precepts of these fundamentals-than I had made in my first fifty years put together; and, please note, since passing the age of sixty, I have made greater gains than I did in the fifties. With these secrets, and at my present age, I would not fear being stranded in a country where I would be unknown and without a friend or a penny. I know that, without undue hardship, I could not rise again to a position off security and comfort.

I am not bragging about myself. I have not done anything, nor am I doing anything, which you cannot do-and in the pages to come, the secrets will enabled me to find peace of mind and material security, will be unfolded to you-and in a manner which you can use in making them your very own.

These things are being told to you at this time to arouse your imagination. I want you to see yourself as you would like to be. Visualize the type of life which would spell complete happiness for you; then... follow a routine which will now be presented.

Earlier you began building a consciousness which enabled you to see that you *can* be a success. I hope you have been faithful-to yourself-by building on the affirmation; I CAN be a success.

Now, just as water in a receptacle on a range will come to a boil as sufficient heat is applied, lay this book aside for a few moments, walk up and down the floor, and with chin out and fists clenched, declare to yourself: I WILL be a Success.

Know that you will be a success because you will take the steps which lead you to success.

Before bringing this revelation to a close, there is one warning I must leave with you. Many times one will think he is following this instruction when all he is doing is running through the motions but not acting upon them fully.

DISCOVERING THE SECRECT SELF

Human personality is immensely complex. A person is far more than a name and certain physical, mental, and emotional characteristics. It is strange that we ever feel we know others at all, when the slightest examination of our own psyche reveals at once that we know scarcely anything about ourselves. We do not even dwell alone in our own bodies, are for the most part a battleground for opposing sides of our nature; and as one assumes command, then another, we present the constantly changing colors of the chameleon.

OUR MANY SELVES

A man engaged in concentrated effort often talks to himself. One part of him sits in judgement on the other, so that he gives vent to little exclamations of exasperation such as, "You can do better than that, Henry, old boy," or "Don't be such a bonehead, you can get it!" In this apparent division of the self, one half assumes a nature that appears above reproach while the other apparently has the personality of a mischievous, recalcitrant child. If you ask Henry which of the two he is, he answers that he is Henry. If you ask him who is talking to Henry, he achieves a look of utter blankness, manages to answer at least that he's only talking to himself.

Well, it isn't just a way that Henry has, it's a way that all of us have. We house within us not one nature, but many, not one self, but a whole myriad of selves superimposed upon each other like endless reflections in opposing mirrors; and not one of these selves is our true self, not even all taken together, but another truer being hidden within, timeless and eternal and unchanging.

The conflicts and oppositions of the many sides of our surface nature are directly responsible for the prevalence of that psychological disorder called schizophrenia. The schizophrenic is disoriented with the world and himself through intense inner conflicts waged by several of his different natures. In extreme cases, one, then the other, takes over, so that he is possessed of several distinct personalities, each as different from the other as night and day. A number of clinical cases of this nature have been studied extensively, one has even been made into a best-selling book, so that by and large people are finally becoming aware of the wavering, mystical being each of us really is.

The psychologically sound person is one who takes charge of his own personality, refuses to allow himself to be influenced by the wind, imposes a discipline upon himself predicated on the goals he wishes to achieve. Yet despite this "taking charge," despite the discipline imposed upon the surface nature and inner parts of the psyche, the psychologically sound person must remain subservient to an inner hidden part of his being, that indestructible and bright core within that sustains him and gives him life. If he does not, then a sickness of all his parts aggrandizes his ego, disassociates him from reality, causes him to assume the psychologically functional disorder known as paranoia. His blown-up ego has shut him off from supporting and sustaining Secret Self, and he is heading directly for destruction. Most of the dictators of our modern political systems have been of this type, carrying their countries and themselves to destruction in a blind and headlong rush.

INFINITY IN THE FINITE

It becomes obvious, once we give it close consideration, that man not only is at war with nature, but actually is at war with himself. We are such battlegrounds within that often we cannot contain our turmoil and our entire psyche becomes permeated with a sickness that makes it of little use to the world or ourselves. Whatever the human being is, he is more than a physical body, and the misty shape of his invisible aura is something that cannot be contained within boundaries or assigned categories or weighed or measured or counted. All that we are and can hope to be is mental, is the essence of some gigantic intelligence in the lap of which we nestle and from which we are fed and nurtured as if from subterranean springs. This gigantic intelligence is the Secret Self of the universe; it is also, paradoxically enough, the Secret Self of each of us.

No amount of rhetoric prevails against disbelief; no argument dissuades the man of faith. Still, the enigma is there. How is it possible that something infinite is size and scope, like a universal mind, can be housed within the tiny, finite body of an individual man? To be infinite is to be one. More than one of anything infinite automatically is not infinite, for anything infinite occupies all the space there is and therefore does not leave room for anything else. Thus, anything infinite is exactly the same as anything within it, for all of anything infinite has to be at each particular place and each particular time. Now this may be pretty hard to swallow, but it is perhaps as scientifically sound as the Quantum Theory of physics, and what is essentially means is this: if there is intelligence behind life, and there is every reason to believe there must be, then all of that intelligence is innate in each creation of that intelligence. Thus, universal mind or the Secret Self is complete and entire within each of us. We have only to discover it for its power and performance to be ours.

But neither the search nor the finding are easy. We are so steeped in out egotism, so encysted within our myriad surface selves, that vision to penetrate the illusion is hard to acquire, is developed only by arduous mental effort and spiritual discipline. Underlying all the turmoil, supporting the contest between the surface selves, giving each life direction and purpose, is the garden from which springs personality, the Secret Self, a place of calm and certitude within each of us. There is no struggle in the Secret elf. It *knows*. Its mere act of perception is an act of creation, for seeing precedes being in this most mental of all places where thought and idea are always prior to physical fact.

BEHIND THE WALL

Carl Jung has stated that most people confuse "self-knowledge" with knowledge of their conscious ego personalities, so that anyone with any ego at all takes it for granted that he knows himself. Actually, he knows only the ego and its contents and seldom has little if any knowledge of the vast and shadowy areas of the subconscious from whence all the impulsions and compulsions that form his active life spring. No man is free who feels that his motivations originate in his conscious ego personality. He is moved about in life like a puppet by the subconscious, and all his elaborate reasonings and painful arrival sat conscious perceptions are made after the fact of his commitment to certain ideas and actions, never before. Between the surface self and the Secret Self lies an opaque wall, impenetrable to the gaze of the ego and yielding its secrets only to one who has expanded his consciousness beyond the limits of his conscious mind. The materialist who prides himself on never accepting anything but a proven physical fact has merely accepted blindness as a condition of his being, and what he thinks is freedom is simply servitude of the highest degree. Turning one's back on the subconscious does not obliterate it. The individual is sprung into being not by an effort of self, but comes performed by something other than the ego that fronts his consciousness during life. The questions is, who is the true resident within, the ego that grows from experience, or the life force that animates from the beginning? Reflection leads us inescapably to the conclusion that the true person within is the hidden dweller in *all* things, that the ego is only a mask doomed by this dweller for a moment in some inscrutable play being acted out for its secret delight.

The constant search of the psyche of man, as long as it confines itself to the ego and the surface nature, must continue to be fruitless, for it concerns itself with a wraith. To truly know man, his actual nature, origin, purpose, destiny, the deeper regions of the conscious must be probed. These are all subconscient, make up the vast, jumbled, tremendously powerful, even frightening mental area below consciousness. Who knows what things are possible to this area of man's being? Sigmund Freud, having exposed its awesome powers, is reported to confessed that he created the dogma of his sexual theory of human behavior because some powerful bulwark of reason was needed against the black flood of occultism that might spring from the subconscious. Yet it is just that occultism, just that black flood that most needs to be studied, for the Secret Self lies there.

312

THE UNUTTERED PART OF LIFE

The Ouija board and divining rod are not just parlor games or the tools of crackpots but are the best of illustrations that within us there is a being enormously different from our surface selves and which has powers of perception and knowledge vastly greater than our conscious minds. A man with a forked hazel stick can find water beneath the surface of the ground, and this remarkable feat is true not because there is any affinity between the water and the hazel stick, but because there exists in the subconscious of the man a means of perceiving that water underlies a particular piece of ground. The stick turns downward and points out the water because of unconscious muscular reactions on the part of the man, but he will swear it foes so of its own violation; and to the degree that the turning down is originated by the Secret Self and not by his surface self, his claim is true. In any case, the stick turns down, the well is dug, and water is there. The man couldn't have seen the water, the stick couldn't have known it was there. Some other thing, some invisible force was at work. That thing, that force, is the Secret Self.

Thomas Carlyle wrote, "The uttered part of man's life, let us always repeat, bears to the unuttered, unconscious part a small unknown proportion. He himself never knows it, much less do others." We wend our unheeding oblivious ways through life, captives of forces we neither understand or are aware exist, and we labor under the delusion that we are free. This blindness has not been forced upon us because of our relationship to life, nor is it necessary in order to preserve our sanity or individuality as some casuists would have us believe. It is simply an inevitable step in the evolution of mind over matter, and even now is being transcended by those individuals sufficiently evolved to correctly perceive the Secret Self and its existence within. Mind seeks to know; its goal is a constantly increasing awareness. Expanding consciousness is apparent wherever we look, almost as if a mental explosion had taken place in the heart of the universe and now speeds outward in all directions, encompassing everything.

LIBERATION FROM BONDAGE

The surface mind is not the true mind, but is the barest fractional part of the true mind, and we never know our power and effectuality until we turn away from this troublesome false self and originate thought and action on the deeper planes of our being. Then we become as a power doubled upon itself, have "hitched a ride" on illimitable energy. Below the surface self and the conscious mind, sustaining and supporting both but remaining infinitely greater than either, is universal subconscious mind, the vast mind that springs into being all living things, that underlies life like a great and infinite ocean of intelligence and energy. This subconscious mind is not just a hodgepodge reservoir of instincts, urges, and long forgotten memories individual to each man, neither a kind of cell energy of pain or pleasure as some psychologists would have us believe, but encompasses infinitely more, the whole scope of creation, of space and time and knowledge and purpose, and all of this mind is in every person and no one has a larger share of it than others, and all of it is available to each of us this very moment, is actually the sustaining self of every one of us.

Frustration and suffering are the human lot in this stage of evolution because we have separated ourselves from the root source of our power. This has been done as a consciousness that has evolved into self-consciousness, for the particular stage of self-consciousness at which we have arrived is embryonic, is only self-consciousness in the narrowest sense of the word, delimits itself by the boundaries of the physical senses and therefore males itself a tiny speck in the infinitely large and living universe. It is small wonder that we are blinded to the beginnings and ends of life, so tiny is our newly acquired sense of being. Yet even now it reaches groping and hopeful hands toward an alliance with its greater self, and it is this alliance that will firmly liberate it from bondage to the flesh, from the limitations of space and time and matter.

THE OTHER PERSON IN YOU

All this may sound pretty obscure, even occult, and since the average person today is so grounded and steeped in materialism, there may be those of you who balk at this point and say, "Prove it. Show me evidence of Universal Subconscious Mind." There is evidence aplenty.

Various hypnotic techniques are continually exposing layers of the subconscious that indicate that they are not the personal property of the person under hypnosis. For example, Miss Jones may be hypnotized and recall intimate details of a life not her own, so that the unwary researcher will be led to believe that she is recalling a life lived previously. Such evidence is continually offered in support of the reincarnation thesis, but no such actual proof has been forthcoming. People under hypnosis have spoken languages they neither consciously understood nor ever had heard, described in detail places and times where they had never been, and could not have conscious knowledge of, literally performed all manner of clairvoyant feats that indicate the amazing power and scope of the subconscious; and the indisputable evidence is of a single entity only, existing in all persons but the individual property of none.

Someone else lives in your body other than the surface mind, which you have long regarded as yourself, a bigger, finer, more dynamic, more gifted, and powerful person than you have ever imagined yourself to be, but your true self nevertheless, the real you. Its action and power are behind every though and move you make, and if your conscious mind is opposed to this real self, then you are torn on the rack of indecision and opposition and meet nothing but frustration and disappointment wherever you turn. But once your conscious mind and surface self are lent as tools to this subconscious self, then of a sudden you are a whole and glorious thing and you find yourself proceeding along life's pathways with surety and power.

YOUR SENIOR PARTNER

To fully uncover the Secret Self is no doubt the final goal of evolution. When the inhabiting spirit has fully emerged from matter, then the Godhead will be revealed at last with all its conscious power and infinite realization. The man who joins the irresistible tide is swept onward by unsuspected energies to accomplish feats far beyond his poor mortal self. He has hitched a ride on cosmic power, and his energies and inspirations spill over the boundaries of his surface self and touch all those whom he associates. He becomes a leader, a doer, a creator, and achieves a kind of omnipotence because he is led in performance by an infallible and irresistible force.

You can talk to the Secret Self. You can go into a conference with it much as you might consult an all-wise and benevolent father or the president of the business that employs you. Once you have the hang of it and come to fully realize beyond any shadow of doubt its potentiality and possibility, then daily conference will be as natural and fitting to your mode of living as the act of breathing. This is "the Father that dwells within you," spoken of by Jesus. This is the senior side of your dual personality, the detached one that judges the action and is untouched by it. This is the subconscious mind referred to by psychologists, the mind that never sleeps, thinks when all is still, works with surety and calmness in the midst of great turmoil. This is the talisman that delivers you the "hunch," that brings you fortune, the idea for your book, painting, or composition, an inner vision, a new path to tread. This is the deep center of your being to which you retreat in meditation and prayer, where joy, serenity, and bliss reign because all is known and truly understood.

Haven't you ever contacted it? Set that right at once. As soon as you know the Secret Self is there, your close relationship to it is assured, for who would turn his back on the source of his redemption from pain and suffering and frustration?

AN EXPERIMENT

Take a simple finger ring. Tie it to a thin thread about twelve inches long. Hold the loose end of the thread between your thumb and forefinger. Let the ring dangle. Now tell the Secret Self that you are going to ask it some questions, that if the ring moves in a small circle you will understand the answer to be "yes," that if it sways back and forth in a linear path you will understand the answer to be "no." Ask the question aloud; hold the ring and wait. Don't try to stop it from moving, and make no attempt to start it moving. It will move. At first, the movement will be erratic, but soon it will settle into a back and forth or circular motion. Eventually, your questions will be answered instantaneously. Then you will have made a direct contact with the Secret Self, and you will realize with comprehending awe that someone infinitely aware dwells inside you.

There is no limit to the power of the Secret Self. Your whole effort from the moment of your realization of its existence should be to become acquainted with it, to explore its infinite facets and discover the keys that unlock its powers. Once you begin to guide your life in accordance with its perceptions and motivations you will begin to take on an infallibility in works that bodes success in every undertaking, every relationship. You will find that you are accompanied always by a feeling of inner joy and energy and well-being where before you were always gnawed at by vague anxieties and fears and feelings of lethargy and fatigue. The color of the sky will change; the world will take on a new and meaningful and exciting aspect. You will have placed yourself in tune with the guiding and motivating force of the universe, and it will buoy your spirits heavenward. No task will appear too great, no obstacle insurmountable.

SUPPORTER OF THE WORLDS

Arthur Schopenhauer wrote, "Every man takes the limits of his own field of vision for the limits of the world." And it is this blinding quality of the surface psyche, that it cannot see beyond the limits it imposes upon itself, that gives inherent characteristics of weakness and incapability to every mortal man. Even so, the degree is markedly different in the limitations men impose upon themselves. Some men build towers to the sky, challenge nature in her most inaccessible places, make their whole lives a constant attack on mental and physical barriers. Other men accept all the limitations they encounter, live in fear of self-manufactured ogres, cannot challenge, expand or grow because they are slaves of the tiny surface self and have not glimpsed or understood the giant within them. There is hope for the man who aspires; his place among the gods is assured. But he who hangs back and never dares and never takes action is withering on the tree of life, and all his wishes will not change anything as long as they are not strong enough to prompt him to attack his fear-created walls.

Once you have discovered the Secret Self within, then it becomes a gradual process of turning over your work, your goals and aspirations to it. You cannot build a perfect life on the imperfect foundation of the surface self. It will not support even the flimsiest edifice, will crumble under the slightest pressure. All must be built on the Secret Self, which already supports the worlds and the universes and will support your life, be you savant or saint, and without the slightest tremor.

> Of all the causes that conspire to bind
> Man's erring judgement, and misguide the mind,
> What the weak head with strong bias rules,
> Is pride, the never-failing vice of fools.
> -Alexander Pope

FACING FEAR

It is vanity, or pride if you will, which is the true enemy of the Secret Self. For with consciousness centered in the surface self, with the vanity that self-centeredness brings, an opaque veil is drawn over all spiritual perception, and a man lives isolated from the well-springs of his being. He may struggle through life many years in this manner, attacking his problems and pursuing his goals with the persistent energy of an enterprising fly, but eventually he must be brought up short by the realization that he simply is ineffectual and he had best find a new blueprint of thought and action or give up the ghost altogether. One ant alone does not topple a rubber tree plant. Only the concerted effort and teamwork of thousands of ants make this feat possible; and the energy and effort of one human being is nothing by itself, but is everything when it proceeds from the source of all energy, for then it is attuned to the tides and forces of the cosmos, becomes in a manner an irresistible force, a kind of infallible action.

Success stories often are fictions concocted by the human desire to achieve supremacy over circumstance. Most people fit into a kind of equation. They react a certain way when confronted with certain circumstances, and therefore must act a certain way always when confronted with those same circumstances. For example, suppose a man is afraid of groups of people when he is unacquainted with them and expected to circulate amongst them and communicate. If early in life he gives in to his fear and avoids new groups, such behavior becomes a habit and one that he eventually finds impossible to break. Therefore, all through his life, when confronted with a strange social situation, he will avoid it through one pretense or another, simply because he has built up a habit of acceding to fear. He is absolutely predictive because he is not free, because he is a slave to his fears. He has become an automaton led around by the nose, a victim of circumstances because he is not a master of his feelings. He tends to regard circumstance itself as the evil, says, "People in groups are uninteresting. They bore me." They don't bore him at all; they scare the hell out of him; so much so that he avoids them at all costs, leaves a large blank in a portion of his psyche and its completely frustrated in this area of his growth. And it is his own fault. He simply cannot bring himself to muster the courage necessary to face his fear.

OVERCOMING WEAKNESS

"You cannot run away from a weakness; you must sometime fight it out or perish; and if that be so, why not now, and where you stand?" Fittingly enough, these lines were penned by a writer bedfast through illness, but he turned that illness into a great victory, eventually recovering his health and giving the world masterpieces of literature. His name-Robert Louis Stevenson.

We must not be soft with ourselves no matter what our goals or positions. All things fare best when they are constantly tested by opposition. The sturdiest grass is that which must grow through concrete. The coddled lawn burns clean away at first exposure to sun or wind. If we have an aching muscle we must learn to exercise it, not to rest it, and we will find the muscle soon healed. If our psyche is closing us in, cutting us off from life and growth and expansion, then we must learn to test and use and expand that psyche. If we do not, the psyche will atrophy, cut off completely all normal ties with life. Still, to be human is to be weak, is to be subject to sin and suffering and error, and as long as we live we never truly overcome any of these; but as long as we live we must try, for we truly live only when we try. What we finally have to learn is that we cannot expect an ultimate or even a satisfactory victory over our infirmities when we meet them one by one, but only when we have found a way of assembling all on the same field of battle for one final showdown. What results then must be a complete step forward in our evolution as human beings, for no one is ever defeated who gathers courage to face his assembled weaknesses.

"How is this possible?" someone may ask. "How does one gather all his weaknesses in one spot and overcome them?" It is not simple or even apparent. In isolated areas, yes. If you have a tendency to be afraid of new situations, then you can build up confidence about them by forcing yourself to enter into them. Sooner or later you are bound to meet each new situation calmly, if not eagerly, for the general condition of newness has become familiar. This exercise of will power, however, while it will tend to give you courage in every aspect of your life simply because you have met a fear in one area and defeated it, nevertheless will not overcome a tendency to be lazy, for example, or untruthful, or disloyal, or even to eat too much. As a matter of fact, it can readily be seen that his helter-skelter treatment of the unwhole psyche is much like a man trying to plug in a dike with his fingers. Eventually all ten fingers will be occupied, and still the new leaks come.

THE UNIVERSAL AUTHOR

What is needed is a new approach to the psyche, one that treats it as a single thing and not as a group of aberrations or incomplete perceptions, and the approach which gives one hundred per cent cures in one hundred per cent of cases is one in which the individual comes to know and be aware of his Secret Self.

Each of faces life with an undeveloped psyche. It is underdeveloped because it is less than whole, because it is only a partial manifestation of something greater than itself. Only insofar as it approached awareness of this greater does it approximate wholeness or self-sufficiency. That sense of self which we use in our daily rounds of effort is useful only insofar as it is larger than the task we undertake. It is perfectly up to peeling potatoes, for instance, but when something large is asked of it, then it may cower in the corner. Bridges are built by the Secret Self and not by the surface ego of man. Towers and highways and planes and automobiles and televisions are wrought by the Secret Self. All books are written by the same author, all pictures painted by the same artist, all music written by the same composer. The ego of the individual is simply not up to such tasks, and as long as a man lives entrapped in bondage to his surface self, then his efforts can only be crowned by such puny results as fit his ego. Only when he tears himself away, divorces himself from vanity and conceit and ego and surface self can he at last perceive the true dimensions of the being that dwells within him. Then he knows his true self, then he turns his life over to it. Then his efforts take on a grandeur and purpose that are bound to achieve noble and vigorous ends, for the power that engrosses him proceeds from outside him and carries him along on its surging tides and is greater than he in every way.

Any man or woman whose life is aimed at creative effort is bound to discover the Secret Self sooner or later. No one can closet himself in the nebulous realm of the mental and spiritual without early coming to know that there dwells within him a mental being of enormous dimension and power, contact with which has the power to ennoble and illumine each moment. The author seeks his muse with all his heart. The painter pauses with raised brush, awaiting inspiration. We are moved from within toward each aspiration, provided it is loftier than the limitations of the surface self; and so, the world belongs to those who aspire, who dare, who try, for all aspiration is only effort against the prison of the surface self, and all such effort is the alchemy by which the common clay of our little egos is transmuted into something

319

transcendental and precious.

AN ARTIST FINDS HIS TALENT

A number of years ago there lived in a poor section of a large city a man who had given up the years of his youth to perfect his art. He lived meagerly on what few pennies he could earn making charcoal sketches in waterfront bars, and he spent every moment he could spare in front of his easel. He painted ships, every conceivable type and kind, at sea, becalmed and in storm, in port, loading and unloading, ships under sail, ships under steam, sleek yachts, wallowing freighters, men o' war. He loved the sea and loved to paint, and by the amount time he had spent at each he should have mastered his art very well, but he hadn't. Somehow it escaped him. His paintings were not amateurish: they exhibited the hand of a craftsman; yet they always seemed to be clichés, as if they were saying something that had been said a thousand times before. People would look at them and even comment that they had seen them before. They hadn't, of course. The paintings just contrived to look like others that had been done.

The painter realized this fact only too well. His work was intensely dissatisfying to him. He often would relate that when he was first struck with an idea for a new subject he would be deeply elated and would set to work with a vengeance. Then, as the work progressed under his hand, he would gradually come to see that it was not a thing of inspiration at all, but wooden, pat, said before, a reproduction, and even before the work was finished he would be gripped by a depression so intense that he could scarcely finish. Still, he drove himself unremittingly. He felt a talent was within him, and he was determined to get it out. Once, in a rage at himself, he burned all the paintings in his studio, nearly setting fire to the building. Another time he was so furious at his hand for its clumsiness that he badly lacerated his fingers, intent on cutting them off. All this, of course, would indicate that our friend was not psychologically stable, but perhaps it was simply that his provocation was great, so enormous was the creative urge that constantly goaded him.

Like most of the great lessons that life teaches, his enlightenment came dear. When war broke out he had just finished a period of deep dissatisfaction with his painting. Disgustedly, he decided to turn his back on it forever. He shipped out as a merchant seaman aboard a freighter bound for Murmansk. The convoy was attacked by German planes and submarines as it skirted the Norwegian coast. Our painter's ship was sunk, and he wound up in a lifeboat on the frigid and stormy Artic Ocean. For days and nights, they drifted, fighting the freezing cold, trying to stay alive. At one juncture, the skies cleared long enough for them to be sighted by German planes, and they were bombed and strafed. Five men were killed, three others seriously wounded, dying that night. A day later, two more died from exposure. Finally, there were left in the boat only the painter and the ship's purser, an elderly and apparently frail man who surprisingly still survived.

"It's no use," said the painter at length. "There is no hope for us, and we might as well slip over the side right now and be done with it."
"That's not for us to decide," said the purser.
"Who's then?" asked the painter.
The purser sat calmly, and his eyes were kind. "Do we decide to be born?" he asked. "Do we decide our nationality, our race, our heritage? Someone or something else does, I think. Get yourself quiet and listen. Perhaps you will hear a voice speak within you. Then you will learn whether you are to live or die."

The end seemed near. Surely it was useless to struggle further. For the first time in his life the painter was able to give over direction of his destiny to something other than his own ego. The bitter cold of approaching night descended on them. Just before dusk a British seaplane swooped out of the fog with a roar, saw them, landed on the sea, took them aboard. They were in a London hospital that night.

After some weeks of convalescence, our painter once again tries his hand at his easel. What emerged from the canvas startled him. It was as if a hand other than his own guided the brush, chose the colors, as though a mind other than his own envisaged the scene. Viewing the complete painting he felt a surge of joy. This was the talent he had fought to bring forth, and now it was flowing! In rapid succession he completed six paintings, packed them off to a London art dealer where they were received with open arms. They were an instantaneous success, launched him on a long and remarkable career.

Years later he was asked about his early period of struggle and how his talent happened to mature.

"It didn't mature," he answered. "It was there all the time. I just never could bring it out because I thought it belonged to me. As soon as I was able to see that it belonged to a being greater than I, it emerged of its own accord and used me, where before I had been trying vainly to use it."

Mystical, yes, a kind of cosmic perception by the artist of his muse, but a far greater secret is hidden here. Our painter stumbled upon the psychological relationship of ego to Secret Self that brooks no failure, that inevitably leads to success, for it is a relationship in which all thought and action proceed out of a universal intelligence and omnipotent power that makes each work absolutely effective.

FALL FROM GRACE

Our consciousness is anchored falsely in our surface selves, and it is this delusion that is our fall that is our fall from grace, for by it we do not know who we truly are and fancy ourselves as tiny isolated selves in a vast and overwhelming universe. The gradual opening and unfolding of consciousness to that point where the vistas within our psyche are revealed is the goal of evolution itself, as life and Intelligence and being manifest out of matter, eventually control and dominate matter. As long as we remain chained to the illusion of the surface self we are but puppets of sensation, reacting this way or that to every situation that confronts us, little more that absolutely predictive ciphers in an equation aimed at producing the free, thinking, omnipotent man. Yet this condition of freedom and omnipotence needs only perception, for without a doubt the mere act of perceiving the Secret Self is akin to becoming one with the Secret Self. How then shall we see? How shall our eyes be opened?

Perhaps the most important step in discerning the Secret Self is disillusionment with the effectiveness of the surface self, for how is it possible to see when we still rejoice in our blindness? So, it is a spiritual awareness, psychic enlightenment, seldom come to one in youth, for youth is preoccupied with the senses, pursues all manner of sensual inamorata, and is for the most part completely oblivious of the prison which the senses have erected. Passing years bring the disappointments, frustrations and inadequacies that cause the seeking soul to cast about within psychic realms for a new foundation on which to erect a more reliable and effective essence of self. When this comes, eventual enlightenment is assured, for no one seeks but he finds, knocks but the door is opened. The mere act of turning away from the senses and the surface self seems sufficient. The veil is removed, the blinder disintegrated, and an event in physical life that was brought about by suffering and frustration and disillusionment turns out to be a great blessing in disguise. A new world is revealed. The death of the surface self actually turns out to be a new birth. Resignation of the senses from control of the person turns out to be a seizing of the reins of the life by a new and dominant and effective force. When the inner eye of the soul is opened there descends upon the whole being a unity of parts and force, a vitality and serenity that remake that life completely, that lend magic and grandeur to everything that is touched or taken into consciousness.

Who sees with the equal eye, as God of all
A hero perish or a sparrow fall
Atoms or systems into ruin hurl'd

322

And now a bubble burst, and now a world.
-Alexander Pope

PATH TO ILLUMINATION

While it is true that perception of the indwelling Secret Self ordinarily comes to harassed mortals only after much suffering and disillusionment, nevertheless there is a path by which such suffering may be avoided in the main, provided that first the soul is dedicated and sincere in its desire to make the discovery. The Secret Self is never discovered alone within, but at the same time is discovered in all places, in all beings, and is found to be the same in all. Different forms of life are merely disguises donned for the moment by the single self that underlies all, that truly is all, a play in which for the moment the Divine is hidden, in which for the moment by the single self that underlies all, a play for which at the moment the Divine is hidden, in which for that moment it actually has become in entirety each of the things it has become. All the power and effectiveness of the Supreme is within you, is yours to use, and is also in everyone and everything else, existing there behind the curtain of egoconsciousness, waiting to be discovered. Therefore, there is a tremendous underlying equality to all things under the sun. Each is sprung from the same substance and has inherent within it the same omnipotent being, and we are not each of us different and individual and separate insofar as we are incomplete. To be complete is to be the Secret Self, whole and entire, without reservation or error.

The most painless path to illumination, to perception of the Secret Self, is thus to arrive at a desire to know the truth that lies behind the surface façade of the senses and to seek this truth not only within but without, in every person you meet as well as in yourself. Once this sense of absolute equality of things and people begins to make itself known to you, then you will detect a presence in each stone and clod, in each tree and plant, in each animal and person you meet, locked in a prison dictated by its form to be sure, but a presence pure and simple of the Secret Self, which has chosen the masquerade for its own purposes and is not truly locked away from consciousness of its real self but even now is developing it as we brush at the veil that separates us from our heritage.

Once a man senses the presence of the Divine in all things he is able to arrive at a sense of equality that makes him in some secret and inviolable corner of his being untouched by victory or defeat, pleasure or pain, position or prestige. He becomes so intent on doing the work of the Secret Self that he abandons almost altogether the uses of the ego and so achieves a kind of selfishness in his appearance to the world. Equality is the perfect psychic position, but it is impossible to the ego which seeks forever to be better than all the egos around it, and if it is not better it is convinced it is worse and so either becomes a blown-up and blind or wounded and fearful and thus provides the worst of all psychic bases for dealing with life, love, and accomplishment. To be equal is to be unafraid. To know that there inhabits all others the same beings that inhabits you is to achieve psychic confidence that enables you to place your life and hopes and energies in the hands of this being without a qualm, with absolute certainty that you will be guided to perform that work that you must do, in the best of all possible ways, at the best of all possible times.

THE PHANTOM MATERIAL WORLD

It is an established fact that our five senses perceive but the tiniest portion of the almost infinite spectrum of vibrations that prevails in the universe, that a million times more remains untold about each thing than can possibly be perceived by sensual means. Whistles can be made which are imperceptible to the human ear but are easily heard by certain animals. The frequency of vibration we know as light is strictly bounded as to the range that has an effect on the human eye, but nevertheless we know there are variations in what people can see-some are color-blind, others near-sighted, others farsighted, some have an artist's vision, to others materializations appear, as to Bernadette at Lourdes. In short, the materialist who prides himself on accepting nothing but the evidence of his senses is accepting the sketchiest of evidence; he actually prides himself on his blindness, accepting things as facts on the basis of knowing a mere one billionth of their total qualities. He would not dream of entering a business deal with a meagre knowledge, but accepts the world and others and himself on such evidence and rears like a reluctant stallion when it is suggested to him that he lives among phantoms.

Focusing attention on the ego and the evidence of the senses the veil that hides the Secret Self. The senses themselves are not the veil, only the impression they give that they are conveying to the observer the total aspect of things. Nor is ego inherently a veil, only the impression that it gives through completely dominating the consciousness that it is the actual self of the person. Hung up in his sensual world and totally immersed in the ego, a man has no chance to perceive the Secret Self. The clarion call sounds but his ears are not attuned. With his tiny and incomplete knowledge, he keeps entering into things without perceiving their true nature and ultimate destiny and therefore his path through life is marked mainly by suffering and defeat, though occasionally the purposes of this ego will coincide with the ends

324

of the Divine, in which case he willingly falls victim to his own duplicity, convinced that his little machinations have moved the world. The end of his ego is certain still, for it is but flotsam adrift on a surging tide and sooner or later destroys itself by pursuing its separate ends.

RESIGNATION AND ASPIRATION

To let go of the ego is the thing to be done. To get outside of and free from the grip of the senses is the only path to discovery of the Secret Self. Many people are brought to their knees by life before they let go of self and achieve equality through resignation. Many of the most brilliantly illuminations have happened in this manner. Out of the utmost defeat and degradation of the human soul have arisen its most inspirational moments, but it is doubtful if any human would willingly choose such a path for an end that is vague to him in the first place. Mystics who have discovered the Secret Self through mental and spiritual concentration report that even they have experienced "a dark night of soul" as the ego was surrendered. Evelyn Underhill chronicles many such transfigurations and all were preceded by a period of deep spiritual and emotional depression, such as Christ had in the Garden of Gethsemane. It is no easy thing to surrender the ego. It is a kind of death. But it must be done before life can be enlarged by the expanded consciousness that results from complete possession of the individual by the Secret Self. The quality above all things that is required is courage. You must push off, the jump must be taken. Lyrically, it is almost exactly as recorded by Dustin Smith, a free fall parachutist.

"The first time you go into a free fall is the weirdest. You have no idea what is going to happen. You are terrified on the first step. Then you look down, like God. And the ultimate is going away from the plane. In this you're free and you're purely responsible for yourself. There is a real moment of truth when you reach for the cord. You come down absolutely elated. You've done something that in one way seems ridiculous, but in another way, makes great sense."

Now it is not recommended that any seeker after truth adopt parachuting as a means to illumination, but there can be no doubt from Mr. Smith's observations that pushing off from the safety of an airplane into the unknown dangers of the sky is almost exactly like the spiritual step of pushing away from the ego and surrendering one's life to the unknown guidance of the Secret Self. They both require courage; they both exemplify a search. They both typify man's aspiration to pierce the veils that blind him.

THE COUNTRY BEYOND

The end result of transfiguration, of illumination, is for the ego to be properly subordinated to the Divine, but before the Secret Self can even appear to the aspiring soul there must be a prior period of time in which the edge of the importance of the ego is gradually whittled down until it no longer occupies the whole consciousness, until there is room within the awareness for light to enter, for the Divine to be revealed. Some people are so immersed in the workings of the ego that they haven't the faintest idea what is meant by subordinating it to another principle. To them the ego is the beginning and end, the sum of all existence, and according to how they gratify this surface self by power and position and victory they feel they have achieved success in life. The truth is that the surest way to assure *against* success in life-the success of arriving at a grasp of the meaning of existence- is to continually gratify the ego. What results then is a blindness by limitation, for the ego, being small, cannot see beyond itself.

Jesus, a great mystic and a master of spiritual knowledge, pronounced it to be more difficult for a rich man to enter the kingdom of heaven than for a camel to go through the eye of a needle. This observation of his, of course, is largely parable. It is not strictly rich men Jesus referred to, for some rich men are not spiritual, but rather men who live to gratify the senses and their ingrown vanity; these are the ones whom expanded consciousness is unavailable. It is denied for no moral reason, but a purely scientific one. If one chooses to look through a crack in the wall there is revealed a partial world. If one goes *through* the wall, the true aspect of the country beyond is revealed at last. Forsaking ego and uniting with the Secret Self makes this view possible to the aspiring soul.

EXPANDING CONSCIOUSNESS

Consciousness is the key to discovering the Secret Self. To become aware that consciousness is the same in all people is a big step in the road to illumination. Once you have become struck by the enormity of this situation you will never again be the same, for you will innately perceive that at work in the universe is not a multitude of aspiring and searching souls, but one individual only, and you are it and it is all others, and so in a very real sense you and your neighbor are one. Once the magnificent implications of this fact have come home to you, you will see that the secret of effective living is not the exerting of your individual will as you have always supposed it to be, but rather in growing to know and understand events and objects so that you can correctly perceive their true purpose and destiny. And you will not do that by observing the surface facts as recorded by the ego self, but only by expanding your consciousness to the point where objects and events become a part of you, as they surely are in actuality, for both you and they are the Secret Self.

To expand consciousness infinitely would be to grow into oneness with the one force, the one power, the one mind that truly exists. Perhaps this goal in this age and at this stage of evolution is impossible, but nevertheless we can expand our present consciousness a thousandfold, if not to include the universe, certainly to include our friends and neighbors and the events and circumstances that surround us. By a process of identification, we can come to know other things and other people and outside events even as we know ourselves, and possessed by this knowledge we can act in the midst of all things in complete accord with their true nature and destiny, and so our actions take on a kind of omnipotence, our works a kind of absolute effectiveness, so that we appear to be molding and changing the world about us when in truth we are only acting in conformity with its real but unrevealed nature.

MAGIC ALCHEMY

"It is not I, but a power greater than I" is the first acknowledgement we must make to the Secret Self. Once this is done, we have by a kind of surrender placed our fate where it should be, in the hands of something infinitely more informed and more capable. To forsake the urgings and promptings of the surface nature and ego is the first step, for as long as we are bound to this ineffective and tiny microcosm we cannot be effective in our works or serene in our spiritual development. We must turn away from that which we have always considered self and embrace that which we have always considered other than self and embrace that which we have always considered other than self, and in that turning away and in embracing lies our salvation. "It is not I who doeth the work," stated Jesus, "but the Father that dwelleth within me." And when his transfiguration was complete: "I and the Father are one."

The surface self will not surrender lightly. It struggles and misguided urgings will be constant. Wise is the man and extremely enlightened who manages to control his ego at all times. To be human is to be subject to error, but to discover within the image of perfection and joy is to find a way out of the morass of physical sensation in which we find ourselves entrapped in life. Salvation for all of us is as near as ourselves, for there dwells within each of us a hallowed light, a hidden self that can relive our sufferings and frustrations, no matter how painful or enduring. We have only to discover and embrace it, for it to become our true selves and to work its magic in our lives.

REVELATION #34
ADVERTISING CAMPAIGNS

Whatever industry you engage in you are going to use some degree of advertising which will require a scope of broad knowledge. Success will depend upon many critical decisions.

If you observe every successful company that advertises you will become enlightened as to the awesome power advertising has in every industry. There is no limit to how big can produce dynamic research. The shrewd wealth seekers in business either know or soon discover the need to boost business activity. Now you have a smathering of the necessity to be educated in advertising.

Of course, there is lots more to learn and realize-your success and wealth depend upon that know-how!

There is a CD that is very extensive with the facts that will develop your expertise, the cost is insignificant when you consider the cost of advertising that must be effective or the entire business may be doomed. The CD is called "Effective Advertising Campaign" and the cost is only $20.00. If you do not obtain it. You are in for the biggest gamble ever. And of course, the purpose is to make money so the education is vital simply to assure big success.

The subject matter necessary to be learned includes the data to become sharp making expert decisions. It is necessary to know how to calibrate results to make sure you are choosing the best audiences and delivering your message to produce extraordinary returns resulting in substantial profits.

By utilizing the tremendous power of effective advertising. The business architect has to employ the best brains. Even if an advertising agency is engaged, the final decisions have to be made by the principle running the business.

Decisions have to be made as to how many things such as to the best media, whether it be newspapers, magazines, truck journals, direct mail, flier distributed, radio, T.V., internet, website, Facebook, google, search engines, airplane banners, press releases, demonstrations, bulletin boards, lectures, sales teams, house parties, free press release, advertising specialties, caps, shirts, key rings, pens etc.

The allocation of capital formula has to calculate smartly. What method of distribution, where?, When?, How? Lots of decisions have to be made with expertise-not just random.

Sales literature has to be written and the quality has to be attractive and dramatic to achieve profitable results! Money should not be squandered or failure will be the result.

PRESS ON

NOTHING IN THE WORLD CAN TAKE THE PLACE OF PERSISTENCE. TALENT WILL NOT; NOTHING IS MORE COMMON THAN UNSUCCESSFUL MEN WITH TALENT. GENIUS WILL NOT; UNREWARDED GENIUS IS ALMOST A PROVERB. EDUCATION WILL NOT; THE WORLD IS FULL OF EDUCATED DERELICTS. PERSISTENCE AND DETERMINATION ALONE ARE OMNIPOTENT.

The Colonies did not make Spain rich

At one-time Spain was the leading power in our world. The Spanish Sovereign was the King of Kings. In his empire, the sun never set. Spanish merchants and explorers went around the globe, took back spices from the Indies, ivory from Africa, and fine silk from China. The Conquerors Cortez and Pizarro overpowered in Middle and South America the mighty tribes of the Maya and Inca and took from the population huge quantities of gold, silver and jewels. What came in to the Spanish Crown were enormous riches-but until our day, Spain was to be a poor country. You may ask why?

Ben Franklin remarked: "The colonies did not make Spain rich, for they spent more than they took in." Many believe it is necessary to make a lot of money in order to get rich. This is an error. Wealth does not necessarily come from a large income, but from the difference between income and outgo. Even more simply: wealth is the money you don't spend.

The first rule of finance is to establish a worthwhile difference between income and what you spend. As long as you do not learn to have some savings from the money you earn, it is no use to strive for more money. It is the difference between what you earn and what you will spend that decides whether you will be wealthy or poor. If you spend all of your money, you will not become rich. The money that counts is 50, 100 or 200 dollars that are left at the end of the month.

How to amass money

"The art of getting money", says Ben Franklin, "depends first of all upon saving it. Not every man has the ability to amass money, but it is within the power of everyone to make some progress in that respect."

All wealthy people are great savers. John D. Rockefeller, billionaire and richest man of his time, was a genius at saving. When only nine, he already had a "saving box," the famous blue bowl. When he was an apprentice and a bookkeeper, most of his small income was saved. It was his objective to be a good business and therefore he saved every cent and every dollar he could. When he went into business at the age of 19, saving had become a habit. He saved at everything: time, money, manpower, freight rates, raw materials, administration. This is the secret that turns pebbles into gold.

All rich men are tight with their money. Paul Getty, the fabulously rich oil man, for years lived in middle class hotels to save money. J. Pierpont Morgan, king of finance, scribbled his daily personal expenditures into a notebook. S.S. Kresge, the chain store tycoon, carried his lunch in a paper sack. If you do not learn how to save money, you will not achieve financial success. Take what you can receive by honest business methods and keep it. That is the secret that turns pebbles into gold.

Mighty oaks from acorns

A plan to save even 100 dollars each month may appear small in terms of saving. You might think that it is not much money. You may even come to the conclusion that all of this saving business leads nowhere, and that you might as well start spending all you earn. Nothing could be further from the truth. If you accumulate small savings and resist the temptation of spending all your income, the result can soon be surprisingly substantial. Ben Franklin said: "Do not despise small savings. Molehills piled one upon the other will rise the mountains."

The history of many great businesses shows that many of them were started with a very small investment of money. All men who grew rich initially possesses at the start, not much more than an idea and a knowledge for making money. These are men such as Carnegie, Rockefeller, Ford and thousands of other successful business men. Frank Woolworth started selling articles priced at 5 and ten cents. Today, Woolworth chain stores are around the world.

When you begin to save, you may put aside only a few dollars each month. That will do for a start. Then you'll develop methods to increase your income and thus increase your savings. Soon, you will accumulate a thousand dollars or more. With this you can make an investment, and buy some business that will be the basis of more gains.

Concentrate on your work

Take full command and concentrate upon your work. Soon you will learn that work is no hardship, but one of life's greatest joys. Ben Franklin said: "Diligence does not need wishes." And one of Franklin's neighbors said: "The diligence of this Franklin surpasses anything I have ever seen in my life. When I return from my club, I see him at work. And he is up early in the morning long before others come out from the feathers."

If you have the feeling that you earn less than you deserve, then think over whether you do your work with enthusiasm and joy. You can only prosper and earn with enthusiasm. Then you'll begin to make more money too.

Don't build two chimneys

You will not succeed if you try one thing today and another tomorrow. By so doing, you split your interests and your power. Franklin said: "It is easier to build two chimneys than to keep one burning all the time."

You can make easier by concentrating your efforts on one chimney and then building a huge fire under it. The masters of wealth built their fires to a giant size. Thru concentration, Rockefeller with oil; Gillette with razor blades; Max Factor with cosmetics; McCormick with farm equipment; Ford with automobiles.

The steel magnate Andrew Carnegie said: "Put all your eggs in one basket and watch that basket with all your might." He also said- "The average man invests only 25% of his capacity in his work. The world respects people who devote 100% of their capacity to work." Give your best to receive the best in return.

You can make money in any field, trade or profession. And you will earn a lot of money by building a chimney and keeping the fires burning. If you can concentrate upon this and do not try to build many chimneys.

Perseverance

Sensational news went around the world about South Africa diamonds as large as dove eggs. They lay upon the yellow sands of Kimberley and need only bend to pick up your fortune. From all parts of the world men came in droves to acquire these riches. Then the success stories ended when the yellow sands surface were combed clean of diamonds. Below the sands, the hard-blue soil could hardly be penetrated by the sharpest spade. The diamond diggers left their claims. They were overjoyed when a young fool bought their land for good money. They laughed up their sleeves thinking they had fooled this greenhorn. But, their laughter stopped when the young man, Cecil Rhodes, tore up the heavy blue soil with earth moving machinery. And now, diamonds came to daylight, which the astonished world had never seen before.

For Cecil Rhodes, the diamond mines of Kimberley were the foundation of his fortune. And, he used his wealth to develop the economy of South and Central Africa. All this, because he was a man to dig three feet deeper.

No success is possible without perseverance. McCormick sold less than 100 automatic threshing machines in his first 17 years. But he persevered and became a giant in the industry. The famous inventor Edison, tried 6,000 materials for filament, before he found the right one for his electric bulbs. He made 28,000 experiments in order to substitute lead in storage batteries.

Awareness of the master's eye

Even the most diligent man is unlikely to get rich from the work of his hands alone. The working capacity of two hands is limited. But, you can get rich by multiplying your working power with manpower, using machinery and leverage systems.

Franklin said: "The master's eye does make more work than his hands." The secret is for every business man to hire good men who materialize his ideas and multiply his efficiency. All leaders of industry know they must strive to inspire their associates and employees. When all the world worked 72 hours per week, Henry Ford inaugurated the 8-hour work day, and paid his men better than average. When the Chicago Fire totally destroyed the store of Marshall Field, the great Chicago merchant said: "At this place, we shall build the largest store in the world." And so he did!

For anyone who wants to get ahead in life it is necessary to learn how to lead people, how to inspire them and give them new ideas. You learn this from practice, by exercises, or by trial and error which is very costly. But, you can learn from others, also. Franklin said: "Experience is a school which costs a lot of money. Fools learn in this school and they may not even profit from it. But the wise man learns from the mistakes of others. One is happy who profits from the experience of others."

Success from smiling

When Franklin opened his book store, he had two men. One did the work, the other greeted the customers. When the man who greeted received a raise, the other man complained. Thereupon Franklin remarked: "A smile gets more sales than efficiency. The purse is closer to the heart than to the head."

Many do not earn more because they do not know how to get along with people and how to influence them. Therefore, learn how to win friends and build personal contacts which may prove very important to you. Therefore, learn how to win friends and build personal contacts which may prove very important to you. Charles Schwab's smile created his fortune. He was paid one million dollars every year by the steel magnate Andrew Carnegie. He was nicknamed "Smiling Charley" and with his grand smile, he sold J. Pierpont Morgan the idea of a great steel empire. And just recently, "Smiling Jimmy Carter" became president of the United States.

Talk with everyone as if he were a special friend. Make it a rule never to argue with anyone. Never make statements which might provoke anger. Instead, admire the arguments of your opponents. Bu doing this, you make friends; whereas others create enemies. Ben Franklin's art of handling people was so highly regarded, that he was sent to Paris to arrange contracts with France and England. He became one of the best know men in the Old World. He knew the power of his smile. What others could not get by fighting, he won by diplomacy.

Build credit and confidence

When Rockefeller began trading in grain, as a very young man, he had only about $1,000. As his business expanded, he needed more money. He went to a banker and told him of his problems. Back in his office an hour later, he waved his hat and cried: "I am worth $2,000! I have obtained a bank loan of $2,000." At that time, this was a small fortune. Why had Rockefeller been able to borrow this money?

In a town the size of Cleveland, at that time, most businessmen knew each other. Bankers and other businessmen knew how seriously Rockefeller took his responsibilities. Money that was due was collected. Bills that were due were paid promptly. Everyone knew young Mr. Rockefeller as a diligent and unceasing worker who was thrifty, did not use profane language, and went to church regularly every Sunday. All of these things were important in establishing credit, and the credit of Rockefeller increased tremendously. In his first year, he borrowed so much money that his net sales passed more than half a million. Later on, he borrowed far more, as the needs of his business increased.

Franklin said: "The good paying master is master on the purse of other people. When one is known as a punctual payer, he can obtain all the money he requires at any time."

Quality pays off

A man named William Lever had a tiny shop in a small town in England. To earn more money, he began to make soap from fat and sodium. To give his customers a better product, he used only the best materials obtainable. Instead of sawing the soap in front of his customers, he sawed it at night when his shop was closed. He wrapped each piece in paper upon which was printed: "Sunlight," one of the first trademarks.

Soon housewives learned that this special soap really made their washing clean. This was quite different from the products of other merchants which were cheaper, but of poorer quality. The soap "Sunlight" became so popular that William Lever could concentrate exclusively on producing soap. At first 50 workers and later 100 workers were needed. The soap "Sunlight" soon conquered England, and afterwards Europe and North and South America. William Lever bought and built sodium and soap factories, founded shipping lines, and built cocoa plantations to give him an ample supply of raw materials.

So, from the tiny shop in a small town in England grew the mighty Unilever Company, one of the business enterprises in the world, selling over one billion dollars worth of products each year. William Lever became Lever-hulme. And all because an able businessman had the idea of serving housewives by giving them cleaning materials of high quality.

No one can become a financial success, if he does not, in the first place, give something which is of use to others. Ben Franklin said therefore: "If you wish to earn you must first serve. The higher your service, the higher your income.

Money Breeding

From all goods without life only money has the ability to grow. From the facts alone it can be mathematically realized that a sum of money has the ability to earn more money. If you put $100,000 in a savings bank, you will receive interest of $6,000 per year. The savings bank can pay you 6% interest because the bank loans your money to industry at higher interest rates. Industry, in turn, uses the money and earns a rate of return higher than it must pay the savings bank. Franklin said: "Never forget that money gets more money. And this gets more money in turn. If you kill a pig, you kill all of her little pigs and so forth, as to a thousand generations. When you kill a dollar, you destroy everything this dollar could bring forth-sometimes thousands of dollars."

Imagination-the magic elixir

The power of your imagination can make you rich. Everyone possess some degree of it. Imagination is applicable to every field of endeavor, trade or profession. It is unlimited, and as vast in scope as the mind can perceive.

Every man can achieve a great deal, depending upon the burning intensity of his desires and the keenness of his imagination. To develop your imagination, it takes only regular exercise. Let yourself relax, and allow your mind to wander-thinking about the goals you desire. If you wish, write down all ideas that pop into your mind. Then explore, mentally, each idea, and develop it. The more you do this exercise, the easier it becomes, as one idea usually brings another. You may exchange ideas with an associate, this is referred to as a 'brainstorming session' wherein each one becomes a bouncing board-so to speak-which reflects ideas with different views and reflections.

Your mind is an amazing tool, never used to its full capacity, and capable of an unbelievable production of work, to acquire success. It is a sleeping giant that needs only to be awakened. Michelangelo's famous statue of David, is an example. The statue was fashioned from a block of marble that had been spoiled in the quarrying, and cast aside as having no value. The great creativity of the artist utilized his imagination. First, he built up his mind's eye a vision of what was possible to use the spoiled marble block. Working with his mind and hands, he transferred thought into reality. Such is true of all artists. In business, it is simply a matter of developing the right idea, business, invention or product promotion. In sales, imagination, may be the planned approach suitable for the buyer's mood-a new concept or innovated presentation.

Many people find that the early morning is an especially good time for new-idea and creative sessions. Many of us seem to be fresher and more able to think clearly at the days start. Others may find best results from late evening sessions. Try and experiment until you find the best time for you. Go about your daily routine, try to observe more. Look at everything with increasing imagination. Read as much as possible. Many excellent ideas come to mind while reading, for this is when idea connections are made, and creativity develops.

Realize-your imagination has the dynamic power to increase your business success and over-all happiness. It's really a magic power sleeping inside your head. Keep it working.

Time to spend

The study of time is very important to the aggressive person. Time well spent, will produce wealth. Time lost, is gone forever, never to earn or be recovered. One must utilize all the available minutes and hours to the most productive degree. Idleness is wastefulness, and produces only failure.

You won't keep time in your wallet or deposit it into your savings account. You never can borrow it. Time can neither be earned back or stored. In fact, all you can do with it is spend it. Time, however is universal and equally available to all.

The use of Time can be analogized and compared to an iron bar worth $5.00. This same bar of iron, when made into horse shoes, will be worth $10.00. When used to make sewing needles, it becomes worth $350. When manufactured into pen knife blades, it becomes worth $3,300. When made into mainsprings for watches, that very same $5.00 bar is created into a value worth $250,000. Thus, time is worth what you do with it, to obtain the end result.

Many starting businesses require more time put in, then capital. Investing time at this stage, may be more important than investing money. Of course, too, one must realize it is not just the amount of time put in, but more important, what is put into the time spent. In other words, how the time is spent.

In the business of production, the time to produce goods will determine whether a profit or a loss will result. Time then, is a measure of money. Don't waste it.

Set your goals

You wouldn't attempt to cross the country without first knowing where you are going, when you would arrive and how you are going to travel! So, it is, with a goal to be attained. One must pinpoint in his own mind, precisely what he wants to achieve. If it is wealth that you seek, then formulate a vivid picture in your mind as to a plan to reach your goal. Work out a defined procedure, set up a timetable of reaching certain plateaus or stages of progress, within a determined time period. Concentrate on highlighting all the essentials to be worked on. Anticipate the possible obstacles, and work alternate plans to by-pass any stumbling blocks. In other words, plan all your moves and strategy. Outline it on paper and study it many times; be aware of where you have been, and where you are going.

Perhaps your goal is a specific income, or acquiring a sum of capital for a particular purpose. It is very important that you continually visualize yourself as reaching that goal in the length of time projected. This is a psychological motivation to drive you in that direction with almost a magic force.

Proven Recipe

The late Bernard Baruch was indeed an expert on acquiring wealth. He not only was an advisor to Presidents, he formulated advice for the little man desirous of success. 1. Make up your mind that it is possible to become rich. 2. You have to work at it while you are awake and even when you sleep. 3. Seek a field of work that can make you happy. 4. You may fail at first, but don't stop, because you have failed forward. 5. FIND A NEED AND FILL IT. When you find it, the nurse it, cultivate it and stay with it until you succeed!

Specialization

To be good at one thing, it is good to know something about many things. One should concentrate on one subject and become a specialist. This will make him unique, and his services in high demand. Specialization reduces conflicts and competitive factors. It makes one's work more interesting, profitable and enjoyable.

Agenda

For the successful man, it is vital to maintain an agenda. All items needed to be attended to, are written in a notebook or on a clip-board. The important items are keyed with a star. As the items are accomplished, a single, non-obliterating line is crossed thru. This keeps a record of accomplished items. Then you simply continue adding items and crossing thru. The important ones are done first. This method is continuous and keeps the wheels turning in an organized manner. Accomplish first things first.

This simple secret is worth money. The head of the Bethlehem Steel Company, Charles Schwab, actually paid with delight, $25,000 to an efficiency expert who helped institute this procedure in office operating procedures. The result was an immense increase in the organizations efficiency, and well worth the fee.

The Success Attitude

Success is dependent upon the individual's attitude. Don't become complacent and passive. Instead, be determined. One must strive to develop all the many qualities combined that attract success. Be optimistic. Never lose hope-no matter what happens. You must sail your ship in storms, as well as in calm waters. Optimism is positive thinking. Diligence cannot be substituted by any other attitude. It is a vital element for success. Work painstakingly with a meticulous, sustained effort. This makes for the most industrious accomplishments.

Persistence is the endless effort and never-ceasing action enduring all obstacles, never to give up! It was the attitude of persistence that made seemingly impossible dreams come true. Perseverance is the stamina, determination and tenacity to withstand the opposition and difficulty in a pursuit toward a goal. Courage- There are no hopeless situations, there are only those that are hopeless. Problems become smaller, as you confront them. In the dark, if you walk towards the light, the shadow becomes smaller. Situations of exposure to risk need courage to control. Since there is a degree of risk to almost everything in life, one must be brave and control fear. Initiative- To begin is half the work. Be a self-starter and organizer. Nothing can ever be accomplished, if never started. Love of work- Pleasurable feelings about your work create more input and output. Exacting and methodical slipshod methods, produce slipshod results. Cultivate personality- the biggest asset you can own, and is free of charge. A winning personality can often do what money can't. Fairness- Your fellow-man will follow you to any end, if he believes in your fairness. Be principled in all dealings. <u>Charitable</u>- To give is better than needing to receive. Charity makes the giver feel successful - a very small price to pay for such gratification. <u>Inquisitiveness</u>- to constantly learn new things is a product of inquisition. Be alert, eager and willing to talk and <u>listen</u> – and <u>listen</u> some more. <u>Will Power</u>- in the form of self-discipline, will be the backbone of your entire attitude. It takes a conscious force to maintain and develop all of the success qualities needed for success.

Salesmanship

Everyone who is successful must possess, to some degree, the ability to sell. If nothing else, he must sell himself. Progress can only be made with the help and cooperation of others. A persuasive manner of speaking is needed to motivate others to act beneficially for you. Even a doctor, or lawyer, must have sales ability. In effect, they must sell their image and build confidence by saying and doing the right things. Develop your personal powers by practicing Salesmanship.

Personality can be developed by anyone. All right, suppose you are just naturally a sourpuss. Act like a cheerful, friendly man, especially when dealing with people – better yet, <u>all the time</u>. Yes, it is an act; artificial; but practice and stay with it. In time – not a long time, either – it will be the real thing. You will be cheerful, friendly, confident.

This is not intended to be deceitful. But you cannot practice improving your personality alone; you must practice on others, talking with others. And when you get the results you are sure to get, if you are consistent in your practice, not only will you be the benefactor, but so will your family, relatives and friends. You will notice quite a difference in all their reactions to you.

A pleasant tone of voice is another important part of personality. Everyone can improve the tone of his voice so it is calm and soothing, not harsh and irritating. It reflects or expresses your friendliness; it is not tense, it shows you are relaxed, you have confidence in yourself – and in the other person you converse with.

Personality is what you project; it is what the other person sees and feels. And don't feel that salesmen are the only ones who use, improve and largely depend on their personality. All politicians, or statesmen find a good personality vital to their election, re-election, winning support for good legislation – just about everything. So, it is with all people who meet the public, who must try to influence the public. Improve your personality for success.

340

Use the coat-tails of bigger people. Do work for them if you can. Deal with the biggest and most respected firms (it seldom costs more). Don't fool around with two-bit businesses, or propositions that make less than average wages, and are degrading.

Obtain employment or service the biggest prestige companies. Develop relationships with the upper echelons, when the opportunity presents itself – make the opportunity. Work your way up along with your image. Promulgate your association with the biggies. Cultivate your traits to be sophisticated (not to be confused with snobbery). Carry a nice air about you. Emulate someone respected for his caliber. Elevate yourself to this level of refinement and polish.

Success Image

Everyone likes to go with a winner. Think, look and talk as if you are successful. Then, almost magically, you will attract success. You don't have to become a phony to accomplish this. Simply dress in style, stand erect, and talk cheerfully (not boastfully). Avoid looking and talking the blues. Don't be a complainer; keep it to yourself. Keep yourself looking healthy and spry. Smile more! Try to associate with a better class of people, and gradually work yourself upwards.

Get Into Action

Nothing ventured, nothing gained. Simply the truth. One must try. First study, explore and calculate – but don't stop there. Either proceed further, or drop it for lack of merit. Don't be a half-way operator. If the odds seem favorable, then test it. If the test looks favorable, then don't spare the horses. No one can give you a guarantee on any venture, not even Lloyds of London. Whatever the deal, there are always degrees of risks. There you must be daring and bold. There is no alternative, if you are to make progress. That doesn't mean to imply that you should gamble with just any odds. You should proceed when the odds are calculated to be in your favor. The calculations are to be derived from analysis, employing available statistics, comparisons, laws of probability, alternatives, downside risk measured against upward potential, sound realistic judgement, past experience and business intuition. All approaches considered to determine basically how much you can lose, and how well you can do. Your business acumen and imagination should be prevailed upon for approached to further reduce risks.

341

Judgement

Rules for good judgement cannot be laid down. It is more of an art, than a science. It is a very refined and cultivated form of common sense. A form of power of discrimination and reasoning that guides our minds into domains of thought that are not perfectly obvious.

One must train his mind to accumulate in thought, at one time, all possible alternatives, views, solutions, criteria, various reactions from ascertain different actions. Then collectively, compare the result of all the various views and reactions as experimentally envisioned in the mind. The comparisons should bring forth, with logical and deductive reasoning, exactly which direction would make the most sense for the desired objective. Good judgement could be said to be the fruit of very shrewd common sense. Conversely, bad judgement usually results from a person's laziness to put the mind to work.

One does not have to be a genius, or have a super I.Q. to make good judgements. Any normal person can train and exercise his mind to work at problems and come forth with answers. Thomas Edison said: "Genius is 99% perspiration and 1% inspiration." Therefore, good judgement comes from good mental gymnastics and work! Judgement is dependent upon the ingredients of acquired knowledge and experience. The more knowledge and experience possessed, the higher the grade of tools the mind has to work with, and thus, the easier and better the judgment will result.

Decisiveness

Once the best direction is determined by sound judgement of the facts, it is then in order to cause decision to act (or possibly) not to act. Inaction is also a decision. In either case, one should avoid being in a state of indecision for very long. Nothing impedes progress more than floundering in limbo. It's like a boat without sail, at the mercy of the sea.

Try to anticipate problems and obstacles as far in advance as foreseen. This will allow ample thinking time to make decisions based upon judgements already made. Readiness for decisions is the key to efficient operations. Governments, companies and alert individuals always have alternative plans and decisions made to meet the various problems and circumstances. You too, should be ready to employ a plan A, plan B, and so forth. This type of advance decision making is better than hurried decision.

Ambition

The very potent factor for success is ambition - the desire to acquire riches and honors. The ambitious drive can be an obsession for those who yearn for success. Many sacrifice sleep, health and relationships under the spell of ambitious drive. Some people have too much ambition, and others have not enough.

Nevertheless, ambition is the common denominator of all self-made successful people. Now you ask - How can one increase his ambition, when more is needed? One way, is to be inspired by the feats accomplished by ambitious people. Don't just study the giants of the industry. Examine true episodes of people in your particular field, whether it is real estate, finance, advertising, retailing or manufacturing, etc. You may not become a giant, but it is educational and motivating to read about J. Paul Getty, Henry Ford, Andrew Carnegie and hundreds of others. Then, too, you must realize that hundreds of new millionaires are made every year. The opportunities are available, so you might as well consider yourself a candidate in the running.

Self Confidence

The belief that one will be successful is paramount. The proverb "When hope is lost, all is lost" has true meaning. On the other hand, of equally true meaning in the positive sense is "If you have hope, then you have everything to gain." Which philosophy are you going to choose? Naturally, the positive thinking. You now possess the main ingredient for self-confidence, belief that you <u>can</u> accomplish what you set out to do.

Believing is a powerful natural law that guides and motivates you. It brings every hope within the realm of possibility. This does not mean that merely by believing you will get everything you want. Of course not. But it does definitely mean that once you learn to believe, then the seemingly impossible moves into the area of the possible. Things really start going for you.

Everything hinges on one's learning to have faith. Some people do not seem able to be believers - either in God, or in themselves, or in their jobs. As a result, they never get very far, just go limping along through life. But most have the priceless ability of believing. They are able to have faith and confidence in themselves and in their jobs. And they become the real achievers in this world.

"Never." "Impossible!" "Cannot be done!" How many times have you heard that? Drop the impossibilities and think in terms of the possible – all things will magically move into the area of possibility. Creativity is put into full steam. How does one learn to believe? The secret is to practice believing until you make yourself a believer. Nobody ever learned to master anything except by intensive and persistent practice. So, if you want to be a believer, the kind of person who does so-called impossible things, start now to practice being a believer. Simply affirm to yourself, and say it very positively: "I believe!" and then say it again, and still again. Every day many times, repeat these two magic words. "I believe, I believe."

"CAUTION – Be Sure BRAIN is Engaged Before Putting MOUTH in GEAR!"

[THINK]

REVELATION # 36
WEALTH IS HEALTH

It is important to be healthy simply because wealth is to no avail having monetary means and yet too sick to enjoy life abundantly. It is the person's sole responsibility to maintain good health for themselves and family. It is true that having wealth will make life easier and perhaps, augment maintaining good health and happiness.

It is evident that many people consider wealth attainment before achieving wealth in the monetary sense.

> *By perceiving thy inner perfection*
> *Thou attaineth a vigorous health*
> *For thy body is but a projection*
> *Of thy view of the indwellilng Self*

THE ORIGIN OF DISEASE

Health and well-being are the natural states of every form of life, for all things are rooted in Universal Subconscious Mind which is perfect. Every living thing is but an idea held in the Universal Mind, made manifest in space and time, gifted with consciousness which seeks ever to know more about itself. There is only one intelligence, one mind in all creation, and all things are made from it. According as each thing realizes the perfection in which it is rooted, it attains to perfection itself. *Thus, physical health proceeds from mental peace, and disease and corruption proceed from mental confusion.*

Disease is a product of the confusion attendant upon growing self-consciousness. So, it is that man, the most intelligent of all forms of life, falls constant prey to disease and illness, while the lower forms of life exist in physical perfection, unburdened by mental confusion. The lower we go on the scale of life the scarcer become the evidences of disease until at last we are forced to the conclusion that disease is a product of mental development, most certainly a product of evolving consciousness. Evolving consciousness carries with it an increasing number of conflicts, which project themselves into Universal Mind, which manifests them physically in the form of disease and corruption of the body. Man, who has come on the full scale of self-consciousness but has not as yet evolved the greater consciousness of immortal Self, sees himself as an insignificant dot in a gigantic universe where he has not ordered his existence and cannot stay his death. His highly developed little ego cuts him off from the roots of his being, and he knows fear and futility and hate and bitterness, all of which sets up conflicts between his emotions and his mind, project into universal intelligence, cast his concept of himself from perfection, and return to him as gallstones, kidney stones, ulcers, high blood pressure, hardening of the arteries, cancer, leprosy, deafness, and so on, as infinitum.

Psychology and psychiatry have unmasked this chain of cause and effect so clearly that medical science, devised to treat disease as a physical thing only, now freely admits that eighty per cent of all disease is of mental origin. It will not be much longer before this admission is enlarged to one hundred per sent where it should be. A truth cannot be *partly* right, and it is obvious that *all* things have their origin in something greater than the physical world around us. The bacterial concept of disease is satisfactory for the chain of effects that exists on the physical plane, but *why* do such bacteria enter one body and not another? And why are they harmless in some bodies yet deadly in others? Indeed, why do they exist at all? Any man who considers the origin of anything must come at last to the invisible but very apparent intelligence from which all things have sprung, and concede it to be first cause. Since this intelligence would scarcely be intelligent at all if its normal procedure were to attack itself (such as in microbes attacking the human body), then it must be conceded that it is creating disease in response to *something*. That something is conception, formed by the Conscious Mind and projected into the Universal Subconscious Mind, whence it manifests in the physical world.

It is a rare person who *consciously* desires to be sick, though it is certainly true that a few unhappy people have so completely cut themselves off from the spiritual unity of life that nothing further appeals to them than this form of slow suicide. The vast majority of people fall prey to disease through negative thinking habits and through coping mechanisms established in answer to buried pain remembrances or Prompters. A person who is chronically ill has a subconscious desire to be sick, though to confront him with such a thesis would be to inspire the most vehement denial. And even those of us who are only sick occasionally become so because it is a way of coping with a situation that confronts us. Since we do not know ourselves or even who we are, we do not understand the dynamically creative energy in which we live, nor do we understand our subconscious desires, nor do we understand that each of these desires is delivered to us in reality. So, it is that all disease, all warping of the body from its natural physical perfection, comes because a person holds subconscious feelings of hate, bitterness, resentment, envy, jealousy, greed, self-pity, maliciousness, or any number of countless abortions that corrupt the natural expression of the universe-love.

If a man does not love, he hates, or projects one of hate's deformed brothers, for love is the power of Universal Mind and flows through each person who lives, whether he uses it positively or negatively. If he uses it negatively, as in hate, it is corrupting power, aimed at evil, and it weakens and decays and withers the body. Instead of the power for life, it becomes the power for death.

Once again we see that the commands of the universe are: "Love or suffer! Love or die!"

Love is the power that heals!

Love banishes confusion, roots out the Prompters, brings peace of mind, bars the door to negative thinking, reveals the indwelling perfection of the human soul-not the love of man for woman, or one person for another, but the love of man for God and the love of God for man, which is complete in man when he knows his love is for God.

BODY IS ROOTED IN SPIRIT

Psychiatry is now only a skip and a jump away from being able to put its finger on the various negative emotions that bring on specific diseases. The day is not too far distant when medical books shall list after hate, bitterness, frustration, repression, envy, and loneliness their resultant physical debilities; and mankind will guard its emotions with the same care it now bestows on its physical well-being, pills and potions being replaced by healthy habits of thought.
  Writes Edward Carpenter:

Every organ and center of the body is the seat of some great emotion, which in its proper activity and due proportion is truly divine.

Body is rooted in true spirit, in Universal Subconscious Mind, which is perfect. Body may be cast from perfection only by concepts held in the Conscious Mind, which project into the subconscious and are returned as physical ailments. We do not cause out hearts to beat, nor do we direct the flow of blood to our various organs, nor the acids of the stomach to perform the miracle of digestion, nor the intestines and the kidneys to go about the process of eliminating waste matter. The dynamic source from which our bodies have sprung has inculcated in them these reflexive actions.

The functions of a body represent the movement and concept of intelligence, and when we get our fears and negative desires out of the way, our bodies function perfectly. But every concept we hold of lack, limitation, acquisitiveness, repression, and despair performs its restricting influence on our bodies so that the blood does not circulate freely, the digestion does not assimilate properly, elimination is poor, congestion develops, strange growths appear and represent the distortion of our thinking. Thus, our self-awareness with its attendant doubts and fears and frustrations limits the condition of our health and our lives. We must let go our little egos, take unto ourselves the God-consciousness which is our true being; then the body becomes perfect, for we have become one with that which is perfect itself.

Body is only a manifestation of God's knowledge of himself. It is an idea held ion the Universal Subconscious Mind, an evolving idea which constantly changes. All about us we see the cycle of life's expression-seed, bud, bloom, decay, the giving way to new life. Form must change as knowledge and ideation advances. Thus, body is that which changes, that which manifests ideas, form within the formless, a complete and perfect expression of an idea held in the Universal Subconscious Mind, destined to express the idea and give way to a more perfect idea. Birth and death, infancy, youth, middle age, old age, all are absolute essentials in the progress of evolution by which God seeks to know himself, and death will not be stayed until the journey is complete, for to stop death would be to stop the progress of evolution.

SPIRIT IS PERFECT

Jesus was the first great healer because he saw that body and mind were one, and he knew that body was only a visible result of an invisible cause. So highly developed was his consciousness that he perceived the spiritual perfection in which every living thing is rooted, and he realized that disease could be healed by revealing to an afflicted person the perfection from which he had come. When he met with leper, lame, halt, or blind, he knew at once that some buried pain remembrance within the mind of the unfortunate man had manifested itself in the man's physical condition. Jesus knew that he and the afflicted man were using the same mind, the Universal Subconscious Mind, the Father. So close was his unity with this Mind that he was able to effect instantaneous healing by removing his patient's negative Prompters. "Dost thou believe?" he asked, thus removing the concept of limitations from his patient's Conscious Mind. "Lord, I believe," his patient answered, and receptivity was established. "Thy sins be forgiven thee," said Jesus. "Take up thy bed and walk." The healing was effected.

When Jesus banished sins, he was not erasing from a ledger held in some ethereal realm by a God who kept records for a judgment day when He would reward the do-gooder and punish the evil-doer. The sins that Jesus spoke of were the buried prompters of the Subconscious that were manifesting themselves as bodily ailments. Hid forgiveness of them was simply assurance to his patient that as soon as such buried guilts and hostilities and rejections were forgotten he would be healed. What Jesus was saying was, "The real you is great and good and perfect. Acknowledge this perfection, and your body will become perfect also."

There is no such thing as an imperfect body, for body is always a perfect manifestation of an idea. There are only imperfect ideas. They are imperfect because they are in error, and they may be changed by simply accepting the idea of change. A man who has stifled his divinity in the belief that physical things are first causes is incapable of healing himself until he has changed his belief. If his joints are stiff and his digestion poor, he spends a good portion of each day acknowledging the fact that his joints are stiff and his digestion poor, and he himself is thrusting his body into these very conditions by his concept. He is deluded into believing that he thinks these things *because* he has stiff joints and poor digestion because he *thinks* them. Place him under deep hypnosis and assure him that he can get about like an athlete and has the digestion of a lumberjack, and after he is awakened his afflictions will have flown. Alas, they will not be gone permanently, for patterns of negative thinking are his still and will shortly bring back his poor condition. But the marvelous illustration will not be denied.

The Intelligence that inhabits a man's body will become anything that is projected into it. It will make healthy body if health is projected, and it will make a sickly body if limitation or hate or bitterness is projected. Thus, a healthy body is always a result of a healthy mind, and a sickly body is always the result of a blocked and unhealthy mind. If we would heal our bodies, we must first heal our minds, with love, with recognition of our true being, with meditation at the center of consciousness.

LET GO OF EGO

Worry and tension, guilt and hostility, resentment and vanity lay the foundations for all of our physical afflictions. They spring like growths from our over-developed little egos, which are forever being hurt and frustrated in a world which we set out to beat instead of cooperating with. Victory seems to be all we can think of. We have to outshine somebody, get the better of someone, make more money, be better looking, wear better cloths. How transient such victories are, and how unrewarding. Find a champion and you will see behind him the shadow of the man who will replace him. There is no victory for the hounded little ego, for it is nothing by itself, and it cannot see the larger dimensions of the being in which it is rooted. So, it is hurt and sad and lonely and frustrated, and is forever turning upon itself and rending itself, as if by the self-affliction of pain, it confirms the poor opinion it has of life. Turn to the gigantic Self that dwells within, and you will cease to be concerned with the pains of your ego, which will immerse itself in an untroubled sea and bother you no more.

> *Some of your hurts you have cured*
> *And the sharpest you still have survived*
> *But what torments of grief you endured*
> *For evils which never arrived.*
> -Emerson

The entire miracle of existence and creation lies at our fingertips, yet most of us fill the pathways of our lives with wails of fear for what lies around the corner; we bemoan past mistakes, or dwell forever on the saddest words of tongue or pen-it might have been. Each day is a new birth, unlimited with miraculous possibilities for each man who lives. No matter what your age, situation, clime or time, you need only awaken to know with Kahlil Gibran that "That which sings and contemplates in you is still dwelling within the bounds of that first moment which scattered the stars into space."

FIND A MOTIVATING PURPOSE

Idea is a complete thing, aimed at a purpose, and the body made manifest from such an idea is also a complete thing, aimed at a purpose. It is this purpose which holds together the many interrelated functions of the body, and when purpose disappears from our lives our bodies disintegrate, even as the idea which manifested them is disintegrating. We often are witness to the vigorous business man who, at a mature age, decides to retire to a life of leisure. Seldom is he embarked many months upon this life before all sorts of symptoms of bad health begin to overtake him. A motivating purpose is absolutely essential to good health, for the organs and functions of the body respond to the goal set in mind. When the goal is removed, sluggishness and irresponsibility overtake the body, and it decays and breaks down. Nobody can be whole and vigorous unless the mind that inhabits it is whole and vigorous, for the ideas we hold in mind are made visible through our bodies and the circumstances that surround us. The first step to health is always the creation of interest and enthusiasm on the plane of mind. Aspiring and dynamic thoughts make vigorous bodies, and we must think health in order to be healthy.

Exercise is a case in point. Our physical culturists would have us believe that running, bending, squatting, lifting, and flailing the arms will bring health, and they point with pardonable pride to various outstanding physical specimens as examples of what comes from exercise. But once again we are witness to materialists who point to results and never causes. For the well-conditioned body is not a *direct* result of exercise but only a secondary result. True cause exists in the mind, as always, and a body is conditioned because of mental purpose, which causes purposeful exercise, which results in a vigorous body.

EXERCISE AND HEALTH

Some of the healthiest people of our age get little more exercise than walking from bed to dinner table, and many of our shortest-lived people are our athletes. It becomes increasingly obvious that exercise alone produces neither health nor longevity. Yet the evidence is all about us that men of great purpose live to ripe old ages, so that it becomes an inescapable fact that interests and desire and aspiration are mental conditions that are *always* found in those who are healthy and vigorous. Our materialists may argue that such people have interest and desire and aspiration *because* they are healthy. But many a healthy man has been led into illness when his interest and joy in life waned, and many a sick man has been led back to vigor and health simply through developing a consuming interest and purpose. All things proceed from mind, which is always first cause.

Physical vigor is the result of vigorous thoughts, and physical weakness is the result of confusion. Therefore, a man who accepts the perfection and power of the indwelling Self will find such perfection and power mirrored in his body. Health comes from within, and never from outside.

By all means take exercise if it is fun, but there is no point in taking it if it is distasteful. Exercise merely conditions the body for more exercise. If you lift a hundred-pound weight ten times every day, eventually you will be able to lift it twenty times every day, but the lifting of the weight will not prevent your arteries from hardening, your nerves from fraying or your digestion from going awry. A man may as simply attain health through welding a pencil with the purpose in mind of completing a book as he may through running the measured mile each day, in fact, more easily, if it gives him more pleasure to write the book than it does to run the mile. Our bodies are always perfect instruments of our thoughts, and perfect health may be ours whether we are athletes, professors, lumberjacks, clerks, or housewives, if our thinking is clear with purpose and our hearts are free to love. Exercise makes not the slightest difference.

Physical strength and endurance may be increased through exercise, but lasting health is as much a prerogative of the sedentary life as the athletic life.

PAIN IS A SIGNPOST

The spiritual unrest of the world is evidenced by increasing orgies of over-eating, over-drinking, over-working, over-playing, and under-sleeping. We undertake such a chain of neurotic activity as an escape from the gnawing doubts and fears and frustrations that lay at the crux of our Subconscious. Abuses of the body are always results of confusions in mind, so that a subconscious sense of insecurity may lead a person into eating far too much, or a sense of being unloved may turn a person to alcohol. We sometimes play too hard, seeking to forget the issues of life and death by burying our heads in the sand like ostriches. We often work too hard, seeking to amass a mountain of material gain to provide for our security, but it stays not death, and we cannot take it with us when the transition comes. We seek constantly for the pleasures of the senses, and by surfeiting ourselves, we dull the mystical creativeness of our true being; and when our bodies grow old and physical sensation wanes, the pygmy of our undeveloped soul plagues us with gnawing doubts and uncertainties. Truly, we cannot be whole men, either spiritually or physically, until we have recognized that the roots of our being rest in eternity.

We learn slowly, mostly by pain, and each of our gains in knowledge and awareness is hard won. Pain is that which visits us when we are in error, and through suffering we are turned back to the path of truth. Writes Kahlil Gibran:

> Much of your pain is self-chosen. It is
> The bitter potion by which the physician
> within you heals your sick self. Therefore
> trust the physician, and drink his remedy
> in silence and tranquility.

Until we have learned the great lesson that pain is merely a signpost indicating that we have wandered off the track of truth, we shall continue to fight it and struggle with it, to lend reality to it, and thus to bring more of it into our experience. But once we have come far enough to realize that all pain-physical, mental, and emotional-proceeds from errors in thinking, we are well on our way to filling our lives with vigor, abundance, and joy; and have come a great step toward unity of consciousness with Universal Subconscious Mind. *The ordinary man learns by his own mistakes; the wise man learns by the mistakes of others.*

Over-indulgence in physical things marks an imbalance of the emotions. Fear, hate, and insecurity rest in the subconscious of every person who flees his demon down the murky road of alcoholism, over-eating, or frenetic searches for pleasure and acquisition. Moderation attends all things to him who has been introduced to the center of consciousness. No violent emotions constrict his soul, for he is secure in the consciousness of God. No uncertainties gnaw at the foundation of his being, for they rest in eternity. Confusion has no place in his mind, because he sees the goal of all life, becomes one with it, takes it unto himself as his own purpose. Should disease or illness become manifest in his body, he turns his gaze within, to the perfection and wonder of his true being, and his body is made whole.

And since he kept his mind on one sole aim,
Nor ever touched fierce wine, nor tasted flesh,
Nor owned a sensual wish-to him the wall
That saunders ghosts and shadow-casting men
Became a crystal, and he saw them thro' it
And heard their voices talk behind the wall
And learned their elemental secrets, powers, and forces.
-Alfred Tennyson

DISEASE IS NEVER INCURABLE

An infinite law is at work in the universe; it is the law of ideas becoming things. Since this law is the movement of Universal Mind, it has absolutely no limitation. Therefore, there is no such thing as an incurable disease. A law must work all the time in order to be a law, and the law that governs the intelligence in which we are rooted is the foundation of all things. Disease itself springs from an idea impregnated upon Universal Mind, and will be banished when the idea is banished. Whatever disease science has been unable to find a cure for is not *incurable*. Something causes it; that something may be discovered and removed. Both medical science and psychiatry are learning that the root of all things exists in mind, springs from idea, and idea can be changed. Since there is no limit to idea and to the inexhaustible power of Universal Subconscious Mind, there absolutely cannot be any such thing as an incurable disease.

We must realize that the universe always turns out to be exactly what we think it to be, even as do our bodies. As we reach higher levels of consciousness, we take unto ourselves more perfect ideas, casting of the shackles of limitation, becoming aware that all things are possible. The moment we say something is *impossible*, we make it impossible for God to manifest it through us. And another man with a greater vision and a greater faith will bring it forth, for he will God to work through him. None of us has the right to say a thing is impossible, unless he is foolish enough to place limitations on God.

Perfect spirit within us, willing to manifest perfect health for us if we but call upon it with faith. All disease may be healed by mental and spiritual treatment, by expanding consciousness to encompass Universal Self.

MENTAL HEALING

Each person who suffers from ill health has usually fallen victim to a specific ailment. This specific ailment is the result of some obstruction in mind; some false idea, some erroneous conception. When we heal the body by mental and spiritual treatment, we do not treat the body, *we treat the mind*. This is very important. One cannot get rid of the result without first getting rid of the cause. Cause is always in mind; bodily ailments are the *results*.

A lifetime of study would be unlikely to reveal the specific mental disturbances that cause each disease, but no table of mental and emotional disturbances with resultant physical debilities is needed to successfully conduct mental healing. All things spring from a perfect source, and we need only contact this source and allow it to manifest its perfection through our bodies. Said the Great Healer, "Be thou perfect, even as thy Father in heaven is Perfect." In so saying he pointed the way to the healing of all disease: *recognize your spiritual perfection*.

There is nothing in Universal Subconscious Mind that desires our bodies to be warped away from purposeful functioning for which they were intended. It is our conception of ourselves that visit disease upon us, and when we have conceived ourselves to be spiritually perfect, we become physically perfect. The real you is not your body. Your body is but an infinitesimal extension in time and space. The real you is mental and spiritual, free of the confines of space and time, limitless in power and the capacity to understand and create. When you have recognized your true spiritual self you have become identified with immortal Self, and disease cannot exist in your body, for there is no limitation in Universal Subconscious Mind.

There all disease may be treated as one disease, which is not disease at all, but simply limited thinking, errors projected into Universal Subconscious Mind. We treat disease by refusing to accept it as having any true existence, by affirming the spiritual perfection in which we are rooted. "Perfect love casteth out fear," and perfect faith casts out physical imperfection.

Yet rare is the man who has the perfect love or perfect understanding or even perfect faith. We are all neophytes on the great adventure of expanding consciousness, and by the very nature of this adventure we are unable to go beyond our understanding. We stand at the crossroads, peering into the infinite reaches of space and time, exclaiming yet over one grain of sand on the gigantic beach of existence. But the veil is rent and light pours through with great revelation that mind and spirit are immortal and infinite and are always first cause of everything. If eons of time are yet to elapse before man completes his journey to oneness with God, what does it matter? We are all part of One Mind and truly exist in a place where space and time are nothing. We may call upon Universal Subconscious Mind with the understanding that now is in us, and the Great Creator will respond by creating for us the image of our understanding. If we can find it in ourselves to accept spiritual perfection, Universal Mind will manifest this perfection in our bodies.

Thus, the basis of spiritual and mental healing is affirmation. We deny nothing, waste no time dwelling on that which we do not desire. Our moments of consciousness are directed inward, at our spiritual selves, and are aimed at perceiving the perfection that gives us consciousness. What we see is returned to us. Awareness of the center of consciousness, perception of the Kingdom of Heaven, brings health.

WE CANNOT GO BEYOND UNDERSTANDING

The objection that is usually raised against mental healing is that nobody seems able to set a broken bone mentally so the whole aspect of mental healing is in error. *It is not impossible mentally to set a broken bone!* The fact that it has not been done simply means that we have not yet arrived at sufficient spiritual understanding. Lacking the understanding, we call a surgeon, which is as it should be. Neither do we have enough understanding to heal a ruptured appendix or dissolve a critical case of cancer, so again we call upon the surgeon. Yet these things and all others of the so-called incurable diseases are possible of mental healing, and the day will arrive when evolution will have brought man's consciousness and understanding to the point where disease will be banished from the face of the earth.

Another argument often used against mental healing is advanced by the school of materialists who see life as species preying on species and survival of the fittest. Their theory is that all organisms by their very natures must feed upon each other, that microbes must feed upon the human body; thus life is a disease itself. This hopeless outlook on the miracle of creation keeps God imbedded in the slime of the amoeba, sees nothing but a screaming insanity in life, and projects a tooth-and-fang existence for even the most enlightened of men.

Evolution is the process of individualized consciousness expanding in search of God. The first result of individualized existence is the struggle to maintain life, with its natural outcome of survival of the fittest. The second result is consciousness of self, the identification of one self with another, and the birth of love and cooperation as opposed to competition and preying on the weaker. The third result is the expansion of the consciousness of self to encompass the consciousness of the Universal Subconscious Mind, and it is this step that mankind is preparing to take now. Once it is fully taken, men will see through the illusions of space and time and perceive that material things are but tiny extensions of a far greater reality that has its roots in infinity. Such a consciousness orders the universe, for the universe turns out to be exactly what it perceives. Microbes, which have their roots in Universal Mind, may be banished by banishing the conception. "Hold out thy hand," said Jesus to the man with the withered limb. "The man did; Jesus saw a whole hand; the hand became whole.

PERCEIVING THE TRUTH

It is sometimes difficult for us to believe that a man who lived two thousand years ago in the rude agrarian life of primitive Palestine could have attained the universal consciousness for which mankind seeks so desperately in this so-called enlightened age. Yet there can be no doubt but what the veil was lifted for Jesus. Every word he spoke, every action he undertook, is fraught with his knowledge of universal consciousness. By parable and deed he sought to convey the mighty truth which he held in the palm of his hand, but he spoke to a political-minded people engaged in revolutionary activity, unready for his spiritual perceptions. Only the enlightened power of Jesus has preserved his dialogues for us to marvel at today. He had achieved unity with Universal Subconscious Mind. When he looked at a withered hand and perceived it to be whole, it became whole. Whatever is perceived by Universal Subconscious Mind becomes a physical manifestation, and it is always Conscious Mind that forwards the perception to the Universal Subconscious Mind. Though our consciousness does not attain to that of Jesus, we may approach his healing power through faith in our spiritual perfection and an abiding sense of love.

Disease is a negative though-force, is false, is therefore an illusion of the mind. In mental healing, we simply separate false thoughts from the true, consciously, and by allowing our faith and affirmation to sink down into the Subconscious we admit physical vigor and health into our lives. The principle of existence is the principle of thoughts becoming things. Since this is a law, we do not argue or struggle with it. Some well-meaning friend may ask you why you don't try walking upon the water since you are so all-fired convinced of this mind stuff. All you can do is assure him that it is toward such a goal that you aspire, for either we walk on the water or drown in it; we either master life or defeat ourselves.

RELY ON THE LAW

Mental treatment entails no personal responsibility other than for the idea and its affirmation. All else depends upon the principle of creation that underlies the universe; and this principle never fails. When you affirm your spiritual perfection you are setting universal law into motion, which accepts your conception and the power of your affirmation, and manifests it in the physical world. There is nothing superstitious or occult about this. The law we are dealing with is infallible; it is true reality, besides which all else pales to nothingness.

Since disease is caused by a mental condition, before it can be healed the mental condition must be surrendered. A man must first surrender himself to God, to Universal Subconscious Mind; he must let go, give up the struggle, trust in the invisible roots of his being, so that God-consciousness may engulf him and make him whole. You cannot successfully treat yourself or another person until you are willing to surrender your doubts and fears and hates and hurts. The nagging, gnawing emotional hurts we bottle up inside ourselves are like time bombs laid within. They explode in tumors, cancers, high blood pressure, hardening of the arteries, diabetes, heart trouble, lung trouble, literally riddle our bodies with poisonous thoughts that impregnate Universal Subconscious Mind. We must surrender our fears and frustrations and guilts, lay aside our vanities and our little egos, place all our hurts on the shoulders of the Atlas of Eternity, then we shall be free-free to partake of the beauty and perfection and abundance of the universe.

God is always right where we are, responding to us exactly as we conceive of Him. He is our infinite invisible dimension, of which our physical bodies are but a negligible projection. The power for physical perfection is running over inside of us; we need only surrender to it, accept it, trust ourselves completely to it, and health is ours.

When you treat yourself or someone else for a physical ailment, remember that you are treating mind and no the body. You are assuring yourself of mental and spiritual perfection, you are affirming it, you are projecting it into the Universal Subconscious Mind with complete faith and trust. When you treat someone else you still deal with the same Mind. You treat *yourself* to think perfection of the person you are treating. Do not try to change the other person's thinking by the power of your own thought. Simply treat *yourself* for *your* conception of him. *You* move Universal Subconscious Mind; Universal Subconscious Mind moves *him*. Therefore, whether you are treating yourself or another, the treatment is always the same, though of course in the latter case you will substitute "he" or "she" where you would normally use "I." But always you are treating yourself, your own conception, and projecting it into Universal Mind. When you heal another, you must first be able to completely accept in your own mind his spiritual perfection. When you have done that, the healing will be effected.

THE MENTAL CAUSE OF DISEASE

A partial list of common physical ills follows, with the underlying mental cause for each, so that you may be guided more easily into directing your treatments at mental conditions rather than physical.

Headache:

Confusion is the predominant condition attendant upon headache. Most generally this is brought about by the suppression of some emotion which revolves around the affections. When headache is attended by dizzy spells it is a sign of basic insecurity. Treat for peace, the clarity of the Subconscious, the love that pervades the universe, and the consciousness of immortal Self.

Fatigue:

When enthusiasm and joy desert us, fatigue enmeshes us in its enervating grasp. Joy and enthusiasm are results of mental and spiritual expansion. We cease to expand when we place limits on our thinking and on our conceptions; our goals disappear or seem unobtainable and we accept defeat and its attendant feelings of lethargy and tiredness. Treat for awareness of life and movement and joy and expansion. There are no limitations on God, and God is expressing Himself through you.

Indigestion:

An intense sense of personal responsibility usually manifests itself in digestive upsets. People who work at high speeds and feel they must do everything by themselves often fall victim to excess stomach acidity and stomach ulcers. Their refusal to assimilate on the plane of mind a unity with the underlying Self becomes symptomatic in the difficulty they have assimilating food. Treat for peace and perception of how God is the only doer. Treat for relaxation and trust in Universal Subconscious Mind. Learn how to let go and leave it to God. There is perfect assimilation in perfect spirit.

Constipation:

Fear causes immobility, which brings inaction into life, freezing and constricting, often manifesting itself in constipation. Fear is the basic cause of greed, acquisitive tendencies, unwillingness to let go. Very often fear comes from belief in limitation, in lack, in burden. It brings on excessive tensions, constricts and binds the muscles and the movements of the body. Fear is faith used negatively. Treat for positive thinking, assurance, confidence, the knowledge that you are one with God and God is right where you are, guiding you unerringly to your goals. Banish negative thoughts. Whatever you refuse to accept in mind can never touch you in the physical world.

Obesity:

We become fat because we eat too much, and we eat too much because certain of our desires and longings are frustrated. Seeking solace, we find it in food, for the pleasure of taste and the comfort it gives us. Our frustrations are caused because we have taken unto ourselves false ideas of our personal unworthiness and no longer believe we can achieve our goals. We have lost confidence in our divine roots, and our energies are directed at sensual pleasures rather than at achievement and service. Treat for knowledge of the center consciousness wherein there is perfect order, perfect beauty, and perfect symmetry. Food is a symbol of love and should be eaten with moderation lest gluttony turn love to greed. God is love, and the perfect seed of love lies within you.

Insomnia:

When we sleep we become immersed in the Universal Subconscious Mind. If we cannot sleep it is because we are over-concerned with the material world, and our Conscious Minds have over-ridden the Subconscious and refuse to let go. The physical world is simply a series of manifested results which have all proceeded from Subconscious Mind. We cannot change these results by fighting them, but only by dealing with them in mind where they originate. Thus, holding onto your cares and worries is the worst possible way to overcome them. Seek your center of consciousness before going to bed. Treat for peace and relaxation. Real truth is of the spirit and lies inward. Turn your eyes away from the world and look within.

Intemperance:

Alcohol provides a tortuous trap for those who seek escape from an unwanted belief. It is always some unwholesome or painful picture gnawing on the Subconscious that turns a person to drink. He himself has created this image, and he might change it by creating another, but he lends reality to his self-made monster and flees it down the avenues of alcoholism or drug addiction or senseless pursuits of pleasure. Treat for the dissolution of guilt and personal responsibility. God is in you, and God is not guilty. Mistakes are for learnings, and each day is a fresh start with a clean slate when you learn to forgive yourself.

Colds and similar congestions:

Mental conflicts and repressions attract congestions of the body such as the common cold. Such conflicts are usually first evidenced by depression of the spirits, a bleakness in outlook. Our creative nature demands that we either make a decision on a problem or put it out of mind. When we hold a problem in mind and are unable to come to a decision, we set up congestion in the forces that flow through us from the subconscious. This reduces our energy and activity, depresses the spirit, brings on bodily congestions and colds. Also, our racial conviction that colds are "catching" and caused by exposure to wind and low temperatures sets up creative impulses to manifest them when we encounter such situations. Treat for harmony and the knowledge of the perfection of Universal Subconscious Mind. Each of your problems will be perfectly answered if you will only let go and leave the solution to your greater Self. Treat for poise and assurance and calmness. There is no congestion in perfect spirit.

False Growths:

A seed buried within grows in darkness, and so we carry our guilts around with us. They block us from knowledge of the great Self, warp and distort our consciousness, manifest their falseness by false growths in and on the body. Treat for unity with Universal Subconscious Mind. Let go of your guilts and sins and give them to God.

Paralysis:

Ideas of restriction and limitation may manifest themselves in paralysis or the malfunctioning of the senses. There is no restriction and no inaction in the mind of God, which you may take unto yourself by meditation at the center of consciousness.

Heart trouble and organic disturbances:

The heart is the seat of purpose, and when purpose is centered in spirit and not in the material world, the heart is rooted in perfection. Organic disturbances always come from a man being out of tune with his spiritual nature. Heart trouble and attendant disorders visit our materialists, those who seek their goals, purposes, and pleasures in the physical world. Treat by meditation on the birthless, deathless, ageless spirit from which man springs. Take unto yourself the mantle of God, become one with him, and His purpose will energize your heart.

There is only one mind, one spirit, one power pervading the entire universe, and it is perfect. It is constantly attempting to express itself perfectly through each of us. Because we are newly arrived at the consciousness of our own little egos and have not yet taken unto ourselves the consciousness of the greater Self, we see neither from where we have come nor where we are going, and the gigantic universe seems to threaten and frustrate us on all sides. Our limited vision causes us to create fear and hate and bitterness and apathy which manifest imperfections in our bodies. All disease and distortion of the body may be healed by meditation at the center of consciousness, by knowledge of the love of God, by awareness and use of the unlimited power and perfection of Universal Subconscious Mind.

We advocate that a study should be made of learning all the methods that can help your mental peace of mind and the physical body maintenance to enjoy good health. We recommend the study of our audio lecture Health is Wealth. You can order this from our order form displayed at the end of The Bible of Wealth Secrets.

List of Soon to Be Available Books

Fundamentals of Wealth Building

1001   Bible of Wealth Secrets

B1.   How and Where to Raise Capital

B2.   Professional Salesmanship

B3.   Business Management

B4.   Turn Your Ideas into Wealth

B5.   Develop Mental Mastery

B6.   Success Qualities & Philosophies

B7.   Savvy Stock Investing

B8.   Entrepreneur Success Blueprint

B9.   Real Estate Fortune Strategies

B10.   Beat Inflation-Protect your Savings

B11.   Forecasting Business Trends

B12.   Basic Business Law

B13.   Interpreting Financial Statements

B14.   Effective Advertising

B15.   Earn 18% on Tax Certificates Safely or 0 Risk

B16.   Upper Hand Negotiating

B17.   Power of Suggestion

B18.   Win Over Difficult People

B19.   Retire Early in Comfort

B20.   Bis Wiz Lingo

B21.   Safely Extending Business Credit

B22.   Health is Wealth

B23. Marketing

B24. Making A Better Will

List Of Soon to Be Available Books

Entrepreneur Wealth Opportunities

E1. Lucrative Insurance Agency

E2. Your Own Label Products

E3. Land Development

E4. Lucrative Mortgage Brokerage

E5. Income Properties

E6. Private Mortgage Investing

E7. Builders Trade Secrets

E8. Start A New Business

E9. Collection Agency

E10. Be A Published Author

E11. Public Insurance Adjusting

E12. Becoming A Food Broker

E13. Part Time Home Business

E14. Import/Export Bonanza

E15. Public Relations

E16. Home Computer Business

E17. Manufacturer Representative

E18. Commodity Trading

E19. Country Property Investing

E20. Real Estate Appraiser

E21. Instant Publishing Franchise

www.ingramcontent.com/pod-product-compliance
Lightning Source LLC
Chambersburg PA
CBHW062347220526
45472CB00008B/1730